# Women in Busi...

This book uniquely combines theory, case studies, and the legal issues surrounding the role of gender at work. It provides real-life examples (based on interviews) that help students understand the role gender plays in organizational life. Case studies on entrepreneurship, work-life balance, mentoring, communication, networking, pay-equity, and career strategies offer readers the opportunity to apply theory to actual business situations. In the cases, students are asked to examine their own beliefs about gender and workplace practices and consider the consequences of actions they might take. In addition to sections on theory, cases, and legal challenges, chapters provide additional resources – websites, articles, books, assignments, and discussion topics.

Key features of the book include:

- Engaging case studies embedded in chapters.
- Legal cases that highlight issues and ground the case studies.
- Women's business roles across nations and globally.
- Suggestions for student assignments/projects.

**Martha E. Reeves** teaches in the Markets and Management Studies program at Duke University, where she is a member of the Sociology and the Women's Studies departments. Reeves teaches courses on markets, managers and organizations, marketing communication, international business, and women in business. Prior to coming to Duke, Reeves taught in the Terry College of Business at the University of Georgia, and was Program Director for the Executive Education Program at the Kenan-Flagler Business School at the University of North Carolina, Chapel Hill, where she was responsible for curriculum design and client management of custom programs and delivery of open enrollment programs. For a decade before becoming an academic, Reeves was a human resource manager in several financial services companies, as well as a consultant on human resource issues to business and government, in both the US and UK. Reeves' recent research has focused on the intersection of technology and management, and women's corporate leadership. She is the author of *Evaluation of Training* (Industrial Society Press) and *Suppressed, Forced out and Fired: How Successful Women Lose their Jobs* (Quorum Books).

Thanks to Katelin Isaacs and to all the women who contributed their experiences for the case studies in this book

# Women in Business

## Theory, Case Studies, and Legal Challenges

Martha E. Reeves

Routledge
Taylor & Francis Group

NEW YORK AND LONDON

First published 2010
by Routledge
270 Madison Avenue, New York, NY 10016

Simultaneously published in the UK
by Routledge
2 Park Square, Milton Park, Abingdon, Oxon OX14 4RN

*Routledge is an imprint of the Taylor & Francis Group, an informa business*

Typeset in Garamond by Wearset Ltd, Boldon, Tyne and Wear
Printed and bound by TJ International, Padstow, Cornwall

*Library of Congress Cataloging in Publication Data*
Reeves, Martha E., 1951–
Women in business : theory, case studies, and legal challenges / by Martha E. Reeves.
p. cm.
Includes bibliographical references and index.
1. Women–Employment–Social aspects. 2. Sex role in the work environment. 3. Sex discrimination in employment. 4. Sexual division of labor. I. Title.
HD6053.R39 2010
658.30082–dc22                                      2009047040

ISBN10: 0-415-77802-6 (hbk)
ISBN10: 0-415-77803-4 (pbk)
ISBN10: 0-203-85141-2 (ebk)

ISBN13: 978-0-415-77802-2 (hbk)
ISBN13: 978-0-415-77803-9 (pbk)
ISBN13: 978-0-203-85141-8 (ebk)

# Contents

# Part I

# An Introduction to Gender Equality

# 1 An Introduction to Women in the Workplace

**Learning Objectives**

After completing this chapter, the reader will:

- understand women's workforce participation in the twentieth and twenty-first centuries.
- understand the major thrusts of first, second, and third wave feminist movements in the US.

This book has three primary goals. The first objective is to provide a thorough review of issues important to women in the workplace. The second is to provide one text that covers theories about gender discrimination, case studies to illustrate key themes, and the legal framework for equity at work. In addition to legal frameworks, this text introduces some of the significant legal cases related to workplace discrimination. A third objective is to introduce some comparisons between the position of women in the United States and in other countries. Although this text cannot provide an exhaustive description of the position of women everywhere, it does include several examples of work-related issues for women in other countries, especially European nations.

## Why Should These Topics Be Important to College Students and Others?

Many economists project labor shortages in the coming years as baby boomers retire and as birth rates continue to decline in the US and European countries (Atwater & Jones, 2004). To handle these labor shortages, we will need to harness the talents of all of our people, and part of this effort will be encouraging highly qualified women to enter and stay in the workforce. Whether you are a male or female college student, understanding the contributions of women at work and the obstacles that women still navigate will be important for your success. The latest projections of the US labor force suggest that women make up 48% of the US labor force in 2008;[1] 60% of all adult women in the US were in the workforce in 2000 (US Bureau of Labor Statistics, 2000). The number of women in the workforce has increased dramatically since the 1950s, and today much of the work in corporations is done in teams of both men and women. If men understand the challenges that women face, they will be better equipped to work with them. If women understand the potential challenges that they may face, they will be better able to successfully respond to these challenges.

In addition to the smooth internal functioning of a firm, women's contributions are important to the firm's external performance. As more and more customers and clients become women and minorities, and as these groups have more financial clout, the successful marketing of products is more likely with a diverse workforce. Business people are learning that female consumers have come to expect products that specifically address their needs; arguably, these products are conceived, produced, marketed, and sold by employees who understand their needs – other women.

The successful participation of women in the workplace should be important to all of us, from students to human resource professionals to marketing professionals and to CEOs and senior managers who hire employees and set workplace policies. Moreover, the effective deployment of women in the workforce should be as important to men as it is to women. If men own businesses or work as senior managers in them, they will need to use all available talent, not just the talents of men. Their businesses will be more successful if they pursue an agenda of equality, rather than one of special privilege for some. If women feel short-changed compared to men, their motivation to put in their best effort will be compromised, which will ultimately lead to less than optimal performance for the firm. So we can see that not taking advantage of half of the available talent (women) and not treating women fairly in the workplace will have a detrimental effect on a company's profits. Moreover, effectively deploying the talent of *all* employees is essential for companies in the competitive, global environment of the twenty-first century.

## Overview of Women's Workforce Participation

To better understand the position of women in the workforce, we begin with an overview of women's workforce participation and various factors that resulted in the rate change in women's workforce participation over the last century. This overview shows that there are multiple reasons for women's increased labor-force participation, and for the changes in the legal and political status of women in the US. An increase in women's civil rights and a demand for women's labor opened doors for women in the workplace. The interaction among changes in women's legal rights, the volatility of the economy, and changing social attitudes all played a role in the profound change in women's labor-force participation through the twentieth century and into the twenty-first century. The following section identifies the various factors responsible for the growth of women in the labor market and explains the interplay among these factors.

## Factors Affecting Women in the Workforce in the Twentieth Century

In the early 1900s, increasing numbers of women in Western countries began demanding the legal and political rights that democracies had denied them throughout the nineteenth century: the right to vote and stand for office, the right to hold property and secure access on terms of equality to public institutions. The most formidable and militant of these early feminists were the suffragettes of pre-war Great Britain. By 1919 women had secured the vote in the UK, and in 1920 in the US. (By contrast, women were not allowed to vote in Switzerland as late as 1970.) This early feminist movement has been called *first-wave feminism*. During this time, the demands for women's equality did not extend to the workplace. Most women did not work, and those few who did were restricted to a narrow range of jobs and professions: primary school teaching and nursing, for example. Women lawyers and doctors were few in number, and often had entered these professions to continue a family tradition in the absence of brothers. They were tolerated as eccentrics. Beyond school teachers and nurses, only telephone operators and bank tellers were predominantly female. Although many women did not work, single women dominated the female labor force from 1870 to 1920 (Casper & Bianchi, 2002; Goldin, 2006; Leibowitz & Klerman, 1995; Rosenfeld, 1996; Smith & Ward, 1985).

The demands of World War II dramatically increased women's participation in the workforce, but only temporarily. Between 1940 and 1945, women found themselves in almost all occupations, including aircraft pilots and other non-combat military jobs. From 1940 to 1944, women's participation increased by almost 50%, mainly in war-related manufacturing such as aircraft and munitions factories. An American war campaign stressed, "If you've used an electric mixer in your kitchen, you can learn to run a drill press" (Goodwin, 1995, p. 414). Women also increased their participation in nursing, teaching, clothing manufacturing, and telephone operations (Marshall & Paulin, 1987). Black women made significant gains during World War II by moving into war-related industries and out of agricultural work and domestic service. But with the end of the war and the return of millions of soldiers, men received priority in hiring and women left factory jobs, many without protest. The prevailing attitude of the time was that government and business had an obligation to provide every man who could be employed with a job, and women with employment only if they needed a job to support a family, in the absence of a male breadwinner.

In addition to workforce demands, an important part of first-wave feminism was the struggle for reproductive rights. In the nineteenth century, it was illegal for doctors to provide contraceptive devices. Women could not control their work lives unless they could control when they had their children and the number they desired. Margaret Sanger, an early feminist, was charged in New York State with disseminating contraceptive information. In 1873, the Comstock Act was passed making it illegal to send "lewd" materials through the mail, including contraceptive devices. Although the struggle for reproductive rights began during the first wave, it was not recognized widely as an important part of the struggle for equality until the second wave.

*Second-wave* feminism began as a movement among women to demand equal access to the professions and to positions of responsibility in the workplace. In the 1950s, middle-class, married women were content to remain at home, the economy was stable and one earner was enough for many family units to live comfortably. By the 1960s and 1970s, however, many families felt the pinch of harder economic times; *stagflation*, the term coined for a combination of inflation and a lack of economic growth, burdened the American economy. Women were eager to move into the workforce to supplement the family's income, and many women had begun to acquire educational credentials that qualified them for the same jobs that men had.

In addition to the economic needs of women and families, the second wave was influenced by a change in consciousness of women. The movement was inspired by works like Simone de Beauvoir's *The Second Sex* (1949), which argued that men dominated women and were therefore the "first" sex, while women as the "second sex" were exploited by the standards set by men. Second-wave feminists rejected the notion that women were either specially suited for homemaking or that they were unsuited to work in all areas of the modern economy, including jobs as police officers and firefighters that no one had ever thought before as suitable for women. A second book, *The Feminine Mystique* (1963) by Betty Friedan, grew out of her interviews with her Smith College graduating class. The book uncovered her former classmates' lack of fulfillment as suburban housewives because their identities were bound solely to their husbands and children. Friedan's work became a voice for women who felt trapped by their domestic roles and who wanted to find fulfilling jobs in the paid workforce.

Two separate but interrelated movements during the second wave influenced women's participation in the workforce and gave them more power. The first was the Civil Rights Movement of the 1960s. Women saw similarities between their own subordinate position and that of black Americans, and they were inspired by the rhetoric of the Civil Rights Movement. Moreover, they learned techniques; the organization, leadership, and protests of the Civil Rights Movement became a blueprint for second-wave feminists. In 1966, The National Organization of Women (NOW), with Betty Friedan as its leader, held its first meeting. The group pushed for fair employment, especially in hiring and promotion decisions, access to education, and equal pay. As part of the push for civil rights for women, in 1961 the Kennedy administration initiated the Presidential Commission on the Status of Women, which outlined changes in hiring practices and recommended maternity leave and affordable childcare. In 1963, The Equal Pay Act was passed, making it illegal to pay women and men differently for performing the same work. Title VII of the Civil Rights Act followed in 1964. It banned discrimination based on race, sex, religion, or national origin.

In addition to these efforts to provide women with civil rights, the second movement pushed for equal sexual rights and was marked by the introduction of the birth-control pill. The pill was finally made available to women in 1961, although it was not until the 1970s that its use became widespread in the US. Birth control made it possible for women to plan their pregnancies, which in turn made it possible for them to plan their careers and postpone motherhood, should they choose to.

From the early 1960s to 1980, the movements for sexual and civil rights and women's income needs led to a dramatic increase in their workforce participation; women's participation went from 38% to 52%, with black women having on average a greater participation rate than white women (Cleveland, Stockdale, & Murphy, 2000). Unlike during World War II when women were temporary workers to fill a demand for factory work, women had entered the workforce as permanent participants. Married women began contributing to the household income; by 1985, men were the sole breadwinners in less than 15% of US households (Cleveland et al., 2000). This was a major shift from the pre-war period when married women participated in the workforce at much lower levels than single and divorced women. At the turn of the twentieth century, only 6% of married women were in the labor force compared to 40% of single women over the age of 10 (Folbre, 1991). Scholars attribute the post-World War II rise in female labor supply to real-wage growth for women as well as their increased levels of education and decreased fertility (Leibowitz & Klerman, 1995; Smith & Ward, 1985).

In her discussion of the changing economic role of married women in the US, Goldin (2006) identifies two sources of married women's shift into the paid labor force. First, the demand for more workers pulled married women into the workforce. Second, as female cohorts moved through time and increasingly acquired the educational and other necessarily prerequisites for paid employment, they were better able to respond to the labor demands over time periods. In addition, the declining real wages of men were a major economic force pulling women into the workforce in the latter decades of the twentieth century (Vallas, Finlay, & Wharton, 2009). As men's real wages decreased, married women entered the labor force to contribute to the family wage. Another factor in the increase in women's participation was fueled by an increase in the divorce rates between 1960 and 1980, making it economically necessary for newly divorced women to work.

In this second wave, the agenda of feminism moved from securing basic political rights to demanding a level playing field in the pursuit of economic opportunities. Women demanded access to jobs up and down the employment ladder, and access to the education and training that would qualify them for these jobs. They rejected arguments against equal treatment of women in the economy that were based on women's traditional roles in child-rearing. Second-wave feminists combined their general demands for equality in the workplace with specific attacks on the unequal standards imposed on those few professions and jobs in which women predominated. For example in the airline industry, women cabin attendants, called "stewardesses" (the men were called "pursers"), had been forced to quit once they were married or pregnant. Weight and age restrictions were imposed on them, and they were required to wear high heels

---

### Box 1.1 Sex Versus Gender

In part because women were increasingly seen to be equally capable as men in many hitherto all-male occupations, and in order to undermine claims that some jobs just couldn't be accomplished by women, second-wave feminism undertook to show that traditional distinctions between men and women were not based on biological differences, but in fact reflected cultural differences. These cultural differences were manifest in values, tastes, prejudices, and socially constructed institutions, as opposed to genetics or the physiology of men and women.

In the second wave, feminists and other social scientists began to distinguish sex and gender: the former was held to be biological and the latter was largely a matter of convention, social attitudes, or the politics of women's subordination. "Sex" refers to male and female biology, while "gender" connotes how our biological sex is understood by others and by ourselves. One's sex is determined by biological differences in male versus female genetic endowment, in particular XY sex chromosomes for males and XX for females, which determine genitalia. Even secondary sexual traits distinguish males from females: a lower voice in men, larger breasts in women, and a smaller musculature in women. Gender, on the other hand, reflects the meanings that people ascribe to the male or female sex. Psychologists, sociologists, and anthropologists have studied gender identity and how it affects individuals and societies; for example, gender identity may determine which careers people find suitable for themselves or the domestic roles societies prescribe for women versus men. In the 1950s, psychologists referred to gender identity as anything a person does or says that marks him or her as male or female (Money, 1955). Later, feminists wrote about gender as the societal and cultural processes that led people to identify themselves as having typically feminine or masculine behaviors (Unger, 1979). Since the 1970s and 1980s, the word "gender" has been thought of by many social scientists as largely a social construction – a construction that can be altered with a change in attitudes or behaviors. Gender role expectations are built into the very fabric of our institutions – the family, the state, culture, religion, and law (Lorber, 2005). For example, consider how some religious ceremonies command a woman to love, honor, and "obey" her husband, or how high schools in the 1960s had shop (Industrial Arts) classes for boys and home economics classes for girls. Even clothing manufacturers create distinctions between the sexes by the color of clothing suggested as appropriate for baby girls (pink) versus baby boys (blue). Once we separate the sexes and emphasize their differences rather than their similarities, we open the door for differences in their treatment. Thus, an important aspect of second-wave feminism was the increasing awareness by women and men of the artificial, non-biological-based gender roles that had been imposed upon them and of the political process necessary to change these prescribed roles.

and, on some of the airlines, revealing uniforms such as "hot pants." Stewardesses began to resist these demands. Toward the end of the second wave, women and their male allies sought successfully to open the traditionally male institutions which prepared only men for the most responsible and influential positions in the public and private sectors. In the US, Harvard and Yale, which had formerly been all-male institutions, opened their doors to women, while several women's colleges became coeducational. The movement was also active in Western European countries; like the Ivy League, most of Oxford and Cambridge's all-male colleges began to admit women.

By the 1990s, demographic and cultural changes in the US had spawned a *third-wave feminist movement*. By 1998, 79% of men and 60% of women participated in the workforce, with black and other minority women participating at 64% (Cleveland et al., 2000). In the US, the populations of all major minority groups (Asians, Hispanics, and blacks) had grown; for example, in census comparisons from 1990 to 2000, the Hispanic population increased by more than 50% from 22.4 million to 35.3 million; the Asian population increased by 48% from 6.9 million to 10.2 million; and the black population increased by 15.6% from 30 million to 34.7 million. The figure is higher for blacks if mixed-race African Americans are included (US Census Bureau, 2000). The participation of minority women in the workforce has steadily increased from 1950 to 2007, with a sharp increase from 2004 to 2007. Another major shift occurred from the 1900s to 1999; during this timeframe, service industries grew from 31% to 78%, bringing more women of all races into the workforce (Fisk, 2003).

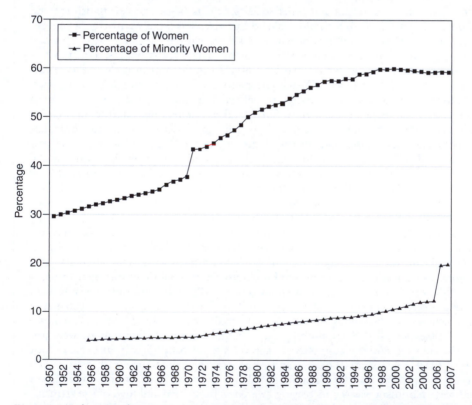

*Figure 1.1* Labor Market Participation Rates for US Women, 1950–2007 (total percentage of women in the US workforce and percentage of minority women in the workforce) (source: Bureau of Labor Statistics, 2007).

Second-wave feminism was a movement largely dominated by white, upper-class educated women from the developed world, and its agenda focused on the interests of such women. A new generation of feminists argued that more attention should be paid to minority women, particularly if a fully adequate conception of women's gender roles and the limitations they impose across all societies, social classes, and ethnicities were to be understood. And they advocated a broader, more inclusive conception of what it means to be female. Third-wave feminists came to treat race, social class, ethnicity, and sexual orientation as social constructions masquerading as real and inevitable divisions between people, whose effects were to foster the exploitation or exclusion of groups classified in those terms. This treatment encouraged third-wave feminists to adapt employment theories originally articulated to understand economic classes in capitalist economies, racial out-groups in apartheid regimes, and discriminated castes in non-Western cultures. These later feminists provided general theories about gender in Western cultures and how gender operates in a globalized economy. Several United Nations Women's Conferences were held around the world that began to alter how women thought about the movement. The first was held in Mexico City in 1975, the second in Copenhagen in 1980, the third in Nairobi in 1985, and the fourth in Beijing in 1995. At these conferences women in Western cultures learned about the issues facing women in developing countries and began to realize that the concerns of Western women were not necessarily the same concerns for all women. Attention shifted from concerns of white women to the empowerment of all women, and to basic human rights. Poverty, education levels, women's health, violence against women, armed conflict, women and the environment, and economic participation of women have all been discussed at these events. During this time, the treatment of women workers in factories of multinational companies also became a concern; US companies use overseas labor in Latin America and Asia to lower their costs of production because hiring these workers is far cheaper than hiring domestic workers. Even though many of these firms pay more than local employers, these workers (usually women) are often subject to long hours and unhealthy working conditions (Pyle, 1999, 2001). The International Labor Office contends that even though more women have entered the workforce, more than half of all working women are in vulnerable jobs that are in less productive sectors of the economy where they are less likely to have a voice at work or basic human rights (ILO, 2008).

By the time this third wave took off, women in the Western economies had entered many of the work roles that second-wave feminists had struggled through the 1960s and 1970s to open up for them. By the late twentieth century, women in Western countries were to be found in all the professions and had made some gains in equal pay with men. From the 1990s onward, with legal protections in place for women and penalties for violations, discrimination had become more nuanced and less obvious than it had been in the 1960s. In the US, women had consistently made gains in the management ranks of organizations, moving from a low rate of 4% of managers in 1990 to 45% in 2000 (see Table 1.1). This increase in management has given them a voice in decision-making and improved their pay.

As the twenty-first century dawned, the agenda of feminism moved away from debate among third-wave feminists about speculative theories of women's subordination in the workplace and the home to concerns about *how* to implement political and economic equality around the world. If third-wave feminism has left an enduring mark outside of the academic world of women's studies, it has been to establish and expand a practical alliance among women across social classes, cultures, and ethnicities, and even to extend it to gay men, undocumented workers, the transgendered, and others still

*Table 1.1*  Percentage of Women Employed in White Collar Occupations
(and as Managers)

| Year | White Collar | Managers |
|------|------|------|
| 1990 | 19 | 4 |
| 1910 | 24 | 6 |
| 1920 | 32 | 7 |
| 1930 | 33 | 8 |
| 1940 | 35 | 11 |
| 1950 | 40 | 14 |
| 1960 | 42 | 16 |
| 1970 | 47 | 16 |
| 1980 | 53 | 26 |
| 1990 | 56 | 39 |
| 2000 | 57 | 45 |

Source: Data from the period 1900–1960, *Historical statistics of the United States: Colonial times to 1970*. Part 1, Series D, 11–25. US Bureau of the Census. Data from 1970–2000, *Employment and earnings*, table 2 from US Bureau of Labor Statistics. Note that the 1900–1960 data include persons 10 years and older. The data from the period 1970–2000 include persons 16 and older.

not fully able to secure their economic rights. Women have been joined by members of all these groups in the effort to find the most effective ways to make use of the advances first- and second-wave feminists helped establish.

## Women's Workforce Participation Today – Current Statistics and Future Challenges

The millennium has passed. We've seen legal advances for women's civil rights and governments have passed equal pay legislation. More women work as managers in America and in European countries than ever before and the rates of women in the workforce have been steadily increasing. For example, in 1970, 43% of women in the US worked in the paid labor force compared to 52% in 1980, 58% in 1990 and 60% in 2000 (US Census Bureau, 2004). The same phenomenon has occurred in European countries. In Belgium, in 1970, 25% of women were in the workforce, and in 1998, the number had grown to 37%. In 2001, 42% of the labor market in Belgium was female (Van Haegandoren, Steegmans, & Valgaeren, 2001). In Greece, between 1990 and 2000, 80% of new job entrants were women, and in 1981, 29.8% of women in Greece worked; while, in 2000, the percentage of women working grew to 38.7% (Kottis & Neokosmidi, 2004). In the Netherlands a similar pattern of increased participation occurred; in 1971, 25% of women worked, in 1990 the number had grown to 39%, and in 2001, 53% of women worked (Tijdens, 2004). According to the Central Statistics Office in Ireland, the participation of married women (as a percentage of women workers) grew from 3.6% in 1971 to 48.2% in 2000 (McCarthy, 2004). Davidson's and Burke's book featuring 20 countries around the world concluded,

> Throughout almost all the countries, the common trend has been over the past twenty years, the proportion of women in the paid workforce (particularly married with children and part-time workers) has increased and today ranges from 30 per cent (Turkey) to 53 per cent (in the Netherlands).

(2004, p. 6)

The dramatic increase in women in the workforce in the developed world is due to many factors, including labor-market shortages that made it necessary for employers to hire more women. In particular, a growing service sector created many part-time and full-time positions for women. In addition, over the decades a greater acceptance of women in the workforce was the result of greater political participation by women. For example, in 1973 in Ireland the marriage bar was revoked. This legislation forced women to resign from jobs in the public and civil service as soon as they married. And social welfare programs in some countries (such as Belgium) afforded many more child-care options, making it easier for women to join the workforce. These legal changes and shifts in cultural attitudes brought women into the workforce in large numbers.

Today women can be found in occupations from which they were previously barred or discouraged from entering, from firefighting to information technology to engineering. Like men, women are gaining advanced degrees from competitive universities; in the US, in 2006–2007 in four-year institutions, 42% of degrees were awarded to men and 58% to women. Of master's degrees awarded, 56% went to women and 44% to men (Knapp, Kelly-Reid, & Ginder, 2008). Parts of the playing field have been made level for women and men in corporations, but women still struggle to balance work life and family life. They continue to have difficulty in attaining higher-level positions in companies in which they work, and they often feel isolated if they are able to move up within an organization. In spite of the gains women have made, 40 years after the United States and European Union countries passed legislation to prevent gender dis-crimination, the glass ceiling[2] still exists in some organizations and in some industries. The glass ceiling can be found in the highest areas of government, academia, and in corporate organizations.

In response to barriers that women and minorities have faced, governments as well as businesses have recognized the importance of equity in the workplace. In the Euro-pean Union, equality between men and women holds a prominent place on the polit-ical agenda. The EU has recognized that its labor force will need women at all levels, as birth rates fall and the population ages. Among the priorities for EU action by the year 2010 are the following: a call for 60% employment rate for women (the rates are currently low for older women and women have a higher rate of unemployment than men); access to employment benefits for women, especially retirement benefits; elimi-nation of the gender pay gap (currently women earn 15% less than men); removal of gender discrimination of immigrant and ethnic minority women; and an increase in women entrepreneurs. Women in EU countries currently have difficulty accessing financing for their businesses (Commission of the European Communities, 2006). Banks and other financial institutions are less apt to loan money to women entrepre-neurs than to male entrepreneurs.

In conclusion, the picture of women in the workforce in the last half of the twenti-eth century and early twenty-first century is mixed. In spite of the lack of significant representation of women at the very highest levels in organizations, some women have made it to the top and many women have made significant inroads into lower and middle management. To reflect these advances, two scholars have proposed that a new, more updated metaphor – a labyrinth – is in order to replace the old glass-ceiling metaphor. Rather than a ceiling that is absolute and impenetrable, Eagly and Carli suggest that women can attain leadership positions but often travel through a laby-rinth, a complex and demanding path rather than the more straightforward path that men travel to leadership positions (2007). Around the world, women's participation in the labor force and their education levels have continued to increase. The challenge for companies and governments in the developed world is to afford women more opportunity at the top of organizations, in positions of significant decision-making responsibility, and in jobs where they can influence corporate strategy. In poorer countries the challenge is to provide decent employment with acceptable working conditions for women and to narrow the significant wage gap between men and women.

## Organization of This Book

Through background information, case studies, and legal cases, each chapter explores a different dimension of gender and/or racial discrimination manifested in the business environment. The first three chapters serve as introductions to the topic of gender and gender discrimination, while the final chapter explains policy prescriptions and actions taken by governments, non-profits, and corporations that have advanced the position of women and other minorities. The middle chapters focus on women in the workplace and the application of the theoretical concepts discussed in Chapters 1 and 2. In addition, the middle chapters turn to cases that relate to the chapter topics. The cases are based on real situations identified through interviews with female business professionals. The names and organizations have been changed to ensure the anonymity of the women and firms treated in the cases.

As discrimination in the twenty-first century has become more subtle (for example, most places of employment do not openly display pin-up calendars or openly harass gay men or women), some of the problems treated in this book are notably more nuanced than earlier problems women faced. Cases concerning sexual harassment are often hard to adjudicate because they involve one person's version of the facts versus another's version. Similarly, in cases of lost career opportunity it is difficult to assign blame to a particular individual. Was it the manager's fault for not putting the woman forward for promotion and not affording her career opportunities, or was the woman ill-prepared because of her own lack of expertise and talent? In these gray areas, students are asked to wrestle with the facts and consider different positions. Following each case, the student is challenged to reflect on various issues raised in a set discussion questions. The questions are designed to help the student evaluate the case from different perspectives and to engage the student in analysis of the possible courses of action the women in the cases could take.

Each of the middle chapters concludes with selected court cases settled in the US and in European countries that relate to the chapter topic. In addition, readings and websites that will augment student learning are suggested.

The organization of the book follows a particular logic. In this chapter we have briefly discussed why gender in the workplace is still an issue after legislation has been passed to rectify problems and make women equal partners with men in organizations. Chapter 2 turns to the fundamental causes of women's continued subordination. Occupational Segregation explains how women have historically occupied the lowest rungs on the corporate ladder. The chapter defines horizontal and vertical segregation and offers explanations for occupational segregation – from a variety of perspectives – socialization and culture, labor market theory, and individual preferences, for example. In particular we have focused on the places where women are still finding it difficult to penetrate: senior levels and board membership. Chapter 3 explains Title VII of the Civil Rights Act and The Equal Pay Act, the two pieces of US legislation designed to protect people from discrimination. By explaining both occupational segregation and the legal framework to combat discrimination, these early chapters pave the way for Chapter 4 – Career Opportunities. If women are segregated from men and given non-decision-making roles in organizations, their chances for career development will be hampered. Discrimination in hiring and in selecting candidates for promotion is examined. The chapter explains the differences between overt and unconscious practices that disadvantage women and discusses how organizational culture affects women's opportunities. For example, exclusion from key social gatherings where business is inevitably discussed and where personal relationships are strengthened will make a woman less visible to senior managers in decision-making roles. Case studies present situations in which women may have been disadvantaged and several legal cases are examined, demonstrating that women are denied career opportunities at both ends of the employment spectrum: in high-end and entry level positions.

Chapters 5, 6, 7, and 8 look more closely at some of the mechanisms of inequality at work, and how they disproportionately affect women. Equal pay issues, lack of influential networks, lack of access to information, differences in communication style, and, finally, hostile work environments all make it difficult for women to reach their true potential. Chapter 5 examines the state of women's earnings versus men's, the factors that lead to unequal pay for equivalent work, and the problems associated with placing a dollar value on individual jobs. In addition to the situation in the United States, the global gender gap in equal pay is discussed. In Chapter 6, the importance of networking and mentoring in the business setting are covered. First, a summary of social network theory is provided. Then the gender differences in accessing networks are reviewed. Through a case study, the chapter examines the issues faced by racial minorities of both genders in finding suitable mentors, and then turns to problems unique to minority women.

Chapter 7, Gender and Communication, explores whether or not men and women communicate differently and how the flow of information (and therefore power) in organizations can circumvent women. In the chapter, cross-cultural communication, verbal communication patterns, and other channels of information – such as electronic and written correspondence – are discussed. Since much of today's communication happens virtually, via e-mail and other methods, the chapter explores the differences and similarities in men's and women's virtual communication.

Chapter 8, Hostile Work Environments and Sexual Harassment, begins with an explanation of what the law defines as a hostile work environment, and continues by explaining the various theories about why sexual harassment persists despite the introduction of legal remedies in the last 40 years. The legal environment, legislation designed to protect victims of harassment, and several high-profile legal cases are discussed. Chapter 9 explores how women balance work and other life pursuits – highlighting the added burden working women typically have in managing a household and caring for children. The chapter highlights the very real problems that organizations have in meeting productivity goals while offering flexibility to their employees, and it examines the burden that women bear for managing a family's needs while holding down a job. Carrying the brunt of responsibility for family can contribute to women's lack of satisfaction with both their family life and work life.

Chapter 10, Women Entrepreneurs: Working *Their* Way, analyzes the current increase in the number of female entrepreneurs in the US, Europe, and in some developing economies, the reasons why women are exiting the formal labor market to work for themselves, and research about the differences between male and female entrepreneurs. Many women discover that, after having worked in organizations for several years, they find more gratification and flexibility in working for themselves. Particular obstacles for women entrepreneurs, such as the lack of access to venture capital and mentors, are discussed. An interview with four entrepreneurs who have chosen to build their businesses in traditionally male-dominated arenas, and a case study of two female entrepreneurs who worked in female-dominated industries, conclude the chapter.

Chapter 11 covers policy decisions and policy recommendations, with a particular focus on the types of programs that seem to have some positive effect on the elimination of gender discrimination. This chapter features work of non-profit organizations, initiatives by corporations, policies and initiatives by federal and state governments, and international efforts.

By presenting the chapters in this order, first the reader sees some of the root causes of, and theories about, inequality and learns about the laws designed to eradicate discrimination. Second, the reader learns how inequality may be expressed in the workplace and its mechanisms for operation. And finally, the reader understands what organizations, governments, companies, and individuals are doing to promote a just workplace.

## Further Reading and Suggested Websites

Becker, G. (1971). *The economics of gender* (2nd ed.). Chicago, IL: University of Chicago Press.

Davidson, M.J. & Burke, R.J. (2004). Women in management worldwide: Facts, figures, and analysis – an overview. In M.J. Davidson & R.J. Burke (Eds.), *Women and men in management worldwide: Facts, figures, analysis* (pp. 1–18). Aldershot, UK: Ashgate Publishing Ltd.

Khurana, R. (2002). *Searching for a corporate savior.* Princeton, NJ: Princeton University Press.

Konrad, A. & Kramer, V. (2006). How many women do boards need? *Harvard Business Review*, 84, 22–24.

http://www.catalyst.org.

http://ec.europa.eu/index_en.htm.

## Discussion Questions

1.  What ideas and events characterize the first, second, and third waves of feminism?
2.  What does the word "feminist" mean to you?
3.  What direction should women's rights go in today?
4.  Do you see any possibility of our civil rights being taken away from us?

# 2 Occupational Segregation and Gender Discrimination

**Learning Objectives**

After completing this chapter, the reader will:

- be able to define segregation and distinguish vertical from horizontal segregation.
- understand some competing theories for workplace segregation.
- understand some of the country-differences of segregated, female employment.

This chapter introduces the fundamental distinctions between two different types of employment segregation, and the evidence for gender discrimination in the workplace. Occupational segregation involves channeling men and women into different occupations, or disproportionately into different occupations, or at different levels within the same industry or sector of the economy.

We introduce some of the leading theories offered to explain why this discrimination still persists. If, as evidence shows, occupationally arbitrary workplace segregation still exits, the patterns of discrimination that produce and maintain it must be well understood. Without a clear grasp of the root causes of workplace segregation, we cannot decide whether segregation warrants intervention to change it, nor can we craft policies that begin to address inequities that might be caused by it.

## Horizontal Segregation

Occupational segregation is horizontal when women are employed in different categories from men in the general economy; for example, when women comprise the vast majority of hotel maids while men occupy the vast majority of auto mechanics, or when men take up most of engineering jobs while almost all nurses are women. Historically women have occupied certain segments of the labor market, including such occupations as clerical work (secretary, administrative assistant), service sector work, and retail sales. One indication of horizontal segregation in the US workforce is that about half of all working women are employed in occupations that are themselves at least 75% female (Dunn, 1997b). Significantly, one of the best predictors of the pay level and status of a job is the proportion of women holding the job; the more women in a particular job category, i.e. the more horizontally segregated it is, the lower the pay (Dunn, 1997a). Women tend to be concentrated in jobs that require interpersonal skills, such as service roles, or nurturing characteristics, such as hospital workers, childcare workers, or teachers; often these jobs are not valued as highly as jobs requiring technical skills, and consequently are not paid as well

(Kilbourne & England, 1997). As more and more women are channeled into these jobs, it becomes the norm to think of women as the legitimate, primary occupiers of these positions.

In the twenty-first century, men and women still occupy different occupations. US census data in 2000 shows that the top occupations for men include drivers, sales workers, first-line supervisors, managers of retail sales, laborers, material workers, carpenters, and janitors. The top occupations for women included secretaries, administrative assistants, elementary and middle school teachers, nurses, cashiers, and retail salespeople. Out of the total number of wage earners, 18% of employed women worked in the service area, while 12% of employed men have chosen service work. From the total number of workers, 8.9% of employed women worked in education, training, or library occupations, while 5.7% of employed men worked in these areas. Out of the total number of female workers, 1.6% worked in computer and mathematical occupations, whereas twice as many men (3.2% of all employed males) worked in these same job classifications. Women dominate the healthcare practitioner field: 7.3% of all working women were employed in the healthcare field, while 4.6% of all working men are employed in this field. A total of 3.3% of all men worked in architectural and engineering occupations, whereas only 0.6% of working women chose these fields (Fronczek & Johnson, 2003). Labor statistics from 2008 mirror those of the 2000 census. The top 10 occupations for women in 2008, in order from most popular to least, were secretaries and administrative assistants, registered nurses, elementary and middle school teachers, cashiers, retail salespersons, nursing, psychiatric and home health workers, first-line supervisors of retail sales clerks, waitresses, receptionists and information clerks, and bookkeepers, accounting and auditing clerks (US Department of Labor Statistics, 2009). Although men still dominate mechanical, civil, and electrical engineering, mathematics and physics, in recent years, there has been a gender shift in some occupations. For example, now women earn 74% of all professional degrees in veterinary science and many are now drawn to pharmacy. At the University of California, 77% of pharmacy graduates and 82% of veterinary science majors are women (Hoff-Sommers, 2008).

Horizontal segregation exists in all countries, including those in the European Union. The largest percentage of European women workers are employed in the service sector, while much smaller percentages of women workers can be found in the industrial occupations and in agriculture (see Figure 2.1). Across Europe, less than 10% of skilled construction workers are women. The prevailing view of hiring-managers in the construction trades is that women cannot withstand the physical workload, even though today many of the heavy lifting jobs are done by machines (Clarke, Pedersen, Michielsens, & Susamn, 2005). Even in countries that are known for their equality (Finland and Denmark), there is substantial occupational segregation. Figure 2.1 shows that female employment in Europe is concentrated in domestic service in private households, where they comprise 82% of the workforce, health (79% of the workforce), education (72%) and other community, social, and personal services (59%). Men, on the other hand, are predominately employed in construction (89%), electricity, gas, and water supply (80%), transport and communication (73%), manufacturing (69%), and agriculture (63%).

In 2003 The British Equal Opportunities Commission undertook a two-year study of occupational segregation. The EOC reports, "Despite 30 years of equality legislation, occupational segregation remains as entrenched as ever" (www.eoc.org.uk). Furthermore the EOC asserts that three-quarters of women are still employed in the five "Cs" – cleaning, catering, caring, clerical, and cashiering. The study reports that the UK is failing to provide real choice for women in both entering training and in work. This is ironic in that Britain is experiencing a real skill shortage in some traditionally male occupations. In the Nordic countries, occupational segregation persists and is high compared to other industrialized countries (Anker & Melkas, 1997). Gender stereotyping tends to place women in three main occupational categories: the caring professions, jobs requiring manual dexterity, and jobs doing typical household work. In Norway, Sweden, and Finland, the highly feminized occupations are housekeeper, childcare worker, municipal health worker, and secretary/stenographer.

Women in the European Union countries continue to choose different fields of study from men, which undoubtedly contributes to the phenomenon of occupational segregation. In the age category 25–64, 26.2% of women in higher education choose math, engineering, or science, while 43.6% of men in higher education choose these subjects. The opposite trend occurs in the humanities, arts, and languages, where 64.4% of women following a course of higher education choose these subjects, while 28.9% of men choose them (Trinczek, 2008). This same trend occurs across the board in many countries. In a study of 44 developed, transitional, and developing countries, researchers found an under-representation of women studying engineering, math, and the natural sciences and an over-representation of women pursuing the humanities, the social sciences, and health fields (Charles & Bradley, 2009). In cross-national comparisons of occupational sex segregation, Charles (1992) found that women have greater access to predominately male occupations in countries where birth rates are low and where there are strong equalitarian beliefs.

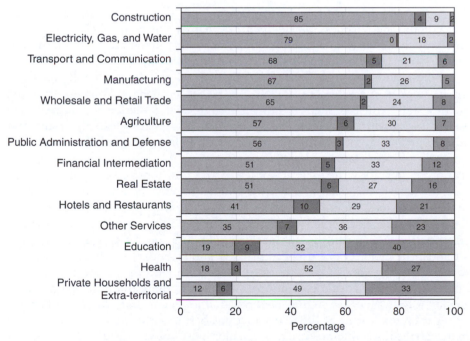

*Figure 2.1* Gender Segregation by Sector, EU (source: the European Foundation for the Improvement of Living and Working Conditions. (2008). *Mind the Gap – Women's and Men's Quality of Work and Employment*).

## Horizontal Segregation – an Issue for Men as well as Women

Just as horizontal segregation keeps women from participating fully in all occupations, men face the same challenge. Because of the social stigma attached to men entering traditionally women-centered occupations, the number of men in nursing, elementary school teaching, home healthcare working, and secretarial work is very low. Of course, part of the reason that men may be deterred from entering these fields is the low pay these jobs command relative to other careers.

## Vertical Segregation

Vertical segregation reflects the view that women have fundamentally different capabilities, skills and emotional strengths than men do, and are therefore suited to different work. Vertical segregation exists when men and women disproportionately occupy different positions within the same general field. This sort of segregation stems from the view that men's capabilities, skills, and strengths qualify them for more authoritative and more responsible positions than women (Charles & Grusky, 2004). Vertical segregation is often referred to as the result of a "glass ceiling" – an invisible or unspoken barrier to the advancement of women beyond a certain level of authority, responsibility, and pay in a job-classification that is not horizontally segregated. Vertical segregation reinforces the idea that women are suited for lower-level roles with less responsibility rather than managerial or professional roles within the same occupational category because they possess certain innate characteristics (passivity, nurturance, emotional sensitivity, for example), or because they have less cognitive capability or fewer higher-level skills compared to men.

Vertical segregation can be found within several job disciplines, including sales, education, medicine, and business management. In many fields men are chosen as managers more frequently than women; for example, in sales, women are more often sales clerks than sales managers. In the realm of business, women managers usually lead less profitable business units and less powerful departments, and female bank managers often work in smaller, more remote branch offices (Stover, 1997). Women are often channeled into staff positions such as human resources and marketing, rather than "line" positions – to which other employees report – that have clear profit-and-loss responsibility. Furthermore, these line positions offer a more direct path to senior management jobs with higher status and pay.

In education, men occupy the majority of leadership positions – principals, superintendents, department heads, deans, etc., while women occupy the lower-level teaching and teacher assistant roles. Women's greater representation in primary education is a direct reflection of what is assumed to be their natural ability with children – transferred from the private sector to the public sphere of education. With the exception of the Netherlands, the majority of European primary and secondary teachers are women. Men, however, dominate jobs in the university system. In Eastern European countries, in the higher education scientific community, women are more likely to be in lower-paid technician roles rather than higher-paid research jobs (Eurostat, 2004). In Europe, vertical segregation is a feature of life in occupations besides education; less than one in nine women certified accountants reaches a senior post (Boyer, 1995). Even in EU sectors where women predominate, such as healthcare or education, a pattern of vertical segregation holds. In the US, the healthcare profession is vertically segregation with disproportionately more female workers in lower-level jobs; according to a 2006 study conducted by the American College of Healthcare Executives, 57% of men work in higher-level general management jobs versus 44% of women. Interestingly, at the management level of the predominantly female healthcare industry, there is also a pattern of horizontal segregation. Women are more involved than men in specialized management areas including nursing, planning, marketing, quality assurance, and home and long-term care. Thus, the pattern of horizontal and vertical segregation can occur several times within a given industry, and one form can be "nested" inside the other repeatedly (American College of Healthcare Executives, 2007).

## Vertical Segregation: Women CEOs and Women in the Board Room

Women have made progress in penetrating the managerial labor market, but much of this progress has been at lower levels or mid-level management positions in American and European corporations. The few highly-visible women CEOs – such as Carly Fiorina, former CEO of Hewlett Packard, Meg Whitman, former CEO of eBay Technologies, and Andrea Jung, President and CEO of Avon – are exceptions to the general under-representation of women at these levels. It may seem that since these women have made it to the top there is no longer a barrier to women's success. However, the progress of women in decision-making roles, such as board-level assignments or senior management roles, has barely increased.

The board of directors of a company and its CEO are the most powerful decision-makers in current business organizations. A company's board of directors governs its affairs, and the company's highest officers report to its board. Women's lack of representation on corporate boards is significant because boards make high-level policy decisions that affect large numbers of people including shareholders, employees, and ultimately consumers. These decisions include, for example, who will be CEO, whether or not to close a part of the business and consequently lay-off employees, whether or not to offer a stock purchase plan for employees, how to remunerate employees, how to respond to the political and legal environments, or whether or not to allocate significant funds to a particular initiative.

Because of the far-reaching power of these positions, the presence or absence of women on boards or as CEOs is a crucial factor in their roles throughout the rest of the corporation. The presence of women board members seems to have a spillover effect on the number of women in senior management positions in companies. In Canada, there is a strong correlation between the number of female board members and the number of senior women in the company (Anastasopoulos & Brown, 2002). A US study found similar effects (Bilimoria, 2006). The presence of women on a company's board of directors is positively associated with gender diversity at the top; the more women on a corporate board, the greater number of women officers with "line" jobs affording significant responsibility, the greater the number of women with "clout" job titles, and the greater presence of women as top earners. Indeed, this phenomenon appears to be present in educational institutions as well. Researchers conducted a study of five Australian universities that have over 30% of their senior management positions filled by women. They found that having a critical mass of other women in senior management was critical to women's advancement to this level (Chesterman & Ross-Smith, 2006).

The statistics clearly show that women are under-represented in top decision-making roles: in 2005 the number of woman CEOs in Fortune 500 companies was nine; in 2006, it became 10; in 2007 and 2008 it was 12; and at the start of 2009 it was 13, just 2.6% of Fortune 500 CEOs. Catalyst, a women's research organization in the US, reports that in 2003, 54 companies in this survey of companies had no women board directors (Catalyst, 2003). In 2005, Catalyst reported that, while the average Fortune 500 company has 21.8 corporate officers, women held 3.6 of these positions. In the three years preceding the 2005 Catalyst report, the average annual increase in the percentage of corporate officers positions held by women fell dramatically to 23% per year, the lowest level in the last 10 years. A total of 75% of Fortune 500 companies reported no women as top earners (Catalyst, 2006b). The status of women on boards of companies in high-growth, entrepreneurial sectors of the economy is also limited; in this sector there is a high likelihood that these types of firms will have an executive team comprised exclusively of males (Nelson & Levesque, 2007). Even when a corporation markets products disproportionately of concern to women, there are often no women on the company's board. For example, although women are more involved than men in the healthcare decisions for themselves and for their families, including which insurance to buy, what pharmaceutical products are available, and the benefits of vitamins and supplements, more than one-third of the world's top 500 healthcare and pharmaceutical companies have no women on their corporate boards (Fallows, 2005).

As in the US, in Europe women's participation at the highest levels of companies is low. In Britain, only 14.4% of company directors in 2005 were women, while the overall percentage of women managers (33.1% in 2005) has tripled in 10 years (Chartered Management Institute, 2005). According to a report by Corporate Women Directors International, almost half of the 92 companies surveyed have no senior women executive officers on their management teams (Corporate Women Directors International Report, 2006). In 2008, only 9.7% of board seats of Europe's 300 top companies were occupied by women. Of the European nations, the Scandinavian countries are best at recruiting women board members; in Norway, 44% of corporate boards are female, in Sweden, 27%, and in Denmark and Finland, 25% (European Professional Women's Network, 2009).

## Norway – Tackling Vertical Segregation in the Board Room

One might ask why Norway is so far ahead of other European nations in recruiting women to boards. The answer lies in recent legislation. The Norwegian government decreed that all corporate boards must be 40% female within two years or force being shut down (Foroohar, 2006). Gabrielson, a conservative trade minister, was largely responsible for changing the gender composition of Norway's corporate boards. The government tried voluntary compliance with little success, so Gabrielson stepped in and pushed for mandatory quotas. "I could not see why, after 30 years of an equal ratio of women and men in universities and having so many women with experience, there were so few of them on boards," said Gabrielson (*Guardian*, March 6, 2008). Gabrielson first hired Benja Fageoland, a female economist, to head-hunt eligible women for board seats. She instituted "Female Future," a six-month institute that provides training for high-potential women who could, with this intensive training, serve on boards. Since March 2008, 570 women have gone through the training, resulting in 1 in 4 women placed on the board of large companies and half gaining board positions in smaller companies. Norway's example, as well as the other studies mentioned above, underwrites the importance of a critical number of women on boards. Having only one or two female board members is less effective, since these women will find it more difficult to push for issues that are of importance to women. It is easier for a single woman board member to become isolated and marginalized.

## Barriers to Top-Level Positions

Although the percentage of women board members is slowly increasing, several factors contribute to their small numbers. Requirements for board membership are significant barriers for women because they include high-level financial management experience, often experience as a CEO and past board membership – credentials women rarely have. Consequently, few women are deemed eligible as candidates. An additional problem seems to be identifying and nurturing female talent. In a survey of CEOs from over 50 countries, only 47% of UK business leaders reported that their company was as good at identifying, retaining, and promoting female talent as male talent (PricewaterhouseCoopers, 2007).

Even when women and minorities have been appointed to boards, the suspicion remains that their presence may be "window dressing," particularly when they do not serve on the most powerful committees. Corporate boards usually operate through committees; the three most powerful and important committees on boards are the audit, compensation, and governance committees. The members of these committees have the most influence on corporate life. The audit committee has responsibility for ensuring that the company's financial statements are accurate and in some cases has the power to hire or fire the external auditors; the compensation committee approves the salaries and benefits of the CEO and other high-level executives; and the governance committee is charged with finding CEO candidates and selecting the CEO. In a study by Bilimoria and Piderit (1994) that controlled for directors' experience-based characteristics, women were preferred for membership on the public affairs committee

---

### Box 2.1 Benefits of Women's Board Membership – Two or Three Are Better Than One

The importance of several women serving at the same time on one board includes improved communication among board members and management, a collaborative approach to leadership, and a greater emphasis on including various stakeholders (Konrad & Kramer, 2006). A study sponsored by the Conference Board of Canada highlights the many differences that three or more women on a board can make. First, 94% of boards with three or more women (compared to 68% of all-male boards) insist on conflict-of-interest guidelines. Female directors pay more attention to audit and risk oversight and financial control, and they are more apt to consider the interests of shareholders. Interviews with board members and CEOs suggest that increasing the number of women board members to three broadens the board's discussion to better represent the concerns of various stakeholders, including employees, customers, and the community. In addition, when there is a critical mass of women on boards, the women are more persistent in pursuing answers to difficult questions (Konrad & Kramer, 2006). On boards with three or more women, 86% ensure a code of conduct for the organization, compared with 68% of all-male board members (Anastasopoulos & Brown, 2002, p. 6). In the same study, 72% of boards with two or more women conduct board performance reviews, while only 49% of all-male boards do these reviews. These statistics carry weight because good corporate governance translates into organizational performance. When board members are active and independent of the company's management, better decisions are made. A 2001 study of Fortune 500 firms in the United States with the best record for promoting women to senior positions and to boards proved to be more profitable than their peer competitors (Champion, 2001).

while male directors were chosen for the compensation, executive, and finance committees.

Since the financial misconduct of CEOs at corporations such as Enron, Tyco, and Worldcom, many companies have sought more independent and diverse board membership to oversee CEOs more closely. Yet the membership of women and minorities on boards is still weak. The status and role identity of women board directors is a subject of interest to many scholars. Some suggest that women view their appointments as simply a reflection of their qualifications for the job (Bilimoria & Huse, 1997; Catalyst, 2003). Others feel that at least one important reason for their appointment was their gender (Sethi, Swanson, & Harrigan, 1981). Female board directors are sometimes expected by other women to advance women's corporate status, yet some women feel uncomfortable in this role. They worry that they may be perceived as having a single focus or be thought of as pushing too hard for a woman's agenda (Burson-Marsteller, 1977; Catalyst, 2003; Mattis, 1997). In fact, according to Harvard University professor Rakesh Khurana, when there is only one woman on a board, she typically follows the opinions of the dominant group (Hymowitz, 2004).

## Progress in Breaking down Horizontal and Vertical Segregation – a Mixed Picture

It is clear that after the 1980s women have had more opportunity to occupy job roles of their choosing. One study compared the progress of women senior executives in Fortune 100 companies between 1980 and 2004. In 1980, there were no women executives in these large, stable organizations, while in 2004 women did hold some of the top jobs. In 2004, the female executives were younger than their male counterparts, rose through the ranks faster than men, and were more likely to hold top jobs in the service sector rather than in manufacturing. Both male and female executives in 2004 were younger and had held fewer jobs to get to the top. Women executives were more likely to have had an Ivy League education than their male counterparts (Capelli & Hamori, 2004). These changes in the attributes of corporate executives are good news for women. Notably, promotion based on seniority and many years in an organization appears to be disappearing, and talent rises to the top faster. One interesting difference, however, is the presence of Ivy League-educated women in top jobs versus publicly educated men at the same level. If women are perceived as riskier hires than men, perhaps an Ivy League education is a strong signal of their quality.

Some firms are beginning to recognize that having women at senior levels in the organization helps their business. For example, the demographic composition of a company's clients can influence the demographic composition of the firm. Law firms with women-led corporate clients are beginning to understand the importance of having women attorneys who are partners (Beckman & Phillips, 2005). Law firms promote women attorneys when their client companies have women in three key leadership positions: general counsel, chief executive officer, and board director. The effects of promoting women are even stronger if the law firm depends on a few clients. This change may occurs in other business organizations; as more women reach senior management positions, the more their own suppliers and their customers become sensitive to the importance of having women in their own organization at senior levels.

Although some firms are promoting women to the most senior levels, the data show that horizontal and vertical segregation still exist world-wide. Horizontal segregation channels women into positions without substantial educational requirements, for which there are typically many more job-seekers than jobs, in which the individual's work contribution is hard to identify and easy to replace. These are all reason why horizontally segregated women secure lower pay and few opportunities to distinguish themselves and secure promotion. Vertical discrimination shunts even highly educated women who have skills, technical knowledge, and management ability into lines of work that are demanding and important, but which often provide auxiliary support to the organization rather than *critical* support for organizational performance.

## Explanations for Occupation Segregation

The question naturally arises, are these differences in employment opportunity between men and women the result of free choice or symptoms of injustices that need remedies? The answer to this question depends on what explains these differences. This section describes various possible explanations for both vertical and horizontal segregation.

### *Personal Preference*

Perhaps the most common-sense explanation for occupational segregation is due to differences in tastes and preferences between men and women. Women may simply choose to occupy less educationally or technically demanding roles, part-time work or jobs with fewer responsibilities (Anker, 1997; Hakim, 2002, 2006). In one study, university students were asked about salary expectations, career characteristics, and intensity of work. Female students placed a greater emphasis on work–life balance and cultural fit. The researchers suggest that the differences in attitudes revealed by the study may account for women's career choices and pay differentials as compared to those of men (Sallop & Kirby, 2007). In particular, women's preferred role as caregiver to children in particular is often cited as the reason for their subordinated work status; women opt to work part-time and come and go in the labor force as a matter of individual choice. When women do choose more flexible work arrangements, they accumulate less experience than full-time workers simply because they are working fewer hours.

Personal preferences seem to be revealed in actual choices by successful business women. Increasingly, it seems, women who have managed to compete in the world of investment banking are choosing to step off the career track in that field. Janet Hanson, a former Goldman Sachs banker, suggests that the business culture of investment banks is "brutal," and the hours include working weekends and weekdays until 2 a.m. (Anderson, 2006). Many Generation Y graduates (those born roughly between 1970 and 2000) are choosing options other than business, forgoing large salaries for life balance. At almost half the nation's top business schools (which often require work experience prior to admission), there were fewer women in the class of 2007 than in the class of 2003. At Columbia Business School, for example, women represented 36% of the 2003 class, but 34% of the class of 2007. According to Universum, a branding and research firm, 13% of 881 first- or second-year women at top tier MBA programs chose Wall Street as their preferred employer in 2002, versus 6.9% in 2006 (Anderson, 2006).

Many women choose career paths that do not offer opportunities for advancement, even when these opportunities allow for opportunities to raise families. Why would women choose vertically segregated "dead-end" jobs that do not have a clear career path of advancement – for instance, support staff positions or jobs without budgetary or management responsibility? Such jobs have limited prospect for advancement compared to jobs with profit-and-loss or management responsibilities.

It is probable that long before women enter the workforce, their personal preferences have been shaped by "socialization" to the expectations of others – mothers, fathers, and teachers, for instance. Established social norms may channel women into certain types of typically "feminine" occupational choices and away from others, by shaping their personal preferences in ways that may ultimately limit their choices and prevent them from making the most of their real capabilities. A series of longitudinal studies at the University of Michigan followed one birth cohort of fifth and sixth graders and surveyed them again in the twelfth grade and again at age 20–21 (Gender and Achievement Research Program, 2007). Data was collected from 3,248 adolescents, of whom over 90% were white and 51% female. In addition, 95% of teachers from 12 school districts, and 75% of the adolescents' parents were also surveyed. The results from the study indicated that both adolescents' self-confidence and their parents' attitudes contributed to their career choices. From grade 7 onward, the girls had lower confidence in their math abilities than in their English abilities, and also considered themselves less able than boys in math. Parents viewed their sons' and daughters' abilities differently, despite comparable actual performance, and provided more opportunities to engage in science-related activities for sons compared to daughters. In the end, these differences in confidence and parental expectations had an effect on girls' versus boys' choice of courses in high school and their future career choices. Boys more often chose engineering and the physical sciences, girls, if they chose science at all, were more apt to focus on the biological sciences and an aspect of medicine that has contact with people.

If personal preference is the sole explanation for workplace segregation, then women's preferences need to have been established independently of social forces such as educational institutions or the labor market. This explanation would have to demonstrate that a woman's biology shapes her choices independent of influence from society, parents, peers, and other groups. There is little credible evidence that biology alone could shape occupational preference. The Michigan studies demonstrate that schools and parents influence self-perceptions and self-confidence, which ultimately have an impact on career choice. Women's different occupational preferences from men's are most probably something that need further explanation, along with vertical and, especially, horizontal segregation.

### The Discriminatory Structure of the Labor Market

Rather than attributing the differences in occupational categories for men and women as the result of personal preference, Barron and Norris (1991) explain women's subordination by the structure of the labor market. They argue that the long-term needs of employers to solve labor productivity problems generate a duality in the labor market between the primary sector, containing well-paid, long-term jobs with promotional prospects, and a secondary sector, characterized by lower pay, job insecurity, and restricted mobility between the two sectors. The jobs women occupy do not have the potential for upward mobility – instead, they are static. In short, many positions that women occupy are seen as "jobs" rather than careers, without any potential for women to move up the hierarchy. This dual labor market enables employers to concentrate investment in workers who stand the best chance of making a long-term contribution to production, through long-term employment or greater efficiency, or both. According to this view, since women are not as committed to long-term employment as men, they find themselves relegated to the secondary labor market.

Barron and Norris (1991) identify five main attributes that consign a group to the secondary labor market: dispensability – the ease of removal from a redundant job; easily identifiable social differences from workers in the primary sector, such as race or ethnicity; comparatively low interest in training, education, or job experiences; low economism – weaker concern for economic as opposed to other rewards of work; and low solidarism – the degree of collective organization and action that characterize a group. Many of these attributes apply to women as a "class" of secondary workers. They are generally not well organized to fight discrimination, they are easily identified as different from the majority (white males), and many women are less concerned than men with high pay and more concerned with the nature of the work and the atmosphere in which they work.

In many corporations, the training dollars to develop managers are spent at the middle- and senior-management levels, while basic skills training, the training spent at the lower level of the organization, is designed to keep people in routine jobs and make them more proficient at them. Leadership training, for example, is most often spent on employees who are already managing people or on those who have been recently promoted to management. Since many women are seen to occupy "jobs" rather than careers, and because many work part-time, their organizations tend not to invest in their development by offering them further education or training. Doeringer and Piore (1971) describe a type of "internal labor market" where employment decisions are made by members of the dominant group, and rules of thumb or custom are used to determine rules for promotion and advancement. Instead of searching in the larger, external labor market for candidates for jobs and promotions, managers first examine the internal market, those already employed by their company or in their circle of friends from their profession. Such customary practice can be "a serious impediment to achieving efficiency and equal opportunity" (Doeringer & Piore, 1971, p. 8). The psychological behavior of the dominant group creates interdependencies that contribute to the formation of relatively fixed customs and traditions with respect to wage structures, promotions, and other organizational rules that affect groups of workers.

## The Human Capital Explanation

A more sophisticated economic explanation of labor-force segregation holds that owing to their "investment" choices, women have less human capital than males, and this results in differential employment outcomes. Women will naturally find themselves in the secondary labor market if they seek work without equipping themselves for more highly skilled positions. The human capital theory was first advanced by Gary Becker (1964, 1985) who identified one's capital as the result of such things as a person's investment in his or her education, work experience, and training. The theory purports to be neutral in respect of class and gender; in other words, all economic agents are assumed to be equally rational, though with differing assets and preferences. If one uses a human capital explanation for differences in career outcomes between men and women, women are disadvantaged in the labor market as compared to men because they have not invested as much in their education, training, or time and energy on the job. They may have less human capital than males because they prefer marriage, children, or domestic pursuits more highly than paid work. Becker asserts that, although the division of labor between men and women may be an efficient way of running a household, it is responsible for income inequality between men and women when they have the same level of talent and education. When women are responsible for housework, childcare, and food preparation, they have less to offer on the labor market:

Since childcare and housework are more intensive than leisure or other household activities, married women spend less effort on each hour of market work than married men working the same number of hours. Hence, married women have lower hourly earning than married men with the same market human capital, and they economize on the effort expended on market work by seeking less demanding jobs.

(Becker, 1985, p. 33)

Since Becker's original explanation of human capital, more contemporary scholars have used this explanation for men's and women's differences in the labor market. Some research suggests that even well-qualified women are unwilling to invest as much as men in their human capital by putting in the number of hours required for senior-level business positions. Charles O'Reilly, a Stanford University Business Professor, studied the career success of MBA graduates. His findings suggest that men compete harder than women; although men and women are equal in ability, skill, and intelligence, men simply put in more effort to reach the top. O'Reilly says:

From an organizational perspective those most likely to be promoted are those who both have the skills and are willing to put in the effort. Individuals who are more loyal, work longer hours, and are willing to sacrifice for the organization are the ones who will be rewarded.

(Tischler, 2004, p. 55)

Some scholars suggest that women do have less human capital than men because of the discontinuity of their work experience, driven most often by their caring for children (Bowles & McGinn, 2005; Mahoney, 1996). Women with children are more likely to not work or to work fewer hours than women without children; however, men with children are more likely to work more hours than men without children (Kaufman & Uhlenberg, 2000).

In addition to intermittent employment or reduced hours, scholars have examined institutional factors that contribute to women's lack of human capital. Women are less likely to receive formal job training than men and have fewer developmental opportunities (Knoke & Ishio, 1998; Morrison & Von Glinow, 1990; Powell & Graves, 2003) and they are less likely to be selected for management experiences abroad, which are generally deemed to be developmental experiences (Adler, 1994; Linehan, 2000). Moreover, women are not as often in positions of responsibility in organizations, which affects their level of experience. Women are often clustered in supporting functions such as human resources management, accounting, and marketing, rather than positions where they have profit-and-loss responsibility for a business unit (Bowles & McGinn, 2005). In 2007, only 27% of women in Fortune 500 firms held positions with profit-and-loss responsibility, while 73% of women held staff positions without profit-and-loss responsibility (Catalyst, 2007d). The Catalyst organization writes that these profit and loss positions are "the gateway for promotion" (p. 1).

In developing countries, there is most likely a stronger argument for women's lack of human capital. Women receive less formal education, and in developing countries men are more likely to receive degrees in higher-paying fields. Women's intermittent labor force participation lowers their average years of total work experience, which in turn leads to lower human capital (Cohn, 1996; Jacobsen, 2008; Polachek, 1981). Employers, rightly or wrongly, may assume that because women work fewer hours they have lower skill levels.

If there is a major problem with human capital theory it is that it does not entirely explain the data about men's and women's assets or workforce participation. Contrary to human capital theory claims, women in Western economies such as the US and Europe have as much education as men to prepare them for challenging work roles. In the US, women earn 58% of undergraduate degrees, 59% of master's degrees, and 47% of doctorates (US Department of Education, 2005). Bielby and Bielby challenge Becker's belief that women put in less effort on work-related tasks because they expend too much effort at home (1988). Using two large surveys, they found that women allocate substantially more effort to work activities than men, either because the typical male cannot draw on extra reserves of energy that apparently women have, or that they choose not to draw on these reserves. They argue that *effort* should not be viewed as a finite resource, where only a certain amount is available for work and domestic activities. Some researchers have even suggested that women's work commitment is equal or more than men's (Marsden, Kalleberg, & Cook, 1993). Bielby and Baron (1986) studied men and women in a large number of firms and found that human capital theory explained only 15% of the variance in sex segregation. Furthermore, human capital theory tends to ignore realities of the market. It assumes that the labor market is a competitive one in which neither employers nor employee have "market power" – i.e. the ability to force others to pay the prices they set, instead of simply being "price takers." This is almost never the case, since there are usually a large number of workers offering to supply labor, and a smaller number of employers who demand it. This imbalance is a recipe for imperfect competition, in which employers have some power to set wages instead of having to bargain with workers. Where employers as a group or individual employers can control the labor market and workers – individually or collectively, there is considerable scope for non-economic factors, such as prejudice and stereotyping, to play a role in employment decisions. Since the employment market is in fact a highly imperfect one, it will be no surprise that there is scope for inefficient and unjust discrimination.

In fact, in practice, it is difficult to disentangle the causes of occupational segregation – how much of it is due to an imperfect labor market, human capital differences between men and women, or personal preference? In reality, it is most likely the interplay among all of these factors – women's personal preferences to work part-time or intermittently may influence their human capital (or assumptions that employers make about their human capital) which in turn may influence labor-market decisions.

## Stereotyping

Human capital theory, like much classical economics, assumes that all economic agents – males and females – are rational, that they seek to maximize their well being, usually by maximizing their wealth or income, and sometimes by making choices that sacrifice monetary rewards. In a society characterized by significant work-relevant differences between the genders, it will be rational for employers to pay attention to such differences in order to make the most efficient business decisions; and it will pay for employees to do so as well in order to secure employment. Rational employers unable to spend scarce resources to establish the nature of such employment-related differences between men and woman will seek less-reliable but more widely available and lower-cost "information" about such differences. In other words, social stereotypes, gender prejudices, and generalizations of varying degrees of accuracy, may provide employers with guidance about whom to hire for what sorts of positions. Even if somewhat inaccurate, unfair, and superficial, such widespread impressions and assumptions

– what we call stereotypes – fill a void in decision-making made by ignorance of the real facts about men's and women's potentials as employees. For example, assume that an employer has a choice between two equally qualified candidates, a male and a female – both 23 years old and both single. If the employer is concerned about being short-staffed or paying for maternity leave, he or she may conclude that the woman, if she marries and gets pregnant, is more likely to leave the workforce to take care of a young infant. Although unfair to make this assumption, as the woman may not marry, may not get pregnant, and even if she does, may not take much time off work, she is still more likely than the male to do so.

And if widespread belief in these stereotypes has an impact on women's decisions about appropriate education, family obligations, and workplace expectations, then the stereotypes become established social facts to which employers adapt their decision-making.

Higher-level managers who are the majority group (let's assume white males) are more culturally attuned to job applicants like themselves (other white males). They have a better understanding of the capabilities and productivity of their own group and know less about any other minority group (African Americans, women, Hispanics, etc.). Because these managers are risk averse, they bid more for the white males than for any equally qualified minority. Economic theory therefore suggests that the white male will offer more to another white male than a minority candidate or a woman, even if he is not racist or sexist. Related to this idea is the notion that managers consider employees as a class, rather than as individuals. This class could be based on age, race, or gender. Doeringer and Piore describe this phenomenon in this way:

> [E]ven at entry points where it would seem most likely that wage rates and worker productivity should be closely related, employment and wage decisions generally apply to *groups* of workers rather than *individuals*. The group may be defined by characteristics such as age, race, or education as is common at entry points, or by seniority and job classification as in the case of jobs filled internally. When wage determinations are made for groups of workers, the influence of economic constraints – labor costs, productivity and so forth – is estimated in terms of *expected value* for the group as a whole and not for individuals.
>
> (1971, p. 8)

For example, if as a group women are seen to be naturally "care-givers" rather than "leaders," they will be channeled into the caring professions such as nursing, social work, or teaching. If men and women are socialized to treat housework as a woman's aptitude, when employers seek to fill jobs as cleaners and maids, the rational among them will discriminate in favor of women. Women are perceived to be good at tasks requiring manual dexterity; thus, they are good candidates for sewing, tailoring, and light machine work. It will be cheaper to simply offer such work to women than to examine the abilities of male applicants. If women are prized for their attractiveness and non-confrontational, pleasing personalities, they will be channeled into secretarial or receptionist duties or customer-service work. Employers save time and money by exploiting stereotypes, even when they are only partly representative of actual abilities in the workforce.

Stereotypes about what women are *not* suited for or innately good at also work against them for higher-paying, more responsible jobs. If women are viewed as non-confrontational, how will they be able to discipline employees, manage or influence others? If they are seen to be physically weak compared to men, why would they be suited to physically demanding work such as construction? If they are deemed to be less able in science and math, why would they be considered for engineering jobs? Even where people do not consciously buy into such stereotypes, the culture reflects their hold on us in many ways. Simply open a woman's magazine to see stereotyped portrayals of women presented. Women are still depicted as masters of the household, responsible for everyday chores such as cleaning, cooking, and taking care of the children. Images of women in advertising more often than not portray women as sex objects rather than professionals. The sheer number of women secretaries in companies leads us to think of a secretary as naturally female rather than male, which in turn may lead us to think of women in supportive, rather than executive, roles. The processes and practices of everyday life reinforce gendered work organizations (Lorber, 2005). When women are overwhelmingly depicted as nurturers, support staff, sex workers, cleaners, and cooks, this social construction of gender becomes embedded in the culture – emphasizing the differences between men and women instead of their similarities.

Gender stereotyping also happens among men and women at the very senior levels of organizations. In a study of 296 corporate leaders (most of whom were CEOs), both sexes practiced gender stereotyping. The study included 128 male leaders and 168 female leaders. Both the men and women characterized women as more effective than men at "caring skills" such as rewarding and supporting people, and men as more effective at "taking charge" skills such as delegation and influencing upward. Both men and women perceived men to be better at problem-solving (Catalyst, 2005). Because problem-solving is associated with leadership, this finding is particularly troubling. Since males are more often responsible for hiring others for top jobs, and since they characterize men as being more effective at problem-solving than women, women will be strongly disadvantaged when they compete for senior level jobs.

A similar study of 935 European senior managers attempted to examine whether gender stereotypes persist in four cultural environments: Germanic, Latin, Nordic, and Anglo groups. Regardless of these cultural backgrounds, managers agreed on the behaviors that distinguish women and men leaders from each other. Respondents perceived women to be more adept at "taking care." As in the US study, across cultures managers perceived that women leaders outperformed men most at supporting others, men were perceived to be more effective at "taking charge," and in almost all cultures, the male respondents perceived that male leaders outperformed females at problem-solving. Women from all cultures perceived that male leaders outperformed women most at influencing upward (Catalyst, 2006). In other words, men were perceived to outperform women at influencing those at a higher rank than themselves.

The study isolated the leadership behaviors that are considered most important to European managers. They are "inspiring others," "team-building," and "delegating." A majority of managers from all cultures ranked "inspiring others" as a highly important leadership attribute; "team building" was also ranked as a highly valued leadership behavior by Anglo, Latin, and Germanic managers. A majority of Nordic managers ranked "delegating" as a highly valued leadership behavior.

The Nordic and Anglo (native English speaking) groups downgraded women's effectiveness at the highly valued leadership behaviors. Nordic men judged women leaders to be less effective than men at delegating – a trait important among Nordic managers. Anglo men perceived women leaders as less effective than men. As in the US example, it is easy to see how European women will be disadvantaged by these stereotypes, since the ones most associated with leadership are thought to be male traits.

As a follow-up to these two studies, in order to better understand how women deal with these stereotypes, investigators from the organization Catalyst conducted in-depth interviews with 13 women leaders who had been surveyed in the previous studies. Being evaluated against a male standard of leadership puts women in a double bind – or a "no-win" situation. Three predicaments emerge for women: first, when women act in ways that are consistent with gender stereotypes, they are perceived to be too soft and less competent as compared to men; yet, when they act more like men, they are perceived to be unfeminine and too tough. Second, the women in the study reported that they face higher competency standards compared to men and that they are forced to continually prove themselves. Third, the respondents said that when they act in stereotypically male ways (assertively), they are perceived to be competent, but less effective at interpersonal skills than women who behave in a more stereotypically female way (Catalyst, 2007a). In another study, women were penalized in mock hiring situations when they were perceived to be agentic without being sufficiently "nice" (Rudman & Glick, 2001). Agency refers to a person's belief and actions that suggest their ability and power to achieve what they want. People with agency typically act assertively and with self-confidence. The researchers concluded that women will be disadvantaged in the hiring process unless they temper their agency with "niceness."

## How Stereotypes Are Imposed

Gender role stereotypes are imposed when authoritative institutions in societies and individuals within societies share a common view about appropriate roles for men and women. Gender roles explain how men and women *actually* behave, but also suggest how men and women *should* behave, thus gender roles are both descriptive and prescriptive (Cialdini & Trost, 1998; Prislin & Wood, 2005). When women or men are trying to fit in, gain social acceptance, or avoid disapproval, they will remain within the gender role that is consistent with their biological sex. Many forces reinforce separate gender roles – athletic contests that separate men from women, attitudes about cognitive development (men are better at math and women better at languages), and the media. Television programs have routinely shown men in employment-related occupations more than women, and women more often in interpersonal roles with friends, family, or romantic interests (Lauzen, Dozier, & Horan, 2008). In a study of the images of women in *Seventeen Magazine*, young women were depicted as entertainers – fashion models, singers, and actresses – rather than as other professionals, while men were shown as occupying more powerful roles (Massoni, 2004).

This tendency of people to stay within prescribed gender roles in Western societies leads men to project themselves agentically – by behaving competitively, assertively, and with dominance – and women to project themselves communally – by being nurturing, friendly, expressive, and sensitive to others. Deviating from these roles can be costly – think of the little girl who is scolded by her parent who worries because she seems bossy, loud, or domineering, or the little boy who is teased because he prefers playing inside in his mother's kitchen rather than competing in outdoor games. Researchers have found that these gender-stereotypic roles develop early; in middle school and beyond, children ascribe gender-specific traits to themselves (Gilligan, 1982; Ruble, Martin, & Berenbaum, 2006).

## How Stereotypes Are Reinforced

It is easy to understand how gender stereotypes are reinforced by the very people they regulate. Boys have been reinforced for behaving assertively, while girls have been encouraged to behave in a non-threatening, nurturing way, so each sex does, in fact, behave according to the stereotype. Stereotypes are reinforced even by those who should disavow them because it is to their disadvantage; several experiments have demonstrated this tendency and been labeled as "stereotype threat" situations. Steele and Aronson (1995) first investigated how performance is affected when racial stereotypes are reinforced. Subsequent experiments showed the effects of gender stereotypes. In one such experiment, women and men were told that they were about to take either a math test or a problem-solving test. Women reported more anxiety and poorer scores when told they were taking a math test (Johns, Schmader, & Martens, 2005). Stereotype lift – improved performance for the sex that is deemed superior at something – can also occur. For example, if men are competing with women in, let's say, a chess match and are given a cue beforehand that they are good at logical thinking, they may achieve a boost in their performance. However, the stereotype lift phenomenon is generally weaker in effect than the stereotype threat effect (Walton & Cohen, 2003).

Because we are socialized to believe women to be more caring, supportive, and nurturing than men, and men to be more assertive, authoritative, and analytical than women, gender becomes practiced unconsciously in many environments – including the workplace. Employing three different scenarios, Yancey-Martin shows how both men and women unconsciously *practice* gender at work. Seemingly insignificant acts – who is expected to answer a telephone in an office or who is expected to hold a door open for another, for example – reinforce gender stereotypes. Yancey-Martin argues that men and women socially construct each other at work through a two-sided dynamic of gendering practices – gendered actions of individuals at work and individuals' reactions to those gendered actions. For example, a male manager may do something at work that is influenced by how he perceives a woman's role (for example, asking his female colleague to photocopy something rather than doing it himself) and a woman may react to this gendered activity by analyzing an appropriate response (should she challenge the man's assumption of her role or should she let it go?). Yancey-Martin further explains how these gendered interactions, which are fueled by stereotypes, significantly affect women's and men's experiences at work and how challenging these gendered interactions will produce insights about how inequalities at work are reinforced (Yancey-Martin, 2003).

Several researchers have investigated the nature of gender discrimination in situations in which women occupy jobs that have been traditionally held by males. A total of 242 undergraduate men and women subjects participated in three experimental studies to investigate the reactions to a successful woman in a male gender-type job (Heilman, Wallen, Fuchs, & Tamkins, 2004). The researchers created workplace scenarios of males and females holding the same job title, Assistant Vice President of Sales for an aircraft company. The job was gendered by the products mentioned in the job description (engines, fuel tanks, and aircraft parts) and the fact that eight men held the post versus two women. The exact same description of job performance was given to the male and female job-holders. In the first set of studies, women jobholders who were acknowledged to be successful were less liked and more personally derogated than equivalently successful men. A second study was conducted in which similarly situated men and women were in a job that was not obviously gendered as a male position. In this study, women were not disliked, thus the dislike of a competent, successful woman only occurred in work arenas that were typed as "male." The authors comment:

> The fact that negative reactions to successful women occurred only when the job was male in gender type, but not when it was female or neutral in gender type, argues for the idea that these negative reactions derive from disapproval for

stereotype-based norm violation. Success for women is OK, it seems, unless it is in an area deemed off-limits for them.

(p. 423)

In the third part of the study, respondents gave employees who were disliked but competent fewer organizational rewards than employees who were liked and competent. The authors discuss the negative effect for women in male-dominated jobs when they are likely to be disliked, simply because they are in a male-gendered job category. The respondents withheld salary and special job opportunities from those employees categorized as competent and successful but disliked. In another study, gender stereotypes were found to influence the credit women were given in team situations; women as members of successful teams didn't receive as much credit as their male counterparts, nor were seen as influential as men at bringing about successful outcomes (Heilman & Parks-Stamm, 2007).

The overall problem with stereotypes is that, while they may generally accurately describe a group, they won't accurately describe all individuals within that group. Women (more than men) may prefer cooking and secretarial work, but this does not mean that all women want to cook or be administrative assistants. Worse, stereotypes force people into behaviors that they may reject or shape attitudes that prevent people from realizing their real potential. Negative effects of stereotypes can be countered with counterevidence (women make good mathematicians and men can competently take care of children), and through a gradual change of societal norms and attitudes. Today, we are far more accepting of women pilots and male nurses.

The gender stereotypes uncovered in all of the aforementioned studies play an important role in workplace discrimination; in this day and age, it is less common for one individual knowingly to discriminate against another. However, when gender stereotypes are part of the social fabric and are practiced by both men and women in an unconscious manner, a more subtle form of discrimination takes place. If both men and women believe that certain behaviors are more appropriate for men and other behaviors more appropriate for women, it is easy to see how these attitudes could be translated into what are considered appropriate occupational roles for men and women. It is also interesting that many women themselves buy into these stereotypes; the women in the Catalyst study perceived men to be better "influencers" than women. In the end, what may be perceived as a woman's personal preference for one occupation over another or the choice of one job role rather than another may in fact be caused by strong gender socialization.

## Pygmalion, Galatea, and Golem Effects

Related to stereotyping, which often occurs at the group level, the Pygmalion (or Galatea) and Golem effects operate at the individual level. Both the Pygmalion and Golem effect suggest the power of self-fulfilling prophecy.

Both of the names "Pygmalion" and "Galatea" derive from an ancient myth. A sculptor named Pygmalion sought to create a statue of an ideal woman – which he named "Galatea." She was so beautiful that Pygmalion fell in love with her. He prayed to the goddess Venus that Galatea would come to life; she granted his wish and they lived happily ever after. A more modern-day equivalent of the myth is in George Bernard Shaw's play *Pygmalion*, in which Henry Higgins believes he can take a Cockney, lower-class flower girl named Eliza Doolittle, and with some training transform her into a duchess. Higgins believed that he could turn Eliza into a lady and he transmitted to Eliza a sense of confidence so that she too began believing in herself.

The Golem effect is, in effect, the opposite of the Pygmalion effect because it produces negative consequences. Several experiments of American classrooms during the 1960s explain how a teacher's low expectations of a student result in poor performance by the student. The name Golem is derived from Hebrew slang meaning oaf or fool. The term originated from a Jewish legend in which a creature is created to eradicate evil but instead becomes a monster. It is easy to see how the Golem effect translates to a management situation; a manager with low expectations of an employee will produce negative behavior in the employee.

The effects of self-fulfilling prophecies were further explored in 1957 by Robert Merton, a well-known sociologist, in his published work entitled, *Social Theory and Social Structure*, in which he explained that "a false definition of the situation evokes a new behavior which makes the original false conception come true."

In the context of a management situation, a manager may have a false expectation of an employee (for example, a female employee is not capable of performing a set of tasks), and even if this expectation is not accurate, the employee will act in ways that are consistent with this expectation. In other words, the manager's expectation of the employee has an effect on that employee's behavior. The Galatea effect refers to the positive effect a manager may have on an employee. If a manager has a positive expectation of an employee, his or her behavior will rise to that expectation.

The Golem and Pygmalion effects could contribute to subordination of women and occupational segregation in the workplace. If a male manager has low expectations of women as compared with men, even if these expectations are unconscious, he may place them in lower-level jobs or give them less-challenging tasks. The female employees may even begin to work only to the level expected by their managers – in other words, women may in fact perform at a level worse than their male counterparts because of the low expectations of their bosses.

## Socialization, Leadership, and the Male Model of Work

In addition to the effect that management expectations can have on performance and rewards, the routine practices of institutions may dictate what women are expected to do. People become socialized by the institutions to which they belong; for example, if female subordination is routinely practiced, it becomes institutionalized in a firm. Employees will become used to women in subordinate roles until it becomes their "natural" place; conversely, if women are in influential roles in a firm, the firm's employees will see women as legitimate holders of these roles. A study of the founders of Silicon Valley law firms tested this theory by examining the representation of women in founder firms and the experiences of the founders in the firms in which they previously worked. Founders from parent firms that historically had more women in leadership positions, such that female leadership became institutionalized, were more likely to establish firms that promoted women into prominent positions. Conversely, founders from firms that historically had women in subordinate positions, such that female subordination became institutionalized, were less likely to promote women into prominent positions (Phillips, 2005).

Just as founders of companies are influenced by their experiences, business professionals have been influenced by beliefs about leadership. Many of the beliefs arose from male experience in the military, which is based on competition and control. The so-called "Great Man" theories identify powerful individuals as the shapers of human destiny. Since the proponents of these theories have been men, and their examples have been male, the understanding of leadership they elaborate has a male bias. The notion of leadership, the idea of who could be a leader, and the attributes for successful leaders, arose from studying great *male* military or political leaders – people like Napoleon, Alexander the Great, Churchill, and Franklin Roosevelt, for example. As with political and military history, the way work has been envisioned and the way in which leadership is understood in the workplace has been skewed toward a male model. Moreover, over time, the male perspective for *how* work is structured and *how* it is accomplished has become the standard. As a society, we have adopted a model of work that is male-centric – working continuously (without career breaks) until retirement. A woman's standpoint about the nature of leadership and the structure of work would have surely given us different models. From a woman's standpoint, rather than constant work throughout one's life, work could be intermittent to accommodate child-rearing. Work could be accomplished from home or from an office. Instead of this female perspective, the way we structure work and what we value in the way of work has traditionally reflected a male perspective.

Researchers have explored how gender (as a standpoint) shapes beliefs, attitudes, and decisions of legal professionals (Yancey-Martin, Reynolds, & Keith, 2002). A study surveyed the positions of male and female judges and attorneys on several factors: their attitudes toward property in divorce settlements, their beliefs about rape and domestic violence, and their general level of feminine consciousness. In this case, "feminine consciousness" can be defined as the degree to which an individual identifies with a female point of view on these issues. According to this research, women judges and attorneys observe significantly more gender bias, particularly in the areas of gender harassment and sexual harassment. Significantly more male legal professionals accepted rape myths, while women professionals were significantly more likely to reject them. Statements about rape on the survey included: 1. Any healthy woman can successfully resist a rapist if she really wants to. 2. When women go around braless or wearing short skirts and tight tops, or go hitchhiking, they are just asking for trouble. 3. Many women falsely report rapes to get back at a man, to protect their reputation after a pregnancy, or simply to gain some attention. 4. If a woman engages in necking or petting and she lets things get out of hand, it is her fault if her partner forces sex on her.

The rate of male agreement with these statements was significantly higher than women's assent to them. The survey also revealed that women judges have a higher feminist consciousness about divorce property rights, negative stereotypes about women, and domestic violence than do male judges. One might expect these effects to be minimized by age of the respondent (younger men being more sympathetic to women because of less-traditional attitudes) or by marital status (men being married). However, these effects of gender consciousness remain even after the influences of age and marital status are taken into account. The researchers conclude that "a judiciary made up solely of men differs from one made up of more equal proportions of women and men because men and women have different standpoints, and standpoints have consequences" (p. 665).

A final part of this social explanation of women's subordination in the workplace is often referred to as "the breadwinner" ideology. "Breadwinner" is the term used to describe the individual who brings in all or most of the family income and provides security for the family. Historically, for example in nineteenth-century Britain, debates about breadwinning often focused on employers who were expected to provide enough income so that men could support their families (Horrell & Humphries, 1997). Thus, even today, men, who hold the position of power in most organizations, may assume (either consciously or subconsciously) that women are secondary to their husbands as earners. In other words, women work for additional spending money, not as the main income earners in their families. Where this attitude persists, it is easy to see how women might be offered less money than males for the same position, or how they might be assumed to be appropriate for part-time versus full-time employment. In situations where organizations may be forced to downsize their workforce, the breadwinner ideology may have serious consequences for women employees since they may be seen as less dependent on their income than similarly situated males (Charles & James, 2005). Of course, this attitude is out-dated since many women are the main breadwinners of their families, or are the sole supporter of their household in the case of single parenthood. In addition, most families in the Western world require two full-time incomes to maintain a reasonable standard of living. Because the pattern of women's and men's work has fundamentally changed in the twentieth and twenty-first centuries, the male breadwinner ideology no longer holds: the service sector has grown and opened up many new jobs that women occupy; Western countries have gone through a period of deindustrialization where "male" factory jobs are no longer the norm; and there are higher rates of employment for women in many sectors of the economy (Creighton, 1999). Moreover, the security of work and full-time jobs for many groups of men has ended (Strangleman, 2005). Today, more often than not, couples employ a dual-breadwinner model where both the male and female contribute equally toward their living expenses (Warren, 2007). In a study of European workers, dual bread-winners were not unusual; in Denmark, 50% of female employees between ages 25 and 55 earn 45% or more of a couple's pooled wages, followed by Italy at 47%, Greece, Finland, and France at 43%, 42%, and 42% respectively (Warren, 2007). In spite of the changing nature of work, and the fact that more women are represented in the workforce world-wide, stereotypes about men's rightful place as breadwinner may persist.

It is important for both women and men to be aware of these potential attitudes; women may be shortchanged if employers think they are only working for "a little extra income," and males may be affected in a number of ways. First, their wives or partners may be shortchanged, affecting their family incomes; and second, if they are employers and pay women less than they are worth, they will experience morale problems with employees, fail to hire the best person for the job, and in the worse case be subject to lawsuits.

## Unequal Job Opportunities – a Complex Issue

The unequal job opportunities for women are most likely the result of a combination of personal preferences (for example, talented women with young children choosing to work part-time, off the fast-track to promotion) and stereotypes that maintain images of women as less-able, less-interested, and less-committed to organizational careers than men. Leveling out this uneven landscape for women will require a change in women's own attitudes that no doubt shape their preferences, new company policy pre-scriptions that help to eliminate real bias, and enforcement of existing laws. The next chapter highlights the most important of these anti-discrimination laws.

### Further Reading

Anker, R. & Melkas, H. (1997). Occupational segregation by sex in Nordic countries: An empirical investigation. *International Labour Review*, 136(3).

Charles, M. & Grusky, D. (2004). *Occupational ghettos: The worldwide segregation of women and men*. Stanford, CA: Stanford University Press.

Gonas, L. & Karlsson, J. (Eds.). (2006). *Gender segregation: Divisions of work in post-industrial welfare states*. Aldershot, UK: Ashgate Publishing.

## Discussion Questions

1.  Which of the explanations for occupational segregation seems most plausible to you? Why?
2.  Look around your community or your college and university setting. If you see evidence of occupational segregation, in which job categories is it present?
3.  How do you think women can counter the effects of stereotyping in employment situations?
4.  Do you think men and women in Generation Y are shunning high-paid jobs in favor of a more balanced lifestyle? Is this preference unique to women?
5.  Read the following article, Yancey-Martin (2003). "Said and done" vs "Saying and doing": Gendered practices, practicing gender at work. *Gender & Society, 17*: 342–366. Can you think of similar examples from your own experience that demonstrate gendered practices?
6.  Scan several women's magazines such as *Cosmopolitan*, *Elle*, and *Vogue*. How are women depicted in the magazines' advertisements? How do these images reinforce stereotypes?

# 3  Employment Discrimination Law

**Learning Objectives**

After completing this chapter, the reader will:

* understand Title VII of the Civil Rights Act, the Equal Pay Act, and the Pay Check Fairness proposed legislation.
* understand the role of the EEOC in combating workplace discrimination.
* understand employers' responses to allegations of discrimination.

Several laws in the US, UK, and Europe make discrimination based on sex, race, national origin, and, in some countries, sexual orientation, illegal. These laws have been amended over time as the courts have gained experience with them; these amendments have generally broadened the scope of the legislation.

## Laws in the US

Two key US laws supporting equal opportunity employment are Title VII of the Civil Rights Act (passed in 1964) and the Equal Pay Act (passed in 1963).

### Title VII of the Civil Rights Act

Title VII prohibits discrimination against an individual based on his or her race, color, religion, sex, or national origin. Interestingly, Howard W. Smith, a Virginia Democrat, opposed the Civil Rights Act. Smith thought that, by adding the inclusion of gender to the bill, northern Democrats would vote against it. In spite of Smith's efforts, the bill passed. In the 1970s, the courts began to hold that sexual harassment was a form of sexual discrimination, and in the 1990s same-sex harassment was recognized under Title VII.

The law recognizes two different kinds of discrimination: disparate treatment discrimination and disparate impact discrimination. The former involves directing discrimination toward an individual, treating him or her unfairly because of his or her sex, race, color, religion, or national origin. Sexual harassment from one individual directed toward another individual is an example of disparate treatment discrimination, or intentionally not hiring the best qualified candidate because of his or her race. Disparate impact occurs when an employment practice has an unfair impact on a category of employees (blacks, Muslims, or women, for example). Advertising employment openings only in magazines read primarily by men would create a disparate impact on women. In one case, the Supreme Court ruled that requiring laborers to have a high school diploma when this qualification was unnecessary for the laborer role had a disparate impact on blacks.

Until recently, the Title VII required an individual to file a complaint of discrimination within 180 days of the discriminatory act or the right to file a lawsuit could be denied. This requirement proved problematic in situations in which an individual was unaware of the discrimination until several months after it occurred. In 2009, Congress overturned this time requirement with the Lilly Ledbetter decision.

There are narrowly defined situations in which employers are allowed to discriminate on the basis of a trait that may be associated more with one sex or another – height or strength, for example. Three conditions must apply to this "BFOQ" (Bona Fide Occupational Qualification) employer defense. First, the trait must be necessary for a particular occupation or job category. Second, it must be central to the operation of a business. Third, there is no alternative to using this trait. When an employer argues that strength is a necessary job requirement (lifting very heavy objects, for example), he or she may prefer to hire males rather than females. When employers hire same-sex locker room attendants (males for the men's locker room and females for the women's) they are within their rights under the BFOQ requirements. However, many of these defenses have been struck down; for example, formerly there was a minimum height requirement for police officers and a strength requirement for firefighters. Neither trait was proven to be essential for the job. Hooters used the BFOQ defense unsuccessfully as it attempted to justify the hiring of only women servers. The courts determined that Hooters is primarily a restaurant, rather than a sex business, so found that sex was not an essential requirement for its business operation.

Title VII of the Civil Rights Act does not specifically provide protection to individuals based on their sexual orientation. Because of this omission, some states have provided such legislation. A total of 20 states have enacted legislation to explicitly forbid discrimination in the private sector based on sexual orientation and 13 states have enacted legislation protecting transgendered people.

### *The Equal Pay Act*

During World War II, many women took on jobs in the war industries. Because of this increased effort by women, the National War Labor Board asked employers to voluntarily make pay adjustments so that women's rates of pay would be more comparable to men's rates of pay. Not only did employers ignore the request to raise women's pay, but after the war ended they also pushed women out of the workforce to make room for returning service men. In addition to this type of discrimination, want ads routinely listed jobs as either "Help Wanted – Male" or "Help Wanted – Female" with higher rates of pay for the so-called male jobs.

These inequities in the 1950s and 1960s ushered in the Equal Pay Act of 1963.

The most important provisions of this act are the following:

(d)(1) No employer having employees subject to any provisions of this section shall discriminate, within any establishment in which such employees are employed, between employees on the basis of sex by paying wages to employees in such establishment at a rate less than the rate at which he pays wages to employees of the opposite sex in such establishment for equal work on jobs the performance of which requires equal skill, effort, and responsibility, and which are performed under similar working conditions.

In essence this provision requires that when men and women compare their jobs for equal pay purposes, they must be for equal work, which requires that the jobs be identical or nearly identical jobs in the same organization.

The Equal Pay Act does specify some exceptional situations in which women and men doing the same work may be paid differently. Men and women doing the same work may be paid differently based on merit (for example, the evaluation of their work), based on the quantity or quality of their production (for example, in factories, employees may be paid based on the number of goods they produce and the quality of the goods), or based on seniority (employees in the same job may be paid differently if one has more years of service than the other).

A woman pursuing an equal pay claim must compare herself to a man doing the same work or nearly identical work. This comparison becomes more difficult to make as women advance in their careers, because jobs become more specialized and few are identical. For example, all managers in a company do not have exactly the same job responsibilities or complete the same daily tasks. (Chapter 5 on Equal Pay discusses the concept of "comparable worth" introduced by some as a way of dealing with this issue.)

## The Employer Response to Allegations of Discrimination

Employers fighting equal pay cases most often use either the exceptions clause of the law (for merit, seniority, or quantity and quality of work) or the fact that the jobs are not similar enough to be compared. If they can demonstrate that one employee performed better than another, or the employees conducted different work, this may be enough to persuade a court that a claim of unequal pay is unwarranted. In sexual harassment cases, the burden of proof is on the alleged victim to prove that sexual harassment took place. The employer's response to unequal pay allegations, discrimination in hiring and promotion, and sexual harassment are covered in detail in subsequent chapters of this book.

When faced with a charge of discrimination, many employers chose to settle out-of-court, offering a financial settlement to the alleged victim. They do so for a number of reasons. First, the cost of drawn-out litigation both in terms of time and money can be burdensome. Second, the evidence may favor the plaintiff, making a court case too risky. And, third, a court case raises the risk that employers' reputations will suffer. These out-of-court settlements do not require the employer to admit guilt. Proactive employers monitor their workforce regularly to ensure that laws are being upheld, and many hire employee-relations specialist or ombudspersons to help adjudicate employee–management disputes, some of which may deal with alleged discrimination. These efforts prevent costly lawsuits and often improve employee morale. In addition, proactive employers educate their employees about sexual harassment and other discriminatory practices.

## The Pay Check Fairness Act

Some members of the US Congress have deemed the Equal Pay Act inadequate to address pay inequities between men and women. They have initiated two bills to correct these problems (although as of the publication of this book neither bill has passed): The Pay Check Fairness Act, introduced by Senator Tom Daschle (D-SD) and Representative Rosa DeLauro (D-CT), and The Fair Pay Act, introduced by Senator Tom Harkin (D-IA). Both bills were designed to close loopholes in the Equal Pay Act that make it relatively easy for employers to circumvent the law, and both were offered as amendments to the Fair Labor Standards Act (of which the Equal Pay Act is a part). The Pay Check Fairness Act has several features that would strengthen equal pay legislation.

Although the Equal Pay Act allows for back-pay awards, it does not allow a plaintiff to recover compensatory or punitive damages. Without this extra stick, employers may be more willing to fight a case and prolong it, given the fact that the risk of losing may not be very high. The Pay Check Fairness Act proposes to allow plaintiffs to recover compensatory and/or punitive damages.

The Equal Pay Act is also silent on the issue of improving information about pay. The Pay Check Fairness Act would require employers to provide the EEOC with information about pay by race, sex, and national origin of employees. Furthermore, the act would prevent employers from punishing workers for sharing pay information with one another. It also directs the US Department of Labor to set up guidelines to help employers share information regarding pay rates for different jobs.

The current Equal Pay Act makes it difficult to proceed with a class action suit, in which employees from a particular firm come together to sue an employer. The Equal Pay Act requires employees to "opt in" to a class action suit, placing the onus on employees to find out about a legal action and request to be part of it in writing. The Pay Check Fairness Act calls for the opposite; a class of employees would be part of the class unless they "opt out" of it in writing.

Under the Equal Pay Act, an employer can assert that a male is paid more than a female in a comparable job because of "factors other than sex" (see Section 3, D1). A seniority system, merit pay, and the quantity and quality of production are three examples given as factors other than sex. As discussed earlier in this chapter, these factors can reflect previous conditions of injustice. The Pay Check Fairness Act attempts to eliminate these loopholes by allowing only non-sex-related factors such as education or relevant job experience.

Under the current law, a wage comparison can only be made between two employees in the same "establishment" (see Section 3, D1). However, employers of large organizations with subsidiaries or divisions may claim that the two jobs are not part of the same "establishment," therefore The Pay Check Fairness Act eliminates this rule. Finally, The Pay Check Fairness Act calls for more education and training of EEOC and US Department of Labor employees and the establishment of an award to recognize employers who eliminate pay disparities.

## The Role of the Equal Employment Opportunity Commission

At the same time that Title VII was passed in the US, a new federal agency was established. The Equal Employment Opportunity Commission (EEOC) was set up to investigate discrimination claims. Table 3.1 shows that, from 1997 until 2007, the number of charges for claims of sex discrimination by individuals has vacillated between a low of 23,904 in 2005 and 25,536 in 2002. In 2008, the number jumped to 28,372. This increase has been partially attributed to the recession. Over the years, the number of complaints based on sex has represented about 30% of all EEOC claims of discrimination. Other charges may have been based on religion, age, or national origin. Charges under the Equal Pay Act have been fairly consistent from 1997 to 2008, from 1.4% to 1% of all EEOC claims. It is important to recognize that not all of these claims of discrimination have been found to have merit. The EEOC investigates claims and makes a determination of whether discrimination appears to have been present; for example, of the complaints for unequal pay in 2008, 56% were found to have no merit.

*Table 3.1* Total Charges for Sex Discrimination and Unequal Pay, 1997–2008

| | FY 1997 | FY 1998 | FY 1999 | FY 2000 | FY 2001 | FY 2002 | FY 2003 | FY 2004 | FY 2005 | FY 2006 | FY 2007 | FY 2008 |
|---|---|---|---|---|---|---|---|---|---|---|---|---|
| Sex Discrimination | | | | | | | | | | | | |
| Charges | 24,728 | 24,454 | 23,907 | 25,194 | 25,140 | 25,536 | 24,362 | 24,249 | 23,094 | 23,247 | 24,826 | 28,372 |
| Percent of Total Claims | 30.7 | 30.7 | 30.9 | 31.5 | 31.1 | 30.2 | 30 | 30.5 | 30.6 | 30.7 | 30.1 | 29.7 |
| Equal Pay Act Charges | 1,134 | 1,071 | 1,044 | 1,270 | 1,251 | 1,256 | 1,167 | 1,011 | 970 | 861 | 818 | 954 |
| Percent of Total Claims | 1.4 | 1.3 | 1.3 | 1.6 | 1.5 | 1.5 | 1.4 | 1.3 | 1.3 | 1.1 | 1 | 1 |

Source: US Equal Employment Opportunities Commission, http://eeoc.gov/stats.

In addition to adjudicating complaints, the EEOC provides outreach and technical assistance to employers. Free training and information is available from the EEOC on employment laws and fair employment practices. The EEOC produces publications on a variety of topics, including: fair employment practices, ways to file a charge of discrimination, employment rights of immigrants, and questions and answers for employers about their liability in harassment cases.

The EEOC has been under-funded in recent years. Consolidating offices, reorganizing, replacing retiring executives with lower-paid ones, and outsourcing its contact center for all public inquiries have all been used to reduce costs. From 1980 to 2004, the agency's full-time employees have decreased by 934 (Gruber, 2004). Now many argue that the EEOC does not have the staff required to effectively handle all of the complaints that come in, and that having a call center manned by people without knowledge of the law or understanding of local business practices leads to inadequate service and poor advice. In 2004, Leroy Warren, the head of a federal task force on EEOC operations, reported that with the then-current staff levels, the EEOC was unable to provide timely service to federal employees filing discrimination complaints. In a letter to Senate Majority leader Bill Frist (R-TN) and then-House Speaker Dennis Hastert (R-IL), Warren wrote:

> The task force has ... received numerous, unsolicited comments from current and former EEOC employees who are deeply troubled and concerned that the EEOC is on a planned starvation diet, with the long-term result being an agency that will eventually fail or become basically inoperative and lacking in public respect.
>
> (Gruber, 2004)

In 2005, the House granted the EEOC $15 million below their request of $350 million and the Senate allotted them $327.5 million, $23.2 million below their requested budget. Cari Dominquez, the chairwoman of the EEOC, went on record that the EEOC foresees an increase in private sector complaints that, without additional resources, cannot be effectively handled (Gruber, 2004).

Other countries have similar bodies to the EEOC. For example, in Britain the Equality and Human Rights Commission brings together what were formerly three commissions: for racial equality, for disability rights, and the Equal Opportunity Commission (EOC) that focused on sexual equality. In Australia, the Human Rights and Equal Opportunity Commission upholds laws against sexual discrimination and basic human rights. In France, the Women's Rights Service provides the same type of services.

## Legislation in the UK and Other EU Countries

Protection against workplace discrimination came later in the UK than in the US. The Equal Pay Act was passed in 1970 and the Sex Discrimination Act in 1975. These laws are very similar to the US Equal Pay Act and Title VII legislation. One substantial difference, however, is the provision to cover transgendered individuals. The Sex Discrimination Act (as amended in 1999) and the Gender Recognition Act (2004) recognize discrimination based on gender reassignment Furthermore, the Employment Equality Regulations (2003) made it illegal to discriminate on the grounds of sexual orientation in employment and training. One additional law focuses specifically on the governmental sector: The Gender Equality Duty (2007) mandates that public authorities must demonstrate that they are promoting equality for men and women, and eliminating sexual harassment and discrimination. Thus public authorities have to track the progress of their employees to see if any discrimination is occurring against either sex.

European countries have passed legislation on sex discrimination prohibiting unequal pay for equal work, sexual harassment, and other discriminatory hiring processes, although individual countries have passed this type of legislation at different times. In France, the Code du Travail was passed in 1973. Similar to US laws, it covers employment discrimination, equal pay legislation, and sexual harassment legislation. In Germany, similar laws exist. However, in Germany sexual harassment legislation was not passed until 1994 as part of The Second Equal Rights Act. In Spain, it was not until 1990 that the Civil Code was altered to include non-discrimination by reason of sex. In Switzerland, the Federal Act on Gender Equality was enacted in 1995. In all European countries, individuals or employers involved in a sex-discrimination case first take their case to their country's court system. If not satisfied with the first judgment, individuals, companies, or organizations can appeal their case to the European Court of Justice. It is up to the European Court of Justice as to whether or not they will consider a case.

The chapters to follow include examples of legal cases that have been brought before the US courts or European courts, and descriptions of some of the challenges that still exist for women in the workplace. The legal cases illustrate how the courts have interpreted the Equal Pay Act, Title VII and European anti-discrimination laws. Many of the challenges for women are presented as case studies at the end of the chapters.

## Further Reading

For information on the current law in the US and activities of Congress, consult: National Women's Law Center, www.nwlc.org.

For international information on employment discrimination law, country-specific laws and statistics, refer to: The International Labour Organization, www.ilo.org and search under research and publications.

Rutherglen, G.A. (2007). *Employment Discrimination Law* (2nd ed.). New York, NY: Foundation Press.

## Discussion Questions

1. Review the complete wording of the Title VII legislation and the Equal Pay Act at www.eeoc.gov. Note that an amendment to the Title VII of the Civil Rights Act was passed in 1991. Review it to see what it has to say about punitive damages for intentional discrimination and unlawful harassment.
2. With current legislation in force in the US and many other countries, why do you think there is still a problem with unequal pay and workplace discrimination?

## Other Activities

1. Internet research project: Switzerland's equality laws came late compared with those of the US and UK. Compare Switzerland with the US or the UK on the following features: how many women are in management positions in the two countries? What sorts of occupations are women prevalent in within the two countries?

# Part II
# Women in the Workplace

# 4 Career Opportunities

## Recruitment, Selection, and Promotion

**Learning Objectives**

After completing this chapter, the reader will:

- understand the differential treatment that women may experience in recruitment, selection, and promotion decisions.
- understand the explanations for differences in career outcomes.
- understand the institutional practices that cause inequities.
- understand what organizations and individuals can do to promote equitable work environments.

As we have seen from the previous three chapters, women and men experience different career outcomes: women are often in lower-level jobs or in different occupations that offer fewer rewards. These career outcomes are the result of different experiences at various stages of their careers and during various organizational processes. In this chapter, we explore the differential impact that some of these organizational practices have on men and women. These organizational practices can contribute to vertical segregation, in particular. We begin with a discussion of how men and women are recruited and selected into jobs. Next, we explore what happens to men and women once they are employed: whether or not they receive challenging assignments, how they are evaluated and how they are promoted to positions of greater responsibility. Because women have been in the workforce at management levels for many decades and have gained educational credentials equal to that of men, we can assume that their human capital is equal to men's human capital. The success of corporations will require using everyone's human capital, equalizing career opportunities, and ending vertical segregation. Corporations that use the talent and potential of *all* employees will have a distinct competitive advantage over those that do not.

## Recruitment and Selection Decisions

Companies typically have procedures for recruitment and selection decisions: human resource professionals or managers define a job's skill set and responsibilities, advertise it internally and externally, screen resumes, shortlist applicants and interview candidates, check references, and finally choose the most suitable person for the advertised position. As firms have become larger and more complex, these procedures have become routinized; having policies and procedures for recruitment and selection is an attempt to make the processes objective, or at least to reduce subjective factors in these processes. In much the same way that Frederick Taylor advocated the one best way to do a task in a shop-floor environment during the early 1900s, human resource departments have tried to institutionalize the best way to recruit and select employees. Firms have sought to control these processes in part because of expensive lawsuits due to discriminatory practices in hiring, and in part to make recruitment and selection more efficient and more productive. Larger firms and government organizations, in particular, have instituted procedures to make their recruitment and selection processes uniform. They have been able to lower costs of recruitment through standardized practices. Smaller firms have been less likely to do so since their costs for recruitment and selection are not as high, and because they most probably do not have large human resource departments. Although intended to make the playing field even for all candidates, the uniformity of recruitment and selection processes has not completely achieved its goal. Human error, lack of compliance with procedures, and bias inevitably enter into these decisions. This is one reason vertical and other sorts of segregation persist.

Women and minorities have often been disadvantaged by recruitment and selection procedures that may be overtly, covertly, or unintentionally biased. Formal procedures can easily be contraverted – positions may not be advertised, only a select few or even one individual may be asked to apply, and the so-called "search" for a suitable candidate will be biased if decision-makers have one individual in mind for a job that is supposed to be open to many qualified candidates. Human resource departments may have solid recruitment and selection procedures that they make available to managers. These procedures may include written guides to assist interviewers, suggested testing, reference checking, and formal training on recruitment and selection. Yet in some companies managers can easily circumvent these procedures, hiring whomever they please without considering a field of candidates. Even where corporations have a stated commitment to diversity of candidates, and especially to providing opportunities for women and minorities, social processes in these organizations may take over and largely dictate unequal outcomes for men and women.

Selection decisions are among the most "high-risk" and "high-reward" decisions employers make. These decisions are high-reward because a highly competent employee can make all the difference between a business unit's success or failure. They are risky because a bad choice may doom the most promising business to failure. Almost always, the information about candidates on the basis of which such decisions must be made is often incomplete, unreliable, or not particularly relevant to the position that is to be filled. Achievements are easy to exaggerate on resumes and often hard to verify. Former employers are reluctant to offer candid evaluations for fear of lawsuits, and sometimes will give favorable recommendations just to be rid of an unwanted employee. Track records in one kind of job may not be good indicators of effectiveness in others, and educational credentials are often only a small measure of ability to learn a new job, and not a reflection of relevant education. Where employees are difficult to discharge, the problem of selection becomes the gravest one a business can face. In fact, it is widely held that the lack of job growth in the European Union is due to the uncertainties unavoidable in hiring combined with the difficulty of firing an unsuitable employee.

In general, employers have strong incentives to reduce the risk associated with hiring. But many of the strategies they employ not only reduce their chances of hiring the best candidates, but raise barriers to women in particular.

## Bias in Recruitment and Selection Decisions

Many managers believe that the best way to minimize employment risk is to seek out others with whom they are comfortable, others whom they know, or those who come highly recommended to them. In work environments where managers are primarily men, it is easy to see why more men are hired and how women lose out. The process of men seeking others like themselves is largely unconscious rather than a deliberate effort to discriminate against women. Male managers interact with men more than they do women, and are more likely to ask for and accept advice from their male colleagues. If women are not well-connected to those individuals in the organization who do the hiring or those who do the recommending, they will be less likely to be considered as viable candidates for jobs.

One short step away from hiring individuals one already knows is hiring the same *kind* of individual with whom one is familiar. For example, a male manager wishing to fill a computer programmer job may develop a vision of the ideal candidate in his mind. He thinks of the current job holders in the information technology department who happen to be mostly male. His prototype for the new position will naturally have masculine characteristics. He will then favor male job candidates over female candidates because of his vision of the successful job holder. Managers hiring to fill jobs in the construction or building trades will also think of the job in stereotypically masculine terms (aggressiveness and physical strength, for example); the result will often be the hiring of males. The same phenomenon happens when the job in question requires stereotypically female characteristics. A largely female secretarial pool will produce the ideal prototype of a female secretary and those hired to be secretaries will be women.

Just as mental prototypes influence hiring decisions, it also appears that the sex of the interviewer can have an effect on selection decisions. Interviewers favor applicants of their sex over applicants of the opposite sex because interviewers are apt to feel and have more in common with them and therefore will like them better. This likeability factor will influence both how the interviewer and interviewee behave. The interviewer will ask more questions of the candidate, receive more information about the candidate, and make the candidate feel at ease. Feeling at ease, the candidate will look confident and relaxed, providing the candidate with an edge over others. Interviewers are apt to remember good things about a candidate whom they like (the "halo effect") and bad things about a candidate whom they do not like (the "horn effect"). For example, a candidate who is initially viewed favorably may answer one question well. Subsequent questions he or she answers will be interpreted favorably regardless of whether they are good or bad answers. The reverse is true for those who do not make a good first impression; regardless of how good their answers are during the rest of the interview, they will probably be seen as poor prospects. *Liking* a candidate has been shown to influence evaluation in several situations (Graves & Powell, 1996; Tsui, Egan, & O'Reilly, 1992).

Gender stereotypes have been found to influence selection decisions in many cases. Data from large US law firms in the mid-1990s showed that when selection criteria include a greater number of stereotypically masculine traits, more men are hired, and when they include stereotypically feminine traits, women are disproportionately hired (Gorman, 2005). Women are associated more with lower-end restaurants and fast-food establishments, whereas men are associated more with upscale restaurants where the pay and tips are higher. These associations have had a negative impact on women who wish to work in high-end restaurants (Neumark, Bank, & Van Nort, 1996).

Another study revealed biases of human resources practitioners as they evaluated identical resumes of male and female candidates (with identical qualifications and experience) (Smith, Tabak, Showail, McLean Parks, & Kleist, 2005). Human resource managers suggested lower salaries for the female candidates, and penalized men more than women for gaps of employment. Similar studies have shown how "black-sounding" names versus "white-sounding" names bias interviewers as they screen resumes. These interviewers overwhelmingly chose the white candidates (Bertrand & Mullainathan, 2003).

Just as names may elicit prejudice, so too may a person's physical attributes. Although looks should not play a large role in selection decision, some studies show that looks *do* matter. A study by Cable and Judge (2004) found that each inch above the average height for both men and women had remunerative advantages; each additional inch above the average added $789 a year to one's salary. Controlling for gender, age, and weight, the study showed that someone who is 6-feet tall earns, on average, almost $166,000 more over a 30-year period than someone who is 5 feet, 5 inches. The researchers controlled for gender by using the average height for men of 5 feet, 9 inches and the average height for women as 5 feet, 3 inches. Shorter men are at a slightly greater disadvantage than shorter women. Height is most important in fields that require social interaction such as sales, management, technical, and service careers.

Other studies have found that weight and hair color can bias an individual. Blondes can suffer from the "dumb blonde" stereotype and heavier people earn less than people who are average weight for their height. Among Caucasian women, an additional 65 lbs. accounts for a 7% drop in earnings (Cawley, 2004). A University of Michigan study of 7,000 men and women reported that the net worth of obese women is as much as 60% less than women of average size. It is significant that the earnings penalty for being overweight did not affect men (Fonda, Fultz, & Jenkins, 2004). Of course, the earnings penalty is not entirely due to the bias of employers. Overweight women are also less apt to marry, and when they do they usually marry below their socio-economic group. Tiggerman and Rothblum (1997) asked overweight male and female respondents why they had not been selected for a job. Of the overweight men, 40% mentioned they suffered discrimination because of their weight; 60% of women suggested weight was the reason. Various studies have manipulated photographs of hypothetical job candidates, adding more weight to individuals, to see if obese people are discriminated against. These studies have repeatedly found that obese people are consistently discriminated against, with women suffering prejudice more often than men (Puhl & Brownell, 2003). Overweight people suffer the stereotype of being less productive, less ambitious, less professional, and less self-disciplined.

Bias obviously occurs when there is really only one specific person wanted for a job. In these cases, managers are simply going through the motions of fair selection when they have already decided on a candidate. In some cases, job descriptions are written with a specific candidate in mind. While this candidate might be the most suitable, the managers have a preconceived idea about who should be offered the job and, therefore, might eliminate other suitable candidates.

In addition to these biases in interviewing, other organizational practices can lead to discrimination in selection. Generalizing from the experience or performance of one or a few women, or one or a few men, can lead to sex discrimination. Let's assume a male manager hires a female manager who performs poorly. His reaction might be, "I won't hire another woman for that job. The last one didn't work out." The reasons for her lack of success could be complex; she may actually not have had the ability to do the job or her lack of performance may have been due to organizational factors that made it difficult for her to succeed. Unfortunately, predicting or generalizing from the performance of one female to all other female candidates is unreasonable and illogical.

There is nothing much a woman or minority job candidate can do to mitigate the effect of a sexist or racist interviewer. Interviewers who consciously or unconsciously view women as eligible for certain jobs and men eligible for other jobs discriminate against individuals who attempt to violate this sex-role stereotype. A woman may find it difficult to be treated fairly when she applies for a job as a construction crew member or electrician, roles more typically held by men. Providing information to the employer that would help counter the stereotype may help. For example, a women applying for a job in construction could emphasis her health and physical strength and stamina. Employers must keep in mind that biased recruitment reduces potential profitability, for it means they may not hire the best possible job candidates.

We turn now to a discussion of decisions taken by firms once employees are hired.

## Promotion Decisions

There are a multitude of reasons organizations may have for promoting individuals. Promotions are a way of rewarding employees and keeping them committed to the company; they are a way for the organization to deploy talent and meet organizational goals; they are a way for the organization to signal its values; and they can be a method to develop "high fliers" for even more promising positions.

Studies of how organizations promote individuals are rare, in part because the reasons may be highly sensitive and confidential. Decisions may be hidden for several reasons, including legal liability or compromises that were made among decision-makers. However, one study of 64 promotions in three different Fortune 500 companies sheds light on the subject (Rudermann & Ohlott, 1994). The reasons why certain people are promoted vary. Many promotions are based on individual efforts and abilities. Some promotions are made based on context or situational factors. One of these context factors has to do with the opportunity structure,[1] or being in the right place at the right time. Individuals who are already situated in visible jobs and who have formerly had an opportunity to prove themselves will be more apt to be chosen for promotion than those who are not, regardless of effort or ability. Those who have proximity to the decision-maker or have been groomed for promotion have a better chance at succeeding than those who have not.

In Rudermann and Ohlott's (1994) study, decision-makers relied on intuitive, subjective data about a candidate, their personal knowledge of the candidate, and the opinion of others. Two areas that were given considerable attention were "potential" and "comfort level." Individuals who were expected to have the potential for the next role were often promoted, and those individuals with whom the boss felt comfortable, someone the boss knew and trusted, were promoted. Rational selection would indicate that there are multiple candidates for a job, but this study showed that in 43% of the cases there was only one true candidate. The study found only a few cases where a formal procedure identified candidates for a job.

Other researchers have noted that most promotions are based on social negotiations where connections and interpersonal influence play key roles (Ferris, Buckley, & Allen, 1992; Leicht & Marx, 1997; Mencken & Winfield, 2000). In other words, getting promoted depends on what you know, but also on who you know. In a large US study, black women had less access to social capital resources,[2] such as drawing on personal contacts for job opportunities, than white men or white women (Parks-Yancy, 2006). White men were also more likely than black women to be promoted as a result of using social capital resources. Judge and Ferris (1992) also noted that people hire people with whom they are comfortable; decision-makers may think they hire based on who is most fit for the job when, in reality, similarity of interests between the job candidate and the hiring manager plays a role, as does personality, background, attitude, and appearance. A boss's comfort level often has to do with how similar the individual is to the boss.

Lack of social capital contributes to employees being stuck in lower-level jobs, because they do not have the personal connections that would help them receive other job offers. Without the prospect of outside offers, employees are not able to press employers for increased wages. A large-scale British study found that women were likely to be promoted at the same rate as men, but they receive a smaller wage increase consequent upon promotion (Booth, Francesconi, & Frank, 2001). The authors of the study propose a "sticky floor" model of pay and promotion, suggesting that women are often stuck at the bottom of a pay scale for the new promotion grade, and that they stay there because they have fewer favorable, outside offers of employment. Males, on the other hand, can use outside offers of employment as a bargaining chip to boost their current wages within a company. The "sticky floor" hypothesis has support in other studies as well. Rainbird (2007) found that training and self-improvement for women at the low end of the pay scale will not improve the position of women when there are structural problems in an organization. However, some authors have described the "sticky floor" as the result of self-imposed limitations that women erect. Baker (2003) notes that being female, disabled, or a minority does not reduce a woman's chances for reaching a high level in the field of law except when she works fewer hours or has less experience than her male counterpart.

Whether or not employees get promoted depends on both their abilities and on the opportunities they have been afforded in the workplace. Unless a highly skilled individual is challenged by visible projects or work that is deemed critical to the organization, he or she will have little chance of moving up. Thus, for example, international assignments are often visible and challenging ways to move up in a large corporation, yet since women managers are chosen less frequently for these assignments, their promotional opportunities are reduced (Catalyst, 2000). In a study of turnover and retention of senior-level women in US corporations, women cited lack of opportunity and an unclear career path as reasons for leaving (Catalyst, 2006c).

Several studies have shown that, when controlling for the variables of experience, education, and job tenure, racial minorities and women are given fewer opportunities in the labor market compared to white males (Elliott & Smith, 2004; Kluegal, 1978; McGuire & Reskin, 1993; Nkomo & Cox, 1990). A study of white men, white women, and minority men and women indicated that for each group, the processes leading to promotion are different; the differences stem largely from minorities' greater need to accrue more time than white males in their total work experience, job-specific experience, and number of years with their current employer (Smith, 2005). These differences suggest that minority women and men need to devote more time and energy to expect the same pay-off as white males. In the study, white males' promotion chances were enhanced more by network assistance, such as help from friends and associates in recommending them for jobs, while minorities and women needed to demonstrate commitment and performance credentials more than white males.

There is also evidence that white women have fewer opportunities due to existing organizational power structures and lack of organizational support for promotion aspirations (Cassirer & Reskin, 2000; Wright, Baxter, & Birkelund, 1995). Blau and Devaro (2007) examined the differences between male and female promotion rates by sampling 3,510 establishments from four different US cities: Atlanta, Boston, Detroit, and Los Angeles. The researchers were able to control for factors that might have influenced their data, such as performance and ability differences of the research subjects and firm characteristics (such as size of the firm, non-profit or for-profit status, and the type of industry). In the analysis the researchers used job-specific performance ratings rather than educational attainment or job tenure. The results of this study indicated that women had a lower probability of promotion than men and that organizations reach down further in their organizations to promote men, which will mean that when women are promoted they will be of higher quality than men (Blau & Devaro, 2007).

Several scholars have studied the impact of promotions when organizations are experiencing change, such as restructuring or reduction in force (RIF).[3] RIF slows promotions for men and women who are retained in the corporation because it ends employment growth, upon which promotions depend. Pathways for women into senior management jobs are blocked, leaving women in lower-level jobs (Acker, 1992; Reskin & Padavic, 1994). Women advanced during the 1970s and 1980s because firms were growing and performance-management systems focused more on equity. During this time, many corporate programs for the advancement of women were initiated to counter the "glass ceiling" effect. However, in the 1990s and 2000s, firms restructured and reduced their labor forces due to economic pressures. RIF and restructuring have made discrimination more likely to occur because male managers place women (either consciously or subconsciously) in labor queues behind other males for the most desirable jobs (Dencker, 2008; Reskin & Roos, 1990). Furthermore, during reorganizations, managers are not as closely supervised as during periods of stability; this lack of supervision may increase the likelihood that women are discriminated against. Human resource departments that are responsible for enforcement of equity principles are often cut back and managers are left to make their own decisions about whom to promote and hire (Meyerson & Ely, 2000).

## Bias in Promotion Decisions

Many of the same types of biases that were discussed in the section on recruitment and selection (pp. 49–51) also apply to promotion decisions. Women can be adversely affected by managers who believe that men are less risky promotional prospects than women, or by outdated attitudes about the suitability of women for leadership roles. Organizations that prefer males for higher-level positions and females for lesser roles exhibit built-in prejudice. Consider a male director thinking about who would be appropriate for the next promotion to management. He thinks about the current managers, most of whom are male, and draws up a list of their characteristics. This type of mental framing activity leads him to unconsciously prefer males for the position rather than females, since his reference group is primarily male.

The impact of stereotypes in assessing what has often been referred to as a person's "organizational fit" cannot be overstated. The lack of person–job fit has been used to explain gender bias against women in organizational performance assessments (Heilman, 1983, 1995, 2001). If women are associated with certain jobs and not others, then they will be perceived as lacking "fit" for the jobs with which they are not associated. As a consequence, these negative associations will have a detrimental effect on how their work is regarded and evaluated, which in turn will have an effect on their chances for promotion. Eagly and her colleagues (1992) found that women in leadership positions have been devalued relative to their male counterparts, especially under three specific situations. First, when women carry out their leadership role with a masculine style (being autocratic and direct, for example), they suffer from poorer performance evaluations compared to men. Second and third, they are more apt to be devalued if they occupy a male-dominated role and when they are evaluated by men. A recent qualitative study examined the evaluations of 22 male and 22 female executives through interviews with their bosses and peers (Lyons & McArthur, 2007). Although the questions asked did not in any way deal with gender, gender became a salient variable in the responses and in the evaluations of the women (119 of the 345 interviewees made gendered comments about the women executives). The comments suggested that women do not readily fit in to the executive suite because good leadership is associated with male behavior. A woman's gender is perceived as an obstacle to her success. Lyness and Heilman (2006) conducted an experiment to see whether the performance ratings for women and men would be different depending on whether or not they occupied *line* or *staff* jobs. Line jobs have been associated more with men, as more men have occupied them, and the holder of a line job has profit-and-loss responsibility for a line of business. Staff positions, on the other hand, do not have profit-and-loss accountability because they support other parts of the organization. Jobs in marketing and human resources, for example, are staff positions because they support other parts of the organization. In the study, performance ratings for women in line jobs were significantly lower than ratings for women in staff jobs, men in line jobs, and men in staff jobs. Furthermore, the composite performance ratings were related to actual promotions that managers received during a two-year period subsequent to the evaluations, after controlling for age, education, organizational level, and organizational tenure. Moreover, the study indicated that the standards for promoting males were more flexible than the standards for promoting females; women who were promoted received higher performance ratings than promoted men. The findings suggest that gender bias from assumed person–job fit can affect the performance evaluations and promotional opportunities of upper-level women managers (Lyness & Heilman, 2006).

The former studies point to male bias in evaluating women, while other studies suggest women devalue their own work. In several studies comparing female with male managers, female managers have attributed their success less to their ability than to hard work. In addition, in the Rosenthal study, female managers gave credit to their subordinates for their success. Men have been more forthright about taking ownership for their success and on identifying it with their abilities (Rosenthal, 1995; Rosenthal, Guest, & Peccei, 1996). This sense of modesty may have a harmful effect on women's performance appraisals, since managers often ask their subordinates for a self-appraisal of their performance before they write up their performance review.

It should be noted that not all studies of performance evaluations find that women are rated lower than men. Wren (2006) found only one difference in ratings by supervisors that actually suggested women were rated higher on developing social relationships with customers, peers, and supervisors. Other dimensions (knowledge, skill, and planning) showed no statistically significant difference in the supervisors' ratings of men versus women.

## Promotion: the International Perspective

The results of unequal career outcomes for men and women in promotional decisions are prevalent in other countries as well as in the United States. A study of Finnish metal workers indicated that women are less likely to be promoted than men who started their careers in similar tasks. Moreover, women become more productive after the initial job assignment both in promoted and non-promoted groups (Pekkarinen & Vartiainen, 2004). An International Labour Organization survey of 6,700 companies in Japan revealed that the reason women have not been promoted as rapidly as men with the same qualifications is the perception that women lack a commitment to work equal to that of men (International Labour Organization, 2004). Traditionally, there has been a two-track system in Japan: men are hired for managerial tracks and women for clerical tracks – even women with college educations are often hired to assist male colleagues with similar qualifications. Women are often assigned to departments that are seen as less strategic to the company; this further prevents them from acquiring valuable experience that might put them in the pool of management candidates. Of the companies surveyed, 54% agreed that women tend to be in jobs that did not lead to management positions, and 19.7% said that women do not necessarily want promotions, preferring jobs that they can balance with their lives outside of work. These statistics don't tell us the underlying reason why Japanese women are not in management positions in greater numbers. Japanese women may prefer to devote more time to outside interests and less to their careers, they may be subjected to the negative stereotypes about their work commitment, or be unprepared for management roles because of lack of experience and opportunity. The answer may be a combination of all of these factors.

A comparison of 30 countries shows that in none of them did the representation of women in managerial jobs exceed more than 45% (International Labour Organization, 2003a). Of all the countries with data, surprisingly, Lithuania had the highest percentage of women in management. South Korea, with women's share of managerial jobs at about 5%, came in last. In Italy, about 20% of managerial jobs are held by women; in Spain, just over 30% are held by women; and in Switzerland, less than about 28% are held by women. In fact, in the newer countries to join the European Union – Latvia, Estonia, Lithuania, Hungary, and Poland, for example – the percentage of women in management is higher than in other parts of Europe. These statistics suggest that women in EU countries are not hired or promoted into management at the same levels that men are. By contrast, in the newer EU member countries, which were formally socialist, the rate of women in management positions is significantly higher. This is no doubt due to a period of state-controlled economies when the proportion of women in the labor force was higher, and when there were state-enforced equal-pay laws. The differences today in these formally socialist countries reflect the long-term pattern of greater equality in pay between men and women, and greater numbers of women in the workforce at all levels. In the Middle East, women have advanced in management, but still have career constraints due to strong gender roles and Islamic culture (Metcalfe, 2006). In the 1970s, Virginia Schein researched the impact of stereotypes on women as they struggled to advance to management positions; she revisited her former research by reviewing the progress that has been made in dispelling damaging stereotypes in the three decades that followed (Schein, 2001, 2007). She finds that "think manager – think male" is an attitude that persists across time and national borders. The view that men are more suitable to management and that women are less likely to have the requisite skills is commonly held in the US, UK, Germany, Japan, and China.

Researchers have been interested in how the general sex composition of a job category affects women's ability to move out of a non-supervisory job into a supervisory position. Maume (1999) studied the effect of the percentage of either males or females in a job category to the chances of men or women moving into a supervisory position within the job category. His findings showed that the percentage of women in a job category positively affected the chances of men moving into a supervisory position. Women, however, were disadvantaged by the percentage of women in a job category; their chances of attaining a supervisory position decreased with the higher percentage of women in the original job category. The phenomenon of men being promoted over women in typically female occupational categories has been called "the glass escalator" effect. In a another study of 76 men and 24 women from four different metropolitan areas of the US in the female occupations of nursing, social work, librarianship, and education, men were consistently promoted over women or steered into the higher-paying areas of education (Williams, 1992). Generally, the men viewed their status of males in a female dominated field as an advantage in hiring and promotion, and many reported having male bosses with whom they had a good, close working relationship. The author concludes that men in female-dominated professions have structural advantages that are often absent for women in these fields.

Other researchers have been interested in how the general sex composition of managerial levels in organizations affects the promotion of male and female managers. Cohen, Broshak, and Haveman (1998) used longitudinal data on all managers in the California savings and loan industry to see what effect sex composition might have on hiring and promotions. They tested three hypotheses: that the likelihood of a woman being hired or promoted into a job will increase with the proportion of women employed above the level of that job; that the likelihood of a woman being hired or promoted into a job will increase with the proportion of women employed at the level of that job; and that the likelihood of a woman being hired or promoted into a job will increase with the proportion of women employed below the level of that job. They discovered that women are more likely to be hired and promoted into a particular job level when a higher proportion of women are already there. The relationship between the proportion of female managers and the number of female *promotions* was stronger than for hiring decisions. In addition, women were more likely to be hired and promoted when there were few women above the job in question. At the time of this study, this may have been due to the pressure to appoint token women. The researchers also found evidence that women are more likely to be hired and promoted when higher proportions of women hold positions below the focal job level. Other studies have produced similar results, suggesting that having many women at high levels of the hierarchy may lead to more women at other levels. For example, having a female college president leads to more female, senior-level college administrators (Pfeffer, Davis-Blake, & Julius, 1995). College administrative positions are more often filled with women when the incumbents of these positions are female and when there are higher proportions of women at similar levels (Konrad & Pfeffer, 1990). In law firms, female decision-makers fill more vacancies with women than do male decision-makers (Gorman, 2005).

Just as stereotypes exist of women being unfit for managerial roles because they do not have the male characteristics necessary for these roles, stereotypes of women being too aggressive, too powerful, and too masculine work against them as well. A study of women executives at Westpac, an Australian firm, reported that Westpac's women executives felt they were wrongly typecast as domineering power maniacs. The women indicated that this stereotype is most prevalent among older males who may feel threatened by younger, powerful women (Beck & Davis, 2005). These stereotypes of women being, on the one hand, too weak for management roles yet, on the other hand, too overbearing for them, leave women in a catch-22 situation. Women find it difficult to know how they should act to ensure their best chances for promotion.

## Institutional Factors that Promote Bias in Selection, Recruitment, and Promotion Decisions

Findings like those above support the idea that the corporate structure influences career outcomes. This may be true for a number of reasons. First, where an individual is situated in the wage hierarchy determines his or her chances of being aware of opportunities and acting on them. Employees at the lower end of the spectrum will have fewer contacts at higher levels, and will therefore be less apt to hear about job openings or attain training necessary to compete for these openings. Conversely, those at higher levels will have the contacts essential for hearing about career opportunities and may have influential people opening doors for them. Second, the presence of many women in a particular job category suggests that the role is an appropriate one for women; when this occurs, both men and women will be more apt to see the job category as a legitimate one for women. Third, as more women occupy higher levels in an organization, they will have more authority over promotion decisions and may be more likely to put women into senior-level jobs.

In addition to where women are situated within the employment structure, certain prerequisites for managerial and other higher-level jobs may be barriers to women. A length-of-service requirement in a particular job role is sometimes a prerequisite to apply for a higher-level position. If males in the organization have had more opportunity than females, then chances are they will have been in higher-level positions for a longer period of time than women have been. A length-of-service requirement can be an artificial barrier that keeps women from applying for certain positions. If management experience is a prerequisite to obtaining a management position, this may disqualify many women. Examining skill sets such as project management and communication skills instead of length-of-service may be more effective in securing the best candidates for management roles.

Many companies use assessment centers to determine who should be promoted to the next level.[4] Assessment centers usually employ a variety of selection tools – interviews, employment tests, psychological questionnaires, and job-related role plays – to assess candidates' skills and fit for a particular job. In theory, assessment centers may be objective ways to determine promotions, but in practice they can be discriminatory.

As part of the assessment center approach, standardized verbal and mathematical reasoning tests and job–knowledge tests are regarded as useful ways to determine whether or not an individual has the cognitive ability or skills to do the job in question. If tests are designed properly and measure actual job skills or cognitive traits that are essential for jobs, then they can be very useful tools. However, if test administration is not consistent for all candidates, and if the test chosen does not measure skills or knowledge necessary to do the job, then the test will not be a valid measure. Psychometric questionnaires and psychological tests measuring personality characteristics may be a good predictor of job performance if they measure psychological factors that are necessary or desirable for job performance. Many organizations use commercial personality profiles as part of their selection processes or as part of their career-development initiatives. Companies that can isolate personality characteristics for specific job categories, such as extroversion for a salesperson or helpfulness for a customer-service agent, may find personality profiles helpful in selecting candidates. They can be useful tools, provided that the organization chooses an appropriate personality profile for the job category.

Managers who use psychometric tools need to understand that differences between men and women on certain items may not be statistically significant. For example, a comparison of three different psychometric tests used in Britain for graduate selection showed very little difference between men and women on personality dimensions; women's averages are slightly lower on some items than men's averages, but these differences are negligible (Ones & Anderson, 2002). If the manager were to attribute too much meaning to these differences, he or she might disadvantage women candidates.

---

### Box 4.1  An Example of Employment Testing

A recent study by Muchinsky highlights many of the problems associated with testing in the business setting (2004). This study illustrates how organizational practices, in particular the way that power and influence, and how the organization's presumed knowledge about test construction, can have a negative impact on what is intended to be an unbiased process. Muchinsky analyzed the decision of one manufacturing firm to use employment testing as a substitute for seniority in determining promotion of machine operators to maintenance mechanics. Instead of relying on outside industrial psychologists to construct a valid test, the company decided to construct the test internally. Creating the test was deemed a simple enough process. The company did not like the test items constructed by the psychologists. Moreover, having company employees design the test would save the firm money as well as give the test designers a sense of ownership of the process. The company identified employees who could act as subject matter experts to construct the test items. As it turned out, the constructed items reflected the power of the most influential person in the group, the maintenance director. When reviewing the items to edit or delete from the test because they were not well-constructed, the lower-status individuals felt uncomfortable challenging the items written by the higher-status individuals. Many of the subject-matter experts were too attached to the items they wrote and became defensive when their items were challenged. Others constructed test items to cover content areas for which it was difficult to write straightforward questions – these subject-matter experts ended up writing ambiguous questions for these content areas. Some of the test items seemed to favor candidates who had recently had some sort of academic preparation, even though this knowledge was not important to the maintenance mechanic position. The test consisted of discrete content areas that could have been scored independently. Scoring for each part of the test would have yielded more fine-grained and more useful information, yet the human-resource department simply reported a pass/fail grade. Finally, when the organization attempted to validate the test, it did so with too small a sample. Small sample sizes may lead to erroneous conclusions about the predictive validity of a test. In this case, the small sample led to lowering the average test score, increasing the likelihood of miscalibrating the level of knowledge desired for the job candidates.

---

In addition to formal rules such as length-of-service requirements, assessment centers, and employment testing, informal organizational practices can disadvantage women. Treating candidates differently before an assessment that determines a promotion is one example of such an informal practice. Men may receive more information, advice, and coaching than women, especially if they are close to the hiring manager or know someone who is. These informal interactions may influence who will be shortlisted or selected for a position. Coaching some candidates and not others may result in hiring a less-able candidate who simply comes across better in the interview process. More importantly, it may also result in not considering the candidate who would in fact be most suitable for a job.

Organizations may indirectly discriminate against women by failing to keep them informed about job opportunities while they are on a medical or family leave. This is important for all employees, but especially women as they may be away from the workplace for several months while caring for a newborn. Large organizations with websites that employees can access from home can eliminate this problem because these sites describe available new job openings, short-term project assignments, and training opportunities, and allow individuals to apply online for them.

In addition to providing information and coaching to employees, another informal mechanism that tends to help people get ahead in organizations is their inclusion in social events. Although not *directly* related to how promotions are decided, when women are excluded from organizational social events, they lose an advantage. Social events give lower-level employees the chance to talk with more-senior-level employees and a chance to make an impression on a company's clients. Jim Copeland, former CEO of Deloitte & Touche, a large US accounting firm, recognized that this type of bias against women can be largely unconscious:

> I was sitting there thinking about an outing I was going to that weekend, a guys' weekend out. The Atlanta partners went and invited a lot of the clients. It has become a very popular event, and sort of a bonding event between partners and clients. And there were no women. It had never occurred to me to ask.... I had assumed that no woman would want to go to a golf outing where you smoke cigars and drink beer and tell lies. It's one of those things where you hit your forehead and say, "How can we have been so stupid?"
>
> (Rosener, 1999, p. 4)

## What Individuals and Organizations Can Do to Make Recruitment, Selection, and Promotion Systems Fair

Individuals need to be aware that bias may play a role in their career prospects or career progression once inside a company. If an individual thinks that bias may be occurring, he or she could address it during the job interview. Attempting to counter stereotypes head-on might work to change the perception of the interviewer. For example, a 50-year-old female job applicant for a management job who is worried that the interviewer holds a stereotype that older workers do not having enough stamina to do the job might say:

> I know you may think that because I am obviously not a twenty-year-old that I do not have the energy for this job. Let me assure you that I do. I get up every morning at 6 a.m. and accomplish more than most people do by noon.

Job candidates need to know their rights. For example, interviewers can legally ask only job-related questions. Questions about whether or not an individual is married, questions about age, whether or not an individual has children, or whether or not an individual plans to have children are illegal because they are potentially discriminatory.

Individuals should recognize that contextual factors play a role in advancement. Individuals who want to be promoted need to take on additional responsibilities and challenges so that they are perceived to be in the candidate pool when promotions become available. Women need to observe what qualities and experience are required for promotion and examine their own career interests. If they are unsure about what qualities and experience are needed for promotion, they should ask people who are in responsible positions about what is required to attain higher-level jobs. Individuals need to be aware that job searches take planning, time, and energy. Making a list of job assignments that would increase one's value to the organization and then pursuing them is one way to plan. Job-seekers should also let others know about their career aspirations so that they can gain help and support. Women tend to have fewer business contacts than men, so they may need to make a concerted effort to develop a broader network of individuals who can help them with their careers.

Organizations can also play a role in opening up career opportunities for all individuals. To ensure fair *recruitment* practices, the organization's leadership should do the following:

- advertise widely and in different media to attract a broad range of candidates for jobs.
- train employees on interview skills and make them aware of situations that could create bias.
- include women and minorities on any shortlist of candidates.
- make sure that the process of recruitment is transparent to all employees.

To ensure that employees are given career opportunities that may lead to *promotion*, the organization should:

- monitor the progress of women and minorities.
- analyze data to see if there could be inequities in certain departments of the organization.
- analyze the processes leading up to promotion. For example, are men mentored more than women? Are women receiving challenging job assignments that would lead to promotion?
- make the procedures for promotions transparent to all employees. For example, if assessments centers are used, explain this process to employees.
- post information about job opportunities so that all employees have access to this information.
- analyze exit data. Find out the reasons for individuals leaving the organization. For example, do individuals leave because they perceive a lack of career opportunity?
- find out how employees view the culture of the organization. Is it perceived to be one that is providing opportunities?
- provide managers with information about the positive effects of a diverse workforce.

With more and more women completing post-secondary degrees, and with more women participating in the workforce than ever before, it only makes sense for employers to use their talents. According to the US department of education, 58% of all undergraduates of post-secondary institutions are women; 59% of master's degrees are conferred upon women; and 47% of doctorates are earned by women (2005). Women are gaining leadership positions in non-profits and in the military, and they have managed to juggle work with family. By using the knowledge and experience of all employees, including women, employers can gain a competitive edge – and those that don't will lag behind.

The following three cases illustrate different aspects of career opportunities. The first describes a new recruitment-center procedure; the second examines an assessment-center approach in which men and women are competing for promotion; the third examines a woman's opportunity for a challenging job assignment that could help further her career.

# CASE STUDIES

### Case Study 1: Recruitment at Capstone Media – Part A

*March 8, 2009*

Julianna Carson had a hard time sleeping. Once again, her job was on her mind. It seemed that just when she had accomplished putting a new program in place, writing a new policy or revising an old one, something went wrong. As Director of Human Resources for Capstone Media, a company that provided computer storage systems for other companies, she never experienced a dull moment. She always had a full plate with salary surveys to do, payroll management, recruitment and selection, and employee communication programs. She was trying to bring best practices to Capstone Media in the area of human resources management but she sometimes felt that the world conspired against her.

### *Several Months Earlier – January 2009*

Julianna had spent months instituting new recruitment practices. Capstone Media had grown very fast in the previous two years, from 200 to 400 employees, and it was time to institute more standardized employment practices. This would include a new system designed to ensure equal access to job openings for all employees by making the process more transparent and more systematic. The procedures would be centralized in the human resources department. When managers had a new job to fill, they were to come to human resources to work with an HR specialist on writing up a job description, outlining the duties of the job and the qualifications sought (see Appendix 4.1, p. 64). The HR department would streamline the process so that all jobs would be posted in a similar format and be advertised online for at least 30 days before candidates were interviewed. The new procedures did not increase the paperwork for managers and the HR department would handle all of the postings of jobs on the website. The recruitment procedures were an important step in ensuring that employees had a fair chance to act on the new job opportunities, and it would ensure a larger pool of candidates. These changes would be good for individual employees, and good for the corporation.

Before rolling out the procedures to managers and employees, Julianna met with Greg Faison, Capstone's CEO. He strongly endorsed the new procedures for a number of reasons. First, he sincerely wanted to open up the pool of candidates for jobs, and second, he had been worried about the potential of a lawsuit. He knew that if recruitment procedures were inconsistent and unsystematic, the organization could be opening itself up to a discrimination suit. He told Julianna:

"This is an important step for us. I think this will streamline the process for everyone. We just need to make sure that the communication to managers and employees is clear so that they know the procedures are now in effect."

Julianna agreed to organize a series of half-hour meetings with managers to explain the procedures and answer questions. She also sent out a briefing memo (Appendix 4.2, p. 65) to all managers to summarize aspects of the new procedures. The meetings went well; no one objected to the new procedures and there were very few questions about the process. Generally, Julianna was greeted with cautious optimism. The managers seemed to be on board as long as they would still be able to make the final decision in the hiring process and did not have to complete more paperwork. One manager remarked:

"I am up to my eyeballs in forms for just about everything from requisitioning new computer equipment, filling out performance appraisals, to filling out budget worksheets. Whatever you propose is fine as long as I don't have to fill out one more form!"

After the manager meetings were held, she had two of her staff, Joe Stearn and Tasha Wilson, inform the employees. Joe and Tasha walked the employees through the process, showing them examples of job postings on the HR website. Employees were instructed to send their resumes directly to HR from the job-posting site, citing the job number for which they were applying. The employees were happy with the new procedures; many remarked that in the past they had no idea how jobs were filled. After the meetings were held, Julianna wrote an article in the company newsletter to highlight the new procedures.

### February 15, 2009–February 26, 2009

Two weeks after the roll-out of the new procedures, Julianna took a well-earned vacation. She and her husband flew to the Caribbean for a 10-day holiday in the sunshine. During her absence, Joe and Tasha were deputized to handle any problems that might arise. In addition, Julianna took her Blackberry with her. Although she did not like being attached to the office by this technology, she told her employees that they could contact her in the event of an emergency.

Julianna arrived back at the office tanned and relaxed. She didn't stay relaxed for long. On her first day back, she met with Joe and Tasha to have them debrief her on what had transpired in her absence.

"So how did it go while I was gone? I didn't hear from you so I assume everything went smoothly."

"We didn't have any real emergencies, except for one issue which we didn't consider an emergency," said Joe.

"What was that?" Julianna asked.

"Well," chimed in Tasha, "Stewart Alvarez hired someone without posting the job to the website and without calling us. We called him, but he didn't return our calls. His secretary said he had been very busy talking to a software vendor and with the new IT rollout."

"I can't believe this! Everyone was informed about the new procedures. How could this happen!"

Stewart was the Vice President of Information Systems. He was well respected for his technical knowledge and his department, one of the largest and most important in the company, ran smoothly. Julianna felt that she had a distant yet cordial relationship with him. She and Stewart had never had any unpleasant confrontations.

Julianna excused Joe and Tasha from her office and decided to phone Stewart right away to find out why he didn't use the procedures.

"Stewart, this is Julianna. Have you got a moment?"

"Sure. I understand that you just got back from a cruise in some sunny place. Must have been nice. Hope you had a great time. What can I do for you?"

"Stewart, I am calling to ask you about the new hire you made."

"Terrific guy. We were absolutely fortunate to get him. He has a fantastic background and just the skills we need right now to get this network conversion done."

"Stewart, did you know about the new recruiting procedure that HR developed?"

"Well, I think I read something about it, but I am not sure. Didn't you send a memo out?"

"I did send a memo out and all managers were supposed to attend a meeting we had several weeks ago."

"Well, I have been so busy with getting this conversion done, I haven't had time for meetings."

"Stewart, we asked that all managers use the new procedures. All job openings are to be posted on the website and then employees have an opportunity to post their resumes for positions they want. It is good for everyone."

"Anyway, I am sorry about that. I needed to act fast on this one and we were so lucky to get this guy. He had other offers. I really couldn't go through a lengthy process or I would have lost him. You know, Julianna, I know employees in this company well and there was no one else that compares with him. You will like him. His name is Samir Ganeshe. He's a great guy. He doesn't start for another month, but he has signed the contract."

"Stewart, I am sure he is a nice guy, but that's not the point. We want the process to be more open and available to employees."

"Well you were out of town when I hired him. I couldn't have contacted you anyway."

"Stewart, I have two very capable managers who would have been able to help you. You know Joe and Tasha. They were handling things in my absence."

"Well Julianna. I did not know. Besides, senior managers cannot be expected to attend all of these meetings, especially when they are working on critical stuff. I really can't keep track of all the HR rules. I have a big system conversion on my hands that has to run seamlessly. And all of our client data had to be secure during and after the conversion. I am sure you can appreciate that."

"Of course, I understand that. In any case, I'd like to meet with you to explain the procedures."

"I can't meet for at least two weeks. I'll try to make time after that. And I'll look over the memo you sent about the recruitment procedures right away. Can you call Karen and get on my calendar?"

"Fine, I will do that."

Julianna could see that she was getting nowhere with Stewart. She wondered about whether she had made mistakes in the roll-out or whether Stewart was the problem. The policy seemed straightforward enough and it really didn't add more work for managers. She worried about the impact that this new hire would have on employees. After all, they had just been told that the process was going to be more transparent and fair for everyone. How would she explain this to employees who complained? And, how could she get the most senior managers to comply with HR policies?

***Appendix 4.1***

**Human Resources – Position Description**

Job title: _____

Job #: _____

Location (department): _____

Supervising Manager: _____

Full or Part Time: _____

Grade Level: _____

Salary Range: _____

Job Description:

Summary:

Work Performed:

Minimum Qualifications: Education and Experience Required:

**Appendix 4.2**

January 15, 2009

**Interoffice Memo**

**To:** Capstone Managers

**Fr:** Julianna Carson
Human Resources Director

**Re:** New Procedures for Recruiting Employees

Now that Capstone Media has grown to over 400 employees it is important for us to streamline our recruitment practices. We need to have all managers adopt the same procedures to ensure efficiency and fairness for all employees. We hope that you will see that these procedures will save you time. Much of the initial work to get your job postings advertised will be done by the human resources department. The recruitment process is going to be fully automated and online. This memo outlines the procedures that will take effect January 31st.

1. When you have a job opening, come to the HR department to get assistance in writing up the job description. We have one form for all job openings. (See the attachment to this memo.)
2. The posting will be required to be up for 30 days so that employees have time to react to it and send in their resumes. Once the 30 days has passed the listing will come off the HR website.
3. Once the 30-day period has passed, we will begin interviewing candidates. The HR department can assist in this if you would like help. For example, we can shortlist candidates that you interview.

In the next few weeks we will be scheduling mandatory half-hour meetings to answer any questions and to review the forms that will go on the website. If you have any questions about this process, please do not hesitate to call me on X4321 or e-mail me at Julianna@ Capstone.com

Thank you for your time and cooperation.

Julianna Carson
Human Resource Director

Attachment: Human Resources Position Description

**Discussion Questions**

1. If the CEO backs the new recruitment methods, what else could he do to show his support for them?
2. What else could Julianna do to ensure compliance with the new procedures?
3. If you were Julianna, how would you deal with Stewart?
4. How is the problem with Stewart potentially symptomatic of a larger problem in the company?

**Case Study 1: Recruitment at Capstone Media – Part B**

After Julianna left his office, Stewart looked through his files to see if he could retrieve the memo that Julianna had sent. With help from his assistant, he found it in his "administrative tasks file."

Julianna's memo clearly stated what managers were expected to do.

Stewart wondered how he could rectify the situation. He had already offered the job to Samir, an outside candidate. And he couldn't rescind the contract offer – nor did he want to. He looked at the attachment with the position description form.

"I could simply back-date the form for a month before the hiring date, and put it on the website now. That would solve the problem. If anyone complained, we could simply explain that there had been a computer glitch and we assumed that the posting was up. In any case, most likely no one would notice. I doubt that anyone in the company would have applied for the position anyway because I can't think of anyone who is qualified for it," Stewart thought.

He decided to go to the Human Resources Department with the completed form the next day, March 6.

When Stewart entered the Human Resources Department, he approached the administrative assistant, Sean Belkins.

"Hello Sean. Can you put this job posting up on your website? I'd appreciate it."

"No problem. Be happy to."

*March 7*

Julianna was back in her office after a series of meetings. She checked her voice mail to see what calls had come in during her two-hour absence. There were a couple of messages from employees about mistakes in their pay slips, and then a final message came from a caller who said,

"Julianna. I am sorry I missed you. This is Tom Thompson. I am upset that I seemed to have missed a job posting that I just saw yesterday for an information technology position reporting to Stewart Alvarez. I couldn't have missed the deadline for this job. I am sure that this posting was not up before, even though the date on it indicates that it was. I have been checking the job postings every other day. I really want to talk to you about this. I think this job would have been perfect for me."

Immediately after checking her voicemail, Julianna checked the Human Resource Department website. Indeed Stewart's listing was up on the site, with a back-dated posting to February 1.

Julianna called an impromptu staff meeting with Sean, Tasha, and Joe to find out what had happened to allow the back-dated posting to go up. As she waited for her staff to come into the conference room, she thought about what she would say to Tom and what generally she would do about this problem.

**Discussion Questions**

1.  What are Julianna's choices now?
2.  If she chooses to "cover" for Stewart, what risk is she taking?
3.  What are the pros and cons of discussing this issue with the CEO?

## Case Study 2: To Be Or Not To Be Promoted?

The phone rang in Jane Preston's office.

"Jane, this is Dave Pearson. I am happy to tell you that you made the first cut for the director of marketing. We plan to have a two-day assessment to determine who the director will be. Congratulations on getting this far. There were many qualified candidates and we have now narrowed it down to three. Please mark your calendar for Thursday and Friday of next week. We'll need you the whole of both days."

As she hung up the phone with the senior vice president of human resources, she reflected on how well her career was going. She had been a successful middle manager for the head office of a major hotel chain, was well respected by both her peers and those who reported directly to her, and always gave 100%. She was excited about this new opportunity to direct a whole department and to manage a team of marketing professionals. Before she could celebrate, however, she needed to go through the company assessment process designed by the company's human resource professionals working with senior-level managers to help them assess the shortlist of candidates. She would undergo some role plays, some verbal and mathematical ability tests, an interview, and a personality profile to see if she was suitable for the position. The selection committee would assess the results of these tests, exercises, and interview, and would evaluate her experience and education in marketing against an "ideal job profile" for the position. She was one of three others competing for the job. Matt Stevenson and Joe Stern had also made it to this final step.

Before the two-day assessment, Jane reviewed the position description for the role of marketing director. The position description was written by the HR department. It read:

### Marketing Director

The position requires the following skill-set and experience. The individual will manage a team of professionals and support staff – six marketing professionals who will each have a set of responsibilities and two marketing coordinator positions. The individual will establish a strategic marketing plan that includes but may not be limited to marketing research objectives, advertising and promotion objectives, and public relations initiatives. The individual will execute the plan with internal marketing resources or outside resources such as advertising and PR firms.

The person will have deep knowledge of our customers as well as knowledge of our internal structure, especially our major hotel properties. The person should have a track record of successful marketing experience (at least eight years) and experience managing a team. The individual should be a self-starter who takes initiative to plan and execute difficult projects. The person should be able to influence individuals from various parts of the company to embrace the marketing mission. People skills are a must. The individual will work closely with other senior-level managers.

Jane felt well-qualified for the role. She had been a marketing professional for nine years. She had handled several individual marketing projects for the company, which included a variety of tasks such as marketing research, advertising concepts, dealing with agencies, customer analyses, hotel promotions targeted at past customers, and contests targeted to the hotel staffs. As a marketing manager, she had successfully managed a team of four people and she felt confident that she could handle a larger team with broader responsibilities. Her performance reviews had singled her out as a high achiever in the top one-third of managers in the company.

### The Assessment Process

Jane was not worried about the ability tests; she had done very well on the verbal and mathematical portions of the university entrance tests and taken advanced math courses in university. She was used to interpreting data in her current job where one of her assignments had been a major marketing research project. She had also managed a budget and was comfortable with numbers and balance sheets.

During another part of the assessment process, four senior-level managers – three men and one woman – interviewed her about her career, her motivations for wanting the position, and her strengths in terms of managing people. Jane talked about her democratic style of management, her ability to help her team work through conflicts, and her high standards. In her tenure as a manager, she had an excellent record for retaining good employees. Jane also talked about her track record of success. She had been recognized for her management skills and had produced a marketing campaign that had increased sales of five of the hotel's struggling properties. Additionally, she had been nominated for this position by her boss, Fred Markum, who had the highest regard for Jane. Jane felt somewhat uncomfortable with the line of some of the interviewers' questions. She recalled them and her answers.

Jake Storm, one of the senior vice presidents, had asked her, "How would you deal with some of our opinionated hotel managers, Dan, Mike, or Ross, who think they know how to market their properties better than the head office? Do you think you could deal with their personalities?"

Jane replied, "I have never had insurmountable difficulty dealing with difficult people. I just keep the dialog going and use facts to support my position. I don't think I would have any trouble, but if I did I would ask for support from the head office to back me up."

George Montgomery, another senior vice president, had asked, "In this business we sometimes need to take a firm hand with employees. You have a reputation of being a democratic manager. How do you take a firm hand with your staff?"

Jane was caught off-guard by the question, but replied, "I find that if I set expectations upfront and hold people accountable for results, I don't need to take much of a firm hand. My teams have always really wanted to achieve because they know I will recognize them for their hard work both monetarily and in other ways. I try to be fair."

George continued, "Well, you must have had to discipline an employee at some point?"

Jane countered, "No, I can't recall having to. Perhaps I've had to spend more time training someone who was not up to speed, but I can't recall having to discipline anyone. I've hired some outstanding people and they have performed very well. If you hire the right people and work with them, you don't have problems."

Jake Storm asked, "Do you think you could manage a budget worth several million dollars?"

Jane replied, "I do. I have the organizational skills to manage it and I have managed smaller budgets where the same principles apply."

After the interview, Jane reflected that these two senior managers seem to proceed with the assumption that Jane would have problems with the new position. She was worried that they had already formed a negative opinion of her. The other two managers' questions seemed more straightforward and allowed her to talk directly about her strengths.

The personality profile part of the assessment process did not cause Jane any trepidation. The industrial psychologist who administered the questionnaire told her that they would debrief each candidate on her or his results since they wanted this to be a developmental process for the candidates. She had taken many personality profiles before, and actually enjoyed learning more about what makes her tick. She answered the questions honestly. The industrial psychologist explained that her strongest dimensions of personality were the following:

- affiliative (values friends, likes being around people).
- democratic (encourages others to contribute, is a good listener).
- data rational (uses data to support views, operates with facts).
- worrying (is anxious when things go wrong, anxious to do well).
- achieving (results focused, career centered).

Her weakest dimensions of personality were:

- controlling (takes charge, directs, supervises).
- traditional (conventional, uses tried and true methods).
- tough-minded (thick-skinned, difficult to upset).
- competitive (wants to win, wants to beat others).

The psychologist mentioned that her weakest dimensions were around the mean for women managers. He explained that he wasn't surprised at her weakest dimensions of personality because the norms for women differed significantly from the norms for men in the following categories: controlling, tough-minded, and competitive. In other words, men see themselves as more controlling, tough-minded, and competitive than women see themselves. He stressed that the questionnaire simply highlighted how individuals viewed themselves and that he was not placing any value judgment on whether some dimensions of personality were better than others. He continued to explain that the importance of using personality questionnaires in an assessment process was to have a clear idea of which personality characteristics are important to do the job effectively. These personality characteristics would have been validated as important for job performance by the actual track record of current or former job holders.

"For example," he said, "I wouldn't want to hire a sales person who was not out-going and socially confident because these are critical personality characteristics common of successful salespeople."

### Roleplays and Other Exercises
Jane was asked to react to some company customer data and make marketing recommendations based on the data. This was something that she routinely did in her current marketing role so she felt very confident about her recommendations.

Each candidate for the marketing role was paired with a senior manager assessor for a role play. Jane was to role play a situation with George Montgomery where she took the role of the marketing director and he played one of her underperforming staff. Her task was to analyze his performance. In the role play, she opened the meeting by explaining the reason for it: to discuss his underperformance in recent weeks. She asked him what he liked and disliked about his job, and whether or not he understood what was expected of him. She also inquired about whether or not he felt he had the training to do what he was asked to do. She was attempting to uncover whether the reason for his poor performance was a lack of motivation or a lack of ability. As George played his role, he was not disclosing anything. Jane found this frustrating because in real situations at work she was able to get her staff to open up and discuss issues. She continued to ask George questions which he refused to answer and finally she succumbed to telling him that he was underperforming and would have to change. She laid out her expectations for his performance and then closed the meeting. At the end of the role play, she couldn't help thinking that none of her employees in the past had behaved this way. She felt George had overplayed a belligerent employee and was possibly just giving her a hard time. He played a role that had effectively sabotaged her ability to demonstrate any management skills.

### *The Announcement of the New Marketing Director*

Jane eagerly picked up the telephone. She had been waiting to hear the news.

"Jane, this is Dave Pearson. I want to thank you for taking the time to apply for the Marketing Directorship. You performed solidly during the assessment process. We have, however, decided to hire Joe Stern. He is an extremely good fit for the role. We know that you will support Joe in his new role."

"Thank you for letting me know," Jane said. She hung up the phone in disbelief. She thought she was the best candidate and had performed extremely well in other marketing roles. She debated whether or not to seek clarification about why she wasn't chosen.

### Discussion Questions

1.  Assuming that Joe, Matt, and Jane had similar backgrounds and experience, what potential bias was present in the assessment process?
2.  Do you think that Jane was a good fit for the job? Why, or why not?
3.  If you were Jane, would you drop the matter of not being offered the job or would you seek clarification on why you were not chosen? Why, or why not?
4.  Describe Jane's management style. Is there any evidence in the case study that her style would be an obstacle to her success?
5.  How might Jane's style of management clash with George Montgomery's?
6.  Assess the role of HR in designing the assessment process. Is there a potential problem with the HR department's role in designing the assessment process and senior managers being on the selection committee?

### Other Activities

Companies often use 360-degree feedback questionnaires, questionnaires designed to elicit feedback on managers from a variety of sources: the manager's direct reports, the manager's peers, the manager him or herself, and the manager's boss, for example. Consulting firms often sell these questionnaires to companies as development tools for managers. Look at the 360-degree questionnaires offered by The Center For Creative Leadership, www.ccl.org, under the "Products" tab. Make a list of the categories that are used on these questionnaires. In your opinion, are these categories gender-neutral or do they show a bias toward a male style of management?

## Case Study 3: Jill Saunders' Career Opportunity

Jill Saunders, a business development manager for Blanton Corporation, was looking forward to her first trip to Japan to explain to a potential client, Japanese company, exactly how Blanton's newest products would benefit the medical supply company. Using ozone, Blanton had recently patented sterilization products for hospitals. Blanton had high hopes to capture the Japanese market using a highly respectable Japanese distributor, Keiresu Corporation. Jill had been fostering a relationship with Keiresu for several months by exchanging written correspondence. The presentation she intended to make to Keiresu was one she had delivered many times to US clients; she was very comfortable extending the presentation to transnational issues. No one in her firm spoke Japanese well enough to do the trip without a translator; but this was not an issue since the company had retained a translator for all of Jill's correspondence with the company. Representing the company abroad would be a great opportunity for Jill since she wanted this international exposure and loved to travel. She knew that having this experience under her belt would make her more marketable within her own organization and lead to a promotion at some time in the future.

Jill had spent the last several months learning about the key players at the Keiresu organization and had developed a good understanding of their business. Keiresu had links with all of the major hospitals in Japan, dealing mainly with equipment for operating rooms. Most of her communication had been with Kenzo Shimizo, one of the senior executives of the organization in the new product area. She had corresponded with him via e-mails and conference calls, using the interpreter for all correspondence and phone conversations. Their conversations were always very formal. Jill was careful to treat Mr. Shimizo with the utmost respect. As in other client situations, she let the client do most of the talking and tried to demonstrate where her company could help his operation.

Barry Stevens, one of Jill's direct reports, had been very helpful collecting data on the company, assisting her in writing a business proposal and, although he did not contribute to the telephone meetings, he listened in on all conference calls. Jill considered Barry her right-hand person on the project.

Jill was to meet her CEO to review the details of her trip. Stefan Blackwell was a California entrepreneur, immensely proud of his company, which had grown from three employees and a sheet of legal paper in which he sketched out the company's product and mission statement, to a company of 500 employees and $312 million in sales revenues. He was very excited about having cracked the Japanese market, and saw this new contract as an entry into the wider Asian marketplace.

### The Meeting with CEO Blackwell

"Have a seat Jill. First, I want to tell you that we are immensely proud of your efforts over the last several months with Keiresu Corporation. You and your team have worked very hard pulling this deal together. This deal, if we get it and I am confident that we will, represents a large part of our future business.

"I do have one concern, though. You know the Japanese culture is very different from our own and, frankly, I am concerned that if we send a woman to make the presentation it may affect the outcome, not in a positive way. I know you are very committed and you have been the driving force behind this project, but I am reluctant to send you as our spokesperson. It's nothing personal; it's just that Japanese businessmen may not accept you and that could put the whole deal in jeopardy. Barry Stevens has worked with you on the project, hasn't he?"

"Yes, he's done a fine job, but he isn't completely up to speed with it," Jill said.

"Well, we are going to need to send Barry to make the presentation. I'd like you to work with him in the next couple of weeks to get him ready. Of course, I'll provide any support that you need."

"Mr. Blackwell, I appreciate what you are saying, but I have had no problems at all dealing with Mr. Shimizo over the last several months. He has accepted my expertise willingly."

"I know that. But the presentation has to be made to a committee and we don't know the other key players. We just cannot risk losing the business."

Jill suggested that they test the waters during a video conference call with Mr. Shimizo by explaining that she would be coming to Japan. "I think I can read his body language to see if he has any issue with it."

"Jill, I really do understand your frustration. But the Japanese are hard to read. I am not sure that you would get an honest read on the situation. And I don't think we could come right out and ask him. He would find that embarrassing. We just can't risk losing the business. Jill, I would send you both but I don't see the need for two people to go from one department. The trip is expensive and the client won't bear the cost. We also need to send our translator and pay his consulting fee."

Dumbfounded, Jill walked out of the office. She wanted Mr. Blackwell to stand up for his principles of treating men and women equally and let her go to Japan. In a company meeting, he had publicly committed to helping women and minorities progress in the company, but now his public acknowledgement seemed hollow. Furthermore, she thought, "He should trust my judgment that the client will not be offended. After all, I've been working with a senior-level manager of Keiresu for months without any problems. He trusts me. Bringing someone else in at this stage could ruin the deal."

### Discussion Questions

1.  Who is right, Mr. Blackwell or Jill? Why?
2.  Should Jill drop the matter or try to continue to convince Mr. Blackwell? Why?
3.  What could Jill do to provide evidence for her view?
4.  In matters of culture, should companies adhere to their own culture when doing business abroad or should they adapt?
5.  If Jill does not go to Japan, how might this affect her career?

# LEGAL CASES DEALING WITH RECRUITMENT, SELECTION, AND PROMOTION

## The Ben E. Keith Company

In April 2004, a Texas-based beer distributor settled a case out-of-court, agreeing to pay $131,508 to deal with a complaint about discriminating against women who were denied interviews when they were equally, if not more, qualified than male candidates who were interviewed for the same positions. The unfair hiring practices were discovered not by the women, but from a routine compliance evaluation by the Department of Labor involving companies that have federal contracts.

## Hynix Semiconductor Company

In 1999, a California recruiter who owned his own business filed suit against Hynix for violating an antidiscrimination law (McDonald, 2002). The Oregon computer firm dropped Jeff Abraham's recruitment firm because he continued to refer women for jobs at the plant after the company's hiring manager told him to stop sending women. Abraham testified that Hynix's Korean owners did not want to hire women or blacks. Abraham was awarded $14.7 million; the company denied any wrongdoing.

## Abercrombie & Fitch

The retailer has been accused of discriminating against minorities in one of their California stores (Johansson, 2003). The lawsuit, filed in June 2003, alleges that five Asians were cut from employment at the same time three white employees were hired. One Asian woman was told that the lay-off was necessary because the store wasn't doing well. Abercrombie & Fitch has come under fire for "appearance hiring." Store employees have been told to try to recruit blond, blue-eyed, preppy-looking women and men for the retail salespeople, excluding anyone else who might be interested who does not fit that appearance description. Abercrombie has paid out $50 million to settle three class action suits that allege an appearance policy kept certain individuals from working in their stores (King, Winchester, & Sherwyn, 2006).

## *Jespersen* v. *Harrah's Operating Company*

Harrah's casinos have a "Personal Best Policy" that requires female bartenders to wear make-up (face powder, blush, mascara, and lip color) and male bartenders to keep their hair no longer than collar length and their fingernails neat, trimmed, and clean. Jespersen, a female bartender, filed a suit in the Ninth Circuit Court claiming that the policy interfered with her self-image, and because she never wore make-up, was an undue and unfair burden (King et al., 2006). The court ruled against her because the policy was determined not to unfairly burden one gender over another (men were also held to an appearance standard). In addition, the policy did not seem to burden any race more than another. This case, though not related to recruitment practices, shows how Abercrombie was held accountable for its actions while Harrah's was not; though both of the cases had to do with appearance, the Abercrombie case was deemed to be discriminatory because it eliminated the prospect of hiring for individuals of certain races, while the Harrah's case was not.

## Hooters

In 1992, Hooters paid an out-of-court settlement to several males who alleged that they were discriminated because Hooters advertised for "Hooters Girls" as servers. Seven men from Illinois and Maryland filed a class action suit claiming their rights guaranteed by Title VII had been violated. Hooters countered by saying that female sexuality was a "bona fide occupational qualification" because it was offering its customers "vicarious sexual recreation." Hooters had difficulty supporting this contention since they had advertised itself as a family restaurant rather than an entertainment venue (Holt, 2004). The restaurant agreed to pay $3.75 million to settle the plaintiffs' suit and consented to fill future positions such as bartenders or hosts without regard to gender.

## The Bell South Company

In 2002, Bell South was sued by five African Americans for racial discrimination for using unvalidated tests and administering those tests in what was alleged to be a discriminatory fashion in order to deny employment opportunities to African Americans (United States District Court for the Northern District of Alabama). The suit claimed that African Americans were subjected to the test while white employees were excused from it. The plaintiffs also alleged that items on the test did not reflect the skills needed for the jobs for which people were applying.

## The Sanofi-Aventis Case

Four women sales representatives have pursued a class action lawsuit against the French drug-maker, claiming that they were barred from promotional opportunities and received lower pay than their male colleagues (Kim, 2007). In August 2007 a US Federal judge gave the plaintiffs permission to pursue a class action discrimination lawsuit, meaning that together women can bring a suit against their employer and, as such, have much more power in defending their claims than if they tried to do so individually. One of the women said that the explicitly sexual language that was used in e-mails and during after-hour happy hours created an inhospitable environment for women, and that twice she was denied promotion. The women are asking for a settlement of $300,000,000.

## The Wal-Mart Case

The female employees of Wal-Mart are on the opposite end of the pay continuum from Wall Street advisors. In July 2003, six female former Wal-Mart employees claimed that Wal-Mart systematically discriminated against them by preventing them from obtaining promotions and by paying them less than men for equal work. The Wal-Mart case was recently certified as the largest class action sex-discrimination case in history – with about two million women eligible to join the class action against the company.

Lawyers for the women have reported that 72% of the sales associates are women, while 90% of the store managers are male. Among Wal-Mart's top 20 officers, only one is female. One black female, one of the original plaintiffs, has alleged that male managers at Wal-Mart treated her harshly and demoted her after she complained and requested training to become a department manager. Prior to this request, she had earned two promotions and two raises. Wal-Mart denies the allegations, stating that their payroll data highlight different findings. Moreover, the company says its operations are de-centralized, giving each store manager discretion over hiring and promotion. The point here is that Wal-Mart claims they never systematically or deliberately kept women out of management; however, the company did not post job vacancies for many management positions. Employees who wanted to apply for a store manager position had to do so by getting the approval of their district manager (usually a male), and there was no objective criteria or oversight for salary decisions. Wal-Mart is appealing the case and it may go to the Supreme Court.

## The Morgan Stanley Case

On July 12, 2004, Morgan Stanley, one of the most prestigious investment banks on Wall Street, agreed to pay $54 million to settle a suit brought by 340 women who alleged sexual harassment and lack of access to promotions (Mulligan, 2001). This was the second-largest suit taken up by the Equal Employment Opportunity Commission in history. Approximately $12 million of the $54 million has to be paid to Allison Schieffelin, who alleged that she had been denied a promotion to managing director because of her sex. Ms. Schieffelin was a bond saleswoman who earned more than $1.3 million a year.

The women in the suit alleged that Morgan Stanley excluded them from social events, such as golf outings and Las Vegas trips, that could have helped them further their ties with clients. Schieffelin further claimed that her supervisors regularly organized trips to topless bars and strip clubs where they sometimes invited Shieffelin's clients, but excluded her.

In addition to the monetary settlement, Morgan Stanley has been ordered to offer diversity training to be conducted by an outside agency to help remedy the promotional opportunities of women. The company has agreed to spend $2 million on these training programs.

Some of the more notable cases that have to do with lack of job opportunity and promotion arise from women working on Wall Street. Many of these cases were settled out-of-court, without companies admitting any culpability. It is clear that these types of lawsuits cost companies millions of dollars, affect companies' reputations and the morale of employees, and take the time and effort of company executives. In addition, publicity of these cases may encourage other groups in the same company or industry to come forward if they feel discriminated against; once one case was successfully litigated against a large Wall Street Firm, others lawsuits followed.

## The Merrill Lynch Case

A class action suit was filed by 900 female Merrill Lynch brokers. The suit alleged that women brokers were systematically denied access to lucrative accounts from departing brokers, leads, referrals, and walk-in business. One broker from Anchorage, Alaska, said that she was dismissed after she complained of unfair treatment. Since male brokers were routinely given leads and referrals, and because brokers depend on commissions from client sales for their livelihood, the company was alleged to have discriminated against the women brokers.

## The American Express Financial Advisor Case

The American Express Financial Advisor case is very similar to the Merrill Lynch case. Seventeen female financial planners alleged that the company discriminated against them in terms of equal pay, advancement opportunities, the distribution of customer leads, and the assignment of customer accounts. The attorneys for the women cited violation of three federal laws: Title VII of the Civil Rights Act, the Equal Pay Act, and the Age Discrimination in Employment Act. American Express agreed to pay $31 million and also consented to institute practices that would help further the careers of female advisors; the company agreed to hire a diversity officer and increase the percentage of newly hired female financial advisors from 25% to 32%.

## The CostCo Case

CostCo, a large discount retailer like Sam's Club, has a similarly sex-segregated force to Wal-Mart. Women make up about half of CostCo's 78,000 employees in the US, yet only one in six managers is a woman (Legal News Watch, 2004). All of CostCo's operations vice presidents are male, and only two of 30 executive and senior officers are women (Goldman, 2004).

Shirley Ellis filed a sex-discrimination suit against CostCo in October 2002 with the Equal Employment Opportunity Commission and the California Department of Fair Employment and Housing. Ellis claimed that after she complained about Cost-Co's practices, she was transferred from a store in Aurora, Colorado, close to her home, to a store in Douglas County, Colorado. The job transfer required her to commute three to four hours a day. Since the Ellis case, a class action suit against CostCo has been filed on behalf of many women who claim that the company's policies and practices contribute to the lack of women in management. The company did not announce openings for managerial positions; instead, the women contended that promotions were made by top-level executives picking other men for advancement (Legal News Watch, 2004).

## The Marriott Hotel Case

In 1991, the Marriott Corporation agreed to pay $3 million to eligible claimants of a class action sex-discrimination case. The suit was started by two female restaurant managers who claimed that they were passed over for promotion in favor of male workers, and was extended to include eligible female managers, management trainees, and supervisors in Marriott's food and beverage divisions (Carlino, 1991). As part of the settlement, Marriott agreed to internally publish all management promotion opportunities and offer career-path alternatives for food and beverage positions. The company also agreed to develop written job profiles so that employees could better understand positions that are available in the organization and what these positions require in terms of experience and skill level.

## Minnesota State College and University System

Some suits have caused organizations (in this case, a university) to deliver back pay to employees because of the bias in promotions. St. Cloud State University in Minnesota was ordered to pay approximately $600,000 to 250 female faculty members who alleged that they earned lower initial salaries than similarly situated male faculty, received fewer and slower promotions, and worked in a sexually hostile environment (Borrego, 2001; Latto, 2001).

## International Court Cases

As in the United States, financial institutions in Britain have been hit with recent lawsuits. Women bankers, insurers, traders, and financial analysts earn an average of 43% less than their male colleagues, according to the Equal Opportunities Commission. Many women complain of unequal opportunity in terms of access to key clients or new business.

A former head of European private banking for Merrill Lynch, Stephanie Villalba, is suing the company for £7 million for alleged victimization, sex discrimination, and unequal pay. During a cross-examination, she said the bank was "institutionally sexist" and she further claimed that she had been bullied and undermined after being promoted. Villalba says she earned substantially less than her male counterparts at the firm and was belittled by her sexist boss who told her to serve drinks and sit in the "stewardess seat" on a business flight. Merrill Lynch executives claim that she was underperforming in her job and repeatedly needed guidance from her boss.

Two other cases demonstrate lack of opportunity for women. Arianna McGregor-Mezzotero won her case against BNP Paribas in June 2004. After she returned from maternity leave, McGregor-Mezzotero's bonuses were cut and she had her job responsibilities reduced. Julie Bowers won $2.5 million in 2002 against Schroder Securities, a London firm owned by Citigroup, for blocking her advancement. Her boss had described her in an e-mail as "had cancer, been a pain, and is now pregnant" (*Business Week*, September 6, 2004, p. 65).

# 5 Equal Pay

**Learning Objectives**

After completing this chapter, the reader will:

- understand the reasons why women still lag behind men in terms of pay.
- understand the differences in the gender gap in pay in various countries.
- understand the differences among equal pay legislation, comparable worth legislation, and pay for performance compensation.
- understand the relationship between equal pay and negotiation skills.

## Introduction: the Pay Gap

A report by the American Association of University Women (AAUW) showed that, just one year out of college, women working full-time earn 80% of what their male colleagues earn, when they work in the same field (American Association of University Women, 2007). Ten years after graduation, the pay gap widens: by that point, women are earning 69% of what their male colleagues earn. Even after controlling for hours, occupation, parenthood, and other factors known to affect earnings, one-quarter of the pay gap remains unexplained. In addition, the AAUW report showed that college-educated men have more authority in the workplace than do their female counterparts and are more apt to be involved in setting employee pay.

Over the course of her life, a young woman graduating from high school will make $700,000 less than a young man graduating from high school. A young woman graduating from college will earn on average $1.2 million less compared to a man with the same college degree. The difference increases as women and men gain further credentials; over the course of her life, a woman with an MBA, law degree, or medical degree can expect to earn $2 million less than a man receiving the same degree at the same time (Women's Policy Inc., 2007). In fact, on average, in the US, women with master's degrees still make less than men with bachelor's degrees (US Census Bureau, 2005).

Although over time women have made progress in reducing salary differences, these statistics show that they still lag behind men (see Figure 5.1). This is true at every level of the wage hierarchy, and within races. For example, in the US, Asian women earn 81% of what Asian men make; white women earn 80% of what white males earn; African American women earn 89% of what African American males make; and Hispanic women earn 88% of what Hispanic males earn (US Bureau of Labor Statistics, 2007). The wage gap in the US increases as women grow older, as

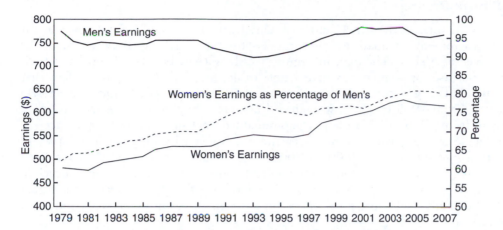

*Figure 5.1* Median Usual Weekly Earnings of Full-Time-Wage and Salary Workers in Constant (2007) Dollars by Sex, 1979–2007 Annual Averages (source: US Bureau of Labor Statistics. (2007). *Highlights of Women's Earnings in 2006*. US Department of Labor, September, p. 4).

they earn more degrees, and as they gain more experience. Between the ages of 16 and 24, women earn 95% of what men earn; between 25 and 34, women earn 88% of what men earn; but between the ages of 45 and 64, women earn 73% of what men earn. In all of these comparisons, full-time working men of the same age group were measured against full-time working women of the same age group (US Bureau of Labor Statistics, 2007).

Women earn less than men in many areas, from service-related jobs to management and professional occupations. The gap becomes greater in professions that pay more and in professions or jobs that are stereotyped as "male," such as higher-level management roles and production, transportation, and materials-moving jobs. The gap between women and men is lowest in traditionally female occupations such as administrative support – secretaries, typists, receptionists. Technological change sometimes results in men entering traditionally female occupations as their traditional male occupations become obsolete. Men entering such traditionally female job classifications often have to accept the prevailing wage, which is determined for a largely female population. If they did demand more, they simply wouldn't be hired, because women are available for these jobs at the prevailing, lower wage rate.

*Table 5.1* Median Weekly Earnings by Occupation

| Occupation | Women ($) | Men ($) | Pay Gap ($) |
|---|---|---|---|
| Services | 390 | 484 | 94 |
| Production, transportation, materials moving | 426 | 601 | 175 |
| Natural resources, construction, maintenance | 518 | 660 | 142 |
| Administrative support | 557 | 619 | 62 |
| Sales and related occupations | 467 | 761 | 294 |
| Management, profession and related | 840 | 1,154 | 314 |

Source: US Bureau of Labor Statistics, *Highlights of Women's Earnings*, September 2007, extracted from pages 11–14.

## The Rate of Progress

In the US, in spite of the EEOC and the many bills in state and federal government that try to remedy inequalities, the progress toward equal pay between men and women has been slow. The data in Figure 5.2 show that, between 1960 and 1965, the pay increase for women was barely noticeable, most likely due to the fact that the Equal Pay Legislation was launched in 1964 and the EEOC founded shortly thereafter. From 1965 to 1970, women did not make any progress relative to men, and again from 1970 to 1975 the pay gap remained unchanged. In 20 years since the Equal Pay Act was passed, women's earnings advanced by only 4.6% relative to men's earnings. Even from 2000 to 2005, when much progress might have been expected due to media attention to inequalities and women's advances in education, there was only modest improvement: a 3.7% gain over five years. Clearly, the Equal Pay Act has only had a marginal effect on the gap in earnings between men and women.

A report in 2002 by the US General Accounting Office (GAO) noted that women's pay relative to men's in certain industries had declined from 1995 to 2000, and in other industries had increased (Dingell & Maloney, 2002). In seven out of 10 industries, the pay gap had widened between male and female managers. For example, in the entertainment and recreation services industries women earned 83% of male managers' pay in 1995 and 62% in 2000. In communications, female managers' pay fell compared to males' pay from 86% to 73%; in the finance, insurance, and real-estate sectors, female managers' pay fell from 76% to 68%; and in professional medical services, women's pay went from 90% to 88%. One reason for the pay decline in these areas could be due to the use of automation in these job categories and a general trend toward de-skilling in these industries. The GAO also found that in only one of the industries, medical services, women accounted for a greater number of managers than men. This is the only industry studied where management and administrative jobs are lower status than professional, non-managerial jobs. Furthermore, in only five out of the 10 industries did women hold a share of management jobs in proportion to their share in the industry. In public administration, hospital services, and educational services, pay rates for women relative to men went up slightly between 1995 and 2000.

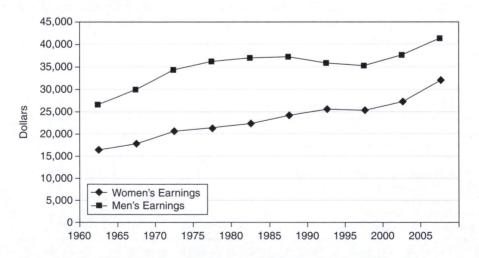

*Figure 5.2* The Wage Gap Over Time (source: US Census Bureau, 2006).

## The Global Case for Equal Pay

As in the US, a pay gap between men and women exists in all of the European Union countries. Although in the United Kingdom women have a large percentage of managerial jobs compared with other EU countries, there is still a pay gap of 21.1% between men and women. Austria and the Netherlands have an even greater earnings gap between men and women; Austria's pay gap is 25.5% and in the Netherlands it is 23.6%. The Scandinavian countries do marginally better than Central European countries: Denmark's equal pay gap is 17.7%, Sweden's is 17.9%, and Finland's is 20% (Eurostat, 2009). In a comparative study of 40 countries, more politically left-leaning governments, such as those in Scandinavian countries, reduced the pay gap more than politically right-leaning governments (Polachek & Xiang, 2006). Such governments are predisposed to enact legislation about equal pay because they are more committed to equalitarian outcomes, while right-leaning governments generally do not favor government intervention in matters of pay.

In Eastern and Central Europe, women's wages are at least 20% lower than men's rates of pay. In economies that have moved from central planning to market capitalism, such as Russia and the Czech Republic, the wage gap has widened since 1989. During the period of state central planning and communist rule, the pay gap between men's and women's wages was lower than it is today. Prior to 1989, trade unions were very strong in the former Czechoslovakia, while today, fewer than 21% belong to unions (International Trade Union Confederation, 2008). This lack of union activity is most likely one reason for the increase in the pay gap, which in 2007 was 23.6% (Eurostat, 2009). The pay gap in formerly communist countries is particularly disconcerting since, according to the traditional free-market view, market forces will be the best mechanism for creating a fair labor market. The widening of the wage gap in countries with transition economies is of special concern against the backdrop of the steep decline in real wages, which makes women who are often trying to support families vulnerable to the risk of poverty (Stepson, 2000). Moreover, in the Czech Republic and Lithuania, the wage gap is largest for the most well-educated women; in Lithuania, female social workers earn 50% of what their male counterparts earn. The overall wage gap in European economies tends to be greater in the private sector than in the public sector, and women in transition economies have been affected more by manufacturing plant closings and economic recessions (Stepson, 2000).

The pay gap statistics represented in Figure 5.3 do not take into account job classification – the statistics are undoubtedly influenced by both lower, middle, and high level job classifications, and the variation in pay for women and men in different industries.

Many managerial jobs in EU countries include such fringe benefits as a company car, cell telephones, retirement benefits, and expense accounts. When women are segregated into lower-level jobs, they miss out on both additional salary and these types of fringe benefits or "perks." Data on pay differences among managers in the EU countries indicates that earnings gaps are the widest the more senior the position. Furthermore, the gender pay gap increases with age, education, and years of service. In the 50–59 age group, the gap is more than 30% compared with 7% in the under-30 age group. Those women with higher education earn 30% less than men, whereas those with lower-level secondary education earn 13% less than men. The wage gap increases as one gains more experience; it is as high as 32% for women workers with more than 30 years of experience (Eurostat, 2009).

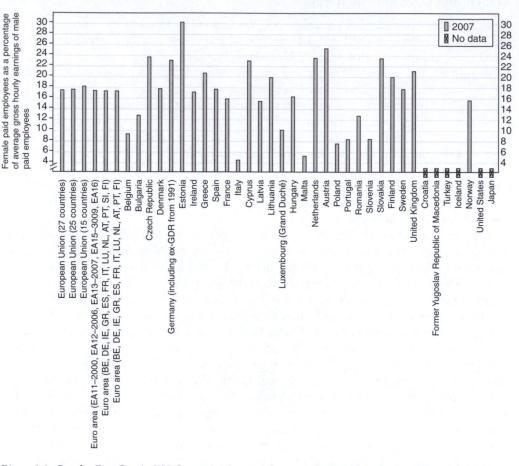

*Figure 5.3* Gender Pay Gap in EU Countries (source: Eurostat, http://epp.eurostat.ec.europa.eu/tgm).

Note

The unadjusted Gender Pay Gap (GPG) represents the difference between average gross hourly earnings of male paid employees and of female paid employees as a percentage of average gross hourly earnings of male paid employees. The population consists of all paid employees in enterprises with 10 or more employees.

## Differences in Labor Statistics across Countries

The differences in labor statistics in European countries can be influenced by any number of factors. Each European country has different rules for how wage statistics are monitored; for example, in Finland any company with 30 or more employees must evaluate pay equity in a yearly workplace equality plan, while in Germany wage statistics are required if the company has five or more employees. In France, gender equity statistics must be reported to work councils or shop stewards in companies that have 50 or more employees. Companies are required to have annual negotiations on gender equity. In Denmark, companies must compile wage statistics for 10 or more employees. In Switzerland, if the pay gap between men and women is higher than 5% in any organization or company, the institution is required to conduct further analysis and take corrective action if needed (Harriman & Holm, 2007). In general, the monitoring and reporting activity has positively influenced gender equity; those countries with stricter reporting and monitoring regulations have smaller pay gaps between men and women.

In addition to monitoring activity, signing on to international conventions in favor of equal pay measures makes a difference. The International Labor Organization (ILO) held a session on gender equality in which over 100 government members voted to endorse the concept of equal remuneration between men and women for work of equal value (2009). Weichselbaumer and Winter-Ebmer compared 67 countries and found that those nations that had ratified such international conventions supporting equal pay had a significant positive effect on narrowing the pay gap in their countries (2002).

The ILO, as well as researchers, cites several reasons for the differences in wage rates among European countries. When a pay gap is small, it is often achieved by only a small number of well-educated women at the top of the labor market. In other cases, progress has been made in low-level occupations such as clerical work, where the gap may be only 3–8%. However, the gap remains highest for female professionals. The gender gap in earnings may be larger in European countries where there is more overall inequality (Blau & Kahn, 2000, 2007). For example, in the United Kingdom the dispersion in the data gives more room for gender inequalities, whereas in Portugal, for example, female employment is probably lower overall and fewer women are pulling down the distribution. The salary distribution is most likely more compressed in Portugal and therefore there is less of a gap in earnings between men and women. Blau and Kahn found that those countries with more compressed male wage structures (a narrower distribution of male earnings) were associated with lower pay gaps. Finally, collective bargaining by unions has been shown to have an overall positive impact by reducing the gender pay gap.

As in Europe, women in Asian countries experience a pay gap. A survey by the Ministry of Health, Labour and Welfare in Japan uncovered several apparent inequalities between men and women. Women graduates earned anywhere from 20% to 40% of men's pay when they earned the same university degrees as the men. In Japan, many women, in spite of advanced qualifications, are in support roles, while men are employed in career track positions. The same situation has occurred in South Korea; in 2000, women with university degrees earned 74% of men's earnings with the same qualifications.

The ILO contends that the reasons for pay disparity among men and women worldwide are complex, and that these disparities are obfuscated by the different methods of reporting wages and jobs. To understand and begin to rectify these reporting difficulties, more information is needed about the distribution of women by their level of earnings, the hours they work, their educational level and qualifications, their access to overtime pay and bonuses, their occupational group, and whether or not they work part-time.

## Explanations for Wage Disparities between Men and Women

### *Lack of Human Capital*

There are several theories about why women are paid less than men. Human capital theory (discussed at length in Chapter 2) suggests that women may be paid less than men because they haven't attained the level of education and experience that men have acquired. Thus, they have built up less human capital than men and are consequently less productive. Therefore they receive a smaller total return since their initial investment is lower. In developed nations, this theory is seriously undermined by the rate at which women are gaining educational qualifications at both the undergraduate and graduate levels, and the fact that the wage gap increases as women gain educational credentials. However, it is possible that some women have less experience than men because they have interrupted their careers for several years when taking care of young children.

Many women decide to take time out from full-time work to devote time to their families, especially if they have young children or if they have elderly parents. In a study of women architects, over half of the participants said that they chose alternative forms of working, including time taken out with children, time for sporting activities, and part-time work (Caven, 2006). The pay gap of lawyers can also be influenced by hours worked; a study of women and men lawyers showed that women worked and billed fewer hours to clients than men. In some cases, the difference in wages can be explained by career breaks that women take and men don't take. Over the decades, women have taken time away from work to raise children, although the percentage of women taking time out is decreasing; in statistics from the US Current Population Survey, Blau and Kahn report that each child under one year of age lowered women's labor supply by 41% in 1980, 29% in 1990, and by 26% in 2000.

When women take time out from a full-time career and then try to reenter the workforce, they pay a stiff price. Women lose an average of 18% of their earning power when they take a break from work. When they spend less than one year away from their jobs, they experience an 11% cut in their salary upon their return to work. If they spend three or more years away from work, they find a 37% reduction in their pay when they return to work (Hewlett & Luce, 2005).

The question remains as to whether this reduction in earnings is really a fair reflection of what women are worth. If women intend to return to work with the same employer after they take time off, they would be wise to negotiate the terms of their reentry before they leave so that they are not penalized upon their return. Staying active in their field while on leave is important for women because it will help demonstrate to their employers that their skills have not degraded in their absence.

## Personal Preference

Another theory suggests that women choose lower-paid occupations and remain in them because of personal preference for these occupations. Occupations such as nursing, teaching, and childcare are low paid compared to other occupations and tend to be occupied disproportionately by women. According to a wage study undertaken for US Senator Tom Harkin, about half of working women work in an occupation that is 70% female while half of working men work in jobs that are 29% female. The higher proportion of "female" jobs are in fact paid less than the "male" jobs. A related explanation for the wage disparity between men and women suggests that women choose positions in industries that are, as a whole, low-paid ones. For example, many women work in retail or healthcare, lower-paid industries rather than the male-dominated oil production or hi-tech, higher-paid industries.

Some believe that women's average rates of pay fall behind men's because of women's role in the family. On average, married men make more than unmarried men make; by contrast, married women make less than single women make. It appears that just being married, especially with children, is an income liability for women. This may be because women fall behind in pay if they decide to take time off to raise children, or perhaps because they choose less-challenging work in order to balance their family obligations with work ones.

## Social Role Theory

This theory suggests that men and women adhere to gender roles that they have acquired early in childhood. These roles are shaped by societal expectations of both men and women that direct them to behave according to a particular gender role (Eagly, Wood, & Diekman, 2000). Thus men behave assertively and women more passively; men are the key breadwinners and women with young children are more apt to stay at home. These societal expectations may have an effect on pay in the workplace in several ways. First, employers may offer men more money because they see them as the key breadwinners. Second, men will act more assertively and they will likely negotiate for more pay. Employers will expect men to negotiate and act assertively as this is a natural aspect of their gender role. Finally, although to their disadvantage, women will naturally fall into their gender role, and not act as assertively as men do. Social pressure and the enduring nature of gender roles over time will make it difficult for women to act outside of their gender role (Vogel, Wester, Heesacker, & Madon, 2003).

Rather than freely choosing an occupation, women are socialized at a young age to prefer "female occupations" that do not pay well rather than male ones that offer more opportunity and remuneration. Guidance counselors and school teachers may even channel women into "female"-oriented careers. A study by Cassirer and Reskin found that men attach greater importance to promotion than women mainly because of where they are situated in the organizational hierarchy; men are more likely than women to be in jobs that encourage workers to expect and hope for promotion (2000).

## Entitlement Theory

Some evidence suggests that the pay gap between men and women is the result of women having lower expectations about the value of their work, thus they make fewer demands for higher pay. Having these lower expectations is part of what women have learned as their appropriate gender role. Several studies have found that women may differ from men in their sense of entitlement – what they believe they deserve to make for equivalent work. In a study by Martin (1989), male and female business college seniors were given the same information about what previous graduates had earned in recent years. The sex of the graduates was not given. The current male and female students were then asked what they expected to earn at their first job after graduation. On average, the amount the female students said that they expected to earn was about $2,000 less than what their male counterparts expected to earn. An experimental study suggests that women feel they have to do more work than men to warrant the same remuneration (Major, McFarlin, & Gagnon, 1984). At the outset of this experiment, women subjects were told that they would earn the same amount as men for a task set by the examiners. Yet during the experiment they worked longer and accomplished the task more accurately than the males.

Fischlmayr (2002) found that the underrepresentation of female international managers compared to male international managers was due, in part, to women's own behavior. When women were asked to consider international assignments, they behaved according to stereotype, and often deferred to their husband's career. If their husband did not want to relocate, the women decided not to accept an international assignment. In addition, women underestimated the value of their own work roles; many believed that they were not ready to accept an international assignment, citing their need for more experience. In a recent study, female managers were three times more likely than men to underrate their boss's opinion of their performance (Taylor,

2009). The effect of underrating one's performance is greater the older the woman; women ages 49–65 underrated their performance more than younger cohorts of women. Taylor proposes several reasons for this underrating phenomenon. First, women do not receive as much reciprocity from their organizations as males do. For example, they are less likely to have received attention from their organization in the way of additional training. Second, they are less likely to have received feedback about their performance, so may assume that their bosses undervalue it. Third, older women may have actually experienced some discrimination or known other women who have experienced unfair treatment. These older women have spent more time working in workplaces in which discrimination was more likely. Their early careers would have been during the beginnings of the feminists movement when few women were in management roles. All of these factors could influence how women think their bosses view their performance.

The effects of women's underestimation of their value can have far reaching consequences. Both male and female employers may expect women to accept a lower wage than men and, therefore, offer a lower wage. In experimental research, subjects charged with distributing money to men and women offered more to men because they believed that women would be willing to accept less (Solnick, 2001; Solnick & Schweitzer, 1999). When asked about women's pay, 48% of managers, 28% of compensation specialists, and 45% of union officials indicated that women's willingness to work for less than men was either a "very" or "extremely" important cause of the gender pay gap (Rynes, Rosen, & Mahoney, 1985). Women who feel that their bosses undervalue their performance will likely be reluctant to ask for more money or more responsibility.

In addition to gender socialization and entitlement theories, there are other explanations for the phenomenon of women undervaluing their work. First, rather than comparing themselves to men, women may compare themselves to other women who also make less money than men, and men may compare themselves to other males (McFarlin et al., 1989; Major & Forcey, 1985). Second, men may make different (and higher) evaluations about what they think their individual contribution is worth. In several studies, women have reported lower aspirations for pay than men. These lower expectations for pay certainly influence negotiation outcomes (Barron, 2003; Zetick & Stuhlmacher, 2002). If women are not given direct feedback about their work, they may be less confident about its value and therefore unwilling to value it highly. When compared with men, women are less sure of their worth and less apt to feel that they are entitled to more than others. They believe that they need to prove themselves on the job more than men do before they deserve a greater salary than others (Barron, 2003). When women are given external feedback about their work, they tend to place a higher value on it.

Clearly, women's own self-perceptions, often shaped by societal expectations, may hinder their career prospects, and ultimately the amount of money they make. (The effects of socialization on men and women are discussed in detail in Chapter 2.)

### Negotiation Skills

The evidence from several studies points to women professionals and managers negotiating lower salaries than their male counterparts (Bowles & McGinn, 2005; Dreher & Cox, 2000; Gerhart, 1990).

Some of this pay gap is due to women's tendency to avoid salary negotiation altogether because they find it distasteful. (Of course, the reason for their attitude toward negotiation is likely influenced by their gender role.) Women are socialized to find negotiation distasteful and they have not grown up practicing it. They may have been brought up to believe that negotiating is too aggressive for women, and even potentially damaging to their careers, if they push too hard or make too many demands. On a more subtle level without specific reference to careers, in general women are encouraged by parents, friends, and the media to be agreeable rather than combative. Some scholars suggest that women effectively advocate for others without incurring costs to their careers, but gender-linked stereotypes and norms prevent them from successfully advocating for themselves. Women have learned that the costs of self-advocacy are too high (Wade, 2003).

Babcock and Laschever conducted several studies about women's attitudes toward negotiation, the likelihood of their negotiating, and the effects that poor negotiation have on their overall incomes (2003). They found that women straight out of college do not negotiate the salary for their first job. Because salary differences become compounded over time, by not negotiating their first salaries they sacrifice over half-a-million dollars over their lifetime. Women have salary expectations between 3% and 32% lower than men for the same jobs. Furthermore, women are less likely to ask for prestigious job assignments or volunteer for opportunities that will give them more visibility. In a sample of 21 studies on negotiation outcomes, men negotiated better monetary outcomes than women. Although the effect was small in this meta-analysis, over time women would stand to lose significant earnings because annual salary raises are determined as a percentage of one's current salary (Stuhlmacher & Walters, 1999).

The willingness to negotiate for salary is linked to one's beliefs and attitudes. In the Babcock and Laschever studies, when women were asked to describe what negotiation was like, they responded with "going to the dentist," whereas men described negotiation as "winning a contest." The authors contend that women don't negotiate hard because they want to be "nice," have been brought up to be less aggressive than boys, and simply fear conflict.

### Sex Discrimination

Sex discrimination provides a further explanation for unequal pay. Once women find their way into corporations, they may encounter glass ceilings, or barriers because of their sex (rather than because of other factors). Opportunities for financial rewards may be limited if those in power discriminate against women employees.

No doubt, the causes of women's unequal pay compared to men's are complex and multi-causal. For instance, a woman's salary may be due in part to her personal preferences which are linked to societal expectations of her, or her manager may treat her differently than equally qualified males.

Rectifying unequal pay situations requires that individuals have correct information about pay rates and job responsibilities so that they can make comparisons among jobs. The next section deals with the difficulty of uncovering such information about rates of pay.

## The Problem of Transparency

How can female employees know whether they are underpaid compared to others if organizations keep pay rates secret? This secrecy is especially prevalent in private, non-governmental enterprises. Some corporations forbid employees to discuss their pay and many do not publish the pay ranges for job categories. Even if pay ranges are publicized, rarely do employees know what individual job-holders make. This lack of transparency makes it difficult for women to find out whether or not they are underpaid.

Bowles and McGinn (2005) compared salaries of male and female job candidates in industries that were low-ambiguity industries versus high-ambiguity industries. The researchers termed industries as having "low ambiguity" when the candidates were well informed about how much to ask for in salary negotiations and "high ambiguity" when candidates had little if any information about salaries. In the low-ambiguity industries, there were no significant differences between the salaries accepted by men and women, but in industries with high ambiguity, women accepted salaries that were on average 10% lower than men's salaries.

Women clearly do better in situations where they have access to information. Without knowing the entire landscape of jobs and pay rates, women will find it difficult to know with whom to compare themselves. Many compensation situations allow for degrees of flexibility by managers, where the rules about who gets what are not well known. Consider how employees receive annual bonuses: managers have latitude in giving annual bonuses to employees and often these payments, which are in addition to basic salary, are secret. Unless employees share information with one another, or the company publishes salary information, it will be difficult for employees to know whether or not their share is fair.

The usual solution to this "lack of transparency problem" is collective action: women may bind together to uncover pay rates, conduct the statistical analysis necessary to compare women's pay rates and job tasks to men's pay rates and job tasks, and put pressure on employers to change pay rates when they are unfair. The US Department of Labor reports that unionized women earn 31% more than non-unionized women workers, female African American union members make 32% more than non-unionized African American women, and female Hispanic union members make 47% more than Hispanic women who are not members of a union (AFSCME, 2007). Unions can often secure fairer job conditions and pay equity for women at the bottom of the wage hierarchy. In Canada, the increase of union participation by women in the 1980s had a significant, positive effect on the wage gap. Doiron and Riddell (1994) found that union participation increased female earnings more than male earnings. Moreover, union participation prevented a further 7% gap in earnings between men and women. In other words, the gap between men and women in non-union jobs was 7% higher than the gap between men and women in union jobs.

In spite of the fact that unions generally improve wages, managers – whether men or women – rarely see themselves as part of union movements.

## Equal Pay for Equal Work

In the US, the Equal Pay Act requires that pay be equal for equivalent work in the same establishment. In its first nine years of enforcement, the US Equal Pay Act did not cover professional, white-collar jobs. As a result there was no incentive to undertake job evaluation, for the purposes of pay equity, for managerial positions. In 1972, Congress enacted the Educational Amendment, which changed the Fair Labor Standards Act to expand the Equal Pay Act to cover these professional workers.

In considering equal-pay cases, it is up to courts to determine whether two jobs are similar enough for comparison by evaluating the skill, effort, and responsibility that the two job-holders possess. By law, the jobs under consideration have to be identical or very similar. This creates a problem for those pursuing an equal-pay claim, especially if their jobs are highly specialized, as they may be the only one in their organization performing the job. At the labor entry point, jobs are very similar – a factory worker or a call-center employee has many colleagues performing the same set of tasks.

But the more education and training employees have, the more likely it is that their jobs will be different from all other jobs in the organization, and therefore not covered by the Equal Pay Act. For instance, two managers, by virtue of the fact that they manage different parts of the firm, are conducting dissimilar jobs; a manager of an accounting department performs different tasks to a manager of a human resources department.

In spite of the intent of equal-pay laws to provide fair remuneration, there is usually enough room for interpretation so that employers can advance arguments against the equality of the work and so rebut demands for equal pay. For example, if extra duties are assigned to one job-holder over another, then that individual can be paid more. If male employees have more seniority and more experience, then that may provide a basis for higher pay than newer female employees in the absence of any difference in the value of their work.

Moreover, if men and women do not do the same or even similar jobs, it may be impossible to apply the Equal Pay Act even when they make the same economic contribution to output.

## Performance-Related Pay

In an effort to deal more fairly with employees, to motivate employees to be more productive, and to recognize individual achievement, performance-related pay was instituted in major corporations beginning in the 1980s. Before then, it was not uncommon to pay employees based on seniority; career advancement was predictable and raises were given annually to employees at the same percentage level. Still the preferred method of determining raises in many corporations, performance-related pay allows managers latitude in deciding the percentage raise to assign each of their direct reports. Managers give those who perform well the highest raises, and those who don't perform well receive lower raises, or no raise at all. Corporations use performance-related pay to attract and retain the best and brightest employees, because high-achievers are attracted to firms where their individual effort is recognized and rewarded. When objectively implemented, the principle of pay for performance serves both organizations and employees well. Jobs in which performance is based on an objective measure, such sales performance, or those with measurable financial targets, such as many jobs in the financial sector, are better suited to pay for performance systems than jobs with more ambiguous, or difficult to measure goals.

Problems arise when pay for performance is subject to interpretation and therefore potential bias. Rubery (1995) contends that the trend toward performance-related pay systems poses a potential threat to the achievement of gender pay equality because, as discretion in pay determination increases, there is no clear relationship between earnings and job grade or classification. Performance-related pay provides fewer opportunities to monitor pay trends and may mask inequalities in the workplace (Elvira & Graham, 2002; Reskin, 2000). Individualized pay becomes a private matter between employee and employer, which reduces the transparency of the labor market. If women are unjustly underpaid, this lack of transparency makes collective responses by women to correct pay inequities unlikely.

Organizations often separate the performance-evaluation discussion from the assignment of pay raises. Many make this separation because they wish to facilitate feedback about performance and employee development, without the more difficult subject of pay raises. However, when performance evaluation and decisions of pay are conducted as two separate processes, and when there is a lack of accountability for these processes, the likelihood of gender bias increases. Castilla (2008) conducted a study in which he analyzed personnel data from a large service organization. He found that different salary increases were given for observationally equivalent male and female employees with the identical performance rating. The subjects in Castilla's study were in the same job in the same business unit, with the same supervisor, and with the same level of education and experience. Castilla reports that this pay discrimination occurs in one of two ways: either the supervisor assigns a rating and recommends a pay raise that is later changed by the human resources (HR) department, or the supervisor recommends a raise to the HR department that is lower than what was warranted by the performance evaluation. The reward bias, therefore, can be introduced either by the manager or by the HR department. However, interviews with HR managers suggested that the bias is most often introduced by the manager who is recommending the amount of pay increase (not the HR department). The HR department did not have the time to carefully review the thousands of salary proposals that they received from managers, so they simply approved the managers' recommendations. As reported by this study, in organizations with performance-related pay systems, those responsible for pay decisions may not be accountable for their actions, nor is the compensation system transparent to all employees.

## Comparable Worth – Equal Pay for Equal Worth

*Comparable worth* is part of an attempt to deal with the problem raised for pay equity by the fact that men and women rarely do identical jobs – especially at higher levels. Comparable worth or pay equity (as it is referred to in Canada) is the practice of assigning equal pay to jobs that involve the same level of skill and responsibility, and are deemed to be of equal value, even though they are different jobs. For example, in a comparable worth case in the United Kingdom, a court ruled that a woman who was a Director of Human Resources (HR) for a retail clothing chain should be paid the same amount as a man who was a Director of the Buying Unit for the same company. The female HR director successfully proved that her job, although different from his, had equal value to the organization. In court, she argued that her job of hiring and selecting employees, instituting health and safety rules in all of the stores and offices, and conducting risk assessments was of equal value to the buyer's job of selecting clothing and other merchandise for the stores (Reeves, 2000).

Comparable worth is a controversial concept. For that reason, it is not a concept employed in US equal-pay legislation.

Proponents argue for its use as part of Title VII of the Civil Rights Act of 1964, which makes discrimination based on sex, race, color, or national origin illegal. In Canada, comparable-worth legislation has been adopted in six of the ten provinces. In these provinces, generally if 60% of a job category is held by women, comparable-worth principles must be applied to it to ensure that the job category is valued fairly compared to equivalent jobs held by men. In these comparable-worth situations, the criteria used to evaluate jobs are skill, responsibility, effort, and working conditions.

## Arguments Against Comparable Worth

Opponents of comparable worth argue that only the market can determine the value of jobs, and that if women occupy lower-paying jobs, this is simply a reflection of the labor market exerting forces of supply and demand, rather than the discrimination of employers. In a competitive economy, an economically efficient market sets the wage rate equal to the employee's "marginal productivity" (the amount of revenue added by the employee), and individual employers and employees cannot influence the wage rate. If women are paid less than men for comparable jobs, then this is a matter of oversupply of potential workers in certain job categories, which drives their pay downward. Moreover, opponents of comparable worth suggest that when discrimination does exist, the inefficiencies it produces will be eliminated in the long run. The market will penalize discriminators because they will miss the opportunity to attract many good employees, pay too much to less-efficient ones, and be penalized by customers who prefer lower prices and perhaps even goods made by non-discriminating firms. This free market view holds that in the long run all wage differences reflect real differences in productivity, and that unfair or inequitable wage differences will be eliminated by market forces' persistent drive for efficiency. This argument justifies large CEO salaries and attendant benefits as fair because the market mechanism determines the correct amount of money – the efficiency-wage – that will attract the best, most-qualified individuals to managerial jobs. Since good managers are extremely scarce, the argument holds, companies must pay large salaries to attract and retain them. During the financial crisis of 2009, this was the argument used to justify bonuses for AIG managers and others.

Opponents of comparable worth further argue that women are free to choose occupations and jobs that have a higher market value. Finally, they argue that the concept of comparable worth is too complicated and too vague to be implemented practically. Even when feasible, the investment in scrutinizing jobs and overhauling current pay systems is too high. Such efforts take time, money, and people resources.

This view about the efficiency of wages dominated the 1990s and 2000s, and led to a decline in comparable worth initiatives in the US. Federal and state courts have routinely struck down comparable worth cases. "[Former Chief Justice] Rehnquist voiced the worry that if courts entertained claims of between-job wage discrimination, it would lead courts into the analytical quagmire of trying to determine what male and female workers in various jobs should be paid" (Nelson & Bridges, 1999, p. 46). The courts are more likely to intervene in clear-cut equal pay cases between two people in the same job. Because of the difficulty of winning a comparable-worth case, the number of such cases brought before the courts has been small compared to equal-pay cases. It has been difficult to prove intentional discrimination on the part of employers in the face of what defendants argue are free-market forces. For these reasons, comparable-worth cases virtually disappeared after the 1990s.

## Arguments For Comparable Worth

Supporters of comparable worth argue that labor markets are frequently inefficient. These inefficiencies make wage rates a poor indicator of one's productive worth. To begin with, some labor markets involve a small number of buyers – the employers – and a large number of sellers – job-seekers. Therefore, the employers can often set the price of labor, rather than it being set by an equilibrium between job-seekers and employers. Employers exercise their market power to set prices and wage rates, and to select employees without real competition with one another. Within a single organization, managers have a great deal of leeway and discretion in setting the pay of their employees. For example, before Sears had a centralized compensation system, salaries for headquarters' positions were determined by group merchandise managers, while salaries for retail positions were decided by store managers. Managers had little if any information about company-wide pay practices and were given great latitude in the determining pay of their workers (Nelson & Bridges, 1999).

Failure of the market to produce efficiency in allocating resources, including labor, has always been accepted as a reason for governmental regulation of the market. Advocates of comparable worth hold that the inefficiencies of the labor market provide an adequate basis for establishing laws promoting comparable worth.

In addition, those who are in favor of judging jobs based on comparable worth claim that, in general, women's jobs are undervalued by society when their roles are measured by wage rates.

Before the 1990s, comparable worth in the US was taken more seriously. In 1984, one study compared the approaches to comparable worth taken by compensation specialists in 360 small, medium, and large companies. When asked whether or not comparable worth was an issue of concern within their organizations, 54.4% answered that it was a concern to them (60% in the large organizations, 51.3% in medium, and 43.9% in small companies); however, these specialists reported that the concern of top management about the issue was significantly smaller: 18.3% (24.8% in large organizations, 15% in medium, and 4.9% in small companies) (Mahoney, Rynes, & Rosen, 1984). Those in top management who were attentive to the comparable-worth issue were concerned about it for two reasons: first, they wanted to ensure company compliance with equal-pay laws and, second, they wished to estimate the potential costs to the company of shifting their compensation policies to encompass comparable worth. When asked how the earnings gap should be addressed, compensation specialist indicated that the most effective way would be for women to prepare themselves for non-traditional, male-dominated occupations where the pay is higher.

---

### Box 5.1  Public-Sector Comparable-Worth Cases in the US

The relatively few comparable-worth suits that have been brought forward are most often initiated by public-sector employees, rather than private-sector ones, because in the public sector information about pay is in the public record. These cases often receive national attention; elected officials, sensitive to women voters, give them their full attention. In the private sector, however, it is more difficult for interested parties to get information on pay rates of men's and women's jobs.

In 1981 the Minnesota Commission on the Economic Status of Women created a pay-equity taskforce of legislators, labor, management, and the general public, whose work it was to estimate how much the predominately female jobs were undervalued based on a job evaluation by an outside consultant. In 1982, the Minnesota state legislature appropriated $22 million for initial pay-equity adjustments for about 8,000 employees (Office on the Economic Status of Women, 1982). Some of the adjustments were as high as $1,600 – in addition to the 8.5% general increase given to all employees. (Because of inflation, in 2009 dollars the amount would be approximately $3,750.) The legislature also changed the state personnel law to make pay equity a primary policy and to compel local governments to implement it. Minnesota addressed the inequities by reevaluating, ranking, and comparing jobs, and then paying its employees based on the job rather than on the sex of who does the job (Women's Policy Inc., 2007). In Minnesota, women's salaries are now much closer to what males earn; female public employees earn 97 cents for every dollar male public employees earn. In a similar case, the Tennessee state legislature passed a bill that increases the damages paid to affected employees for each repeated act of willful discrimination that an employer makes. An employer was required to pay damages of up to double the amount of unpaid wages due the employee for the second offense, and up to triple this amount for the third offense. This type of legislation acts as a real deterrent to repeat offenses.

By contrast, the State of Washington did not handle pay equity between its male and female workers similarly. In 1981, an affiliate of AFSME (the American Federation of State and Municipal Employees), one of the largest unions in the state, sued the state for failing to implement several job-evaluation studies that had been commissioned seven years earlier and that showed a 32% gap between average wages of traditionally male and female jobs. In this case, a federal district judge ruled that the state had knowingly and deliberately discriminated against women by underpaying jobs that were at least 70% held by women. He ordered that back pay be given from September 1979.

The first case to use comparable worth as a theory of pay discrimination under Title VII of the Civil Rights Act was *Christensen* v. *State of Iowa*. Female clerical workers at a branch of the University of Iowa brought the case against the state for paying them less than plant workers (men). The university argued that it raised the pay of male plant workers to rates higher than clerical workers to reflect market rates for physical plant jobs. In addition, it maintained that the two classes of jobs were different and that there were no barriers preventing women from applying for plant positions. The women plaintiffs argued that there was no shortage of potential physical plant employees in the university's employment area and, therefore, no need to raise the rate of pay for employees in these job categories. Further, they contended that the firm, Hay Consulting, that carried out the job evaluation and pay study, had judged the jobs to be of the same value. Many of the male and female jobs had been assigned identical pay grades. Therefore, the plaintiffs argued that the pay disparity between them was evidence of discrimination. The trial court concluded that the women seeking to establish sex discrimination under Title VII had to show equal work, and since the jobs were not shown to be equivalent, the women did not have a case against the state. The case was appealed but the women clerical workers did not prevail. This time the Seventh Circuit Court of Appeals held that job-evaluation studies alone do not prove sex discrimination, and that the market mechanism was a valid approach to setting pay. The appellate court found as follows:

> Appellants have failed to demonstrate the difference in wages paid to clerical and plant employees rested upon sex discrimination and not some other legitimate reason. The evidence shows the UNI [University of Iowa] paid higher wages to plant workers because wages for similar jobs in the local labor market were higher than the wages established under the Hayes System.... We find nothing in the text and the history of Title VII suggesting that Congress intended to abrogate the laws of supply and demand or other economic principles that determine wage rates for various kinds of work. We do not interpret Title VII as requiring an employer to ignore the market in setting wage rates for genuinely different work classifications.
> (*Christensen* v. *State of Iowa*, 563 F. 2d 353 at 355–56 Seventh Circuit, 1977)

The fact that the women were not barred from occupying the plant positions excused the state from any discrimination claims.

Nelson and Bridges (1999) noted several interesting features of this case. The branch of the university in question is located in Waterloo, Iowa – the dominant firms in the area were John Deere and Rath Packing Corporation. Thus, the community viewed itself as having an industrial base rather than an academic one. This perception may have contributed to how the jobs at the university were initially evaluated. When industrial concerns, such as John Deere and Rath, laid off employees, those employees sought jobs at the state university. When they were hired, these individuals began agitating for higher pay. By contrast, female clerical workers were less apt to make collective pay demands.

In addition to the favorable bias given to physical labor performed primarily by men in the community, the university appears to have engaged in institutional discrimination. Men in non-professional positions were paid much higher rates of pay than women. Men often occupied single-incumbent jobs (jobs in which one man held the only position in that job category) that paid on average $2,300 a year more than females in multiple-incumbent jobs. In short, the jobs stereotyped as female jobs, filled by women, were paid less than the jobs stereotyped as male and performed by men. Even after controlling for seniority, salary basis, and local market salary levels, women earned on average 17% less than their male counterparts. There is even some evidence that the university senior managers interfered with the market mechanism that they claimed to be operating to determine wage rates and which therefore absolved them of charges of discrimination. These managers had suggested to women clerical workers if they took "industrial jobs" at the John Deere plant, their prospects for later employment with the state would forever be closed. In addition, one vice president in the university system disclosed that Deere had entered into an agreement with the university not to hire away its clerical employees at higher wages.

Like the Iowa case, *The American Nurses Association* v. *The State of Illinois*, 1986, proved to be high-profile case. Nurses employed by the state of Illinois claimed that the state had intentionally discriminated against them by departing from market measures of salaries on the grounds of sex, and that the state of Illinois had violated Title VII of the Civil Rights Act by failing to pay comparable wages for comparable work. The nurses, who were almost entirely female, were paid less than men in jobs held primarily by men. For example, an electrician (a job held predominantly by males) was paid a monthly salary of $2,826 while a nurse was paid a monthly salary of $2,104. In their argument against the state, the nurses also noted that two different job classifications were given for essentially the same job: a prison clerk (a male job) was paid more than a clerk typist (a female job) although these two differently labeled jobs entailed the same tasks. The plaintiffs lost their case in both the US District Court and on appeal in the Seventh Circuit Court of Appeals. Richard Posner, the presiding judge and a well-known advocate of the use of economic analysis in the law, wrote the opinion for the court of appeals, rejecting the nurses' appeal. Posner's judicial opinion began with the assertion that wage differences between men and women were due largely to women having made less investment than men in developing their human capital, often because they are out of the labor market taking care of children. Therefore they earn less due to market forces, and not to discrimination.

Posner also held for the appeals court that the market mechanism is the most productively efficient way to determine wage rates. Moreover, he held that interfering with the labor market will do harm to women. His reasoning is worth quoting because of its influence in the decline of comparable-worth cases after the 1980s:

> On the cognitive question economists point out that the ratio of wages in different jobs is determined by the market rather than by any a priori conception of relative merit, in just the same way that the ratio of the price of caviar to the price of cabbage is determined by relative scarcity rather than relative importance to human welfare. Upsetting the market equilibrium by imposing such a conception would have costly consequences, some of which might undercut the ultimate goals of the comparable worth movement. If the movement should cause wages in traditionally men's jobs to be depressed below their market level and wages in traditionally women's jobs to be jacked above their market level, women will have less incentive to enter traditionally men's fields and more to enter traditionally women's fields. Analysis cannot stop there, because the change in relative wages will send men in the same direction: fewer men will enter the traditionally men's jobs, more the traditionally women's jobs. As a result there will be more room for women in traditionally men's jobs and at the same time fewer opportunities for women in traditionally women's jobs – especially since the number of those jobs will shrink as employers are induced by the higher wage to substitute capital for labor inputs (e.g., more word processors, fewer secretaries). Labor will be allocated less efficiently; men and women alike may be made worse off.
>
> (Posner, 1986)

Finally, Posner rejected the plaintiffs' claim that the State "willfully" failed to take action to correct discrimination highlighted in its own pay study. He held that merely undertaking the study and then refusing to act on its findings did not show that the state had *intentionally* discriminated against women.

Posner's arguments make some strong claims about the labor market. In general he assumes two things: first, most markets for employees are competitive ones in which there are large numbers of employers and large numbers of potential employees, none of whom has the power to set the prevailing wage rate – the price of labor. Second, all participants in the labor market – buyers (employers) and sellers (employees) – have complete information about jobs and job candidates.

If comparable worth is difficult to establish and unequal pay claims without merit unless jobs are the same, why not use Title VII of the Civil Rights Act to fight unequal pay claims for dissimilar jobs? The reason is simple. The law requires that in order to be illegal discrimination against a class of employees, a practice must be the result of the specific individual *motivation* of an employer to discriminate on grounds of sex. This makes it almost impossible to use Title VII to combat inequalities in pay and gives employers wide latitude to continue policies of unequal pay. An employer may always cite as reasons for such practices beliefs about human capital, or impact on production costs, or some other business reason in order to explain an individual hiring decision or wage-differential. Motivations are notoriously difficult to establish in law.

## Comparable-Worth Evaluations

Other countries have had more interest than the US in evaluating the comparable worth of different jobs. In Switzerland, a system called EVALFRI has classified health-care workers, primarily a female professional group, and paid them according to their value to the organization. Moreover, a recent International Labour Organization statement approved by over 100 governments supports comparable worth:

> Respect for this principle [equal pay for equal value] is essential, because of the sex segregation in the labour market. Efforts need to be taken so that the principle is understood and applied, as appropriate. Job evaluation on the basis of objective and non-discriminatory criteria are one way to implement equal pay for work of equal value.
> (2009 International Labour Conference, Provisional Record, 98th Session, ILO, Geneva)

In its efforts to implement equal pay for equal value, the ILO has worked with the Portugeuse food and beverage sector. In one establishment, women pastry chefs were making less money than the men who sold the pastries at the front of the shop. By assessing the value of these two jobs, the women's pay was readjusted so that it was higher than the male sales clerks' pay. In another case, women hospital workers recording patient information and instructions were paid less than male parking lot attendants in the same hospital. It was successfully argued that the value of the women's jobs was higher than the value of the men's jobs. An error on a patient chart could be far more serious than a mistake parking a car (Hodges, ILO Presentation, July 28, 2009).

## Fair Job Evaluation

Instead of comparing jobs two-by-two as comparable worth requires, job evaluation is the process of assessing the contribution of all the jobs in an organization for productive value. Job evaluation has been used in organizations to promote fairness in pay. A recent ILO publication provides a system for conducting gender-neutral job evaluations for the purposes of establishing pay rates (Chicha, 2008). Organizations should first set up a pay-equity committee comprised of equal numbers of men and women, including representation from female-dominated job categories. Second, evaluators should be sensitive to potential biases in the measurement of job qualifications, effort required in the job, degree of responsibility of the job holder, and prejudices around work conditions. For example, interpersonal skills are often dismissed as a requirement for jobs typically occupied by women, yet nurses need empathy, and secretaries need good verbal communication skills and command of written language. In terms of the physical demands of a job, men are often given credit for lifting heavy objects and for outdoor work (in construction, for example). Nurses are also required to lift patients, cashiers are required to stand for long periods, and seamstresses deal with taxing, repetitive work and noise. Women are often not given credit for the responsibilities they have; administrative assistants need to keep sensitive information confidential and primary school teachers are responsible for the safety of children. Traditionally, responsibility has been evaluated based on whether an individual manages other adults or manages materials or a budget – activities that men have done more than women.

## The Pay Check Fairness Act

Some members of the US Congress have deemed the Equal Pay Act inadequate to address pay inequities between men and women. They have initiated two bills that seek to implement comparable-worth analyses: the Pay Check Fairness Act, introduced by Senator Tom Daschle (D-SD) and Representative Rosa DeLauro (D-CT), and The Fair Pay Act, introduced by Senator Tom Harkin (D-IA). Both bills were designed to close loopholes in the Equal Pay Act that make it relatively easy for employers to circumvent the law, and both were offered as amendments to the Fair Labor Standards Act (of which the Equal Pay Act is a part). To date, neither bill has been passed. The Pay Check Fairness Act has several features that would strengthen equal-pay legislation.

Although the Equal Pay Act allows for back-pay awards, it does not allow a plaintiff to recover compensatory or punitive damages. Without this extra stick, employers may be more willing to fight a case and prolong it, given the fact that the risk of losing may not be very high. The Pay Check Fairness Act proposes to allow plaintiffs to recover compensatory and/or punitive damages.

The Equal Pay Act is also silent on the issue of improving information about pay. The Pay Check Fairness Act would require employers to provide the EEOC with information about pay by race, sex, and national origin of employees. Furthermore, the act would prevent employers punishing workers for sharing pay information with one another. It also directs the US Department of Labor to set up guidelines to help employers share information regarding pay rates for different jobs.

The current Equal Pay Act makes it difficult to proceed with a class action suit, where employees from a particular firm come together to sue an employer. The Equal Pay Act requires employees to "opt in" to a suit, placing the onus on employees to find out about a legal action and request to be part of it in writing. The Pay Check Fairness Act calls for the opposite; a class of employees would be part of the class unless they "opt out" of it in writing.

Under the Equal Pay Act an employer can assert that a male is paid more than a female in a comparable job because of "factors other than sex" (see Section 3, D1). A seniority system, merit pay, and the quantity and quality of production are three examples given as factors other than sex. As discussed earlier in this chapter, these factors can reflect previous conditions of injustice. The Pay Check Fairness Act attempts to eliminate these loopholes by allowing only non-sex-related factors such as education or relevant job experience.

Under the current law, a wage comparison can only be made between two employees in the same "establishment" (see Section 3, D1). However, employers of large organizations, with subsidiaries or divisions, may claim that the two jobs are not part of the same "establishment," therefore the Pay Check Fairness Act eliminates this rule. Finally, the Pay Check Fairness Act calls for more education and training of EEOC and US Department of Labor employees, and the establishment of an award to recognize employers who eliminate pay disparities.

### Further Reading and Suggested Websites

The National Committee on Pay Equity website: www.pay-equity.org/day.html.

For a history of pay inequity and the wage gap: www.infoplease.com/spot/equalpayact1.html.

Babcock, L. & Laschever, S. (2003). *Women don't ask: Negotiation and the gender divide*. Princeton, NJ: Princeton University Press.

Blau, F.D. & Kahn, L.M. (2000). Gender differences in pay. *The Journal of Economic Perspectives*, *14*(4), 75–99.

# CASE STUDIES

---

### Case Study 1: Equal Pay Discrimination or Lack of Negotiation Skills?

The publishing business was undergoing enormous changes and Carolyn Johnson knew that she had to swim with the prevailing tide or drown. Many days it was hard to keep her head above water, but the President of the Corbett Group, a publisher of trade books of all varieties, had made it very clear to all employees that they would have to be flexible and hard-working to survive against the other media, which seemed to be bombarding their customers from all directions. With the advent of the Internet and global competition, Corbett was being forced to go to print with shorter lead times and with new titles.

   Calvin Kuehn was the president of the Corbett Group. The company was privately owned and he had inherited the business from his father. He knew publishing very well and had established a thriving, mid-sized firm specializing in trade books.

### *The Trade Book Industry*

Most publishers of trade books are organized around a similar model. As an individual senior editor, Caroline, like other senior editors, was responsible for a list of titles under a particular category, such as mysteries, science fiction, or romance novels. Caroline's list was mysteries. Typically, senior editors work with a group of authors or authors' agents, encouraging them to write more titles and more marketable books. Senior editors juggle a number of projects at once; they need to drive authors to finish books to meet their publishing deadlines, but they have to be careful to not push too hard. After all, the best authors could go elsewhere. In addition to the editorial side of the business, other major parts of Corbett include the production department (here, employees set production budgets for individual titles and manage the physical production of books from their inception to print), the sales and marketing department (those responsible for advertising, promotion, and sales), the information technology department (employees who handle both internal information technology decisions and the company's Internet presence), and the finance and accounting departments (which manage both internal financial controls and work with the marketing and sales department to set book budgets). To keep pace with technological advances, in the last several years the Corbett Group had begun publishing online versions of some of its most popular titles, as well as downloadable versions of certain books and audiobooks.

### *New Job Assignments for a Few*

Throughout the company, employees were being asked to take on more work. The senior editors were no exception. The added amount of work came without additional staff; everyone was told that budgets were extremely tight and managers would need to find creative ways to get the work done. Two employees, Caroline and one of her senior-editor peers, Jack Dryer, were called to a meeting with the President of Corbett to discuss not only more work but different job responsibilities. Jack managed a list of science-fiction titles. Both Caroline and Jack felt the inevitability of this meeting since they had already been told that there would have to be changes. Although they were dedicated to the success of the company, they dreaded having additional work. They were already stretched too far.

Calvin Kuehn kept his comments fairly brief, "Thanks for coming in. I know that both of you are very aware of how our business is changing. It seems each year the market ups the ante. We have to give our customers as many options as our competitors do, just to stay even. Let me come to the point. I'll need both of you to add more electronic options to your lists and more DVDs. You will need to work with our marketing department to figure out a strategy for distribution. I suspect we can use some of our current clearinghouses to distribute DVDs. We'll use our website for electronic versions of titles. Work with IT on that. Can you come up with a proposal by Wednesday next week to show me which titles you think would be best to put into these formats?"

Although, Calvin asked a question, both Jack and Caroline understood it as a command.

In unison they responded, "Of course."

"OK then, Caroline I'd like to meet with you next Wednesday at 2p.m. Jack, can you come in at 3?"

Jack automatically responded, "Be glad to," even though he didn't have any idea what he had planned for that day. If he had scheduled an out-of-town trip, he would simply change his plans.

"Oh, be sure to include timelines for rolling out new and old titles and a proposed budget."

Calvin Kuehn rose from his chair, a sign that the meeting was over. He shook Caroline's hand and patted Jack on the back.

"Good work, both of you."

### Caroline's Meeting
Caroline had frantically put together a complete document with each title in her list and a suggested rationale for whether or not to expand its distribution to DVD or an electronic book. Before the meeting she had met with the marketing, production, and finance directors to discuss with them the promotion and distribution decisions that would have to be made and the projected costs associated with each project. Each of her recommendations had a timetable attached to it, a budget, and a suggested strategy for distribution. She handed the document to Calvin and she sat down at the conference table.

"It's ambitious, but I think we can do it. All the costs have been cleared with both production and finance."

Calvin nodded and began reading the document. Several minutes later, he looked up.

"This looks good. So you can do three titles by year end. And another four next year. That's great. If you run into any snags you have my full support. You'll need cooperation from just about every one of our departments. If you don't get it, I want to hear about it, OK?" he smiled.

"I don't foresee any problems, Mr. Kuehn, but thank you for your support." Caroline shook his hand as she prepared to leave.

### Jack's Meeting
"I've been working on this steadily since we last met. I think you will be pleased with it. May I walk you through it? I made us both copies," Jack said.

"Be my guest," replied Calvin Kuehn.

In great detail, Jack proceeded to explain how he planned to introduce technology to his book list. Like Caroline, he planned to introduce three downloadable editions this year and four e-books next year. He recommended that one title be dropped; it wasn't making the company much money and it was very time-consuming. He explained that with a little extra time he would really be able to devote himself to thinking more strategically about the list. He mentioned that he thought a good complement to the science-fiction titles would be a few books of fantasy or magical realism. He hadn't really sketched this out, but wanted to test the waters with Mr. Kuehn to get his opinion. Mr. Kuehn seemed receptive to the idea and told Jack that he liked his kind of forward-thinking. At the end of the discussion, Jack said,

"Mr. Kuehn I've worked for the company now for eight years and I have always stepped up to the plate when called on to do extra things. I work long hours and my family and I have sacrificed a lot to make this company successful. This project will increase my workload substantially. It's really a new job role for me. I will need to learn the electronic publishing business and everything that goes with it. That will mean taking on some additional courses to learn selling in this new medium, networking with other publishers in the e-space, and it will require that I learn new production principles that are completely different from our traditional trade books. It's really a new learning curve for me and a new terrain for our company. It will require a huge effort. I am very happy to do this but it has expanded my job role considerably. I think that it warrants extra compensation. Obviously a large raise would be great, but I do understand the kind of financial pressures we are under. It is more the recognition of my hard work that I am looking for."

"Jack, I do know how hard you work. Let me take a closer look at our budget and I will get back to you. I am not making any promises, though."

### Caroline's Lunch Date

Denise Snyder, an employee in the payroll department and one of Caroline's closest friends in the company, called her to have lunch. They found their usual quiet corner in the company cafeteria.

"You can't breathe a word of this because you know I am supposed to keep employee details confidential. This one really burned me up, though, and I thought you should know. Do you promise not to tell a soul?"

"Promise," Caroline said.

"Well, I was asked to amend Jack's employment records. Kuehn has approved adding another $10,000 to his merit bonus. I thought our President just told us we all needed to tighten our belts and pitch in to get the work done. What did Jack Dryer do to deserve such treatment? You work just as hard as he does and in my opinion get more done."

Caroline was astonished to hear this news. She knew that she worked just as hard as Jack did and felt she deserved the same. She couldn't believe that Mr. Kuehn wouldn't do the same for her.

"Now, you can't tell anyone I told you."

"I won't, I promise," Caroline reiterated.

**Discussion Questions**

1. In your opinion, was this a case of Caroline's lack of negotiation skills or a case of discrimination?
2. If you were Caroline, what would you do now?
3. Could Caroline have presented herself better during her meeting with Mr. Kuehn? If so, how?
4. Mr. Kuehn owns the company and is simply trying to keep costs in line and keep his employees happy. Is he unwise to pay Caroline and Jack differently from one another or is he simply making a smart business decision?
5. In pairs, role play the conversation between Caroline and Mr. Kuehn during which she is describing her proposal to him. If you are playing Caroline's role, ask for what you think you deserve.
6. Look at the information on pay comparisons between men and women in this chapter. In your opinion, why do these disparities still exist?
7. Read the article by Gneezy, Niederle, and Rustichini entitled, "Performance in Competitive Environments: Gender Differences" (*Quarterly Journal of Economics*, 2003). Do you think women shy away from competitive situations? Why, or why not? Do you think women's performance slips when they are challenged by males?

### Case Study 2: Splitting Tips or Splitting Hairs? Should Female Wait Staff Complain?

Lauren DeStephano pulled on her work uniform, a pair of khaki pants and a white button-down-collar shirt, with *Luigi's* embossed in bright red on the breast pocket. She mentally prepared herself for a long Saturday evening of being on her feet and smiling graciously to her customers – even the most demanding, unreasonable ones. Lauren began her shift at 6 p.m. and finished by midnight. She worked part-time at Luigi's as a way to supplement her college spending money and to help defray the cost of her textbooks.

Luigi's is a growing franchise restaurant that appeals to middle-income people – families and single people alike. With a wide selection of Italian dishes at moderate prices (pastas, cannelloni, lasagna, and pizza), popular salads, anti-pastas, trendy desserts, and a full bar menu, Luigi's attracts large crowds, especially on the weekends. In keeping with the food, the restaurant has an Italian flair. The walls are painted a creamy yellow with faux-finish designed to give the restaurant a rough-hewn appearance as if it had one time been a Tuscan farmhouse. Italian motifs adorn the walls – landscapes of hill towns, vineyards, and the ever-present Venetian gondola. The wait staff at Luigi's is almost entirely female: eight women servers and two male servers. Those clearing tables, the "bus-boys," are all male, and the three full-time bartenders are male.

When Lauren started her job, she was told that the wait staff pooled their tips with the bus-boys and the bartenders. Bill Myers, the general manager of the restaurant, took all of the credit-card receipts and added up all of the tips that had been added to each receipt. He then took that amount from the cash drawer and added it to the tip pool. At the end of the evening, the money was divided up evenly among all of the wait staff, the bartenders, and the bus-boys who had worked that shift.

When Lauren first started her job, she was too busy and preoccupied with college work to think about the fairness of the tip system; however, as she became better acquainted with her fellow female waitresses, her attention to the matter increased. The women often stayed after work and had a drink together. On a Saturday night after the restaurant was closed, they began to discuss the rationale behind the pooling-of-tips system.

Janine began, "I can understand a system where the wait staff would pool their tips because it is really the luck of the draw if someone who is rich and not cheap sits in my section and not yours, Sal."

"I agree. We can't really control who sits where and how much they might tip. And I think we all work hard so it is fair that we share our tips. But I'm not sure about sharing them with everyone else," Sally offered.

"The bus-boys work hard, but they don't have to deal face to face with the customers as often as we do. Customers don't blame them for anything. When the steak that was supposed to be rare turns out burned to a crisp, we take the flak, they don't," Mary said.

Sally added, "I think they deserve some part of our tips, but we shouldn't have to split them with them. The guys do clear off our tables and get them ready for the next customers that come in. But I agree, they shouldn't get as much as we do."

"Look we make $5.50 an hour and we need all of the tips we can get. I have rent to pay and groceries to buy. I can barely make it on what I bring in. I know we make less because supposedly our tips make up for it, but that just isn't the case." Mary said.

"How much do the bartenders make an hour?" Lauren asked.

"They make $8.55 an hour. Why should we split our tips with them? They make much more than we do!" Sally fumed.

Mary added her indignation, "Besides, they make tips from customers who sit at the bar. They don't split those tips with us!"

"Why don't we try to talk to the general manager about this? We could ask him to meet with us after our next shift," Lauren offered.

"Good idea, Lauren. Will you ask him?'

Lauren agreed to speak to Bill Myers the next day to set up a meeting.

### The Meeting with Bill Myers

Myers was an outgoing, friendly man, younger-looking than his 55 years. He bought into the Luigi franchise five years before and had made a success out of it through working persistently, hiring reliable people, and advertising widely in community newspapers. The restaurant had gone from a small number of patrons to families, college students, and single people, largely because of his efforts. He had instituted happy hours, family meal specials, and once-a-month special events with live music for sororities and fraternities. He was more than willing to talk to the women about their concerns.

"We had an incredible Saturday, didn't we? You all did very well and I think it could have been one of our busiest nights ever. But, you wanted to discuss something with me, didn't you? OK ladies, what's on your mind?"

Lauren began, "We have some concerns about the pooling of tips system."

Lauren waited for her colleagues to pitch in. When they didn't, she continued, "It's just that we don't understand why we have to pool our tips with the bus-boys and the bartenders. It seems unfair."

As soon as Lauren opened up the conversation with their chief concern, the other women volunteered their views.

"Mr. Myers, I've been here three years and it's always bothered me that I have to give my hard-earned tips to the bartenders. They make almost double what I make," Sally said.

"And they don't share their tips with us," added Mary.

"Well, let me address the bartenders' pay first. They make more because their position requires more knowledge. They have to know how to make lots of complex drinks. And they attended a bartending school. In terms of the bartenders' tips, they don't get many. Most of our customers sit at the bar only because they are waiting for a table. We don't get many hard-core drinkers in here."

"Well, Mr. Myers, about the bartenders knowledge.... We also need to know how to serve tables correctly. How to pour wine, which side to serve from, exactly how the food is made, which items are vegetarian, and what comes with each dish, *and* how to deal with customers when they don't get what they expect. Every time the menu changes we have to learn what new items are on it," Sally countered.

Janine added, "We really work hard on a weekend night, running around from table to table. The bus-boys and the bartenders don't have the physical demands we do. We have to have both stamina and a constant, cheerful attitude with the customers."

"Janine, I know you all work hard. So do the bus-boys and bartenders and they count on a share of the tips from the customers. The bus-boys have physical demands like you do. They are on their feet all evening and lift heavy trays of dishes. In this restaurant, we all serve the customers wherever we are, whether we are serving them at the tables like you do or from behind the bar," said Bill.

"So you aren't going to change the system?' asked Lauren hesitantly.

"Look, this is how all of Luigi's franchises operate. The chain is very well run and management hasn't received any complaints from other locations on this issue. I run this restaurant on the principle of teamwork and I think everyone should have a share of the customer tips if they contribute to the service. The bartenders and the bus-boys deal with customers too."

### Job Description for Bus Person
The individual job-holder will support a station in the restaurant, typically six tables, by setting tables with table clothes, silverware, and napkins. The individual will clear tables when customers are finished with their meal and deliver the dishes to the stations located on the sides of the kitchen. Bus-persons will be sure to keep salt and pepper mills full, ketchup and other condiments full and clean on the tables. They will clean tables with clean towels after they are cleared and before new customers sit down. As part of the restaurant team, bus-persons will also help out where needed. This may include filling water glasses when the wait staff becomes very busy or answering customers' questions if they are asked. Because this is a visible position, bus-staff must be courteous and well-groomed, and strong enough to lift trays of dishes.

### Job Description for Wait Staff
Wait staff will manage six tables in their station. They will take orders, answer customers' questions about meal choices, and they will understand our various offerings. This includes everything on the menu, as well as evening entrée specials and desserts that

change daily, and the bar and wine menu. Wait staff will periodically attend training sessions to learn about new wines on the menu and the various new offerings. They will handle customer complaints and special requests so as to minimize attention of other customers and to ultimately "take care of the customer" so he or she will have had a pleasant dining experience. As a team member, wait staff will support one another. This means on occasion taking customers in another wait staff's station to relieve pressure or helping with large parties. This job position requires stamina, teamwork, diplomacy to handle difficult customers, an outgoing personality, and the ability to learn the technology we use to enter and transmit orders to the kitchen staff. Previous experience desired.

### *Job Description of Bartender*

This job requires previous experience as a bartender and a complete knowledge of the range of drink orders, including types of wines, beer, and hard liquor drinks. The position requires speed and accuracy in handling drink orders, which may come from either the bar or from the wait staff when people order drinks from their tables during their meals. The individual must be able to work well under pressure and be a team player, as this position requires working with other bartenders and wait staff. Stamina is required as bartenders remain on their feet throughout their shift. The individual must be personable and well-groomed. Knowledge and enforcement of the law required; bartenders may not serve individuals who are underage or continue to serve individuals who have had too much to drink.

### Discussion Questions

1.  Bill Myers indicates that the male bartenders have more human capital (skill and knowledge) than do the female servers. Do you agree or disagree?
2.  If you were the women, what other tactics would you use to try to obtain a fairer system of compensation?
3.  How is restaurant work gendered? Why do you think this persists?
4.  This case demonstrates some of the problems with the concept of "comparable worth." In what other professions (jobs) do you see making a comparison between a man's job and a woman's job problematic?
5.  Design a program for assigning worth to three positions in this restaurant so as to assign wages and tips more equitably.
6.  Go to www.salary.com for an interesting look at what specific occupations pay around the United States. Enter your zip code and a job title and see the ranges for salary in a particular job category for your area of the country.

# LANDMARK EQUAL PAY AND FAIR COMPENSATION CASES

Two cases have strengthened the US Equal Pay Act, *Schultz* v. *Wheaton Glass* (1970) and *Corning Glass Works* v. *Brennan* (1974), and one, *Ledbetter* v. *Goodyear Tire and Rubber* (2007), has weakened some equal-pay cases.

In *Schultz* v. *Wheaton Glass*, the US Court of Appeal's Third Circuit ruled that jobs that are paid equally need to be "substantially equal" in terms of tasks and responsibilities but not be identical. This case proved significant because most jobs are not identical, particularly as one moves up the hierarchy in organizations. Assembly-line workers may have identical jobs, but managers rarely do.

In *Corning Glass Works* v. *Brennan*, the US Supreme Court ruled that employers cannot justify paying lower rates for women for the same job simply because the market has accepted the rate. In other words, even if women accept lower pay for the same job, the court ruled the practice illegal. Corning Glass Works had been paying women sales executives less than male sales executives.

Wal-Mart has been forced to pay $78.5 million for violating Pennsylvania labor laws by forcing employees to work through rest breaks and off the clock. In this case, "off the clock" is a term used to explain that employees are expected to work without getting credit for all of their time. For example, a maid might be forced to punch out (thus recording the end of her shift), but still work a half-hour or more to clean up. The class action suit was filed by 187,000 current and former employees of both Sam's Club and Wal-Mart (Dale, 2006). One plaintiff, who was fired after complaining about work practices, reported that she worked eight-to-ten unpaid hours a month. In addition to uncovering the practice of not paying for overtime, the prosecuting attorney in the case explained that Wal-Mart's computers were programmed to dock workers for every minute that they signed in late. This practice saved Wal-Mart $26 million in one year.

## *Lilly M. Ledbetter* v. *The Goodyear Tire Company*

Lilly Ledbetter, a supervisor at Goodyear Tire and Rubber's plant in Gadsden, Alabama, worked from 1979 until her retirement in 1998. Her equal-pay discrimination case finally made its way to the US Supreme Court in May 2007. Her claim was dismissed by the Supreme Court based on a narrow reading of the Title VII law, rather than on the spirit of the law, which was written to prevent discrimination based on sex, race, color, religion, or national origin. In January 2009, President Obama reversed the Supreme Court's decision and signed into law the Lilly Ledbetter Fair Pay Resolution Act, making it possible for persons experiencing age discrimination to have their case heard after the 180-day time-limit requirement if they had no knowledge of the discrimination during the time-limit period.

When Ledbetter was first hired, her salary was in line with similarly situated male area managers. Over time, however, her pay fell in comparison to the pay of male managers with equal or less seniority. Ledbetter was the only woman working as an area manager. By the end of 1997, her pay was in sharp contrast to her 15 male counterparts; she was paid $3,727 per month versus the lowest-paid male area manager who received $4,286 per month and the highest, at $5,236 (Justice Ginsburg, 2007, p. 1). Under Title VII legislation, Ledbetter made charges of discrimination to the Equal Employment Opportunity Commission in March 1998. A jury eventually found that Goodyear more than likely paid Ledbetter an unequal salary because of her sex. The court awarded Ledbetter money for back pay, damages, her legal fees, and other costs associated with the judgment. Goodyear took the case to the Supreme Court where Justices Alito, Scalia, Kennedy, and Thomas reversed the lower court's decision. The court held that Ledbetter's claim was time-barred because of Title VII's stipulation that charges of discrimination be filed within 180 days of the alleged unlawful act. The court ruled that it was incumbent on Ledbetter to file charges each year that Goodyear failed to increase her salary commensurate with the salaries of her male peers (Ginsburg, 2007, p. 2). Moreover, the court affirmed that any pay disparity not contested within 180 days becomes impossible for Title VII to repair. Ledbetter narrowly lost her case at the Supreme Court in a five-to-four decision. The dissenting Supreme Court Justices, Ginsburg, Stevens, Souter, and Breyer, contested the ruling for several reasons. Ginsburg, the author of the dissenting opinion, wrote:

> The Court's insistence on immediate contest overlooks common characteristics of pay discrimination. Pay disparities often occur, as they did in Ledbetter's case, in small increments; cause to suspect that discrimination is at work develops only over time. Comparative pay information, moreover, is often hidden from the employee's view. Employers may keep under wraps the pay differentials maintained among supervisors, no less the reasons for those differentials. Small initial discrepancies may not be seen as meet for a federal case, particularly when the employee, trying to succeed in a non-traditional environment, is averse to making waves.
>
> (Ginsburg, 2007, p. 2)

Ginsburg explains that both the pay-setting decision (under the 180-day rule by Title VII) and the actual payment of a discriminatory wage are relevant to the Title VII legislation and its intent to make unlawful the practice of pay discrimination based on sex. The Supreme Court ruling was clearly a setback for women. Often it takes more than 180 days for people to realize that they have been unfairly compensated. Furthermore, individuals may be trying to negotiate a fair outcome with their employer; in this case, they may not wish to file a complaint when they are attempting to rectify the situation by conciliation with their employer. Ginsburg remarked that Ledbetter's experience was more suggestive of a hostile work environment, rather than a single, discrete episode of pay discrimination.

In April of 2008, Congress revisited Title VII, but did not change the 180-day rule. Many Congressional members felt that it would result in a groundswell of equal-pay cases. The statute of limitations is controversial. Some against changing the law suggested that it would actually hurt workers because employers, as the cost of litigation increases, would hire fewer people and pay them less. Ted Frank, an attorney, writes:

> To the extent every employee is a potential lawsuit, that is a cost of hiring an employee. As those costs go up, employers will hire fewer employees, and charge "insurance" to the employees they do hire by reducing their wages to account for the possibility of a future lawsuit. If the misnamed "Lilly Ledbetter Fair Pay Act" passes, the vast majority of workers will be worse off, as money that would have gone to pay employees will instead go to pay attorneys.
>
> (Frank, 2008)

In 2008, several members of Congress introduced the Lilly Ledbetter Fair Play Act, which revised the law to state that prior acts outside the 180 day statute-of-limitations could be included. The bill passed in January 2009.

## Boeing

In the 1990s, Boeing Corporation quietly began to conduct data on pay to see how women were paid in comparison to men for similar work. Several salary studies concluded that women had been paid less than men. In 2000, 38 Boeing female employees filed a class action suit against Boeing. As part of the legal proceedings, the prosecution lawyers requested pretrial documents that Boeing had about gender pay differentials. Boeing's lawyers refused to turn over documents, citing attorney–client privilege as the legal principle. Meanwhile, behind the scenes, employees removed the pay documents. The case was settled out-of-court for $40.6 million. Boeing was ordered to revamp its hiring practices, overtime assignments, criteria for promotion, and its complaint procedures. The maximum award that any plaintiff received in the suit was $100,000.

## Other Equal Pay Cases

In the United Kingdom, Stephanie Villalba, the former head of European private banking for Merrill Lynch, earned substantially less than her male counterparts. She was unsuccessful in suing Merrill Lynch for £7 million in damages as the employment court dismissed her allegations of unequal pay and sexual discrimination. The Industrial Tribunal ruled that she did have a case for unfair dismissal because after she was dismissed from her position she should have been offered an alternative position within the company. There is a monetary cap on unfair dismissal claims in the UK of £55,000.

Liz Pullen, a regional director for Onyx Environmental Group, a French company operating in the UK, found that when she was laid off from her job along with two other male directors, her severance package was significantly less than theirs. She has been offered six months' severance pay while they were offered one year's pay. At the same time, she discovered that she had been underpaid in comparison to them, earning £15,000 a year less. Since severance packages are calculated based on salary and the number of years employed by the organization, not only was she disadvantaged during her time with the company, but also when she was "let go." Pullen managed an annual turnover of £20 million and 300 employees, and had worked for the company for six years.

In 2007, API, a British manufacturer for the graphics and packaging industry with operations in Europe, the US, and Asia, settled an equal-pay case for £25,000. When Bridget Bodman, an accountant with API, was promoted from an accountant to a financial controller, she discovered that her successor was offered £8,000 more than she had made as an accountant, and had received an additional £8,640 in a car allowance and other benefits. An industrial tribunal ruled that the company had no defense for offering her replacement more than she had made. The case highlights the importance of companies' pay rates, even in situations in which an employee has left a job and moved on to another.

In *Mrs. Cadman* v. *Health & Safety Executive*, the UK court ruled that Mrs. Cadman's pay could not be determined based on a length-of-service requirement. Mrs. Cadman filed against her employer when she discovered that she was being paid less than a male performing the same job, based on the fact that he had more seniority with the company than she did. The court said that a length-of-service requirement must be objectively justified to a set of employees, not to a single employee, and that it needs to determine what weight it should have compared to other factors, such as merit. It is easier to justify a length-of-service requirement in managerial roles, where experience may be relevant to performance, than in routine jobs where it is not as much a factor.

# 6  Networks and Mentors

**Learning Objectives**

After completing this chapter, the reader will:

- understand the characteristics of formal and informal networks.
- understand social network theory.
- understand how networks and mentors affect job performance.
- understand how attitudes toward gender affect mentoring and networking behavior.
- understand particular issues for minorities in mentoring and networking relationships.

## An Introduction to Networks

Networks can be defined as interconnected systems of people. Women can increase their chances of career success by establishing relationships with other individuals or by joining network groups. Networks are both a source of information about possible job opportunities and an avenue for influential contacts that can help women throughout their careers. Consider the young, talented individual who is informed about a job opening before it becomes known to others and whose network members put in a good word for him with the hiring manager. This individual will have an advantage over others who hear about the job opening through a more formal, organizational channel such as the human resource department. Imagine the person who is recommended for a high-profile client assignment that will give her the needed experience to advance to the next level or the individual who is given frank career advice. These types of experiences are necessary to reach the highest level of the organization, and they make it easier to navigate the mid-level of an organization.

But networks can also be barriers, like a fishnet strung across a stream – keeping out talented people, individuals unknown to or unwanted by the network members. Women need to understand the value of social networks in order to make use of their advantages and avoid the obstacles they can create. Securing a mentor is one of the first steps for breaking into networks that can help advance one's career. Mentors introduce their protégés to influential members of networks. They also increase their protégés' stature, visibility within the organization, and credibility with others by virtue of their association with them. The popular press is full of examples of successful business women who credit their success to mentors who guided them, providing advice, and opening organizational doors that otherwise would have been closed. This chapter explores the power of networks and their specific relevance for women's professional advancement.

Although organizations have formal rules such as explicit hiring procedures, leave policies, and other employment standards, the informal, unofficial part of organizational life often determines who gets ahead and how. Through informal networks employees build alliances, obtain access to resources, and advance their careers. These networks also allow employees to circumvent or exploit the official rules and formal procedures, giving them an advantage over others (Campbell, Marsden, & Hurlbert, 1986; Lin, Vaughn, & Ensel, 1981). Networks can help women to hear about job opportunities before they become widely known, and may give women access to important decision-makers during a recruitment and selection process. Informal networks provide employees with initial recognition, resources such as the opportunity to gain additional skills, information exchanges, and contacts that help them secure promotions (Bridges & Villemez, 1986; Haythornthwaite, 1996; Podolny & Baron, 1997). In studying networks, scholars have focused on both the characteristics of network members and the nature of social interactions within a network.

## Social Network Theory

People have three different types of capital that help them get ahead in life: financial capital, which includes available cash, lines of credit, and financial investments; human capital, which includes one's positive personal characteristics such as level of education, amount and type of experience, intelligence, personality, and appearance; and social capital, which includes one's family ties, relationships with others, and the impact of race, religion, and other social and cultural factors. One obtains social capital from individual relationships or relationships with networks of people (for example, fraternities, sororities, country clubs, or church groups).

Social network theory departs from other theories that attribute achievement to individual actions, efforts, or skills. It assumes that one's personal relationships (one's social capital) are at least as important in determining personal outcomes as one's individual qualifications, level of seniority, or personality – how much one knows, how hard one works, how long someone has worked in an organization, and whether one is friendly, kind, or compassionate, for example.

Social capital can also be influenced by race or ethnic group. Consider ethnic minorities who do not use standard English, but instead speak in the dialect characteristic of their racial group. These individuals will have a harder time moving up in a largely white business culture because of inbuilt prejudices against their speech patterns and because they may be stereotyped as unsophisticated or less intelligent than those who speak "standard" English. Some people's social capital may be insufficient to break into networks. Even large quantities of human and financial capital may not make up for a lack of social capital. For example, minorities with high levels of both financial resources and education may have fewer relationships with white, male business executives or may not be invited into exclusive clubs. One reason networks are so important is that entering them, often through the intersession of mentors, can make up for an individual's poor social capital or even increase it.

Knowing that social capital and networks are important is a good start for anyone in business; but equally important is understanding the structure and characteristics of networks. The following section turns to examine these aspects of networks.

## Homophily and Networks

Understanding the structure of networks, in which individuals are typically aligned together, and how networks operate can help an employee make the most of them.

Individuals are generally attracted to people like themselves because of the ease of communication and the comfort level of interacting with the familiar rather than the less familiar. "Similarity is thought to ease communication, increase the predictability of behavior, and foster trust and reciprocity." (Brass, Galaskiewicz, Greve, & Tsai, 2004). "Homophily" (from the Greek, meaning "love of the same type") refers to the degree to which individuals who interact are similar in identity or organizational group affiliations (Ibarra, 1993; McPherson, Smith-Lovin, & Cook, 2001; Marsden, 1988; Rogers & Kincaid, 1981). Both men and women seem to reach out to others of the same sex, income, religion, race, and those with similar interests or occupations. For example, in a study of recruitment methods at a call center, both men and women referred people of their own sex for call-center jobs (Fernandez & Lourdes Sosa, 2005).

The desire men often have to interact with those who have power, and the desire of both men and women to interact with those who are similar to themselves (a case of homophily), help explain why men often exclude women from their networks and women exclude men from their networks. Women may be excluded from networks both because they are perceived by others to have very little influence or power, and they, themselves, may prefer to associate with other women who share the same interests and who are at a similar level in the organizational hierarchy. Because of this tendency toward homophily, networks are most often comprised of people who are similar to one another in terms of sex, age, race, socio-economic level, and values.

Researchers have distinguished two types of homophily: status homophily and value homophily (Lazarsfeld & Merton, 1954). The former refers to the tendency for individuals with similar informal, formal, or ascribed status to cluster together; and the latter, to the tendency for people with similar attitudes, beliefs, and values to gravitate toward one another. For example, those of similar economic status tend to live in the same neighborhoods, attend the same schools, and attend the same type of social functions. Those sharing the same beliefs may attend the same church, belong to the same political party, or seek out others as friends who believe as they do. Often status homophily groups overlap with value homophily groups.

## Instrumental Versus Expressive Network Ties

Social network theorists distinguish between two types of ties: expressive ties based on friendship or social relations and instrumental ties based on specific ends or goals. Instrumental ties are connections to resources, benefits (for example, a positive relationship with one's boss) versus expressive ties that provide social-psychological support and friendship but do not provide resources (for example, relationships with one's co-workers). An instrumental tie might take the time to help with a difficult job task, recommend one for promotion, enhance one's reputation by talking about one's achievements, or introduce one to other influential people. Expressive ties, on the other hand, are often between equals who socialize together over lunch, talk about personal matters, and commiserate over work problems.

## Strong and Weak Ties

In addition to differences in the power of individuals within a network, the number of networks to which an individual belongs will also have a bearing on their success. Both strong ties and weak ties have been recognized as important for success (Brass, 1992; Granovetter, 1973, 1982). Strong ties are one's frequent, immediate contacts, while weak ties are through other people and are more superficial. Figure 6.1 shows strong ties between "you" and players A and B and weak ties between "you" and players A(1) and B(1). Weak ties, although not as close, can put one in touch with influential people in other networks, provide resources themselves, and help broaden a person's network to more diverse individuals. If a woman's network is comprised of both strong and weak ties, she will be more likely to succeed. Her strong ties will provide her with frequent contact and support, while her weak ties may expand her area of influence. If a woman's network is composed of strong ties, but very insular – for example, a group of neighborhood women from a small town – these individuals will refer her to individuals she already knows. On the other hand, if she extends herself in many directions – joining a business group, a book club, her child's school–parent organization, and a sports club – she will be interacting with many types of individuals who travel in different social circles and who will potentially connect her to many more people and to other networks different from her own. Uzzi and Dunlap (2005) recommend that people identify the power brokers in their network – those individuals who most often introduce them to others whom they do not already know. In building a network, individuals can cultivate power brokers and routinely stay in touch with them.

## Network Density

A network's density is the extensiveness of contact among its members (Marsden, 1990). If density is "high," all members have close contact with each other – everyone is connected to everyone else in the network and the network is characterized by social solidarity and strong, rather than weak, ties. One feature of a high-density network is the inability of any one player to play off others in a negotiation. When everyone knows everyone else in the network and information flows freely among individuals, it is difficult for any one individual to take advantage of others. In high-density networks, one cannot leverage resources gained in one relationship into an advantage in another relationship and therefore it's more difficult for one individual to exercise power over others (Ibarra, 1993). Women are more likely to belong to high-density networks than men are, because women's networks are often composed of peers who have bonded through friendship.

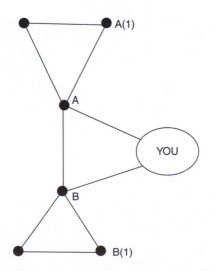

*Figure 6.1* Strong Ties Versus Weak Ties.

Burt (1992) holds that network ties are costly to maintain (they take time and effort) and therefore individuals should be selective about with whom they establish ties. He suggests that individuals should cultivate "structural holes" in their network. A structural hole is defined as the absence of a link between two people who are both linked to the same person. Structural holes link two different social clusters or network groups and, in this way, can provide an individual with new, non-redundant information. Structural holes improve one's social capital because they expand one's contacts, often to many different types of people. The variety of people provides an individual with new ideas. In addition to providing information and ideas, structural holes give an individual more control over information. As the diagram in Figure 6.2 shows, "you" have access to information from both "C" and "D" that others in your network do not have. You can broker relationships between the other players in your network or decide not to. The benefits of both structural ties and weak ties have been borne out by research; structural holes and weak ties in career-advice networks were found to positively correlate with social resources, which in turn were related to promotions, salary improvements, and career satisfaction (Seibert, Kraimer, & Liden, 2001). Similarly, Podolny and Baron (1997) reported that large networks with many structural holes improved career mobility.

## Network Centrality

One's structural position in a network is an important variable in individual job performance. The more one is *central* in a network, the more one is apt to be close to resources and valuable job information. Centrality in networks is measured by the number of ties to others – therefore, the more one is connected to others in a network, the more central one is to the network In Figure 6.3, "you" are connected to all others in the network (five people), while everyone else is connected to three others. Several studies have linked network centrality to job performance; Sparrowe, Liden, Wayne, and Kraimer (2001) studied 190 employees in 38 work groups from five organizations, finding that centrality in networks that provided advice was positively correlated to individual job performance. Centrality in networks of informal communication has been associated with promotion (Brass, 1984).

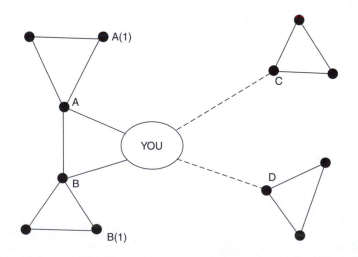

*Figure 6.2* Structural Holes.

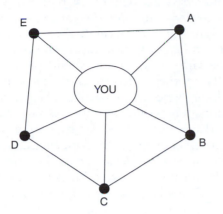

*Figure 6.3*  Network Centrality.

## Networking, the Knowledge Economy and Job Performance

Networks are particularly important in a modern knowledge economy. Networks are those channels of supply and distribution for information needed to produce a company's products. Unlike concrete commodities such as manufactured goods, information in the knowledge economy can be distributed without dilution and with only modest delay as long as the information travels efficiently via technology through people. Consider how fast information flows through the Internet. Developed economies, such as those in the US, Europe, and Japan, rely less on unskilled labor engaged in manufacturing. Instead, their economies have turned to knowledge workers in such fields as bio-technology and electronics. Failure to participate in networks through which business-critical information flows will make an employee less productive. Career success and even career survival require access to those who have knowledge of the inner workings of an organization and access to individuals outside of an organization who have valuable information.

Awazu (2004) envisions knowledge networks composed of four components:

1.  central connectors, those people who identify what knowledge seekers are looking for and guide them in the right direction;
2.  boundary spanners, people who connect one network to another network;
3.  gatekeepers, those individuals who control knowledge that enters or leaves the network;
4.  bridges, those individuals who connect people who do not share common backgrounds, skills, or experiences.

To ensure their access to information, women should be aware of the individuals who are connectors, boundary spanners, and bridges, and they should cultivate them. These key individuals will provide them with critical information and introduce them to others outside their immediate network. Women also need to identify gatekeepers, who may attempt to keep information from them.

Cross and Cummings (2004) studied knowledge-intensive networks within two firms: a petrochemical firm employing engineers and a strategy consultancy employing management consultants. They explored several hypotheses relating to networks and job performance. First, the researchers were interested in whether awareness of colleagues' expertise and one's access to relevant knowledge in more distant regions of a network positively correlated with job-performance ratings. Second, they predicted that the number of ties an individual has, both outside of an organization and to other individuals in different departments within the same organization, would positively correlate with individual performance ratings. Third, they tested to see if ties to more senior people in the organization correlated with job-performance ratings. Their results indicated that, for both engineers and consultants, job-performance ratings positively correlated with information (knowledge) networks and awareness of others' expertise. They also found support for the positive relationship between job performance and the number of ties both outside the organization and in different departments. In terms of performance ratings, ties to senior people in the organization were important in the consulting firm, but not in the engineering firm. (It is likely that in engineering firms people are evaluated more on their expertise and less on their network affiliations.) In both management consulting and engineering, an individual's ability to assemble a diverse set of professionals with relevant expertise cannot be underestimated because work in these fields depends on teams with skill sets that support each individual client assignment. Individuals excel if they are quickly able to harness teams that have the talent and knowledge to solve novel problems. The results from this study as well as others indicate the growing importance of networks in intensively knowledge-based industries such as high-tech, management consulting, and engineering.

## Networking Behavior and Recruitment, Selection, and Promotion

Like the Cross and Cummings study, other research has indicated positive outcomes related to networking. Luthans, Hodgetts, and Rosenkrantz (1988) related networking to promotions, and Michael and Yuki (1993) found that both networking inside one's organization and externally were related to rates of advancement. Middle- and upper-level managers engage in more networking activities, both inside their organizations and outside of them, than lower-level managers. Michael and Yuki also found that networking behavior was related to job function; marketing and production managers networked more outside their organization than did finance managers. The nature of these jobs requires that the job-holders interact more with customers and suppliers, whereas finance managers do not need to interact with others outside their organizations to do their jobs. Networking behavior and career outcomes are also related to job level; in a study of 217 males and 197 females from a metropolitan, municipal bureaucracy, Gould and Penley (1984) found that networking behavior was positively correlated to salary progression for managers but not for clerical and professional staff. Analysis of questionnaires given to clerical and professional staff and managers indicated that managers use a number of networked-based career strategies to a greater extent than either professionals or clerks. In particular, managers reported higher use of seeking guidance from others and networking. The authors do not speculate about the reasons for such disparities between workers, but it is likely that clerical workers have access to less-powerful networks than managers do and therefore invest less in them.

In addition to its relationship to promotion, networking has a positive impact on finding employment, negotiating for salary (especially for high-level jobs), and for assimilating into the culture of a new firm. Most firms prefer to hire someone who comes recommended by a trusted "insider" than to hire a complete stranger, and some organizations even provide incentives to employees who refer others who are subsequently hired. In one study, recruits' social ties to an organization improved their salary negotiation outcomes (Seidel, Polzer, & Stewart, 2000). The results from 3,062 salary negotiations from this high-tech company also showed that these social ties existed for whites, but not for minorities. Two other studies found that assimilation of new employees to the company's culture was enhanced by their network involvement (Jablin & Krone, 1987; Sherman, Smith, & Mansfield, 1986). Being part of a network as one enters a firm not only helps one feel a welcome part of the organization, but also provides a short-cut for learning the accepted behavior, unspoken rules, and norms of the firm.

## Entrepreneurs and Networks

Just as networking is a critical part of an employee's toolkit, it is essential for those working as independent consultants, contractors, or entrepreneurs. Entrepreneurs realize that achieving success depends in large part on their ability to effectively network. Entrepreneurs use networks to explore business ideas, to gain valuable feedback and advice, and as a source of much-needed capital to start a business or to take an existing business to the next stage of development. Through networks, entrepreneurs tap into several sources of advice and funding – so-called "angel" investors (wealthy individuals), bank managers, family members, and friends may provide assistance at various stages of a business venture. When their businesses are up and running, women can use networks to prospect for customers, to seek advice on marketing, or to form strategic alliances with other companies. Alliances are important because they help businesses grow quickly and can provide additional customers, capital, or products. Barnir and Smith (2002) found that the more networking that small-business owners engaged in, the more strategic alliances they were able to form. Many online sites are available to help business owners exchange information, prospect for customers, advertise, and sell their services

## Gender and Networks

Women business owners use networks in much the same way that male business owners do – recognizing that they are important for various phases of their operations, and especially during the planning stages (Greve & Salaff, 2003). However, there are differences in the networking behaviors of men and women and in the benefits that the two genders receive from their networks. For example, women business owners use kinship ties to a larger extent than men do, calling on their family and friends for both financial and emotional support (Greve & Salaff, 2003). In a study comprised of male and female business owners in Raleigh, North Carolina and Milan, Italy, there were many similarities in the networking behaviors of individuals in both countries, yet the personal networks of women in both countries included very few men (Aldrich, Reese, & Dubini, 1989). In a similar study, female entrepreneurs had significantly lower proportions of males in their social networks in the early stages of development of their enterprises, but as their businesses grew their networks began to grow increasingly similar in composition (Klyver & Terjesen, 2007). The study revealed no significant differences between the network size and density between male and female networks. Established female entrepreneurs, however, had a higher proportion of kin in their networks (40%) compared to established male entrepreneurs (28%). The differences in the gender composition of men's and women's networks at the early stages of business development could be due to women's comfort level in seeking out males, or in males' reluctance to join women's networks until they have proven that their businesses are successful.

Several social scientists note gender differences in men's and women's access to networks and in the degree to which networks help men versus women (Ibarra & Andrews, 1993; Ohlott, Ruderman, & McCauley, 1994; Smith-Lovin, McPherson, & Cook, 2001). Women are less likely than men to be part of networks with high-status members or to be part of networks with diverse memberships (Brass, 1984; Burt, 1992; Campbell, 1988; Ibarra, 1993; McGuire, 2002). In McGuire's study of 1,000 financial services employees, gender inequality manifested itself in employees' informal networks. Despite the fact that black and white women had jobs in which they controlled resources and had ties to other powerful employees, they received less work-related help from their network members than white men did. Similar findings demonstrate that both black and white women have a harder time gaining invitations into networks that serve as a valuable part of career development (Bell & Nkomo, 2001).

Forret and Dougherty (2004) studied the networking behavior of 418 male and female business-school graduates from a large, Midwestern state university. The graduates were all working full-time – averaging 51 hours a week, most were white (98%), most were married (78%), and 36% had advanced degrees. Individuals in the sample had an average of 15 years' work experience. The researchers proposed the following hypotheses about the networking behavior of these individuals: 1. networking behavior would be positively correlated to the number of promotions received; 2. networking would be positively correlated to total compensation; 3. networking behavior would be positively correlated to *perceived* career success; 4. gender would moderate the relationship between involvement in the network behavior and objective career outcome (the number of promotions and total compensation) such that these relationships would be stronger for men than for women. Forret and Dougherty defined networking activity in five ways: maintaining contact with others (sending cards, newspaper clippings, faxes, or e-mails to stay in touch), socializing (playing sports with clients or co-workers or engaging in social functions), participating in professional activities (attending conferences, for example), participating in community activities (church, civic, or social clubs), and increasing internal visibility (accepting a highly visible job assignment or going to lunch with a supervisor). Career success, measured by the number of promotions in an individual's career, could be defined as a change in office or type of furniture in the office, a significant increase in annual salary, qualifying for a bonus, incentive, or stock plan, a change in level, or a change in job scope or responsibility. Results of the study showed that engaging in professional activities did not increase women's compensation, yet engaging in these activities did increase compensation for males. Increasing total internal visibility (serving on taskforces or accepting highly visible work assignments) was significantly related to the number of promotions for men, but not for women. Both genders perceived that networking behaviors would be beneficial to career success, even though women did not gain as much from their networks as males did. The authors provide a variety of reasons for the disparate effects of networking between men and women. First, professional activities may be more highly valued when men perform them; second, men may negotiate additional compensation for their professional activities whereas women may not; and third, women's lower status compared to men's status in the organizational structure may make it more difficult for them to maintain contacts, engage in professional activities, and increase their visibility. The results of this study are important to women for several reasons. Women will need to adopt a range of networking strategies and be aware that, as women, they will have to work harder than men on some of the networking behaviors to reap the same rewards. Even then, they may not receive the same support.

Beyond adopting a range of networking behaviors, women must also be aware of falling out of networks because of their greater use of flexible work arrangements and teleworking. Non-traditional work patterns, part-time work, maternity leaves, and flexible work arrangements, including working from home, are a blessing for women who want more options, yet these work arrangements will make it more difficult for women to retain strong ties, that depend on face-to-face contact. Women who choose these arrangements or are absent from work because of maternity leaves or a career break will have to make an extra effort to stay connected to networks.

## Gender and the Status of Network Members

Individuals connected in a network can be considered as either high-status or low-status players. High-status players are those with organizational clout – ones who wield a greater amount of influence and power, and therefore a greater level of status within the organizational hierarchy. Low-status network players, on the other hand, are those without influence, power, or decision-making authority, and those with few resources for exchange. Their lack of organizational power makes them less-attractive network members to other individuals in the organization. Because of these factors, networks with a majority of high-status players will be far more beneficial to individuals who occupy them than those with low-status players.

A study of 108 senior and middle managers in China indicated that most networks that yielded career success for both men and women were composed of power ties with men (Bu & Roy, 2005). Another study of 1,000 financial-services employees helps explain the importance of instrumental ties to both women and minorities. A pecking order exists in terms of who gets help in mixed gender and race networks: white men are at the top, receiving the most help from their network members, followed by white women, then black men and finally black women (McGuire, 2002). In spite of the fact that white women and black women held jobs in which they controlled resources (budgets, staff, etc.), and had ties to powerful employees, they received less work-related help from their network members than did white men. In addition, African American employees had fewer network members than white women did, and both women and minorities had very similar kinds of networks. McGuire indicates that they were networking with lower-status people than white men were, people who had less to give them, fewer resources, less poverty, and less legitimacy.

Since women generally occupy lower-status positions compared to men, they have more difficulty penetrating high-status networks. The organizational structure limits the interaction between high-status and low-status individuals and sometimes even physical barriers limit interaction among high-status and low-status employees. For example, the senior executives may be centralized on one floor of an office building while workers are on other floors. Managers may have offices with walls and doors, while non-managers have cubicles. These physical differences create natural affinities and barriers that both encourage interaction of like-status individuals and discourage interaction between those of different status.

If employees choose members of their network based on their ability to reciprocate or return favors, then women may be considered less desirable members because of their lack of access to resources. If occupational segregation causes women to interact primarily with other women and men with other men, then naturally women will develop networks with women because these are the individuals with whom they have daily contact. Michael and Yuki (1993) note some differences between networking behavior of individuals inside versus outside of their organizations. Network behavior inside organizations is focused on the status of network partners; however, when people network outside of their organizations they are less concerned with the status of other people and will focus on an individual's job function. An individual networking outside his or her organization may pay attention to someone of a lower rank, if this person has a similar job function. Higher-level managers may perceive less risk in befriending lower-level managers outside of their organization (they will not be seen to be associating with a lower-status individual) or they may simply be less aware of status differences when they are outside of their work environment. The point for women is to consider joining networks based on job function (human resources, marketing, information technology, etc.) where they may receive additional support outside of their organizations.

## Gender and Strong and Weak Ties

If a woman's network is comprised of both strong and weak ties, she will be more likely to succeed. Her strong ties will provide her with frequent contact and support, while her weak ties may expand her area of influence. If a woman's network is composed of strong ties, but very insular – for example, a group of neighborhood women from a small town – these individuals will refer her to individuals she already knows. On the other hand, if she extends herself in many directions – joining a business group, a book club, her child's school–parent organization, and a sports club – she will be interacting with many types of individuals who travel in different social circles, and who will potentially connect her to many more people and to other networks different from her own. Uzzi and Dunlap (2005) recommend that people identify the power brokers in their network – those individuals who most often introduce them to others whom they do not already know. In building a network, individuals can cultivate power brokers and routinely stay in touch with them.

   In addition to being aware of how power and status players influence networks in non-virtual environments, individuals need to understand how social networking sites on the Internet can improve their networks.

## Social and Professional Networking Sites

Networking through the Internet is becoming increasingly popular as a way to reach out to perspective employers and as a means to meet influential people. One way of increasing network ties, especially weak ties, is through social and business Internet sites such as Facebook, MySpace, Tribe, Spoke, or LinkedIn. One might ask, how can one have 400 friends? Do these weak ties actually do anything for an individual? The answer is probably both "yes" and "no." The multitude of connections one has online becomes a part of one's identity and status. In other words, with whom you are friends and how many so-called friends you have says something fundamental about your interests and your social and economic status. How you interact with these individuals and what they publicly proclaim about you also contributes to your identity. Building a network of "high-status" individuals identifies one as high status by virtue of the fact that one is associated with these high-status individuals and one's profile is in the public space. On the other hand, what do these "weak ties" actually do for an individual? The answer to that question may have to do with how the social networking sites are configured and the rules under which they operate.

Social and business networks come in two general categories: registration-based sites, where one simply signs up and fills out an individual profile, and connection-based sites, where one has to be invited in as a member by a pre-existing member of the network. For example, in order to become a member of Orkut, a non-member would have to contact a friend or acquaintance who is already a member to ask them to "invite" them to join the site, whereas Facebook only requires that an individual registers to become part of the network. Social networks such as MySpace, Friendster, and Facebook reveal personal information, such as sexual orientation, favorite music, movies, books, and TV shows, general interests, e-mail address, and allow for posting of photos. Business networking sites such as LinkedIn, Spoke, Ecademy, Ryze, and Meetup include professional details such as work history, experience, and education. Via a format or template, all of these sites control the type of information that can be shared. For example, LinkedIn asks for professional details such as job title, skill set, and education, while Ecademy and Ryze make professional details optional. Ecademy's users are generally Europeans, with a predominance of UK participants. The site features information on business meetings, offers a marketplace for selling items, provides information on office space, and offers smaller, local networking groups that people can join. Ryze has several existing networks of interest to women professionals that members can join. Networks with titles such as "Real Women," "Women in Networking," and "Women Business Owners" are open to anyone who wants to sign up. Meetup is a site for business people to form affinity groups for "meetups" offline at restaurants or in other public places. A third category of site exists where companies form their own internal networking sites. Generally, the purpose of these enterprise portals, as they are called, is to improve cross-departmental communication and to share knowledge.

Gender issues on social and business networking sites have not been studied in any great detail, although this is certainly a rich area for future research. Rapleaf (2008), an online research firm, has studied the gender and age composition of several social network sites. The highlights of their research include the following:

- Women aged 14–24 dominate activity on social network sites and have more friends than men in the same age range.
- Men aged 35 and over are more active and have more friends than women in the same age group.
- Men dominate LinkedIn, which is the site most used by business people.

Women's usage on social network sites is highest in the younger age categories, the 14–17 and 18–24 age groups, for instance, on sites such as Facebook and MySpace, which are less often used to network professionally. More research needs to be done on LinkedIn. For example, do professional men connect more with other men or are their relationships on the Web gender-neutral? The invitation-only business sites could open up doors for women or they could keep them closed, depending on how liberally the users invite other in. In a *Newsweek* interview, the CEO of LinkedIn was asked whether he would recommend that users invite anyone who asks into their network. His reply:

> Absolutely not. You should only connect with people you know and have a reason to help. In my LinkedIn profile I have a message at the bottom that says, "Please don't reach out to connect to me unless we went to school together or worked together so that I can serve as a reference or recommend you to somebody."
>
> (Levy, 2007)

If homophily translates to the online environment, we would expect men to interact primarily with other men and to interact at the same general status level. Are women invited into connection-based networks as often as men are? Do men and women portray themselves in similar ways online? In internal company networks, do women participate in the same way that men do? In these internal networks, do cliques of individuals form based on certain social characteristics?

In addition to potential gender differences of online network activity, identity formation is an important aspect of online networks. User profiles are a means of providing an online identity. The type and number of photographs individuals put up on their profiles, the vocabulary they use, and the kind of activities and interests they list, help acquaintances and strangers form an impression of them. This ability to define oneself represents an opportunity for women, as they can control what type of image they want to promote. On business-networking sites, women can specify the type of help they want, from providing references for jobs and building a network of people in a particular business area to providing contacts for sales opportunities, if they are entrepreneurs or in sales.

In summary, networks serve a variety of functions for individuals; they can assist them in finding suitable employment and they help them gain influence once they are part of an organization, which in turn improves their chances of promotion and job success. Networks are critical for entrepreneurs at every stage of their business development, from the planning phase to the maturity phase. Perhaps most importantly, being part of informal networks fulfills a basic human need for connection and a sense of belonging.

## Mentors

The following section highlights the importance of mentors for career advancement. Networking and mentoring are connected in a variety of ways; having powerful, influential mentors increases the likelihood of an individual's being invited into influential networks. Mentors are most often senior members of an organization who provide developmental tools and career guidance to more junior members of the same organization. Mentors can also help an individual decide when to leave an existing network, how to behave in a network, how to ask network members for job-related help, and how give help to others in the network.

In business organizations, in addition to opening doors to networks, mentors provide valuable career advice, give honest feedback about individual performance, and perhaps most importantly, help their protégés understand the internal politics of an organization (Bahnuik & Hill, 1998; Pfleeger & Merz, 1995; Williams, 2004; Woolf, 2004). A mentor might advise an individual about how to deal with a difficult boss, how to secure a promotion, or how to manage a conflict with a co-worker, for example. The help a mentor can provide can be divided into two broad categories: vocational duties such as identifying and finding opportunities for the protégé in her workplace, coaching on job skills and psycho-social duties such as role modeling, providing a sense of belonging to the individual, counseling, and friendship (Offstein, Morwick, & Shah, 2007). In addition to these practical areas of advice, having a friendship link to a prominent person in an organization (perhaps a mentor) tends to boosts an individual's performance reputation (Kilduff & Krackhardt, 1994). The simple association an individual has with a powerful mentor affects the way others perceive the individual.

Mentors, protégés, and companies that organize formal mentoring programs need to understand that individuals will require different help at different points in their careers. A new, young employee in his or her first job will require orientation to the firm and assistance in meeting people, whereas older persons who have been with a firm for a longer period of time may need feedback on their performance, more visibility for the work they are doing, and opportunities to shadow or observe more-senior-level employees. Ideally, mentors should be chosen based on their leadership skills and their ability to help an individual with job-related tasks.

Mentors can be particularly helpful in large, complex organizations where there may be opportunities that are difficult for junior-level employees to see. Well-seasoned, experienced senior managers may know their way around an organization and expose individuals to opportunities they were unaware of. In addition, most organizations have become flatter – with fewer opportunities for climbing the corporate ladder and unclear promotional paths. Having a mentor in these organizations can help one gain the necessary skills and contacts so that, when an opportunity arises, the individual is ready to take it.

## Does Gender Impact Mentoring Relationships?

There is some evidence that the gender of the mentor influences the degree to which the mentor will emphasize some of the functions of mentoring, for example psychosocial support of their protégés. Psychosocial roles of a mentor include role-modeling proper behavior, providing the protégé with a feeling of belonging and acceptance, encouraging and supporting the protégé, counseling the individual through tough situations, and extending friendship. In several studies female mentors were more likely than male mentors to provide psychosocial support (Allen & Eby, 2004; Burke, 1984; Burke, McKeen, & McKenna, 1993; Gaskill, 1991). For example, both Burke and Burke et al. found that female mentors have a greater impact on career aspirations of protégés than male mentors. In one study, 637 graduates (mostly white) from a top-tier graduate MBA program were asked to identify the three most important things mentors could do for their protégés (Levesque, O'Neill, Nelson, & Duman, 2005). Championing, acceptance, and confirmation behaviors were reported as more important functions by women respondents than male respondents. All respondents ranked friendship as least important and all wanted informational support, political assistance, and protection. The authors of the study suggest that dysfunctional corporate cultures are the main reason why help in understanding and navigating the politics of the organization and protection from people who would do harm to one's reputation are important mentoring behaviors. Friendship may have been undervalued because the respondents, MBA graduates, were likely to be socially confident.

One study isolated several function of mentoring relationships to see if there was any significant difference between how women mentors versus male mentors interacted with their protégés (Fowler, Gudmundsson, & O'Gorman, 2007). In the areas of personal and emotional guidance, learning facilitation, coaching, advocacy, career-development facilitation, role modeling, strategies, and systems advice, there were a few differences in the behavior of male versus female mentors. As far as protégés were concerned, the female mentors provided both personal and emotional guidance and career development facilitation to a greater extent than male mentors did. In this study, data were collected from 147 female protégés and 125 male protégés and all four gender combinations were represented in the mentor–protégé relationships. (In all of these studies, it is important to take into account whom the researcher is asking – the protégés or the mentors. In the Allen and Eby study, the respondents were the mentors themselves, and in the Fowler et al. study, the respondents were the protégés.)

Even in e-mentoring situations, where protégés are mentored via e-mail contact with their mentors, female mentors communicate a greater amount of psychosocial support (Smith-Jentsch, Scielzo, & Weichert, 2007). The authors of this study indicate that male mentors may be reluctant to offer psychosocial support to female protégés as it may be misinterpreted as having romantic undertones. In earlier investigations of cross-gender relationships, Kram (1980, 1985) suggested that friendship, coaching, counseling, and other elements of mentoring that involve close personal contact with protégés might be linked to anxiety by mentors because of the perception of impropriety that others in the organization might read into these relationships. In 41 interviews with professionals about their comfort-level with cross-sex friendships at work, respondents indicated that they feared that their sense of humor and conversation might be interpreted as sexual harassment (Peplau & Elsesser, 2006).

There are many possible explanations for this gender difference in regard to emotional, psychological, and career support. Women seem more comfortable becoming close to their protégés without their behavior being misinterpreted as a romantic interest. In addition, women who have reached the stage in their careers where they are able to mentor someone else will most likely have worked very hard to rise to a senior-level position. They may have benefited from psychosocial support themselves or they may have wished they had had more of it. Either way, their perspective on the importance and attention to career development and psychological support will be something they pass on to others. Women may be more accustomed to providing emotional support to others and place a greater value on it than men do; in their daily lives, women provide emotional support to friends, children, spouses, and extended family.

The effect of same-sex relationships is another area of research that has captured the interest of social scientists. Reich (1985, 1986) found that women mentoring other women produced closer relationships than mixed-gender mentoring relationships. In other investigations on this topic, protégés in same-sex relationships reported greater psychosocial support than those in cross-sex relationships (Allen, Day, & Lentz, 2005). Again, as in the aforementioned situations, women and men may simply feel more comfortable with members of their own sex.

## Mentoring in Corporations

Some 60% of Fortune 1000 companies have formal mentoring programs – many of these programs grew out of a dissatisfaction that women workers and minorities voiced because of the lack of female and minorities in top jobs. Ortho Pharmaceutical Corporation, a division of Johnson & Johnson, developed a program primarily for women and minorities which focused on helping these individuals understand the informal rules of the company culture. Lynn Tyson, a minority employee, started a mentoring program at Dell Computer Corporation. She relates that in her 20 years in corporate America, she had very few role models with whom she could identify. Hilton International has a mentoring program for men and women at all levels of the organization. The Hilton program grew out of dissatisfaction with an assessment center approach that was designed to bring prospective employees who were ready for promotion to the attention of senior managers. The mentor program is a way to support employees in their career development and provide them with someone more experienced who can question them, help them to set goals, and listen to them. The president and chief executive officer of the transportation division of General Electric, Charlene Begley, started a women's network in part to stay the exodus of women at GE. Women needed support, encouragement, access to critical job assignments, and more flexibility in their work arrangements (Brady, 2003). GE also used a mentoring program for its effort to drive quality through the organization. In its Six Sigma Quality initiative, GE attempts to reduce product defects down to 3.4 out of every 1,000,000 opportunities for defects. GE assigns a seasoned project leader, with experience in quality management and leadership, to mentor 10 other employees. GE credits part of its success in improving quality with the development of other employees by these seasoned managers, called "Black Belts" by those in the organization (Offstein et al., 2007).

In 1999, women at Goldman Sachs, an investment bank in New York City, initiated a group called 85 Broads – the name refers to Goldman Sach's headquarters which is 85 Broad Street, NYC. The program is designed to mentor current women MBAs as well as undergraduates at leading business schools in the US and Europe. Over 4,800 women graduate and undergraduate business students have joined, and the global network has over 17,000 women participating. As women graduates from business schools join investment banking, they become mentors for the younger generation of students. The 85 Broads network has expanded to Singapore, Tokyo, and London, and now includes The 85 Broads Foundation, which provides economic empowerment to women around the world through its programs.

In addition to corporate programs that offer mentoring programs to women employees, young entrepreneurs can benefit greatly from having a seasoned professional advise them on many aspects of starting and growing a successful business. Among many things, a mentor may give advice on how to secure financing, how to craft an image for a company, how to write a business plan, how to negotiate with suppliers, how to market a business to consumers, and how to network with other business professionals in order to secure customers. It is important for the entrepreneur to select someone who does not view her as a competitor and someone who is willing to spend some time with her.

Mentoring arrangements can be set up in a variety of formats: some organizations may establish formal mentoring programs that individuals are either invited to join or that are open to any interested party. These formal programs attempt to match prospective mentors with protégés by looking for both personality fit and similar occupational interests. Other organizations encourage mentoring but prefer a more organic approach – allowing individuals to find mentors on their own who are suitable for them. Even some career services firms will supply, for a fee, clients with a mentor outside their organization. Some organizations, such as AT&T, have used an e-mail mentoring approach to link minority engineering students with volunteers in the industry in the hopes of boosting the number of African American and Hispanic women in math, science, and engineering. In this program, more than 2,000 mentors from 600 companies have been linked with 2,000 minority students. Similar attempts have been used to increase the number of women in high-level positions in computer science. Women in this industry have few role models both in university and in corporations at senior levels, and generally women progress in these environments at a much slower pace than men do. In a program funded by the American Association of University Women, female mentors either from university settings or from the corporate world were matched with protégés in their organizations. Successful mentoring relationships had the following characteristics: the mentor and protégé met frequently, they respected one another and communicated easily, the mentor was committed to work on whatever the protégé found most important, and the mentor provided the protégé with additional work responsibilities, challenging assignments, or visibility with key people (Pfleeger & Mertz, 1995).

Questions have been raised over whether formal, organization-sponsored mentoring networks can be as effective as informal mentoring relationships because informal mentoring is based on friendship where the mentor willingly helps the protégé while the formal mentorship often involves social pressure for mentors to participate (Chao, Walz, & Gardner, 1992; Keele, Buckner, & Bushnell, 1987). In the former work, three groups were studied: those who were formally mentored, those informally mentored, and those not mentored. Both of the mentored groups reported greater job satisfaction and socialization to their organization, but the informally mentored group had more positively ranked statements than the formally mentored group and received higher salaries. Perhaps this occurs because when individuals chose their protégés, they will put more effort into these individuals and will be more likely to help them seek highly remunerative jobs. Like the former studies, Ragins and Cotton (1999) found that informal mentoring arrangements reaped better rewards for protégés than formal, corporate-sponsored ones. Their survey of 1,162 men and women protégés found that informal mentors provided higher levels of career guidance, counseling, friendship, and facilitating interactions than mentors identified in a formal mentoring program. They also found gender differences in their study: female protégés received less coaching, role modeling, friendship, and social interaction in formal programs than informal ones, whereas male protégés reported receiving similar amounts of these benefits from both formal and informal mentoring relationships.

Ragins and Cotton (1999) also studied the outcomes of mentoring programs; men in their study benefited more in terms of improved compensation than women did. Male protégés with male mentors received the most compensation, followed by female protégés with male mentors, followed by male protégés with female mentors, and finally female protégés with female mentors. This finding suggests that both women and men are better off choosing a male mentor, most likely because men still have the most influence in organizations. Women actually earned more promotions, but did not gain as much financially as men did.

Some experts suggest that an ideal mentor would be someone whose management style is different from the protégé's and someone who is two levels above the individual in the organization. If the mentor is two levels above the protégé, he or she will have more power and influence and therefore be more likely to help the protégé gain visibility and secure challenging job assignments.

## Mentoring Minorities

A limited amount of research has been conducted on the effectiveness of mentoring minorities. Although more needs to be done, one aspect of this research deals with the effectiveness of cross-race development relationships (Kaplan, 1994). Questions arise as to the benefit of pairing protégés with persons of their own racial group, or ignoring racial and gender categories in the matching process. If a protégé is matched with someone of the same race and gender, then she will be able to more easily discuss issues that are unique to women and unique to the racial group to which she belongs (Bell & Nkomo, 2001). On the other hand, some experts suggest that in order for minorities to get ahead, they need to be mentored by whoever is influential in the organization – this often means white males (Ragins & Cotton, 1999). In a survey polling 565 respondents, protégés from a federal agency reported that the assignment process and the frequency of meetings were more important to their satisfaction with the mentor–protégé relationship than pairing them with someone of the same race or gender (Lyons & Oppler, 2004).

To understand the different career trajectories of minorities and whites in organizations, David Thomas studied the progression of racial minorities at three large US corporations. He found that whites are often identified as on "the fast track" early in their careers, whereas high-potential minorities take off more slowly, only after they have reached middle management. Minorities who advanced the furthest had a strong network of mentors and corporate sponsors, whereas those who plateaued in middle management received only mentoring that focused on coaching on job-related skills. By contrast, minorities that reached senior management had more encompassing relationships with mentors, where mentors were more interested in developing them over the long term. In his study of 22 cross-race mentoring relationships, Thomas highlights the difficulties of talking about race at work. Most of the cross-cultural relationships (14 of the pairs) used what Thomas called "denial or suppression" of racial subjects. Neither party discussed race, or if they did so, did so very superficially. The other eight pairs did discuss race openly. Pairs that did discuss race openly were closer in age than pairs that did not. In many of the pairs that did not discuss race, the protégé, if African American, found other outlets for discussing race (Thomas, 2001). African Americans may want to have someone of their own race as a mentor; someone who understands the struggle of being a minority in a predominately white culture. However, given the shortage of African Americans in senior management (especially African American women) this is difficult. Thomas found that corporations fail to achieve a racial mix at the top of the organization because either they have a revolving door for talented minorities in which the best and brightest are recruited in and then leave out of frustration, or racial minorities are stuck in the middle of management unable to move up.

## Mentoring and the Generation Gap

Some research points to the problem of older businesswomen mentoring younger ones; it seems that some younger women do not value, appreciate, or recognize the sacrifices older women made for their careers. Giving up or postponing marriage and children for one's career is not something younger women admire in their older counterparts, and this may cause tension in the relationship between younger and older women (McDonald, 2003). A study by Simmons College and the Committee of 200, an association of female entrepreneurs, found that today's teenagers hold a negative view of women in business suits – many believing that these businesswomen have given up their identity. On the other hand, older women may bristle at the notion that younger women expect to climb the corporate ladder quickly without being willing to pay the price that older women paid. Some women may feel overwhelmed with being asked to mentor many up-and-coming younger women – in organizations where there are few senior-level women, they may be called upon too frequently to help other women. It is important for organizations to encourage communication among older employees and younger employees for the simple reason that older employees will soon be retiring in large numbers (the baby boom generation born between 1946 and 1964) and their institutional knowledge and wisdom needs to be tapped and passed along to the next generation of employees.

## One Mentor or Many? External or Internal?

As companies become more complex, and as people change jobs and even careers more frequently, there is wisdom in garnering more than one mentor. The idea of a network of relationships rather than one relationship is likely to be more beneficial to an individual's career (Dahle, 2004). One mentor might provide psychological support, another may be a great skills coach, and still another may provide access to resources and visible job assignments. Having influential contacts outside of one's work organization is equally important. Many people build a trusting relationship with a mentor in the workplace only to find that the individual moves on to another company in another place. It is possible to outgrow one's mentor – the person who was most valuable to an individual as a young manager will not be the same individual who can help him or her when they reach middle or senior management. Lublin (2004) cautions that, should a woman become identified too much with one individual, colleagues will begin to view her as unable to think for herself. Later in a woman's career, it is important for her to declare independence from the influence of mentors to ensure colleagues and senior managers know that she can make decisions independently. The issue of whether mentors are more useful to protégés if they are in the same organization or in another organization has been studied by some social scientists. Baugh and Fagenson-Eland (2005) examined the responses from employees in two technology organizations to find out whether they valued mentors in their own organization or mentors from a different employment setting. Protégés whose mentors worked in the same employment setting as themselves reported more career and psychosocial support than protégés whose mentors worked in a different setting. Although this study identified internal mentors as more valuable to protégés, it is useful to secure internal and external mentors – mentors who works in the same organizations will understand the culture of their protégés' organizations and will be able to guide them, while mentors who works in different employment settings will be able to provide fresh perspectives and will help broaden the protégés' contacts.

Women are more likely than men to leave the workforce for a time to raise children. Having mentors (and a large network) cannot only help women become reemployed, but can help them when they reenter the same organization after a leave of absence. A mentor can check in with a woman during her maternity leave to keep her apprised of what is going on in the organization in her absence, and can help her adjust once she returns to work.

## Mentoring at a Distance

With cheaper and more sophisticated telecommunications options, establishing a long-distance mentoring relationship, or one that is local but is based on e-mail communication, is possible (de Janasz, Sullivan, & Whiting, 2003; Headlam-Wells, 2004). Although working at a distance prevents a mentor from observing someone at work, he or she can provide advice on workplace situations and career strategy either by telephone or by e-mail. In some ways, this type of relationship is ideal once the two individuals know each other well. Both parties can communicate asynchronously (not at the exact same time), which saves people time and is often more convenient than meeting face-to-face. It is very possible that protégés will have more contact in mentoring relationships that involve e-mail, rather than face-to-face communication, simply because of the ease at which parties can communicate with one another; no one need travel or spend time meeting. Via the Internet, mentors can provide short, specific feedback, when it is convenient for them to do so, on problems that the protégé may be encountering. MentorNet, an e-mentoring program in Canada using volunteer mentors who have professional experience, is a multi-institutional, large-scale mentoring effort to mentor women students in engineering, science, math, and technology. In an evaluation of the program, 80% of students said they would recommend the program to others. They reported that they benefited from improved levels of self-confidence, enhanced knowledge about their field, and knowledge about workplace skills (Single, Muller, Cunningham, & Carlsen, 2004).

## Benefits for Mentors and Organizations

The benefits to protégés are obvious but what about the benefits for mentors? Mentors may benefit in the following ways:

- Giving something back to others is fulfilling and enjoyable.
- Mentors learn a great deal about their own management and coaching style by helping another individual.
- Others (especially older employees) may exchange learning with their protégé who may have more current skills in some areas than they do (technology, for example).
- Mentors may receive recognition by their organizations for their efforts.

Organizations benefit in the following ways:

- Mentoring offers a complementary means of providing learning and development to employees.
- Since corporate mentoring programs use volunteers, mentoring has substantial cost advantages associated with it.
- Invaluable institutional knowledge is passed along through mentoring. Typically this knowledge is not written down anywhere, nor is it included in any corporate training program.
- Mentoring and sharing information among employees provides a sense of continuity for individuals in the organization.

The following two case studies explore issues in networking and mentoring. The first features a situation in which a salesperson struggles with if and how to use a potential network to grow her financial advising business, and the second deals with how best to mentor an African American woman.

# CASE STUDIES

### Case Study 1: Networking in a Sales Organization

Shemane Green had recently accepted a new position as a financial advisor for an investment company. She would be earning a modest salary, plus commission on any financial products that she was able to sell. Shemane had previously worked for the same financial services organization in the corporate strategy department; now she was eager to work on the sales side of the business because she liked interacting with people and truly believed that if people would plan for financial events such as retirement or funding a child's education and invest, they would be much better off. She had thought long and hard about the decision to move from the security of a home office position to the less secure, but potentially more rewarding, sales position.

During her first several months on the job, she had been through an orientation program to learn how the company's products worked and to practice selling skills. She had passed all the required tests to sell insurance and financial products. She was now ready to have her weekly meeting with her sales manager, Charlie Finch, to discuss her sales strategy. Charlie was a terrific sales person and a tireless manager. He had 17 years in the business, was recognized each year as a top earner, and was proud to have helped so many "rookies" launch their careers.

### *Meeting with Charlie*

"Good to see you Shemane. How's it going?"

Charlie's easy-going manner made Shemane feel immediately comfortable.

"Can't complain. I passed all the tests and I am ready to begin really digging into this business."

"Great. OK. Last time we met, I asked you to brainstorm a list of everyone close to you, without thinking of whether or not they needed our services. This is your immediate network. They can help you reach others who you don't know, but who could use our help. The best way to find clients is through other people because they are more apt to trust you if you are recommended by someone close to them. So let's see your list," Charlie said.

"Well, I did come up with several people. Clay, my husband, is a minister and obviously he is well connected to his congregation and so am I for that matter. Then there is Cora who is a very good friend. However, she is retired and I don't know who she is really connected to. Crystal Riley is someone I worked with over a few years on a board. We are very close too. She is connected to other mothers in the school where our kids attend. So those are my closest contacts."

"Anyone at the head office?"

"Most of my friends there are women. We go to lunch every so often. I suppose I could find out more about their networks, but I really don't think they are that well connected to people in high places. We all know each other. And I think they would refer me to people I have already asked for business."

"Let's start with your husband. This seems like a really great opportunity. He has the respect of the congregation, he is seen as a leader, and a good citizen, I am sure. He would be seen as trustworthy, which is important in our business. How many people are in the congregation?"

"We have about 200 active members and 350 members total."

"Wow. Fantastic! You have a great resource right at your finger tips. Could you ask him to sponsor a seminar at the church where you could discuss the importance of financial decisions at various stages of one's life – planning for marriage, retirement, funding college educations, and the like? It would be great service to the congregation and I would be happy to be there and to introduce you. We have a standard presentation you could give with 20 or 30 PowerPoint slides. And we don't try to sell anything during the presentation. It is just informational and it gets people thinking about their finances, but it will lead to business, I am sure."

"I don't know, Charlie. I'll have to ask Clay what he thinks. It makes me a little uncomfortable. It seems I am using his position."

"I know you believe in the company and our products. This is a service that really can help people. If people can save early in their careers, they won't have to worry as they age and they will be able to do the things they enjoy. The way everyone sells is through networks. There is nothing unethical about it."

"I know. . . . I just feel that mixing it with the church seems a bit pushy."

"Do you feel that helping people save money and invest is pushy? Think about how much better off people can be if they begin saving money while they are young."

"I know all that. It's just that we've never done anything like this in our church. We have sponsored charities for talks, but not a business organization."

"Do you feel confident in our products and services?"

"OK, Charlie. I'll talk to Clay tonight and we'll see how he reacts to it."

"Good. Check in with me tomorrow and we can discuss it further."

### Conversation with Clay

Clay typically arrives home about 7 p.m. In addition to preaching on Sunday, he counsels many in the congregation who need support in one way or another. His week might be comprised of helping a married couple adjust, listening to a widower who recently lost his spouse, or running a youth group. The congregation had steadily grown under Clay's leadership largely due to his vision and his energetic and engaging personality.

That evening, over a glass of wine and before dinner, Shemane decided to broach the subject of an investment seminar with Clay.

"Honey. What would you think if I did a little seminar at the church to introduce myself to people who could begin investing? It wouldn't be a sales pitch, but just a seminar on the basics of tax planning and investing. People would be under no obligation to do anything, or even attend for that matter. You told me yourself that one of the major things that breaks up marriages is arguments over how to spend money. Getting couples to talk about money and investing and saving would be helpful."

"That's true, but I wouldn't feel comfortable having my wife even be *perceived* to be selling to the congregation. It's not right, even if it would help people. It puts me in an awkward position. People might feel obligated to work with you because of me."

"Hmm. OK, but I am struggling to tap into a network of people who would trust me and work with me. I can't see anyone doing business with me from a yellow pages ad or from a cold call, can you?"

"Well, no. But you'll just have to find another way. Can't the company help with names? You know, refer you to some people?"

"We are given a list of names to contact, but the way to really grow your business is through personal connections. We do know a lot of people through the church."

"Think about how bad you would feel if the investments you sold to someone didn't do well and you had to see them every Sunday in church. I know I wouldn't like it."

"But the company doesn't invest in high-risk securities. We have a good track record among investment firms. People certainly do better investing with us than saving with a bank or not saving at all."

"Shemane, I'm not comfortable with it."

As if to signal the end of the conversation, Clay got up from the couch and headed for the dining room table.

### Meeting With Charlie the Following Day

"So how did the discussion go with Clay?"

"Not very well. He is opposed to the idea. He feels that it would compromise his position. I did try to explain that we wouldn't be selling anything. He was pretty adamantly against it."

"Well, how would you feel about simply calling people you know in the congregation? They know you and I assume that you have a list of members with their phone numbers. You wouldn't have to involve Clay at all."

"That's true. Clay wouldn't have to be involved at all."

"Or you could follow up on some of the work contacts you have."

"The work contacts I have don't seem to have a lot of connections to people with a lot of influence, and I don't have that many. I want to find some contacts that can put me in touch with lots of other people who are in a position to invest. The two work colleagues who I know the best are single. One is divorced and the other never married."

"Well, think about calling your friends at the church. We can work on a script. Something about your changing careers and that you are eager to work with people like themselves. All you want is a commitment from people to meet with you. Once they see what you have to offer and how hard you work, they will work with you."

"OK, I'll think about it."

### Discussion Questions

1. Do you think it is unethical for Shemane to use the congregation phone list?
2. Should Shemane call members of the congregation without her husband's permission? Why, or why not?
3. How do Shemane's other potential contacts mirror the research about women and networks in this chapter?

## Other Activities

1.  Create a diagram of your own network. (You may have several different networks that do not intersect.) Analyze it in the following ways.

    - How many instrumental versus expressive ties does it contain?
    - How diverse is it in terms of race, ethnic group, sex, and age?
    - How many structural holes does it have?
    - Identify any gatekeepers, boundary spanners, bridges, and connectors.
    - How useful is your network to you?

2.  Looking at your network from Activity 1, think about ways in which you could broaden or improve your existing network. What activities could you add, clubs could you join, people could you meet, and so on?
3.  Compare your network with another student in class. How is your network the same? Different?
4.  Examine your online networks. If you are on Facebook, what proportion of your "friends" are male? Female?

## Case Study 2: Mentoring at Maidstone Corporation

Malcolm Fitzgerald, CEO of Maidstone Corporation, was known as a man of principles with a reputation for treating all employees with dignity and respect. He valued the contribution of women and felt frustrated that some of his key managers seemed hesitant to promote them. He had looked at his company data and scratched his head. While 70% of middle-management jobs were held by men and 85% of senior-level management jobs were held by men, the majority of lower-paid jobs were held by women. Of the 30% of middle-management jobs held by women, minority women had only 10% of them. Of the 15% of women at the top, only 3% of them were minority women. The organization was bringing in highly qualified women but they were consistently side-tracked, rarely making it beyond the middle-management level unless they came into the organization from the outside.

Maidstone provides commercial real estate and office design services to companies in the south-east. The firm offers market analyses, finds suitable properties for its clients, and manages properties. It has 1,200 employees who work across the southern United States, especially in growing urban areas such as Atlanta, Birmingham, Raleigh, Charlotte, Nash-ville, Jacksonville, and Miami. The Head Office is in Atlanta, Georgia.

Perhaps Fitzgerald's sensitivity to women's issues was influenced by his 30-year-old daughter who worked for a large corporation in Washington, DC. She often shared with her father her frustrations about being held back in a male-dominated organization. She felt that she should have been given more opportunities and should have progressed farther than she had in her four years with the company. She had invested in her education, having received an MBA, but was still stuck in middle management.

Although he hadn't directly heard complaints from women in his own company, he decided they were unlikely to complain to him. He knew that commercial real estate had historically been a male domain, but he also knew that women did very well in it. They had shown themselves to have the skills to interact with builders, architects, and developers, and close deals, and they were very good at follow-through. The dearth of women in senior-level jobs bothered him a great deal. The company was not using talent that he believed was buried somewhere in the middle. Malcolm decided to do something about the situation. He considered that the best way to go about it was to establish a mentoring program to help women gain the advantage he could see men in the organization already had. He wanted the program to address several specific issues: giving women an inside track to jobs that might come up, providing them with coaching from someone who is successful in the organization, and offering advice and support when they encountered organizational obstacles.

Malcolm instructed his human resources department to put together a process for choosing mentors and protégés, and a process for training the mentors who were chosen so that they would know what type of support to give their protégées. He decided that, as the head of the company, he would announce and endorse the program himself.

### The Mentoring Program

In his conversations with potential mentors, Malcolm described the importance of the program in this way:

"Our competitive advantage as a company rests on the talents and creativity of all of our people, men and women alike. This program will give our many talented women the chance to excel and strengthen the company. We want to provide them with the same type of experiences and networks afforded to men and we think that one way in which we can do this is by pairing them up with a successful senior manager who will provide them with career advice, access to key people and projects and other opportunities. I feel strongly that we make this program a success and my hope is that you will join me in this effort and consider volunteering as a mentor. The human resources department will be spearheading the effort. In a few weeks they will be asking for volunteers. You will receive training and every effort will be made to pair you up with someone who can really benefit from your expertise."

The human resource department began collecting applications from women interested in being matched with a mentor. The application asked for details about the woman's career history, her career aspirations, her perceptions of her strengths and weaknesses, current performance appraisals from immediate supervisors, and areas she was interested in working on with a mentor (see Appendix 6.1). Women were given two weeks to turn in their completed application before they were notified about whom their mentor would be.

When the two weeks passed, 20 women had signed up to be mentored, while 10 senior-level managers volunteered to be mentors. Malcolm Fitzgerald was somewhat disappointed in the number of senior managers willing to help; on the other hand, he knew that his senior-level people were very busy and he thought that, if the program was a success, more mentors would follow.

The human resources department now had the task of eliminating 10 of the candidates. Fitzgerald intended to call the first group a "pilot group" and announce that, once this first cohort got off the ground, other mentoring groups would follow. He did not want to discourage those women who were not chosen, but he knew that he could not overstretch his senior managers by insisting they work with too many women. In making their selection, the human resources department decided that they would place the largest emphasis on the supervisor performance appraisal and on each woman's stated reasons for wanting help.

### Julianna Roberts' Application

Julianna Roberts was one of the few African American managers at Maidstone. Although three of her staff were black, none of her fellow managers were African American females. She had been with the company for eight years in a variety of roles, from customer-service coordinator and customer-data coordinator to her current position as customer-support manager. In her role, she set policies for dealing with customer complaints and supervised a staff of 10. She held a BA in Business Administration from the University of Georgia.

In her application, Julianna documented her career history, focusing on her strengths – her organizational skills, her ability to deal with people, and her competence with data analysis. She emphasized her deep knowledge of Maidstone's customers, having tracked their concerns for eight years. Under the section on career aspirations, Julianna wrote that she wanted eventually to move into the marketing department. She believed that her knowledge of the customer and her data-analysis skills would be an asset to the marketing department. She would be happy to make a lateral move, but would not consider a position that paid less than what she was making now. In the section entitled "Areas You Wish To Work On With Your Mentor," Julianna wrote the following:

I'd like to understand the various elements of how our company does market research since I believe my customer data analysis experience fits in well with this area. Eventually I would like to understand all areas of marketing.

I would also like to supervise a group of employees in another area of the company.

I think I need to work on forming more relationships with senior managers – I have worked very well with my peers and people reporting to me but I have had few opportunities to work with senior managers. I'd like to understand more of the big picture.

As an African American female I feel isolated. I'd like to be able to discuss what it is like to be a black female in this company with someone I can trust. There are very few African Americans at Maidstone and most of them are men. I think we communicate differently than white people and we have some different issues.

I am thinking about starting a master's program in business administration or in marketing research and I would like some advice on institutions that might be a good fit for me and how to balance further education with my job.

### Choosing a Mentor for Julianna

The human resources department examined the applications from mentors and chose two who could work well with Julianna. The department felt strongly that individuals should not be allowed to choose who they worked with; individuals might choose someone simply because they know him or her rather than choosing someone who could be most beneficial to them. It also might cause some bad feelings among some mentors or protégés who were not chosen. The program did not want to start off by making volunteers feel uncomfortable.

The two potential mentors are described below:

Tom Watson, a 38-year-old white male, has been with Maidstone for 15 years in a variety of middle- and senior-level jobs. After finishing his Bachelor's of Science at Emory University, he started out in the customer service area of Maidstone as a customer-data analyst. Since then he has held positions as marketing coordinator, manager of human resources, marketing communications specialist, marketing manager and is currently Vice President of Marketing. He is a well-respected and very visible member of the senior management group, having served on several company-wide task forces.

In his application, under the section about why he wants to be a mentor, he wrote:

It's time for me to give something back. I've been lucky enough to have a great career with Maidstone and I'd like to help an up-and-coming individual. We have a lot of young talent in this company that has yet to be fully utilized and people in my age group and older need to think about who will be running the organization in another 10 years. I've got plenty invested in this firm (both financially and otherwise) and I want the firm to be well-run after I leave. I also find the energy and perspective of some of our younger employees refreshing. With a little help I think that their ideas can be brought to the foreground.

Delores Campbell is a 45-year-old African American with an MBA. She came to Maidstone Corporation four years ago, from a competitor. She was recruited as an information-technology director, and she was recently promoted to Vice President of Information Technology. In her application, she wrote:

I have a particular interest in helping women advance. It hasn't been easy for me as an African American woman in an almost entirely white workplace. I am interested in helping another African American woman succeed. Four years ago I remember how daunting it was for me starting out here without having any contacts. Our women need a little extra attention so that they can be heard and I think I can help here. I am not sure what I can offer someone who isn't in my functional area in terms of skill development – my emphasis has always been informational technology – but I do think I can help any women understand how this organization works.

The problem HR faced, was who – Tom or Delores – would be the best mentor for Julianna?

**Appendix 6.1: Application for Protégé**

| | |
|---|---|
| **Name** | *Julianna Roberts* |
| **Current Position** | *Customer Support Manager* |
| **Department** | *Customer Relations* |

1.  Please describe your career with Maidstone (The jobs you have held and your various responsibilities). In addition describe any jobs you have held outside the company. (You may attach a resume)

    *1999—2002   Customer Service Coordinator*

    *Analyzed customer service records to track the type of complaints and the timeframes taken to resolve them. Produced quarterly reports for management. Worked with sales teams to find out what type of issues their customers have and the difficulties salespeople have with head office procedures that interfere with good customer service.*

    *2002-2004   Customer Data Supervisor*

    *Managed a team of five administrators whose responsibilities were to compile data on customer interactions and analyze the data for trends. Made recommendations to senior management on necessary organizational changes to improve customer service and track customer interactions.*

    *2004-present   Customer Support Manager*

    *Conduct qualitative focus group research with current customers (primarily developers) to find out their future needs and suggest potential new services for them. Travel to sites to oversee installations of design services to ensure customer service. Manage four customer service coordinators.*

2.  Describe your educational achievement. In addition to degrees earned, include any certificates or continuing education credits earned.

    *BA University of Georgia – Business Administration, Minor in Psychology*

    *With the company I have taken the following courses: Effective Performance Management, Managing People, and I have had some specialized software training from our vendors.*

3.   What career objectives do you have in the next several years?

> I aspire to a senior level job in marketing. I want to use my creative skills, "people" skills, and analysis skill in the role that I have. I also want to go back at some point to University and do a weekend MBA program. I think having an MBA would help me gain additional skills that could be beneficial in any number of management roles at Maidstone.

4.   Why do you want to have a mentor? What would you specifically like to work on?

> I'd like to understand the various elements of how our company does market research since I believe my customer data analysis experience fits in well with this area. Eventually I would like to understand all areas of marketing.

> I would also like to supervise a group of employees in another area of the company.

> I think I need to work on forming more relationships with senior managers - I have worked very well with my peers and people reporting to me but I have had few opportunities to work with senior managers. I'd like to understand more of the big picture.

> As an African American female I feel isolated. I'd like to be able to discuss what it is like to be a black female in this company with someone I can trust. There are very few African Americans at Maidstone and most of them are men. I think we communicate differently than white people and we have some different issues that are easier for other African American women to understand.

> I am thinking about starting a master's program in business administration or in marketing research and I would like some advice on institutions that might be a good fit for me and how to balance further education with my job.

**Appendix 6.2: Application for Mentor**

| | |
|---|---|
| **Name** | Tom Watson |
| **Current Position** | Vice President |
| **Department** | Marketing |

1.  Describe your career history both with Maidstone and with other organizations. (You may attach a resume)

> I started out as a graduate trainee after finishing my degree at Emory. As such, I worked in many areas of the company for two years before I decided on marketing. My first position there was as marketing manager, then Director of Marketing and most recently for the last two years, Vice President of Marketing.
>
> These jobs have involved all aspects of marketing, from planning to execution, to working with our sales force.

2.  Describe your educational achievements. (Degrees, certificates, honors, etc.)

> BS Business Administration – Emory University
>
> I have also taken many of the firm's leadership training courses throughout the years and most recently our Executive Leadership program.

3.  Why do you want to be a mentor?

> It's time for me to give something back. I've been lucky enough to have a great career with Maidstone and I'd like to help an up-and-coming individual. We have a lot of young talent in this company that has yet to be fully utilized and people in my age group and older need to think about who will be running the organization in another 10 years. I've got plenty invested in this firm (both financially and otherwise) and I want the firm to be well-run after I leave. I also find the energy and perspective of some of our younger employees refreshing. With a little help I think that their ideas can be brought to the foreground.

**Appendix 6.3: Application for Mentor**

| | |
|---|---|
| **Name** | *Delores Campbell* |
| **Current Position** | *Director* |
| **Department** | *Information Technology* |

1. Describe your career history both with Maidstone and with other organizations. (You may attach a resume)

   *After finishing my undergrad. degree, I joined Alliance Incorporated, a consulting firm focused on large commercial real estate deals, as an Information Technology Officer. I assisted in an I.T. initiative that involved 5,000 head office employees converting to a new system. From there, I took a leave from work and pursued my MBA. After finishing that, I returned to Alliance as Senior Consultant of I.T. I was recruited to Maidstone as Director of Information Technology and was soon promoted to Vice President of I.T., six months after joining the company.*

2. Describe your educational achievements. (Degrees, certificates, honors, etc.)

   *B.A. University of North Carolina (Chapel Hill)*
   *M.B.A. Fuqua Business School*
   *Executive Leadership Program – Maidstone*
   *Various I.T. conferences across the United States*

3. Why do you want to be a mentor?

   *I have a particular interest in helping women advance. It hasn't been easy for me as an African American woman in an almost entirely white workplace. I am interested in helping another African American woman succeed. Four years ago I remember how daunting it was for me starting out here without having any contacts. Our women need a little extra attention so that they can be heard and I think I can help here. I am not sure what I can offer someone who isn't in my functional area in terms of skill development – my emphasis has always been informational technology – but I do think I can help any women understand how this organization works.*

## Further Reading

de Janasz, S.C., Sullivan, S., & Whiting, V. (2006). Mentor networks and career success: Lessons for turbulent times. In *Contemporary Issues in Leadership*, Westview Press.

McPherson, M., Smith-Lovin, L., & Cook, J. (2001). Birds of a feather: Homophily in social networks. *Annual Review of Sociology*, 27, 415–444.

Ragins, B.R. (1997). Diversified mentoring relationships in organizations: A power perspective. *Academy of Management Review*, *22*(2), 482–521.

Thomas, D. (2001). The truth about mentoring minorities: Race matters. *Harvard Business Review*, *79*(4), April, 98–107.

Uzzi, B. & Dunlap, S. (2005). How to build your network. *Harvard Business Review*, April, 1–9.

## Discussion Questions

1. Why would Tom Watson make a good mentor for Julianna?
2. Why would Delores Campbell make a good mentor for her?
3. If you had to choose between the two, whom would you choose?
4. In your opinion, what else could Malcolm Fitzgerald do to help women advance?
5. Read the following article: Hill, S. & Gant, G. (2000). Mentoring by minorities for minorities: The organizational communication support program. *Review of Business, 21*, 53–57.

In this article, compare the approach taken by Dow Corning and Dow Chemical to that of Maidstone Corporation. What advantages and disadvantages does an employee-driven process have?

# 7  Gender and Communication

**Learning Objectives**

After completing this chapter, the reader will:

* understand the differences in communication styles between men and women and how these differences may result in bias.
* understand how men's and women's leadership styles vary.
* appreciate the importance of non-verbal communication.
* understand how men and women use electronic communication.

Once individuals become managers, they have typically proven to be competent in the technical aspects of their chosen field. What distinguishes them from average performers and helps them move up is often described as their "interpersonal skills" or their "people skills." Both of these seemingly vague descriptions have to do with how people communicate, and how they are perceived to communicate. Individuals' poor interpersonal skills and the inability to form strong working relationships often derail them, even after they become executives. In short, their inability to communicate well and to navigate organizational politics catches up with them. For women, communication skills are particularly critical; once a woman becomes a manager and begins to move up the corporate ladder, her interpersonal skills will be closely observed. Can she adapt her style and conduct to different types of people? Can she manage conflict without alienating people? In the many seemingly gender-neutral descriptions of what it takes to reach the highest levels of management, often little, if any, thought is given to whether or not men and women communicate differently, whether having different motivations influences their communication style, whether the corporate environment favors a "man's" style of communicating versus a "woman's" style of communicating, and whether or not women leaders are held to a different standard when their communication skills are assessed. This chapter introduces each of these ideas, beginning with the controversy about whether men's and women's styles differ.

## Male Versus Female Communication Styles

Many social scientists have identified differences between male and female communication. Generally, they have attributed these differences to either socialization or as simply a reflection of the power differential between men and women. Those who subscribe to the former theory believe that these differences begin in childhood through the socialization process (Gilligan, 1982; Maltz & Borker, 1982; Schaef, 1985; Tannen,

1990). Boys grow up being encouraged to compete with one another, whereas girls are expected to be accommodating and non-assertive. Girls often play in pairs and interact through language, while boys play competitive games and interact through physical activity. Often the games that boys play have a definite winner and loser; the games girls play are often scenario based – such as playing school, playing house, or pretending to be a doctor or patient. When boys do play in pairs, there is often some type of technology separating each participant. Consider how boys play Nintendo, PlayStation, or Wii video games, for example.

All of these researchers note that early socialization processes affect how men and women employ communication later in life. Women frequently communicate to establish connection and intimacy, while men use communication to establish dominance, independence, status, and control over their environment (Tannen, 1990). Since the early 1990s, Tannen (1990, 1994, 1995) has analyzed the speech patterns of men and women at work and found several differences. Her studies of language-use revealed that women used qualifiers and hedges more frequently than men. Words and phrases such as "perhaps" and "maybe we should" can make women appear unsure of themselves. The women in Tannen's studies sometimes used upward inflection when making statements. This made them appear to be asking a question or seeking confirmation for what they were saying. To those listening, the overall impression they made was that they lacked confidence. In an effort to show support for others' views, Tannen noted that women often nodded to show agreement or acceptance of someone else's idea. In contrast, she reported that men often talk to exhibit knowledge, to establish their status in the group, or to give advice to others. Men more frequently played the "devil's advocate" simply to display dominance, even when they did not disagree with an idea. They typically held the floor longer than women did.

Some scholars point out that those who subscribe to the differences in male versus female communication overplay their significance. Aries (1996) contends that the differences between men's and women's communication styles are small and that both men and women display masculine and feminine styles of interaction. She indicates that communication style depends on many factors including status, role, and gender identity. The way in which men and women interact is highly dependent on the situation and their reasons for interacting.

Whether the differences are small or large, men's and women's communication styles reveal very little about their actual job competence, leadership capability, or effectiveness as managers. These different styles, however, create *perceptions* about ability and competence. For example, when a woman uses qualifiers she may seem unsure of herself or ill-informed. Qualifiers, when used by women, have a detrimental effect, but they do not have a negative effect when men employ them. When women qualify their statements, they are considered by others to be less intelligent and to have less knowledge, yet this is not the case when men use them (Cleveland et al., 2000). Frequently agreeing with others may make a woman appear to acquiesce to another's view rather than show support of it. She may simply be encouraging someone to continue talking, yet she can seem to be too compliant. To others, especially men, it may look as if she has no ideas or opinions of her own. These differences in communication are not problematic unless individuals find one style more effective than another. Since males dominate senior positions in organizations, their communication style is often associated with leadership, competence, and management – while traditionally a woman's style has not been viewed in this light.

## Men's Versus Women's Leadership Styles

There is evidence that women and men adopt different leadership styles, at least in part because they communicate differently; women tend to use a more democratic decision-making style and manage by communicating a vision, values, and a purpose for the work (Bass & Avolio, 1994; Bass & Riggio, 2006; Eagly et al., 2000). They try to instill a sense of pride in the work. Women spend more time on motivating employees and forming relationships with their direct reports. This style of leadership has been referred to as *transformational*. All of the above-mentioned behaviors require strong interpersonal communication skills. Men, on the other hand, adopt a more authoritative, autocratic style of leadership and focus on task accomplishment. They use contingent rewards by offering money or other perks for completing objectives. This style of leadership has been referred to as *transactional* (Eagly & Johnson, 1990). If women are more often transformational leaders, it is easy to imagine the way in which they will communicate. To build relationships they will communicate one-to-one with their direct reports and verbalize their support. They will often revisit the goals of the organization and how their team contributes to them. To encourage participation they will ask more questions, solicit feedback, and use words that suggest inclusiveness, such as "we" rather than "I." Male leaders are apt to communicate differently based on their preference for a transactional style. A meta-analysis of 29 studies in the medical field indicated that female primary-care physicians engage in more patient-centered communication, ask more questions, and seek a more active partnership with their patients. They provide more counseling and have slightly longer visits with patients than do their male counterparts (Roter, Hall, & Yukata, 2002). In the business arena, the perception of women's communication style is one explanation for the lack of women CEOs; women's tendency to weigh feelings and the impact on people when making decisions may be taken for weakness (Oakley, 2000).

In spite of the differences in style between men and women, there is little evidence to suggest that one sex or the other is more effective leading.

## The Use of Language – Talking Time and Interruptions

Some social scientists subscribe to the theory that differences in power or hierarchical relations between men and women are reflected in the ways in which men and women use language (Lakoff, 1990; O'Barr & Atkins, 1980). Men assert their dominance in several ways: by interrupting others to change the topic or to disagree with the speaker and by talking more than women. Interruptions have been studied by many social scientists interested in gender dynamics and speech. West and Zimmerman (1975, 1983) analyzed cross-sex conversations and interruptions, finding that out of 48 interruptions, 46 were perpetrated by men. Some scholars differentiate affiliative interruption, or interruption that is intended to support, and disaffiliative interruption, interruption intended to disempower or make an individual appear weak (Goldberg, 1990; Makri-Tsilipakou, 1994). For example, women may overlap someone else's speech in an attempt to agree with or add to an idea of the speaker. Makri-Tsilipakou (1994) identifies three types of affiliative interruptions: 1. minimal responses such as "yeah" and "a-huh" that show the speaker that the listener is in agreement; 2. finishing an individual's sentences or saying the same thing at the same time; 3. supportive reformulations of an idea that overlap with the speaker's words. Disaffiliative interruptions include criticisms, attacks, insults, and changing the subject. In one study with 2,846 interruptions, men interrupted almost twice as often as women with disaffiliative interruptions, while women interrupted almost twice as often as men with affiliative interruptions (Makri-Tsilipakou, 1994). In the same study, when women did use disaffiliative interruptions, they were more apt to be interrupting men rather than women (about 3 to 1). When men used disaffiliative interruptions, they were more apt to interrupt women than men (about 2.5 to 1). In a meta-analysis of 43 studies comparing adult women's and men's interruptions, men were found to use intrusive interruption more often than women to gain dominance of the conversation. This effect was largest when groups of three or more were observed (Andersen & Leaper, 1998). From a gender and power perspective, when women are interrupted by men in a disaffiliative manner, they can appear incompetent or weak – even when the criticism lodged or comment made is unjustified.

Women's verbal performance often leads to them being labeled as followers rather than leaders. By not interrupting high-status individuals, by interrupting others to show their interest, by allowing higher-status individuals to talk more than they do, and by generally being agreeable, women may appear to be too weak to lead. The way speakers question others can be an indication of their status. Males often question in an interrogating manner while females may question to clarify their understanding of something. Additionally, women may add a question at the end of their talk to seek support. Questions such as, "Don't you agree?" or "What do you think?" may make women appear weak and lacking in confidence. Women try to keep a conversation going by obeying the rules of polite conversation, while men interrupt to show their dominance (Fishman, 1978; Kollack, Blumstein, & Schwartz, 1985; Tannen, 1990).

In addition to the study of interruptions, talking time is an area of interest to social scientists who study communication. In Cashdan's (1998) study of student behavior, total talking time was the most consistent indicator of high power, both in men and women, but an even greater marker of status in men (p. 219). Other researchers have noted that women often speak in short bursts, rather than in sustained amounts (Tannen, 1990). Likewise, men have been found to talk more than women when in mixed-sex conversations (Crawford, 1995; Easton, 1994; James & Drakich, 1993). Hannah and Murachver (1999) make the point that in a dyad (two-person communication) the style of communication of the participants influences the talking time. Partners interacting with participants who use frequent minimal responses will speak more than partners interacting with partners who use infrequent minimal responses, regardless of gender. They did, however, find that, over time, men and women in mixed conversations reverted to stereotypical behavior (e.g., men interrupting women more than women interrupting men, and men talking more). This research suggests that, regardless of gender, the initial behavior of a person in a conversation influences the responses of the other party. However, typical gender patterns persist over time: men talk more without interruption and women talk less. Moreover, women increase their use of minimal responses and ask more questions.

There is undoubtedly a relationship between sustained talk and interruption. If women are interrupted more often, it may be hard for them to take back the floor or maintain their train of thought to continue talking. Some social scientists have tested the effects of gender and power to see which trumps the other. Johnson (1994) found that, regardless of their gender, managers talk more, have lower rates of positive interruptions, and use fewer qualifiers than subordinates.

## Non-Committal Language

Just as interruptions pose a problem for women, so does language that is perceived to be non-committal. Women seem to be unsure of themselves compared to men when they qualify their statements with words such as "maybe" or "perhaps," or verbs such as "could," "might," and "may." For example, a female manager says to her staff, "Perhaps we should look at reducing the number of brochures we produce" simply as a way to get conversation started on a topic and to hear people's opinions. Rather than non-committal, this language could be an attempt to bring people on-board with an idea and to test out their reactions to it. As it turns out, these words are either simply conversational "fillers" or they may be attempts at getting others to explore an idea or agree with an action (Tannen, 1990). The danger in using language that is not direct and concrete, however, is that it makes the speaker look unconfident and unassertive.

## Talking in Groups

The communication dynamic can be influenced markedly by the context and the situation; how much women talk, who listens to whom, and the style of talk may change from one situation to another. The ratio of men to women in a group and the subject people are discussing, for example, may influence the participation of members. In hierarchical situations in which people's status is emphasized, men tend to dominate discussions, but in more collaborative environments women participate equally with men (Cleveland et al., 2000). In mixed settings, men and women tend to accommodate one another's style – men dominate less and are less competitive and women are less supportive than they would be in all female groups (Haslett, Geis, & Carter, 1992). However, even in these mixed settings, men tend to be more dominant than women, unless of course, the subject is something they have little experience or interest in. One can imagine that women would dominate in a mixed group that is discussing infant care or clothes shopping, for example.

Aries (1977) suggests that women may compete with women when they are in mixed settings. An increased participation of women in mixed groups is due to women directing their comments to men, rather than to other women, and to men communicating more with women.

## Non-Verbal Communication

It is often said that gestures speak louder than words. Research is divided on the significance of some gestures that both men and women use. Some social scientists suggest that women use many gestures in greater frequency than men and that this signifies their subordinate status. For example, according to Henley (1977, 1995), smiling and nodding are exhibited more often by low-status females than high-status or dominant males. Nodding is particularly controversial; some feel that it is ritualized submission and others assert that it is simply a way of encouraging a speaker. More smiling and closed body postures are thought to indicate submission and ingratiation (LaFrance & Henley, 1997). The body postures of dominant individuals are reported to be more open and expansive (Aries, Gold, & Weigel, 1983; Burgoon, 1991). Women tend to be more restricted in their movements; they sit with their legs crossed rather than open, hold their hands in their lap, and generally keep their arms close to their sides (Dierks-Stewart, 1980; Henley, 1977). In one study, women who were perceived to have higher power than other women had a more open body posture – especially wide open arms (Cashdan, 1998).

Others disagree with some of these findings, reporting that, although women do smile more frequently than men, this gesture does not denote inferiority or lack of assertiveness, but rather intimacy (Burgoon, Buller, Hale, & DeTurck, 1984; Kleinke & Taylor, 1991). In a study of men and women in a university dorm setting, smiling was completely unrelated to perceptions of "toughness" or "leadership" in either men or women (Cashdan, 1998). Some suggest that smiling is a sign of friendliness, affiliation, and happiness, rather than a signal of subordinate status (Coats & Feldman, 1996).

In terms of non-verbal language, one's physical size and how one uses space in a room sends a signal. In general, women's physical size compared to men's puts them at an immediate disadvantage. How does a woman who is 5'5" standing behind a 4-foot-high podium compete with a man, similarly situated, who is 6'3"? A man's or woman's location in a room signals his or her status. When leading a meeting, the chairperson typically sits at the front of the room in order to command attention and respect. Sitting next to a more powerful person than yourself may indicate your association with that person. Women need to be attentive to these subtle markers of status.

Touching can be a way of demonstrating status. In the work setting, men touch women more than women touch men, and may do so to show their dominance. Men more frequently pat someone on the back or shoulder, shake hands, and guide someone's forearm with their hand. Women may avoid touching men because touching may be construed as a sexual advance, rather than a signal of power. Many women interviewed for this book commented that men of higher status had removed a stray hair on their blazer, patted them on the shoulder, or tucked a brand tag in at the back of their neck. These women commented that they would never do the same to men, even if they were carrying a laundry load of lint on their shoulders!

The degree to which people look at others while speaking versus while listening to someone else is another area of interest to researchers of communication. Visual dominance ratio (VDR) is defined as the proportion of time looking while speaking to the proportion of time spent looking while listening (Dovidio & Ellyson, 1985). Powerful (or high-status) individuals typically look at others while speaking, but may not look at others while they are listening – especially if these others are viewed by the high-status person as lower status. In cross-dyadic interactions (interactions of two people of the opposite sex), men show a higher ratio of VDR than women, in parallel with the VDR between high-status and low-status individuals. In other words, men are more apt to look at others while they speak, and are unlikely to look at low-status individuals when those individuals speak. If a woman is speaking and men in the room appear not to be listening because their gaze is elsewhere, this can create the perception that what she is saying is of little or no importance. Furthermore, her reaction to this lack of attention may frustrate her; and this frustration could actually make her communicate less effectively.

## Negotiation Skills

Negotiation skills, which entail both verbal and non-verbal elements, are of particular importance to women. Like men, women need to negotiate with their bosses about their incoming salaries, subsequent raises, performance reviews, promotions, and work assignments. With their work colleagues, women have to negotiate how work gets done and who will do what. Many researchers have examined the difference between male and female negotiation styles (Colley & Todd, 2002; Florae, Boyer, Brown, & Butler, 2003; Kersten, 2003). The research tends to suggest that women are less forceful than men in negotiating for salary and in other negotiation scenarios that are perceived by women to be adversarial. Consequently, women are less effective in attaining their goals. Carnegie-Mellon MBA students are a case in point. In a recent graduating class, the women MBAs had starting salaries $4,000 lower than their male counterparts, and only 7% said they negotiated their salaries, compared to 57% of the men (Kersten, 2003). Women are anxious about confrontational negotiations that involve standing up for themselves. They tend to be better at negotiating on behalf of others rather than themselves (Kersten, 2003).

Several studies have shown that women initiate negotiation conversations less frequently and, because of the opportunity structure in organizations, have fewer opportunities to negotiate (Babcock & Laschever, 2003; Bowles et al., 2007; Roth, 2009; Small, Gelfand, Babcock, & Gettman, 2007). Apparently the language used to encourage women to negotiate influences their decision to do so. Framing negotiation situations as *opportunities* is intimidating to women because this language is not consistent with norms of politeness. However, framing negotiation situations as opportunities *for asking* is less intimidating to women because it is perceived as polite and consistent with their role (Small et al., 2007).

Some scholars suggest that because women are more apt to see themselves in relation to others, they will have a harder time negotiating. Because women often consider themselves, for instance as part of a team, as an employee of an organization, a wife, a mother, a friend of others, etc., they will have a more difficult time standing up for themselves. Women naturally see themselves as having responsibility for others and find it difficult to consider only their own interests (Asherman & Asherman, 2001). In one study, 78 male and female undergraduate and graduate students were given two scenarios, one suggesting that the corporate culture was equalitarian and in the other that the corporation was hierarchical. In both scenarios, women negotiated lower economic outcomes for themselves than men did (Curhan, Neale, Ross, & Rosencranz-Englemann, 2008). The authors suggest that women's economic outcomes were lower than men's because of their relational self-concept.

## Getting Credit

Just as negotiating effectively is a critical skill, women must recognize the importance of receiving recognition for their accomplishments. Because women may receive less credit for the same level of work that men do, they need to be sensitive to the importance of self-promotion and find a way to ensure that they get credit for their organizational accomplishments. Sometimes this requires correcting "the record" either verbally or in writing when a task or project that they accomplished is attributed to another. At other times, it simply means that women should market themselves better by letting others know what they are working on and what they have accomplished. If a woman is not getting the public recognition from her boss, she will have to find a way to let others know the good work that she is doing. She can do this by making sure that important documents she has authored are circulated to people besides just her boss, or by simply informally networking with others.

When women complain that someone ran away with their idea and took ownership of it, it is often the case that the individual developed the idea by adding to it, and by force of his personality took over leadership of it. Women need to do more than get acknowledgment for their ideas. Once a woman comes up with an idea, she can put forth a proposal for the implementation of the idea and suggest that she lead a group of employees to achieve it.

## Electronic Forms of Communication

With so much of modern communication in electronic form, it is critical to examine whether men and women communicate differently when using this medium. Social scientists have analyzed the e-mail correspondence of men and women. They have found gender differences between men and women in both the content of messages and in their writing style. Much of the research about electronic communication has been done outside of work settings, examining chatroom dialogues, discussion lists, e-mail correspondence between friends, and blogs. Some of these studies have involved individuals who have never met one another face-to-face and who have even adopted assumed names. This anonymity will most likely affect the nature of the communication. More research needs to be conducted in actual work settings to see if the same finding about electronic communication research persists in business e-mail communication. One question that needs to be answered is whether women are treated more equitably in electronic modes of communication than they are in face-to-face exchanges because their gender is less omnipresent.

Many researchers have found that men and women adopt a style consistent with gender stereotypes. Herring (1993) analyzed the differences in rhetorical style between male and female postings on discussion lists. Males were more adversarial and "flamed" more than women.[1] Female communication had a supportive tone. Women often expressed appreciation of others and used hedges even when disagreeing with the others. Others have found women to be more self-disclosing, polite, and emotional in discussion forums, and men to be more impersonal and factually oriented (Savicki, Lingenfelter, & Kelley, 1996). In a study of student discussion forum postings, males were more likely to use authoritative language and respond negatively in interactions and females were more likely to explicitly agree and support others, and make personal and emotional posts (Guiller & Durndell, 2007). In her studies of online discussion groups, Ferris (1996) suggested that women are often the target of men's flaming and online harassment. Men frequently relate to one another through using flaming language and unconstructive criticism, while women find this type of online activity intimidating (Franco et al., 1995). Morahan-Martin (1998, 2000) complements these findings. She asserts that men use sarcasm, self-promotion, and put-downs online, while women tend to be more supportive and tentative in their communication. The Internet clearly provides opportunities for uncensored information to be posted online; one example of this is the controversial Juicy Campus in which students from various universities post information about one another anonymously. In another study of electronic communication, females used more intense adverbs, expressed more emotion, gave more information about themselves, asked more questions, gave more compliments, apologized more, and made more self-denigrating comments (Thomson & Murachver, 2001). Colley and Todd (2002) studied e-mail correspondence about a recent vacation between male and female students who were friends. E-mails from women contained more expressions associated with rapport and intimacy than those of male participants. The women also made more references to "we" and "our" in describing their holidays, while the men made more references to "I" or "me." These studies suggest that electronic communication shares many of the same differences that Tannen (1990) uncovered in face-to-face communication.

## Bias against Women and Bias for Men

Although evidence suggests that neither sex is better at leadership or better at verbal, non-verbal, or electronic communication, women will be judged according to the expectation that they are caring, warm, and non-confrontational. Both women and men will be assessed on how they handle conflict among their subordinates and how they manage disagreements that they may have with their peers or with senior management. Women will be judged on whether or not they are collaborative and supportive of others' ideas and on how well they communicate to move an agenda forward. Some scholars note that women are judged more critically for their interpersonal skills than men. For example, in a content analysis[2] of 15 episodes of *The Apprentice*, a popular reality TV show depicting men and women vying for positions in the business world, women were judged more critically for their interpersonal skills while the evaluations of men focused more on their leadership abilities (Kinnick & Parton, 2005). Women will be expected, as a natural part of their character, to be able to harmonize work relationships and to be "good" with people. The Catalyst organization reports that both male and female CEOs and senior-level managers have the perception that women leaders are most effective at supporting and rewarding others, and less skilled than men at influencing and delegating tasks (2005). Women respondents perceived women to be better problem-solvers than men, yet men perceived men to be better at this skill. Since problem-solving is a critical part of managing and leading, this perception will have negative consequences for women. These stereotypes will undoubtedly play into the judgments both men and women make about communication style. For example, if a woman says "I'll do that," she may be perceived as being helpful, whereas a man saying the same phrase may be perceived to be taking charge.

Stereotypes certainly play into our expectations of communication behavior for both men and women. Women are expected to be polite and accommodating. Therefore, we will notice these characteristics in women as they speak and most likely emphasize them, de-emphasizing characteristics that do not fit as easily into our assumptions about women. Or we will sometimes highlight areas that do not fit a gender stereotype to the detriment of that sex (for example, anger in women or nurturance in men).

Similarly, if men are assumed to be commanding and powerful, we will emphasize aspects of their communication patterns that fit that stereotype and perhaps ignore others that do not. Studies in the 1970s by Virginia Schein found that both male and female managers associated masculine rather than feminine characteristics with managers. Several further studies have borne this out. Schein and Davidson (1993) found that both men and women ascribe typically masculine characteristics to managers, and in a later study Schein, Mueller, Lituchy, and Liu (1998) found that sex typing occurred in the US, UK, Germany, China, and Japan among male and female management students. Powell, Butterfield, and Parent (2002) conducted a study with similar results; 348 business students associated a good manager as someone with predominantly male characteristics.

Assumptions about leadership characteristics and appropriate gender behavior present a catch-22 for women; if women act like men, they violate female stereotypes, but if they act like women they won't be commanding enough to warrant leadership positions. These types of assumptions also play into what we feel are appropriate emotions for women. Some scholars have noted that people more frequently have an unfavorable view of women's anger in professional settings than men's anger (Brescoll & Uhlmann, 2008). In a study of only male protagonists (Tiedens, Ellsworth, & Mesquita, 2000), research subjects conferred more status on the male leaders and workers who expressed anger than those who expressed sadness. Following the Tiedens study, Brescoll and Uhlmann set up a series of experiments to test whether or not the same would be true for women. They hypothesized that if women showed anger, they too would be perceived as having status and power. In the first experiment, 39 men and 30 women were shown video clips of a male or female candidate for a job (with exactly the same qualifications) in which the subject talked about his or her current job. The individual either expressed anger or sadness about the loss of an important account due to a colleague who arrived late to a presentation with materials that were critical for the meeting. When the subjects of the experiment were asked how much status or power the job candidates should have, the participants conferred the most on the man who said he was angry, the second most on the woman who said she was sad, slightly less on the man who said he was sad, and the least by a large margin on the women who said she was angry. When asked what the candidates should receive by way of compensation for the job, the participants assigned the angry male candidate $38,000 in salary versus $23,500 for the angry female candidate.

In a second experiment, Brescoll and Uhlmann wanted to see if the results of the first experiment were due to the relatively low employment status of the fictitious candidate. Perhaps, the anger that women displayed was seen as inappropriate to their occupational level. In the second experiment, 180 participants were asked to view a video clip of a job interview with a man or a woman. This time half the candidates (male and female) were described as trainees and the other half were described as CEOs. The participants rated the angry female CEO as significantly less competent than all the other candidates. The participants assigned the unemotional female executive $55,384 in compensation versus $32,902 for the angry female CEO, while they assigned the male candidates, regardless of their emotional expression, $73,643. In a third experiment, Brescoll and Uhlmann tested to see whether delivering a justifiable reason for the anger would mitigate the response to the female job candidates who expressed anger. The angry female who explained why she was angry was awarded a higher salary than a female who did not explain, but was still awarded substantially less than both the male candidate who expressed anger and the male candidate who didn't. On the basis of these experiments, the researchers suggest that women who express anger in the workplace, no matter whether it is justified, will be penalized for showing it.

Much work has been done to analyze the emotional responses of high-status people versus low-status people to either positive or negative events (Tiedens et al., 2000). High-status people (we can infer primarily men) have been found to feel proud when something positive has happened to them, while low-status people have felt appreciation. Rather than attribute a positive event to their own accomplishments, low-status people express appreciation and thankfulness. When something negative happens to them, high-status individuals become angry, while low-status people express sadness in a negative situation. These findings are particularly significant for women. Very competent women may inadvertently signal that they have lower status if they express appreciation for something positive that has happened because of their own actions. If they express pride in their accomplishment, rather than simply appreciation, they are more likely to show agency and leadership.

In spite of this tendency to ascribe certain characteristics as female and others as male, in reality both sexes are capable of a wide range of behavior and emotions and should be allowed to express them without penalty. Both men and women, however, need to be aware of how perceptions and biases form opinions. Women may be misjudged because of how they speak or how they express emotion or show appreciation; similarly, men may be misjudged for violating a masculine stereotype and appearing too nurturing or caring.

## Bias in the Language Used to Describe Performance

Deloitte & Touche, one of America's largest accounting, tax, and management consulting firms, undertook an inquiry to understand why women were not advancing to partner level as quickly as men. Partners in accounting firms make the most money, have an equity share in the business, and have the highest level of status. Among the many findings of Deloitte's observations was that different language had been used to describe the performance of men versus women. Equally talented people were described in different ways: men were described as having the potential to lead while women were evaluated on their actual performance. The language used to describe a promising woman went something along these lines: "She's really good, gives a 100% effort. But I just don't see her interacting with a CFO. She's not as polished as some. Her presentation skills could be a little stronger." The conversation to describe a promising young man with almost identical skills would be: "He's good … he and I are going to take the CFO golfing next week. And I know he can grow into it; he has tremendous potential" (Roessner, 1999, p. 4). When a man was found to lack certain skills, the company made allowances and viewed him as promotable; when the woman was lacking a skill, the deficit was used to cast doubt about her ability to work at the next level.

## Incivility in Communication – a New Type of Discrimination

Several scholars have advanced the idea that incivility toward women in the workplace is the modern form of discrimination against them (Andersson & Pearson, 1999; Cortina, 2008). This incivility can take place in face-to-face interactions or over the Internet. Blatant sexism is no longer tolerated in the workplace because of existing laws such as Title VII, yet discrimination against women can easily be masked by everyday acts of incivility, such as interrupting, behaving rudely, ignoring a woman as she is talking, or failing to include her in professional camaraderie. Andersson and Pearson (1999) define incivility as "low intensity deviant behavior with ambiguous intent to harm the target, in violation of workplace norms of mutual respect" (p. 357). This uncivil behavior more often than not involves communication. The problem with such behaviors is that they can be seen as mere oversights, the result of a person's ignorance, or the personality quirk of an individual without serious intent to harm a woman's reputation or her effectiveness at work. If they are noticed at all, they could even be attributed to the over-sensitivity of the female target. These uncivil behaviors occur under the radar screen and are rarely attributed to an individual's bias or the tolerance of an organization for discriminatory behavior. Several researchers have discussed who might be the most vulnerable to incivility at work. Some find the most vulnerable to be successful professional women and minorities who are perceived to be highly competent and advancing in ways that threaten the dominant majority of white males (Fiske, 2002; Jackman, 1994; Reeves, 2000).

In an examination of the experiences of 4,608 attorneys in the US, respondents were asked to describe uncivil conduct. Many female attorneys described varying forms of disrespect that they attributed to gender bias (Cortina, 2008). Male judges and attorneys tended to cut short, ignore, or exclude female attorneys. According to the women attorneys, they were treated aggressively by male attorneys in depositions, with frequent interruptions. Sometimes women attorneys were treated as if they were not in the court room at all. Cortina makes the point that the incivility could not be a trial strategy offered up by the opposing legal team as the rude behavior seem to come from all sides: judges, court clerks, attorneys, and other court personnel. Cortina (2008) extended the study of incivility to other occupational settings – a city government and a law-enforcement agency – with similar findings. Women and minorities reported more frequent encounters with uncivil behaviors such as being ignored by an individual, information being withheld from them, or failing to be publicly recognized by an individual. As in the earlier studies, these behaviors could easily be labeled as oversight, rather than deliberate bias against an individual.

## Implications

What should research on communication style, leadership behaviors, computer-mediated communication, and incivility mean to women in the workplace?

First, women need to acknowledge that they may face a double-bind. They may be expected to behave like a "female" and exhibit a communication style associated with women – being friendly, cooperative, and non-dominant – while at the same time prove that they can lead. If women exhibit the necessary qualities expected for a leader and a high-status individual – decisiveness, verbal dominance, forcefulness, and even anger – they will be acting against their gender type. A woman risks accusations of "she's too forceful, too aggressive" and she may even be labeled as "bitchy," "strident," or "loud-mouthed." One need only watch how Hillary Clinton tried to walk this double-bind tightrope in her presidential campaign, neither appearing too feminine nor too masculine. In the early days of her campaign, she came on strong to prove her place at the table with the other candidates for president. When she was criticized for being either too angry or too wooden, she toned down the pitch of her voice and began smiling more. In the later stages of the primaries, her feminine qualities seemed to help her more. Many pundits even suggested that she gained support when during the primary in a New Hampshire coffee shop she exhibited strong emotions. When asked about "how she managed to do it all," holding back tears, she responded that it was hard but that she cared so much about her country that she just kept on going.

Second, in the business environment, women will also need to be aware of how they are perceived, and portray themselves as both feminine and competent. Carli Fiorini, former CEO of Hewlett Packard, suffered the same accusations of being too tough, too aggressive, too intense, and unfeeling toward employees. By many, she was viewed as not being feminine enough.

Salon.com, a popular online magazine that deals with many aspects of business and culture, noted that much of the media reporting in business magazines depicts women CEOs are either sex objects or dowdy matrons (Brown, 1999). Rather than reporting on their accomplishments as heads of industry, business journalists emphasize their gender and appearance. For example, Esther Dyson, the multi-millionaire entrepreneur and forecaster of the dot-com stockmarket meltdown, was reported as wearing mail-order jeans. Moreover, young female Silicon Valley entrepreneurs have been depicted as sex objects in technology magazines such as *Wired* or the mainstream business magazine *Fortune*.

This double-bind of managing one's impression is generally something that men do not have to worry about. Men can combine their sexuality with power, yet women who do the same are accused of flaunting their sexuality. Men can be tough without being characterized as unfeeling; witness Jack Welch's philosophy of cutting the bottom 10% of his workforce each year to continually improve General Electric. This philosophy was heralded as a "smart" business practice by the former CEO of GE.

Women need to understand that certain verbal and non-verbal behaviors signal weakness, especially in male-dominated environments: short replies or short bursts of speech, tag questions,[3] qualifiers, and raised intonation at the end of a sentence, for example. Women should be conscious of the fact that certain non-verbal behaviors are likely to be misconstrued as indications of powerlessness: lack of eye contact or too much eye contact, a weak handshake, nodding, and smiling. Only when women become more aware of these rhetorical patterns and mannerisms can they evaluate their effects.

Third, it is up to the leaders in an organization to be sensitive to how women are being perceived in the organization. Are they expected to be "woman-like" – passive, friendly, collegial, non-threatening, and at the same time be assertive, decisive, and commanding? Are women able to act assertively without paying a penalty? An organization's leaders should be vigilant about making sure that the expectations for women's communication are not impossible for women to meet. Senior-level managers have the role of educating others that differences in communication style are simply that – differences. People should be judged on their ability to do a job, not on small nuances of communication style. A company's senior managers should make others in the organization aware that both men and women can have a range of acceptable communication behaviors. Women should be able to raise their voice or exhibit anger when they are passionate about something. If there are subtle forms of incivility in the workplace (rudeness, women being ignored in meetings, or hostile interruptions, for example), management should not tolerate them.

Fourth, women will probably fare better in organizations that already have employed people with diverse communication styles, perhaps Hispanic, Asian, or African American employees. It is important that this diversity be present at all levels of the organization. The acceptance of only a "male" style in one job category or at one level will be more likely if that is the predominant style in that job category or level. When women are being recruited to join an organization, they should look for signs of a diverse workforce at all organizational levels, not just the lowest ones. If they see a variety of communication styles, they should take that as an encouraging sign.

Finally, women themselves can and should begin to change the way people communicate in organizations, especially if they find themselves in an environment where communication is hostile or uncollaborative. When women are in positions of leadership, they can begin to change the nature of communication. Consider a female manager who supervises a group of people, both men and women. She can model communication behaviors that are collaborative and helpful, rather than ones that show disrespect for others. For example, during a meeting, she may solicit other people's views and seek to involve them in discussion about ideas and decision-making. She may also recognize women, when they are not given due credit for their ideas. In general, because she is the leader, the way in which she communicates will set the tone for the rest of the group. At the end of a meeting, she can summarize the team's ideas and give recognition to those who have contributed positively to the discussion. Even when women are not managers or leaders, they can support one another during important business meetings by agreeing with each other's ideas and by verbally and publicly supporting each other's proposals, plans, or agendas. If they honestly do not agree with an idea, they can recognize its positive aspects (in almost all cases ideas, proposals, and projects have some positive attributes), and then make suggestions for building upon it.

## An Opportunity for Women

Many domestic firms in the United States have offices in other parts of the world. As women climb the corporate ladder, they will have opportunities to use their communication skills abroad as expatriate managers. One of the key skills of ex-pats, as they are commonly called, is the ability to communicate across a range of cultural styles. In a PricewaterhouseCoopers Annual CEO Survey for 1999, experience managing multicultural teams was noted as the most valuable attribute of a manager; more so than industry knowledge, company experience, or an advanced degree from a top business school (Dalton, Ernst, Deal, & Leslie, 2002). Women may be more attuned to this than men, as they have had to be cognizant of how they are being perceived by others and are most likely more aware than their male counterparts of managing the impression they are making. Even if a multinational organization is cutting back on ex-pat assignments, communication with others across the firm occurs via conference call, e-mail, or virtual teams comprised of people from different countries who may not leave their country but who work and communicate with one another using technology. The increase in electronic communication in business makes it even more important for women to influence the style and tenor of communication. Specific communication traits such as "openness," "extraversion," and "cultural sensitivity" are essential for cross-cultural assignments; therefore, women can use these traits to their benefit in situations where they are communicating across cultures (Dalton et al., 2002).

Moreover, women can and should use the Internet to their advantage. Online networking can open up opportunities for women by helping them exchange information with one another. The Internet provides a world-wide forum for women to share their experiences, concerns, and knowledge, and to help each other get ahead. With electronic media, women entrepreneurs can now be in charge of their own image by carefully crafting what they want to say about themselves online. The Internet provides an inexpensive way for female entrepreneurs to advertise their services and to build their personal brand. In spite of the aforementioned obstacles for women discussed in this chapter, the Internet can be an equalizer between male and female entrepreneurs. The Internet requires low start-up costs and only a small physical space; women can opt to work from their homes and still have a substantial online business presence as long as they have the appropriate technology (phone, fax, website, etc.). Communication via the Internet opens up contact with suppliers and customers, and allows women to communicate with other female entrepreneurs (Sherman, 1998). Some researchers suggest that the Internet actually helps women entrepreneurs because it hides their gender, emphasizing instead their business offering (Martin & Wright, 2005).

## Further Reading

Asherman, I.G. & Asherman, S.V. (2001). *The negotiation sourcebook* (2nd ed.). Amherst, MA: HRD Press.

Barrett, M. & Davidson, M. (2006). *Gender and communication at work*. Farnham, UK: Ashgate.

Herring, S.C. (2005). Gender and power in on-line communication. In J. Holmes & M. Meyerhoff (Eds.), *The handbook of language and gender* (pp. 202–228). Oxford, UK: Blackwell Publishing.

Lakoff, R. (1990). *Talking power: The politics of language in our lives*. New York, NY: Basic.

Tannen, D. (1995, September/October). The power of talk: Who gets heard and why. *Harvard Business Review*, 139–148.

# CASE STUDIES

### Case Study 1: Communication Dilemma – Getting Credit

Security Financial Corporation is a Fortune 500 company located in New York. It special-izes in financial analysis, stock and mutual funds, and investment banking operations. Claudia Pearson had worked her way up the corporate ladder to a position of Director of Sales Management Development, reporting directly to the Vice President of Human Resources. In this position, she was responsible for training all financial sales advisors and sales managers. The job was demanding; typically, Claudia worked 65 to 70 hours a week and traveled to various Security Financial sales offices around the United States. She had graduated from Columbia University with a double major in English and eco-nomics. She had worked for Security Financial for 12 years, starting her career as a train-ing manager. Eight staff members reported to Claudia, most of whom were training managers responsible for working with sales managers and financial sales advisors.

Claudia worked closely with both the marketing director and the sales director because each had input into her programs. She met weekly with the sales director, Robert Norville, a man who had been in the financial industry for 25 years. All of the eight regional sales man-agers reported to him. His main responsibilities were meeting the national sales force numbers and hiring and retaining sales advisors, who were vital to the business. She had less contact with Ken Peterson, the marketing director, but nevertheless he was an import-ant person for her to consult with before she designed any programs for the sales personnel. At age 35, Ken was about 15 years younger than Robert. Claudia often characterized Robert as "old school" – he had worked his way up in the business to a prominent senior job and Ken as "the young turk" – he had held several marketing jobs before joining Security Finan-cial and was full of new ideas. Although Robert, Ken, and she were all peers, Claudia felt that Robert needed to feel like he was of a higher status than she was. When they met together, she allowed him to feel like he was in charge simply because she found that this was the best way to get along with him. She reminded herself that this wasn't really an issue as long as he didn't make her feel subordinate when others were around. She had tried to deal with him as an equal and it simply didn't work as well as allowing him to feel like he was making all of the decisions. Her relationship with Ken was more collegial and equalitarian; neither of them seemed particularly interested in flexing their "authority muscles."

Claudia and her team had been designing a new program that consisted of 12 courses to be delivered over a year; one course would be offered each month in every sales office. The project had been extremely time-consuming, involving many meetings to determine the content of the program and, once designed, deciding how to launch it with the sales force. This was the biggest training effort the company had ever undertaken, and Claudia was very proud of the result. Each training session had self-study sessions that were downloaded from the Internet, video clips, and classroom exercises. She met with Robert to review the schedule of training sessions and to discuss the roles her managers would play. She showed a draft of a letter that she intended to send out to all sales managers announcing the new program.

A few days after her meeting with Robert, Claudia was going through her inbox of e-mails to find a message that Robert had copied to her. To her amazement and fury, it was nearly the same letter she had drafted and shown to him two days before. The letter was written on Robert's letterhead and signed by him. It announced the program and highlighted the 12 individual training sessions with a timetable for each office (see Appendix 7.1). Although it mentioned that Claudia's team would be delivering the training, the letter seemed to insinuate that the effort was Robert's. Claudia was livid and decided it was high time to confront him.

It was routine in the company that managers sent e-mails or memos out announcing only those activities that they had initiated. She thought that this had been a deliberate move on his part to take credit for something she had worked on for nearly a year or at the very least to look like somehow he had been supervising her efforts.

### The Confrontation

Claudia decided to confront Robert the next day. She called his secretary to get on his calendar. He was free at 2 p.m. and would meet with her over a late lunch. Their conversation began cordially with small talk. Robert told her how excited he was to begin the training program and how much he appreciated her work on the project. This left an entrée for her to discuss the issue of the letter with him.

"Robert, I have to tell you that I was upset with the memo you wrote to the field organization. As head of the training department, that memo should have come from me." Claudia waited for him to respond.

"I thought it was important to get the news out right away. The sales organization has been waiting a long time for the program. I certainly didn't mean any harm by it. Everyone knows that this is your program. I think you're being a little sensitive."

"Robert, it was important to me that the memo came from my office. In this company, when a manager is in charge of a program the news about it comes from that person. Besides you copied it to our CEO!"

"Calm down. I certainly didn't mean to upset you. How is the pasta salad? I would have ordered it but I have to slim down. I'm afraid it's lettuce salads for me for about the next month. I have to rush. I have another meeting at 2:30. Let's talk after the first program is rolled out to review the results."

They finished their lunch in silence. Claudia left feeling angrier than ever.

### Appendix 7.1: Partial Organizational Chart for Security Financial Corporation

### Appendix 7.2 – Robert's E-mail

Dear Sales Managers and Financial Sales Advisors,

The day has finally come. We are ready to roll out the year long training program to all of you. It's absolutely top notch and will move us closer to becoming the high performing sales organization that I know we can be. In the next few days, you will be shipped training manuals, DVD self-study guides, and videos which will all be used in the program. Your sales coordinators will make sure that each individual receives the appropriate materials before your first training session.

We expect a significant improvement in sales as a result of this program and I will be monitoring not only sales results by division, but will also be asking you to evaluate the program as we progress through it. A team member from the management development department will be coming to each sales office to deliver the training.

The schedule for the first series is outlined below. We expect perfect attendance so mark your calendars now! We will be sending you the March schedule very soon. You won't want to miss this opportunity to learn!

| | |
|---|---|
| Divisions 1–4 | Feb. 9 |
| Divisions 5–8 | Feb. 10 |
| Divisions 9–12 | Feb. 11 |
| Divisions 13–16 | Feb. 12 |
| Divisions 17–20 | Feb. 15 |

Best Regards,

Robert Norville

Director of Sales

**Discussion Questions**

1.  Examining the case from the very beginning, what mistakes do you think Claudia made?
2.  Was Claudia being too sensitive? Do you think Robert was deliberately taking the credit?
3.  What damage was done by Robert copying the memo to the CEO?
4.  Examine the memo. If Claudia had taken it to her lunch meeting with Robert, how might she have structured her comments to Robert differently than she did?
5.  What should Claudia do now?

## Case Study 2: Meeting Madness

The Benton Corporation manufactures all types of temperature gauges for a variety of industrial and residential uses. One of its most popular products is the sensory device in home heating and air-conditioning systems. The company also manufactures sensory devices for garage door openers, commercial refrigeration systems, and commercial electric lighting systems.

Meetings at the Benton Corporation are very important; decisions are made in meetings and reputations of individuals become cast in stone based on how they "perform" in meetings. Typically, stakeholders gather for meetings, lasting between an hour to three hours, to hash out their rationales for support or rejection of programs and their opinions for taking one action over another.

### Chandra Patel

Chandra Patel, a quality engineer, was not entirely comfortable in meetings. Her introverted style did not mesh well with the extraverted nature of most Benton managers. Furthermore, Chandra's upbringing contributed to her discomfort. She was not used to speaking out and had achieved the highest grades in engineering school without having to say very much. Although Chandra grew up in the United States and was educated at an American university, her family still felt strongly about their Indian heritage. Chandra was brought up to value her education as a prerequisite to prosperity and happiness, but she was also expected to value her cultural heritage that placed importance on women's duties to family, husband, and the domestic realm. Chandra's grandparents still lived in the Indian state of Gujarat, in the eastern part of the country. Chandra's parents emigrated to the United States before Chandra was born because her father took a job as an engineer with Union Technologies Corp. Chandra's mother was educated up through university in India, but has never worked outside of the home. She supports Chandra's career, but hopes that some day she will cease working, settle down with an Indian husband, and devote herself to raising a family. Though very intelligent, her mother generally defers to her father when they have differences of opinion on a subject.

### Benton Engineers Meeting

Benton's engineers routinely meet to discuss the design of new products and the redesign of old ones. In these meetings, they determine recommendations they will send to senior management about product design, and they set individual responsibilities for tasks. Chandra disliked these meetings because she often felt railroaded into decisions that she did not have enough time to consider. She confided in a friend, "We make decisions too quickly and the loudest voices seem to carry the day. I'm uncomfortable with the whole process."

Chandra prepared for the upcoming engineers meeting by studying the project timetables carefully, and analyzing their feasibility. At the previous meeting it was agreed that these project timetables would be the chief topic of discussion. Together, they would decide which ones needed to be amended.

Chandra arrived at the meeting in conference room B with apprehension. She expected that yet again her voice wouldn't be heard among the other more vocal members. Three other engineers were present: Margo Payne, Jeff Powers, and Michael DePalma. Margo had agreed to chair the meeting.

Michael and Jeff entered the conference room together.

"That was some 18 holes you had last Saturday! Next time I'm going to sign on as your partner for the company tournament," Jeff slapped Michael on the back. "You didn't tell me you were a closet golfer."

"I got lucky. Did you see the drives that Stevenson had? Incredible. He's got amazing power, but then he'd blow it on the green. Boy, was he upset," said Michael.

Margo attempted to get the meeting underway, "OK, let's get started. I didn't have time to e-mail you the agenda in advance, so I made copies for everyone." Margo handed out the agenda, "Jeff e-mailed me and wanted to put the Zanzibar project on the agenda so that is the first item on the list. We won't have time to deal with timetables today so we can discuss that next week. We have to deal with the recall of Zanzibar and what we need to do to correct the problem. The next big item on the agenda concerns the design choices with the new refrigeration unit system. I suggest we start with Zanzibar."

"The problem with Zanzibar rests with the supplier and we need to press them to fix it. I don't see why Benton should bear the cost for their mistakes. Remember the last time this happened? We had a major mess on our hands because we didn't fix the problem fast enough. We can't risk our customers finding out the problem before we recall the product. I just don't see why we should bear the costs. Every project is being scrutinized for efficiency and cost containment and I am not willing to run over on this one. The supplier should fix it," said Jeff.

"That may be true, but I looked into the contract and ..." Chandra began.

She was interrupted by Jeff. "We have been dealing with this supplier for five years and things are never quite right with them. *They* need to fix the problem not us. They are becoming more and more unreliable," Jeff continued.

"I agree, Jeff. They dragged their feet on the last project which put us behind for weeks. I think we need to demand that they bear the costs of fixing the system," said Michael.

"But, the contract states ..." Chandra tried again to find her way into the conversation.

She was again interrupted by Jeff. "These guys have quality standards just like we do and they need to live up to their promises."

Frustrated, Chandra sat back in her chair. She wanted to bring up the fact that Benton had agreed in writing to a cheaper component that did not carry a warranty. At the time, their supplier had told them that it might not hold up. Benton was willing to take the risk since it would make a big difference on their profits.

The conversation continued for several minutes without Chandra's participation. Margo suggested that they write a letter to the supplier detailing the faulty component and demanding that it be replaced. Jeff and Michael continued to describe previous situations with the supplier in which the service they received was not adequate.

Chandra decided to try to bring up the issue of the contract one more time. "Our problem is this ... the contract says that the component is not under warranty. Their proposal to us recommended a different unit. But we didn't want to it use because it was more expensive. I think we better ask them to meet with us to discuss the problem rather than send them a nasty letter demanding payment," Chandra said.

The discussion progressed for several more minutes, with Jeff, Margo, and Michael debating what Benton should do to try to recover at least part of their costs.

Time was running short so Margo interjected, "We need to reach an agreement on how to proceed. We still have to discuss the design choices for the refrigeration units."

"I agree with Jeff," Michael said. "We need to invite them to a meeting to discuss the issue. Sending a letter is too aggressive given the fact that we did sign the contract agreeing to purchase the component. I'll write up a memo and circulate it to all of you for your approval."

"That's settled. OK, let's move on to talk about the design choices," Jeff said.

Chandra was dumbfounded and angry. She found it impossible to contribute anything to the next agenda item.

After the meeting was over, Jeff and Michael left together.

"Do you want to grab a sandwich at the deli?" Michael asked.

"Sure … they have great subs. We can go over the project timetables for next time. I'm not happy with the Garner project. I can't possibly finish it in the original timetable," Jeff said.

"Well, let's have a look at it over lunch. Maybe we can work something out."

## Discussion Questions

1. Describe the communication between Chandra, Jeff, Margo, and Michael.
2. What meeting management techniques could Margo use to make sure that everyone's voice is heard?
3. What strategies could Chandra try in order to be heard?
4. Do you think men's and women's communication styles differ? Why, or why not?
5. What techniques can introverts use to make sure that they are heard in meetings?
6. How does culture affect communication? Give some examples from your own experience.
7. Jeff and Michael have social interest in common. How does this affect their communication at work? What effect does it have on Margo and Chandra?

## Other Activities

1. Examine the communication patterns in your workplace or in a classroom setting by closely observing a meeting or a classroom discussion. Who speaks the most? Who is listened to? Do you notice any gender differences in communication style?
2. Examine the e-mail communication you receive from others. Is there a difference in style among the messages from males and those from females? If so, how do you explain the difference?
3. Since Title IX was passed allowing women to compete in sports in high school, women have avidly pursued their athletic interests. Do you think this exposure to competition has improved their ability to compete in the workplace? Has it made them more eligible for leadership positions or improved their ability to negotiate?
4. Imagine that you are negotiating for a pay raise. How would you prepare? How would you approach your boss? What would your communications strategy be?

# 8   Hostile Work Environments and Sexual Harassment

**Learning Objectives**

After completing this chapter, the reader will:

- understand what constitutes and what causes sexual harassment.
- understand the role of the Equal Employment Opportunity Commission in relation to sexual harassment.
- understand the differences among countries and governments in their approach to sexual harassment.

Although sexual harassment has been with us for millennia, the American public's awareness of it rose to universality during the 1991 United States Supreme Court confirmation of Clarence Thomas when his former employee, Anita Hill, brought sexual harassment charges against him. She claimed that Thomas discussed inappropriate sexual acts with her, referred to pornographic films, and made unwelcome sexual advances toward her while he was head of the Equal Employment Opportunity Commission, and again as an administrator in the US Department of Education. The case was significant not only because of its racial overtones (both Hill and Thomas are African American), but also because Hill was clearly a highly educated woman willing to stand up to a powerful, public figure. She brought the charges against Thomas while she was a law professor at the University of Oklahoma. Since Hill's accusations, sexual harassment has been on the radar screen of all organizations – non-profits, schools and universities, and businesses. The number of complaints taken by the Equal Employment Opportunity Commission have increased substantially. Organizations have had to take allegations of harassment seriously because of their potential financial liability for the actions of employees, and because hostile work environments produce poor morale and low productivity.

This chapter provides the legal definition of sexual harassment and explains how sexual harassment creates a hostile work environment that prevents individuals from contributing productively to organizations. The chapter also explains the various theories that have been used to explain the underlying causes of sexual harassment. Understanding the underlying causes of harassment is the first step in redressing it. Only after sexual harassment is understood can institutions begin to prevent it. Once its cause or causes are better understood, the effectiveness of possible remedies, legal and otherwise, can be evaluated.

## What Constitutes Sexual Harassment?

Legally, sexual harassment can be defined as any conduct, gesture, comment, or sexual contact that is likely to cause offense to any employee, male or female, or be perceived by the employee to place a condition of a sexual nature on employment or any opportunity for training, job assignment, or promotion (Coelho, 2006). Sexually harassing behavior can run the gamut from sexist remarks all the way to sexual assault. The most common forms of sexually offensive verbal behaviors are jokes of a sexual nature, sexual innuendo, sexist remarks about an individual's clothing or body, sexual invitations, bragging about sexual prowess, or inquiries about a person's sex life. Physical forms of sexual harassment include such things as touching someone inappropriately, grabbing or groping a person, staring at an individual's breasts or genitals, or making lewd gestures. Visual and written displays can also constitute harassment; sending unwelcome, sexually explicit e-mails or displaying sexually offensive pictures or cartoons are examples. In all cases, sexual harassment involves the attempt of exerting power of one human being over another; the sexual attention paid to an individual is unwelcome and unreciprocated, and it can be coercive. In some cases, the harasser implies that there is a reward for complying with a sexually explicit invitation, such as a salary raise or promotion. In other cases, a harasser may threaten to deny a job benefit to an individual who refuses sexual advances.

## The Legal Framework for Sexual Harassment Cases

The law recognizes two forms of sexual harassment: quid pro quo harassment and hostile work environment harassment. In the United States, Title VII (under which sexual harassment legislation resides) does not apply to employers with 15 or fewer employees.

Quid pro quo harassment occurs when employment decisions are based on the employee's submission to, or rejection of, sexual favors. For example, quid pro quo harassment would have occurred if a women's supervisor threatened to deny her a promotion unless she succumbed to his or her sexual advances, or if a supervisor changed the employee's work assignments because of a refusal to date the supervisor. The employment decisions could include any number of things such as hiring and firing decisions, salary increases, work assignments, or work schedules.

A hostile work environment can be defined as behavior that focuses on the sexuality of another person or persons in the environment. The unwelcome sexual conduct creates an environment that makes an individual (or individuals) feel intimidated or uncomfortable, or an environment that interferes with work productivity. Supervisors, co-workers, or customers can create such an offensive environment. Although sexual harassment is reported more often by women, men can also be victimized by women or by other men.

In the law, determining whether or not sexual harassment has occurred can be problematic. Some courts adopt the "reasonable woman" standard. The courts ask whether a "reasonable woman" would define the offensive behavior as sexual harassment. The reasonable woman standard recognizes two factors; first, that a man cannot be expected to evaluate whether the treatment a woman receives is offensive or threatening and, second, that the environment determines what a woman might find reasonable. In the first instance, the courts take into account the perspective of the individual who is being harassed. What specific factors would contribute to her perspective of the events as harassing? Any number of factors could contribute to her perspective; for example, her age, cultural background, the frequency with which the alleged behavior occurred, and the severity of it may be significant. In the second instance, the type of work a woman does may have a bearing on what she would find offensive. For example, the reasonable standard of what a woman finds permissible if she were working in a strip club may be different from what a woman may find permissible if she were employed in an office environment. Another circumstance that courts look for is whether the sexual advances were welcome or unwelcome. This often comes down to examining the alleged victim's responses to the harassment. Did she actively discourage the harasser? Did she appear to be traumatized? This standard for determining whether sexual harassment occurred can be problematic because individuals have complex reactions to sexual trauma and harassment; not all women will respond in exactly the same way. Some women will act unfazed by sexual remarks or sexual touching in the workplace when, in reality, they find these actions highly objectionable. Although on the outside they may seem to be unbothered, on the inside they may find coping at work difficult.

## The Equal Employment Opportunity Commission (EEOC)

The United States Equal Employment Opportunity Commission was set up to enforce employment discrimination legislation.

Individuals are not required to use the EEOC in order to seek legal redress, but the EEOC can be helpful in resolving sexual harassment and other discrimination claims. The EEOC investigates charges and issues rulings as to the merits of a case. If a case is found to have merit, the EEOC invites the two parties to a mediation. Mediation often results in a faster outcome than a legal battle and can be less expensive – the EEOC does not charge for its services, although both parties may have an attorney present during a mediation.

In order for the EEOC to investigate a charge, an individual must file a complaint with the EEOC within 180 to 300 days from the last alleged violation (the number of days is determined by the state in which the claim is filed). Of the 12,025 sexual harassment complaints filed in 2006, 15.4% were filed by males and 84.6% by females. In 2006, the monetary compensation paid to plaintiffs of sexual harassment charges based on mediation reached $48.8 million. Of course, this figure is lower than the actual amount that sexual harassment costs employers since many victims pursue their cases in court, without the help of the EEOC. More importantly, sexual harassment reduces worker productivity and discourages well-qualified women from willingly taking on jobs with more challenging responsibilities.

As US businesses expand globally and as more US citizens work abroad, the EEOC found it necessary to define the scope of employment legislation for US companies operating abroad. US employees working outside the United States are covered by Title VII if the employees are controlled by a US employer.[1] If US citizens are working abroad for a US employer, they need to know that they are covered by US law; if they are working abroad for a non-US company, the laws of that country apply. The likelihood of harassment increases in male-dominated industries and in countries in which the culture does not view women as equal to men. (Several court cases involving US women employees working in Iraq are described at the end of this section.)

## Sexual Harassment Legislation in Other Countries

Because most Asian and Latin American countries did not adopt equal employment opportunity laws until the mid-1980s or later, the attitudes in these countries about women in the workplace, especially in influential positions, may not be as hospitable as they are in the United States. A member of the Chinese parliament has proposed that a law be passed to penalize sexual harassment, but some experts in China indicate that before legislation is passed the Chinese need to better define the problem. Sexual harassment is a taboo subject in China. As such, it often goes without precise verbal description, which is a problem for developing legislation. In Indonesia, the Geger Foundation and the International Labour Organization have received reports of women factory workers being verbally and physically harassed by managers. Because many of these women need their jobs, they often will keep quiet about their abuse. Moreover, official information from governments on the reported abuses is difficult to obtain because the women who have been victimized rarely go to the police to file a formal complaint. Additionally, governments either do not keep accurate statistics on harassment or refuse to share them with international organizations. In Japan, equal employment opportunity legislation was revised in 1999 by the minister of labor to include a section covering sexual harassment and company liability. Now the liability for harassment is directed toward the company, if it should have known about the harassment or did nothing to prevent it. The law in Japan closely mirrors US law in that two forms of harassment are recognized: quid pro quo and hostile work environment (Japanese Institute of Workers' Evolution, 2009).

The European Union has legislation similar to the US code covering sexual harassment; however, it was established much later than the US legislation. In May 2002, the European Union Council and the EU Parliament amended a 1976 Council Directive on the equal treatment of men and women in employment, prohibiting sexual harassment. The EU Equal Treatment Directive required all member states to adopt laws on sexual harassment or amend existing laws to comply with the EU directive by October 5, 2005. Unlike the US legislation, the EU Directive requires all businesses, regardless of size and the number of their employees, to adopt the law. In 2005, the EU instituted a new law placing the burden of proof on employers that sexual harassment did *not* occur in their workplace. Employers must prove that they created a harassment-free environment.

Canada has a similar sexual harassment law to the US law, under the Canada Labour Code. The code states that every person who is an employee has a right to equal treatment from the employer, agent of the employer, or by another employee, without discrimination because of sex. This in essence covers an individual's right to a workplace free of unwanted sexual attention. Under Canadian law, after consultation with employees, every employer must issue a policy on sexual harassment and post it where employees are most likely to see it. In Canada, sexual harassment is considered to have occurred if the harasser knew or should have known that the behavior was unwelcome, or if a reasonable observer would consider the behavior to be harassment, taking into consideration the recipient's cultural background (Konrad, 2006).

## The Causes of Sexual Harassment – Alternative Theories

Although there are many theories of sexual harassment, most center around two different causal hypotheses. One is that the primary explanation for sexual harassment stems from sexual desire or one's basic biology. The other is that it comes from unchecked power of one group or one person over another. These two main ideas are often broken down further into a number of competing explanations.

## *Biological/Evolutionary Explanation*

This explanation holds that men are biologically predisposed to harass women simply because they are male and have sexual urges that they find difficult to control. Through the process of evolution, the fittest strategies for leaving more offspring have been subject to natural selection. Since males can impregnate large numbers of females, there has been strong selection on traits that enable males to do so. The best reproductive strategy for females is quite different. Since they can only have a few offspring, their fitness is maximized through a combination of being very choosy about which males to reproduce with, and ensuring these males aid in the long-term care of their children. Nature selects for whatever psychological traits – emotions, mores, willingness to use force or take risks, interest in competition or domination – in males that will increase their chances to employ their optimal reproductive strategy of serving many partners. This process of selection results in a natural inclination to sexually aggressive behavior.

In women, selection has resulted in traits of a different kind which encourage resistance against unwanted sexual demands. Perhaps the strongest evidence for natural selection of this difference in reproductive strategies is the widespread acceptance over a long period across many cultures of a double-standard. Male adultery is treated as less serious than female adultery; societies attach little importance to male virginity before marriage, while female virginity before marriage is considered virtuous. Men are expected to tell off-color jokes, while women who do so are considered coarse and unladylike. On the other hand, this theory suggests that we should expect far more sexual harassment than in fact actually occurs in most societies, including ones that are even more patriarchal than ours.

However, differences between sexes in willingness to use force are well established. Two meta-analyses of more than 100 studies of aggression confirmed that males are more aggressive than females in physical and verbal manifestations. The gender gap is wider for physical aggression than verbal aggression, but exists for both (Eagly & Steffen, 1986; Hyde, 1986). Evidence that males are more likely to partake in spontaneous aggression than females can be seen in the playground. Eagly and Steffen (1986) also found that boys have different expectations about the consequences for aggressive behavior than girls do; females anticipate more disapproval from their parents. Females also feel more guilt for aggressive behavior; both for the harm it may cause another person and because of parental disapproval.

Biological or evolutionary theories of the origin and persistence of male sexual harassment of women are highly speculative. Many social scientists don't feel the need to take sides in the dispute about whether sexual harassment is a matter or nature or nurture. What is clear is that many features of contemporary society, from early childhood experience, encourage or reinforce this pattern of male pursuit of control or domination over females, as well as the resistance of males to changes in women's and men's roles in the workplace or the home.

The following non-biological theories are all similar in holding that one group – men – exercises power over another group – women – in order to acquire and maintain organizational resources, or to obtain status from other males. These theories do not trace sexual harassment back to innate gender differences, but to the perennial struggle over any scarce resource and the coalition-building it produces.

## *Socio-Cultural Factors*

Several elements of our culture and society contribute to sexual harassment. These can be broken down into theories that focus on socialization, patriarchy, male bonding, and the ratio of men to women in a particular setting.

## Socialization

According to this theory, males and females are socialized differently. Boys are taught from an early age to dominate females and to be assertive rather than passive. Girls are taught to be submissive to men and passive rather than assertive. Many social forces encourage stereotypes of both male and female sexuality, suggesting that men are permitted to sexually dominate women and that women, being the weaker sex, will eventually relent. The advertising industry and popular media, such as television and movies, bombard us with images objectifying women as sex objects and depicting male domination of women. Emphasizing the differences rather than the similarities between the sexes contributes to this early socialization process: girls play jump rope on the playground in a cooperative activity, while boys shoot baskets in a competitive one; boys play video games in which they conquer an enemy, often with violence, while girls prefer other forms of entertainment; girl babies wear pink and boy babies wear blue; women rock stars are highly sexualized and male hip-hop stars sing misogynist lyrics. All of these distinctions shape how the sexes view one other.

Two recent studies indicate that sexual harassment is rampant in the educational environment. A 2001 study of students in grades 8 through 11 revealed that 83% of girls and 79% of boys have been harassed. Many indicated that the harassment began as early as their elementary years (American Association of University Women, 2001). The questionnaire on which the study was based provided a common definition of sexual harassment for the respondents. A more current study examining sexual harassment on college and university campuses found that two-thirds of college students report experiencing sexual harassment, while one-third of freshman college students indicated that they had been sexually harassed (American Association of University Women, 2006). If sexual harassment is a common and recurrent practice in elementary, high school, and college settings, it is easy to see how it might occur in the workplace as simply a natural extension of the type of behavior that has been normalized elsewhere. Fraternities on college campuses have contributed to the acceptance of general harassment by allowing initiation rites or hazing rituals. Many of these male-bonding activities degrade their target (the new pledge) and are of a sexual nature.

## Patriarchy

The term "patriarchy" comes from the Greek, meaning "rule of the fathers." According to patriarchy theory, the central cause of sexual harassment, and any discrimination based on gender, is the fact that men have always attempted to hold the power in social, political, domestic, and economic spheres of life and will continue to do so. In terms of their influence, women are more apt to be confined to the private sphere – the domestic sphere – while men occupy the public space (Walby, 1988, 1990). Even though women have gained access to occupations, patriarchy will keep them from exercising any real power within them. Organizations that are hierarchical, with women occupying primarily the lower levels, foster a climate for harassment of women. Men are able to use sexual harassment as one means of keeping women in their place and of maintaining their control of organizational practices and resources.

Catherine MacKinnon, a professor of law at the University of Michigan, has argued that sexual harassment is not the expression of male sexual urges, but the way in which men maintain their power (MacKinnon, 1979). As women enter the workforce in greater numbers and enter male domains, men's aggression becomes a weapon they use to protect their space and to keep women from sharing in organizational rewards. MacKinnon's analysis of the nature of power and group dynamics can be applied to any marginalized group, such as racial minorities.

Some debate has occurred over whether or not patriarchy is a permanent, impervious fact of human nature; Goldberg (1973, 1993) has advanced the argument that patriarchy is inevitable because dominance on average is more biologically prevalent in males than in females, due to the male hormone, testosterone. Testosterone is associated with strength and aggression. Thus, unless male biology changes to reduce the production of testosterone or female biology changes to produce more of it, men will continue to dominate the social structure. Socio-biologists, on the other hand, would believe that both human behavior and physical traits are adaptive and evolve over time. Therefore, patriarchy would not be inevitable – it would depend on the evolution of physical as well as environmental factors. Some socio-biologists note that in many environments, cooperation is more likely to emerge than competition (Axelrod, 1984).

## Male Bonding

Some social theorists suggest that when men are in groups they are more likely to harass women than when men are alone. Stoltenberg maintains that "Male bonding is institutionalized learned behavior whereby men recognize and reinforce one another's bona fide membership in the male gender class and whereby men remind one another that they were not born women" (2004, p. 42). Male bonding is a behavioral code of gestures, speech, attitudes, and routines that separate men from women. Males harass women as one way to bond with other males and to gain status from other men in their group. A group of construction workers making "wolf-whistles" at a female as she walks by them, or a group of male work colleagues standing around at the water cooler commenting on a woman's body as she walks by, are two examples of such behavior. The more patriarchal a culture, the more these aberrant ways of male bonding are acceptable behaviors.

## Sex-Roles and Sex-Role Spillover

When women work outside of their expected sex-role in occupations that are considered to be non-traditional roles for women, harassment is likely to be acceptable behavior. In an experimental study, male and female participants were less likely to perceive incidents of sexual coercion as harassment when a woman was in a non-traditional occupation (Burgess & Borgida, 1997).

Furthermore, when gender roles are differentiated in the home, where women do one set of tasks, such as cooking, cleaning, and laundry, and men do other tasks, such as mowing the lawn, pounding nails, and cleaning gutters, there will be what has been called a spillover effect to the workplace. Because men's and women's roles have been differentiated at home, the same pattern occurs at work. Men will be considered suitable for some jobs and women others. If men subordinate their wives in the domestic sphere and if women take on a gender-specific role in the home, it is likely that these roles and attitudes will carry-over into the work environment (Gutek & Morasch, 1982). In terms of sexual harassment, the problem occurs when women are treated badly in the domestic sphere; if women are abused and treated as inferior at home, this type of treatment will carry-over to the work environment.

## Misconceptions of Women's Friendliness

Some social scientists have pointed out that a man may mistake a woman's friendliness toward him as a signal that she is attracted to him. When this happens, the man may make a pass at the woman, thinking she is inviting it. One particular study found that males misconstrued women's flirtatious behavior to be sexual, whereas the women meant it to be "fun and relational" (Henningsen, 2004). The study proposes that people flirt for a variety of reasons: for sex, fun, exploration, as a way to relate to each other, and for their own self-esteem. Men tended to view flirting as more sexual than women did, and women attributed more relational and fun motivations to flirting interactions than men did. No gender differences arose for the other motivations.

In addition, researchers have found that men and women label the same action differently. For example, a man inviting a woman to lunch or complimenting her appearance might be interpreted as menacing by the woman, but the man may think his actions are simply friendly gestures. A woman who doesn't resist advances immediately might do so out of fear of losing her job, whereas the man may take this lack of resistance as a signal of her acceptance of the advances. Two online studies (of 238 young adults in the first study and 198 in the second) evaluated the misconception of sexual and romantic interests of friendships between men and women. Males over-perceived and females under-perceived their friend's sexual interest in them (Koenig, Kirkpatrick, & Ketelaar, 2007).

Other studies have replicated this general finding concerning different perceptions of female friendliness. Men have been shown to more likely attribute sexual desire to women during friendly interactions (Abbey & Melby, 1986; Johnson, Stockdale, & Saal, 1991). In scenarios depicting verbal and physical harassment of women, women are more apt to label actions of a male as harassment than men (Osman, 2004). Especially in situations where women are subordinate to a male harasser, the women may smile or act friendly in an attempt to deflect the harassment and in an effort to maintain a positive work relationship. Unfortunately, this behavior on the part of the female may send exactly the wrong signal to the male.

## Personality and Fairness in Organizations

The likelihood of men harassing women can be influenced by both their personality and their perception of organizational justice (Krings & Facchin, 2009). Organizational justice can be described in several ways: distributive justice is the fairness of an outcome such as a raise, promotion, or an assignment; procedural justice is the equal treatment in procedures used to make decisions and determine outcomes; and interpersonal justice is fairness in the way people treat each other during an organizational process, perhaps how two employees treat each other. In one study, men who felt disrespectfully treated by their supervisor (interpersonal justice) were more likely to sexually harass. In addition, men who were prone to "low agreeableness" – impulsiveness combined with hostility – and sexism (measurable personality traits) were more likely to experience negative emotions and aggressive reactions that would be directed at women (Krings & Facchin, 2009). Similarly, Skarlicki, Folger, and Tesluk (1999) found that individuals who perceive their treatment by the organization and co-workers to be procedurally and distributively unfair were more likely to retaliate against women co-workers. It is easy to understand why a sexist man who feels mistreated by a woman would be more prone to harass her than a non-sexist man who encounters the same situation. Similarly, a sexist male who perceives that a woman was unjustly promoted ahead of him would be more likely to harass than a non-sexist male confronted by the same circumstances.

*Types of Harassers*

Harassers can be divided into two broad types: those who harass in public and those who harass in private (Dzeich & Weiner, 1990). The former often flaunt their sexist attitudes with colleagues and subordinates, while the latter are far more careful about public displays of discrimination. They are interested in finding their target alone where they can intimidate and threaten the individual without being discovered.

Although most reported cases of sexual harassment are male-on-female, it is not unheard of for men to harass other men and for women to harass men. In a case involving a Denver Chevrolet dealership, several men alleged that two male used-car salesmen touched or grabbed their genitals, thrust their pelvises against the buttocks of other male employees, used derogatory and crude language, and exposed themselves in the workplace (EEOC, 2000). The case was settled out-of-court for half-a-million dollars. In another case, a man was harassed by his female manager. A female supervisor of Domino's Pizza continually caressed a male employee's shoulders and neck and pinched his buttocks. The case went to trial in Tampa and the male employee was awarded $237,000 in damages (*EEOC* v. *Domino's Pizza Inc.*, 909 F. supp. 1529, M.D. Fla. 1995).

The cases of female-to-male harassment, although not as common as male-to-female harassment, are becoming more frequent because women are in positions of authority and power that were unheard of many years ago. In addition, with more awareness of the problem and legal protections, men may be more apt to report harassment than they were in the past.

## Employer Liability

A critical element of sexual harassment cases is the determination of employer liability. An employer may be liable for the conduct of employees if the employer knew, or should have known, about the sexual harassment and did not take any corrective action. Employers may be liable for the actions not only of their employees, but also of their customers and independent contractors, if they knew that sexual harassment by these individuals had occurred, since employers are expected to protect the civil rights of their employees at work. In recent years, companies have been forced by the courts to pay women large settlements for not attempting to prevent harassment once they had knowledge of it. An employer may be expected to know about a hostile work environment if someone complained to management or if the harassment is practiced openly and is well-known to others in the company. In the contemporary organization, management is expected to establish a policy against sexual harassment and distribute it to all employees. Many corporations take the added step of training all employees about the nature of sexual harassment and informing them of their rights. *Faragher* v. *Boca Raton* provides an example of the liability that organizations bear; in spite of management's lack of knowledge about harassment of female lifeguards, the City of Boca Raton was held to be liable (see case description under Landmark Cases, p. 184).

## Workplace Romance or Sexual Harassment?

A workplace romance between two adults that is consensual is not deemed to be sexual harassment and is not illegal, although some employers discourage workplace relationships, especially when the parties are working in the same business unit or when one is supervising the other. According to a report by the Society for Human Resources

Management (Parks, 2006), only about 18% of companies surveyed had written policies about workplace romances. Companies that did have such policies particularly discouraged romances between supervisors and subordinates, and public displays of affection in the workplace.

In cases involving workplace romances, both parties want the attention they are giving to one another, and presumably neither party has been coerced into a romantic or sexual relationship. Problems arise, however, when one individual wants to end the relationship, while the other wants to continue and persists in sexual advances toward the person who no longer wants to be involved. In these situations, it may be hard to judge exactly when the relationship fractured and whether or not sexual attention was wanted or unwanted by either party. In other cases, the presence of workplace romances may make other non-involved parties uncomfortable. In a California State Supreme Court case against the Department of Corrections, Edna Miller, an employee with one of the state's prisons, filed a lawsuit alleging a hostile work environment because Lewis Kuykendall, the prison warden where she worked, was sexually involved with three of his subordinates, giving them preferential work treatment, helping them advance in the organization, and fondling them in view of other workers (*Edna Miller et al.* v. *Department of Corrections*). These relationships were among consenting adults.

## Individual Responses to Sexual Harassment

Individual responses to sexual harassment vary. A person may ignore a sexual comment or not be offended by it, while another individual may find it difficult to work in a situation where sexual jokes are the norm. In addition to the responses that individuals have to harassment based on their personalities, the general work environment influences individuals' willingness to come forward and complain. When employees are generally treated in an unprofessional and disrespectful way, it is unlikely that they will be treated with respect if they file a sexual-harassment complaint (Bergman, Langhout, Palmieri, Cortina, & Fitzgerald, 2002). Their complaints are unlikely to be taken seriously, especially if they are against a supervisor or higher-level manager.

Fitzgerald, Swan, and Fischer (1995) argue that many people explain women's responses based on the degree of assertiveness, or their willingness to confront their harasser or the organization. According to the authors, this one-dimensional scale does not accurately reflect the possible responses to sexual harassment. Instead they suggest two classifications of responses: internally or externally focused responses. Internally focused strategies are those used by women to manage their emotions and thoughts related to the event or events. These include such things as enduring the harassment, denying it is happening, detaching from it, re-attributing the harassment by defining it as something else, or blaming oneself. Internally focused strategies, though many seem destructive to the individual, are intended to help the person cope. Externally focused responses are those focused on actively solving the problem. These strategies include avoidance of the harasser, appeasement, assertion, attempts to seek organizational help, and attempts to seek social support outside the organization. Each sexual harassment event is unique and each organization different, so it is unwise to dictate exactly how someone should respond to harassment. It is important for women to think through the implications of whichever action (or inaction) they take.

Many studies have demonstrated that sexual harassment takes a toll on individuals and organizations because victims suffer stress, low morale, inability to concentrate at work, and, ultimately, lower productivity (Fitzgerald et al., 1995; Schneider, Swan, & Fitzgerald, 1997). The psychological literature provides examples of the type of mental

problems people face because of sexual harassment. A study of 262 women in counseling settings showed evidence of their mental stress and loss of confidence (Crull,
1982). Moreover, studies of women in the military associate in-service sexual harassment with post-traumatic stress disorder (Murdoch, Polusny, Hodges, & Cowper,
2006). For women in the armed forces, the presence of sexual harassment will undoubtedly feel like a violation of their government-protected civil rights. They signed on to
serve their country and protect others in a setting where service people are supposed to
look after one another, yet they are victimized by their "comrades" and often not sup-
ported by their own government.

Some women may wish to file a formal grievance or informally complain to
someone, but they fear retaliation. This retaliation could take many forms. For
example, the harassment could become worse. This outcome is most likely in organizations that generally turn a blind eye to discrimination of any kind. Because the harasser
knows that he will not be punished, he intensifies his efforts as a way to get back at the
woman who complained about him. A more subtle form of retaliation occurs when the
woman is labeled a "trouble maker" in the organization – although this label is not
outwardly expressed. She is simply less apt to be promoted and may be otherwise marginalized. Some women fear making their case public even if they know they plan to
leave an organization; they worry about obtaining good references from their employer
or are concerned that the news of their complaint will be informally spread to other
organizations. This may make it difficult for them to secure employment elsewhere,
even if the sexual harassment was acknowledged to have happened. Future employers
may be worried about taking on someone who has a record of suing or pursuing litigation against a company.

A recent study about sexual harassment prevention training and its impact on
responses to harassment is relevant to the question of whether or not individuals feel
comfortable reporting harassment (Goldberg, 2007). The study, conducted with 282
full-time professionals – 55% male and 45% female – used a pre- and post-test format
to see if individuals altered their intended responses to sexual harassment. Both a
control group and an experimental group were asked to complete surveys twice – and
both groups received sexual harassment prevention training in a lecture format
between the first and second surveys. The lecture covered relevant legislation, key court
decisions, fundamental definitions of harassment, employer liability, policies, and
grievance procedures for victims of harassment to report the behavior. The experimental group, however, had additional content – their training emphasized the potential
negative ramifications of formally reporting a sexual harassment incident, while the
control group did not receive this information. Participants in the experiment group
expressed a lower likelihood of confronting the perpetrator of sexual harassment than
did control-group subjects. Apparently, participants weigh the pros and cons of confrontation against the potential of retaliation and decide against confrontation. Participants in both groups would not report gender harassment or sexual attention if they
were prone to avoid conflict.

Other studies have shown that people with few personal resources (or power) are less
apt to be assertive in situations involving social sexual behavior (Gruber & Bjorn,
1986; Knapp, Faley, Ekeberg, & Dubois, 1997). Many sexual-harassment policies,
including the US Equal Opportunity Commission's Policy Guidance, suggest that
individuals should first try to confront their harasser and tell him or her that the harassment is unwelcome. Indeed, Powell and Graves (2003) report that this approach
improves conditions for 60% of female victims and 61% of male victims (p. 176).
Given the results of these studies, sexual-harassment trainers need to manage the fears

that conflict-avoidant individuals have about reporting sexual harassment while at the same time painting an accurate picture about what one might expect after filing an internal complaint (Goldberg, 2007, p. 71). Goldberg (2007) did not indicate that harassment training increases the likelihood of seeking external advice; therefore offering sexual-harassment training does not seem to invite litigation.

Data collected from 41 studies and 70,000 respondents in a meta-analysis report that sexual harassment is one of the most damaging barriers to career success and satisfaction. Representing many different types of organizations and job roles, women in these studies describe decreased job satisfaction, lower organizational commitment, decreased mental and physical health, post-traumatic stress syndrome, and withdrawal from work (Willness, Steel, & Lee, 2007). It is not difficult to understand how unwanted sexual attention at work could interfere with one's career. Victims of harassment are more often preoccupied with fending off their harasser on a daily basis or avoiding contact with him or her altogether, than they are with work tasks or future career opportunities.

## Organizational Responses to Sexual Harassment

In business settings, most companies have sexual-harassment policies that describe what women should do if they have been harassed. The worst of these policies will suggest that a harassed women speak to her supervisor if she has been victimized – using the chain of command to resolve the problem. This procedure is ill-advised as the supervisor or someone in the management chain may be her harasser. The best policies identify a neutral person (for example, an ombudsperson whose job it is to investigate employee-relations issues) or a neutral employee group to conduct an investigation, while protecting the identities of both the alleged harasser and alleged victim. In practice, of course, protecting anonymity is difficult because some individuals in the organization will be interviewed to try to ascertain if, when, how many times, and where the harassment occurred. It is difficult to keep the rumor mill from churning. Both the alleged victim and alleged harasser may be surprised to find out that a confidential investigation has turned public. Those who investigate claims need to insist that individuals keep confidentiality for several reasons – individuals' privacy and rights need to be protected. Additionally, morale and productivity may be adversely affected if other employees begin discussing a case.

Company managers have an obligation to intervene if they witness sexual harassment or if they receive a complaint. If they do not take action, the company may be financially liable for the harassment. Company policies typically define what actions managers should take. In the first instance, they should listen to the complaint and document exactly what the individual says to them. Then they should notify the appropriate person or persons who will investigate the charge, and at the same time make the policy clear to the alleged perpetrator.

James and Wooten (2006) studied the responses of organizations to both racial- and sexual-discrimination claims. The authors propose that there are two general theories that relate to how organizations handle discrimination crises: threat-rigidity theory and institutional theory. Threat rigidity occurs when an organization's initial response is to gather and search for information. Soon, however, leaders reach their cognitive capacity and abandon their search for new information about the case. At this point leaders become less flexible and potentially risk more because they block out any new information that might come along. Institutional theory suggests that organizations become similar in their approach to a discrimination claim and that they follow basically the same pattern of response. In sexual-harassment discrimination claims, organizations will initially deny a claim. When outside stakeholders become involved and mobilize against an organization (women's groups, the press, etc.), they retaliate against the plaintiff, perhaps by firing the person or attempting to intimidate her. In addition, they retaliate against the legal process by attempting to manipulate the process (shredding or not providing documents, and using delay tactics, for example). Most notably, the organizations that were studied had a different response in racial- versus sexual-harassment cases when outside stakeholders (agitators, women's groups, racial justice groups, etc.) became involved:

> What was surprising was the variance in the presence or absence of informal (non-legal) coercive pressures over types of lawsuits, and the ways in which firms responded to these pressures. For example, firms accused of gender, age, disability, or religious discrimination experienced no informal pressure from externally mobi-lized groups. Yet groups were actively mobilized against firms accused of race dis-crimination and sexual harassment. Moreover, in race-based discrimination lawsuits, activists who held little to no legitimate power over organizations were particularly influential in how the latter responded to allegations of discrimina-tion. In these cases, firms were fairly quick to accommodate the demands of such groups. To the contrary, rather than succumb to mobilization pressures, firms in sexual harassment cases were more likely to engage activists in fairly combative ways. A reasonable conclusion based on this finding is that there is a proclivity to respond with fear to accusations associated with racial matters, whereas accusations of harassment directed toward women evoke anger.
>
> (James & Wooten, 2006, p. 1116)

The authors hypothesize that the difference in response to sexual-harassment cases versus cases involving race is because sexual-harassment cases have a high burden of proof on the part of the plaintiffs, and lawsuits can easily be construed as personality conflicts between two people rather than civil rights issues. Given the burden of proof and the ambiguity of many cases, organizations will adopt an antagonistic response to the plaintiff, the legal process, and any outside stakeholders. It could also be that racial justice groups are perceived to be more powerful opponents than women's rights groups.

## When It's Not Sexual But Still Harassment – Incivility and Bullying

Many forms of harassment are not legally recognized because they do not have a sexual component. Abuse of one person by another by bullying, verbal, or psychological abuse are examples of behavior that may not be sexual in nature, but are as destructive as forms of sexual harassment. Bullying, aggression, and verbal abuse are perpetrated on others for the sheer pleasure of exercising power. Women as well as men can be bullies, and many perpetrators choose someone of their own sex to victimize (Namie, 2007). Often if an organization knows about the behavior of the bully when the bully's target is of the same sex, the behavior is perceived to be a personality clash between two people, rather than a serious problem that requires intervention.

Verbal abuse in front of others is one way to bully another, but perhaps an even more potent and manipulative way is to make calculated moves to render the target unproductive and unsuccessful. This can involve spreading rumors about the person's competence, or setting the person up for failure by withholding critical information from them, or denying them resources to effectively do their jobs. Because bullies are often in positions of higher authority over their victims, these activities are easy to conduct. Bullies are usually very adept at managing upward and maintaining positive relationships with their superiors, making it even more difficult for victims to complain. Workplace bullying is characterized by repeated actions by the bully rather than an isolated incident, and an escalation in terms of the seriousness of the bully's abuse. Frequently the victim is subjected to abuse by the bully for a year or more (Keashly & Jagatic, 2003).

When the bully is male and the target female, the actions of the bully may be the result of general animosity toward women, and women may be seen as an easy target for aggressive behavior. For example, in the UK, females became targets in a fire brigade that was composed of primarily male firefighters (Archer, 1999).

Few countries have specific laws against bullying behavior. In the US, although several states have introduced legislation against bullying, there are no federal or state laws against it. Sweden is the only country in Europe with legislation specific to bullying. Sweden's Victimization at Work ordinance falls under its Occupational Safety and Health provisions. In Australia, employers can be fined up to AUS$100,000 for failing to adequately manage bullying behavior. Some provinces in Canada, for example Saskatchewan and Quebec, have laws against workplace bullying. In the UK, the "Dignity At Work" bill is designed to specifically address the problems of bullying in the workplace. Although it has been introduced as legislation, it has yet to become law. Clearly, nations need to recognize that bullying is a form of harassment, and can be just as psychologically damaging as sexual harassment.

### Suggested Websites

http://apa.org The American Psychological Association website features many articles about sexual harassment. Type "sexual harassment" in the search box.

www.abanet.org The American Bar Association website is a useful resource for understanding the law and for specific reference to sexual-harassment cases. Type "sexual harassment" in the search box.

www.eeoc.gov/facts/fx-html This is the Equal Employment Opportunity Commission's website that contains a factual guide to sexual harassment.

# CASE STUDIES

## Case Study 1: Sales at Syntec Corporation

Megan Green was excited about her new sales position. She had interviewed among stiff competition for the job with Syntec Corporation and was elated to find that she was offered a position in the south-eastern territory. Unlike other sales positions for which she interviewed, Syntec offered a salary plus generous commissions and a benefit package that included healthcare and retirement benefits. Syntec was an up-and-coming software provider that sold its products across the United States. Syntec's suite of real-time accounting software was its number-one seller, but the company also sold payroll-system software. Megan felt that Syntax was a good fit, not only because her undergraduate degree was in business administration with an emphasis on information technology, but also because she liked the informality of the company. When sales representatives were not meeting with clients, they dressed casually; the men wore khakis and dress shirts but left their ties at home, and the women wore slacks instead of dresses or business suits.

### Megan's First Several Weeks

Syntec prided itself on its sales training program for new employees. Megan would be paired with another sales representative, Mark Henderson, and her district manager, Jeff Amundson. For three weeks they poured over training manuals introducing Syntec's products and a standard approach for demonstrating them. Over these early weeks, Megan learned to answer client questions about the software, to sell to both individuals and to committees, and to handle objections effectively. She was videotaped during various role-play situations designed to teach her how to deal with a variety of personalities and myriad products. Megan felt lucky to be paired with Mark Henderson since he had already had sales jobs in the software industry and was clearly more experienced than she was. He was taking the training primarily because he was required to learn Syntec's products and Syntec's way of selling. Mark, a 26-year-old, had a background similar to Megan; he had attended a state university in the Midwest, graduating with a degree in business.

Jeff Amundson had been present in the final stage of her interviews and he seemed genuine about wanting Megan to succeed with the company. He was in his mid-30s and had been with Syntec for 10 years. Jeff had trained many salespeople over the years, and his veteran trainees had spoken to Megan about how fortunate she was to have him as her immediate sales supervisor. In the last two weeks of the sales training program, Megan and Mark traveled with Jeff to observe him with clients and prospective clients. He was adept at establishing immediate rapport with prospects and converted approximately 50% of them into clients. Megan kept track of questions clients asked and how Jeff responded to them. With her notebook of questions about technical support, product costs, licensing, computer upgrades, and compatibility with other programs, she felt prepared to handle queries that might come up. After these client meetings, Jeff, Mark, and Megan would de-brief each situation over drinks and dinner in their hotel. All three typically repaired to the hotel bar, where they reviewed their day. Megan was careful to only have one drink (she wanted to maintain an image of professionalism), while Jeff and Mark had several and remained in the bar well after she left at about 10 p.m.

### Back at the Sales Office

Back at the office, Jeff was busy with the rest of his team: five men in their twenties and thirties. Megan was not the only female sales representative, but she was the only woman on

Jeff's team. Cynthia Johnson, Pam Peterson, and Divia Patel were on different teams, reporting to other district sales managers. She had not had much contact with these women only because she had been so busy with her training schedule. When things slowed down a bit, she intended to invite them to lunch and compare their training to her experiences.

After the training had finished, Jeff scheduled a meeting with Megan and Mark to let them know that he was comfortable having them go out on calls without his supervision. As he put it, "Burn up the territory and meet your monthly sales quota in the first two weeks! You two are definitely ready to start making some real money."

Because many of Syntec's prospects were located in Atlanta, he suggested that they schedule a trip there to make their first calls together. Megan and Jeff decided that they would travel together, but call on prospects separately. Both of them wanted to test out their own sales skills without possible intervention from the other. In addition, both felt this was a better use of their time and neither wanted to split commissions if they did manage to sell something. Megan and Jeff agreed that, at the end of each day, they would meet to discuss how their sales calls went and to share anything that they had learned.

### The Atlanta Trip

After the first long day of sales calls, Megan felt encouraged. With her rental car, she had navigated the city well and met with three potential customers: the first a hospital administrator; the second the manager of a large hotel chain; and the third a director of a conference center. She was eager to swap stories with Mark and to find out what sort of experiences he had had. After a quick shower and a change out of her business suit into more comfortable clothing, she met Mark in the hotel restaurant. They sat down to a leisurely dinner and then retired to the hotel bar.

"Wow, you look great in a pair of jeans. A lot more relaxed," Mark said.

"I feel more relaxed. What a day! I'm pretty upbeat but I'm glad it's over."

"OK, so tell me how it went," Mark said.

Megan began a brief summary of her first call. "I felt very confident with the hotel manager. I knew the software well and I was right on with suggestions for how to deal with his data-management problems. At the start of the call, I was worried that he wasn't giving me his full attention. You know, grabbing the phone every few minutes to take calls. Then I asked if we could find a conference room where he wouldn't be interrupted. He agreed. From that point, I really think he liked the product and our approach. Anyway, I didn't close him. He has to go through his IT manager, but I think I am at least halfway there. He thinks we can probably do a follow-up via a conference call in about a week.

"The call with the hospital administrator was tougher. I really don't know his business that well. Aside from getting my appendix taken out as a teenager, I don't think I've ever been in a hospital."

Mark leaned across the cocktail table and touched her arm, "I'm sure you were very brave. Can I see the scar? I bet it's as beautiful as the stomach it sits on."

Megan withdrew her arm and tried to ignore the comment. Instead, she made light of it, "It's too ugly for words. I wouldn't want to put you through that. Let me tell you about this hospital guy. He kept throwing out acronyms. I had no idea what they meant so I just nodded my head, acting like I knew what he was talking about."

"Don't be afraid to ask him to explain them. Next time tell him that you want to learn everything about his operation. He'll be impressed if you take notes. Besides you're a good-looking woman who could easily sway him. Just sit a little closer to him and wear a low-cut blouse," Mark laughed.

As they continued to discuss their days, Mark ordered another gin and tonic, while Megan stuck to her glass of wine. She was getting helpful hints from Mark about handling client situations. She didn't like his references to using her sexuality to sell or his comment about her stomach, but she felt awkward about saying anything.

After Megan finished talking about her calls, Mark talked about his. He had met with four customers, all business owners. He had successfully closed two of the calls; one was a "maybe" and the other a definite "no."

He leaned over to Megan and whispered in her ear, "I don't waste my time with someone who doesn't want to do business with me. There are other fish to fry. Anyway, enough business talk. There's a band playing next door. Let's go over and check it out."

"OK," Megan replied.

They walked to the Elysian Fields, a dance club directly opposite the hotel. Megan enjoyed dancing, but rarely did these days, because she felt uncomfortable going into a dance club alone or even with a few women friends. It felt too much like a meat market. She and Mark danced for about half-an-hour, until Megan looked at her watch and was surprised to find it read 11:00.

"Mark, I'm really tired. I think I need to get back."

"Too bad. You're a great dancer. I like the way you move," Mark said.

"I have a lot of early appointments tomorrow and I really need some sleep."

"OK, let's meet for dinner tomorrow night, say about 7."

"Fine," Megan replied, "I'll see you then."

### Megan's Second Day of Appointments
Megan saw three prospects the next day. She had used a couple of Mark's tips that seemed to work well. One prospect out of the three seemed genuinely ready to buy the software, but as in her experience the day before, he needed to secure approval from his boss first.

As planned, Mark and Megan reviewed their respective sales calls over dinner.

Megan began, "I felt much more confident today than I did yesterday. One guy I met with was clearly just interested in a free lunch. I don't think his organization really needs what we can provide and he is too far down the corporate ladder to make the decision anyway. I did have a good meeting with a Director of Information Technology for a retail chain, though, and he told me that he was genuinely interested. It was a little frustrating because he needs to get approval from the Vice President of IT. This means I either have to try to do a conference call from the office or come back to Atlanta in two weeks."

Mark thought for a moment, "OK ... you need to get to the decision-makers, if at all possible, on the first call. It will improve your likelihood of a sale and it won't waste your time."

"How do I do that?" asked Megan.

"When you're setting up the appointment, ask the person you are talking to if anyone else should be at the meeting. Ask the person if he or she can make the decision to buy. Be blunt. Ask them who has the authority to make the buying decision and request that they attend the meeting. If that doesn't work just wear a low-cut blouse," he leaned over towards her and laughed. "You could even wear that one and just unbutton that button there." He pointed to the third button from the top of her blouse.

She ignored his last comment, "Won't asking them seem a little pushy?"

"Not at all. Try it."

"Mark, I'll see you tomorrow morning. We've got an early plane to catch. We need to be at the airport by 8:00 so I'll meet you down in the lobby at 6:15."

As she got up to go, Mark grabbed her arm and said, "We've been having such a good time together. Is there any chance you might want to come to my room tonight? You look like you need a little fun."

Embarrassed, she said, "Ah, no … I'm really tired and have to get some sleep." She rose and walked briskly toward the elevator, leaving Mark at the table.

### Back at the Office

Megan was still troubled by the incident in Atlanta and felt awkward around Mark Henderson. She avoided him altogether, making sure that she parked far away from him, did not meet him in the hallway, and left after he did. She even avoided the breakroom where other sales reps ate their lunch or just chatted together. Worse still, Mark sometimes walked by her cubicle and just stared at her before moving along to talk to someone else. She wondered who she could talk to about the incident in Atlanta and her discomfort in the office. She couldn't decide whether to confide in anyone at all.

She thought about talking to Jeff but she didn't know how he would respond. He seemed to like Mark and they often went out for drinks together after work. As a new employee, she worried about rocking the boat and causing any kind of controversy within her district, especially because she knew Jeff Amundson was the best sales manager in the region, whose people did extremely well. All of Jeff's people were making more money than new representatives in other districts. She was worried about whether or not they might assign her to another district if she complained. She also knew that if Jeff had to choose between a rookie salesperson like her and an experienced one like Mark, he would choose the latter. Mark was the most successful sales person in the district. She needed this job and didn't want to put it in jeopardy in any way. On the other hand, she thought Mark had overstepped a boundary and had come on to her when she didn't invite him to do so.

Megan knew that she had to do something; she just didn't know what.

---

### Discussion Questions

1. Study the legal definition of sexual harassment on page 161. Do you think Megan was sexually harassed? Why, or why not? If you were defending the company against a sexual-harassment lawsuit, how would you argue that sexual harassment had not occurred and that the company was not liable?
2. In your opinion, was Megan partly responsible for Mark's actions? Why, or why not?
3. Identify the various approaches Megan could take and their possible costs and benefits.
4. With whom could Megan discuss her situation? What should she say to each?
5. Which of Syntec's organizational practices might encourage a climate for harassment?
6. If you were going to write up a Sexual Harassment Policy for a sales company like Syntec, what important points would it cover?

## Case Study 2: Homophobia at Klein Corporation

Ellen Ryan was the marketing manager for Klein Corporation, a mid-sized food-distribution company located in Roanoke, Virginia. Klein served owners of family restaurants and franchisees of mid-sized restaurants. Its line of food included entrees such as chicken cordon bleu, salmon with béarnaise sauce, and vegetarian lasagna, and side dishes such as prepared salads and fruit dishes. Restaurants with high turnover used food-distribution companies like Klein because the company's product line enables them to serve dependable, high-quality dishes without a lot of preparation.

Ellen had been with the Klein Corporation for two years. Before joining Klein, she had worked for a larger food distributor and then taken a break from work to pursue an MBA degree. Klein had given her the opportunity to forge a stronger bond between the sales and marketing divisions of the company. Ellen's position required preparing all of the marketing literature for the sales force about the various food products that Klein offered. She worked with the sales force whenever there was a new product launch, helping them understand how to position the product with other products in Klein's line. In addition, she helped the salespeople work with individual restaurant owners to improve their profits by pricing and displaying products appropriately. Ellen felt strongly that the company could improve its own bottom-line by improving the bottom-line of its customers. As a supplier, Klein advocated working in partnership with the restaurants it served.

Ellen was a lesbian. She had been living with the same woman for nearly 10 years. They considered themselves partners for life. Although she did not make her sexual preference known to anyone in the company, she did keep her eye out for other women who might share her sexual orientation. She often felt isolated and would have welcomed knowing if there were other gays or lesbians in the organization. She felt it best to stay in the closet in an environment that consisted mainly of men. She was careful not to display pictures of her partner in her office and she did not talk about her social life with her colleagues.

In order to foster better communication between the marketing and sales divisions, Ellen was occasionally invited to the annual sales meetings, not as a participant but as an observer. She was looking forward to the upcoming sales meeting in New Orleans in two weeks. Sales meetings were always an opportunity for her to see how marketing literature was used by salespeople. She was able to influence how salespeople used it and she was often given good ideas for ways to revise the literature so that it would be even more effective with Klein's client base.

### *The Annual Sales Meeting*

Ellen attended the sales meeting along with 20 male and five female sales managers from around the United States. Usually before the meetings officially started, everyone gathered for a continental breakfast in the meeting room of the hotel. The atmosphere was lively and informal. Clearly the sales managers were well-acquainted with one another; some had known each other for years.

As they ate breakfast, the men's banter soon deteriorated into sexist remarks about women.

"So, Carl, are you going to get any action tonight? There are some pretty good looking women down on Bourbon Street. Some even have moustaches and are about your size," Phil joked.

"Yeah, Carl. Every year you threaten to bring one of them to the closing dinner, but it never happens. Haven't you been able to score?" Stan added.

"You should talk, Stan. When was the last time you were successful catching anything? The only thing you've been able to dredge up is a fish out of Lake Pontchatrain when we all hired that boat. The high-class hookers in the casinos wouldn't even talk to you last year!" Carl said.

"Talk about catching stuff. Did you bring your penicillin with you again this year, Phil?" Stan laughed.

"No, my wife forgot to put it in my kit this year when she packed the condoms."

The men continued joking about "their inability to get some action." Ellen sat there embarrassed, offended, and speechless, hoping the subject would end. The female sales managers, who were probably more accustomed to this type of bantering, seemed to ignore the men and talked among themselves. Bob Evans, the Sales Director, was present but had not been participating in the jokes. Finally, he called the meeting to order. During the meeting, the managers acted professionally, discussing sales targets as well as products that seemed to be more difficult to sell. Each manager reviewed his or her sales progress against their target. At noon the group broke for lunch.

### The Lunch Break
When Ellen arrived in the dining room, all of the seats were taken except for one. She joined a table of six male managers for lunch. Again, the discussion turned to sexual innuendos and jokes. This time it was even more directly offensive to her.

Stan began, "Did you hear about the new brand of tennis shoes for lesbians called Dykes? They have a long tongue and it only takes one finger to get them off."

The men burst into laughter.

"Speaking of dykes. Did you see Roseanne Barr on TV last night? Now that's a dyke I wouldn't put my finger into," said Phil.

"Yeah, but Ellen DeGeneres and whoever her girlfriend is … that's a pair I'd like to be a fly on the wall of," said Stan.

"Yeah, you should know, faggot. Look at those beads around your neck. They're sooo sweet," one of the men chuckled while grabbing the Mardi Grad beads around Stan's neck.

"Now come on … I'm wearing these to be in the New Orleans spirit. We went out partying last night. I'm not gay just because of a few beads! In fact, I threw a few of these beads at some of the rather well-endowed ladies on the floats," he countered.

The gay-bashing discussion went on between two or three of the men as they ate their sandwiches. Ellen couldn't tolerate the comments any longer. In disgust, she left the table before finishing her meal. She decided something needed to be done. The best course of action, she thought, would be to call the corporate head office's Human Resources Director to explain what was going on. After all, the company had a policy against this kind of thing. She called the Director's office and asked the Director's secretary to try to set up a conference call with both the Director and Vice President of Human Resources. She explained that she needed urgently to speak to both of them about a confidential matter. The secretary, noting the emotion in her voice, scheduled a conference call for that afternoon.

During the call Ellen explained in detail what had been said and by whom in both the morning session and during lunch. The HR Vice President advised her in the following way:

"We don't support this kind of behavior at Klein. I think you should feel free to personally confront those individuals who have offended you and tell them what they said and why it was offensive to you. The only way they will understand how their behavior is affecting you is if you make the complaint personally. They need to hear how their behavior affected you. I will support you if you decide to do this, but it's up to you. You need to think about what you'd like to do and then do it," he said.

Ellen decided she would bring up the sales managers' behavior the first thing the next morning. But first she needed to inform Bob Evans to make sure he would support her actions. When she discussed the matter with him, he encouraged her to say something about it at the outset of the morning session.

### The Morning Session

"Before we get started Ellen wants to say something about our meeting yesterday. I fully support her in what she has to say," said Bob.

With that, Ellen began, "Well, I'll be completely candid with all of you. I found the behavior of several of you and the jokes that were being traded back and forth completely unacceptable. In particular, Phil and Stan, I found your jokes about lesbians and 'getting some action' deeply offensive. I see no place for this kind of behavior in a business setting. Furthermore, our company has a policy against it."

The room fell silent for several minutes. Finally Stan spoke up.

"Well, I certainly didn't mean to offend you. What I said wasn't directed at you," he said.

"Neither did I. If I knew it bothered you, I certainly wouldn't have told any jokes. You see, Ellen, we are just used to being together in an informal setting and unwinding a bit. We know each other pretty well. We didn't mean any harm to you or anyone else," Phil explained.

Ellen continued to explain that there was no place in a business meeting for these kinds of remarks. It demonstrated disrespect for women, period, she reiterated. After she had made her points, the Sales Director called the meeting to order and the group turned to business issues.

### Two Months Later

Ellen was preparing for her annual performance appraisal. As part of this process, the company asked her to circulate questionnaires to gather feedback from various people in the company. She received feedback from her boss, her peers, and other employees with whom she worked – including the sales managers. Ellen's manager collected the feedback and evaluated her performance, in part, on what others reported about her.

When her manager discussed her feedback with her, she was shocked to find that he had gathered quotes from some of the sales managers criticizing her behavior during the annual sales conference. She was said to be intolerant of others' opinions and generally disruptive. Her manager read two of the comments to her:

"Ellen works hard, but she needs to learn to be more flexible and accommodating to others' styles. She also took us off-track during the sales meeting in New Orleans when she was meant to be there as an observer only. At the conference, we had a limited amount of time to deal with the issues and her interruptions did not add any value."

"Ellen needs to better understand the sales managers' jobs. She sometimes gives the impression that she is intractable in her views. She needs to be more tolerant of other people."

Ellen sat stupefied as she listened to these criticisms. Her manager continued discussing her performance:

"Ellen, I discussed these comments with Bob Evans to see if he shared the same perspective as these two individuals. I am sorry to say that he did. He also thought that during the conference you took the group off-track when they had important things to discuss. He told me that you needed to develop a better rapport with his guys."

Ellen began to feel angry as she listened.

"You know that the relationships you have with the sales managers are very important to the work that you do. I think you need to work on them a bit more. Perhaps meet more often with the sales managers just to find out what they think and how they operate. You met or exceeded every objective that I set for you this year, but with this kind of feedback I cannot give you the top performance rating. I know that this must be disappointing to you, but I am giving you an 'average rating' based on the information I have from others. Perceptions are very important."

She wondered what she should do about this feedback. Explain to her manager what had happened? Approach the Sales Director about these comments? Talk to the Human Resources Department?

She was convinced that there was a campaign of retaliation against her, one in which her manager was either knowingly or unknowingly participating.

**Discussion Questions**

1. Evaluate the company's success with its policy against harassment. What type of policy and actions would be effective in this type of environment?
2. According to the definitions of harassment at the beginning of this chapter, which type of harassment had Ellen experienced?
3. Evaluate the Director and Vice President of HR's actions. Is there anything else they could have done to support Ellen?

**Case Study 3: Smart Zone Office Supply**

The Smart Zone Office Supply Headquarters is located in an outer-ring suburb of Minneapolis, Minnesota. It houses approximately 90 staff members who oversee all of its products and services. Not only does it equip many businesses in the area with their paper, envelopes, mailing labels, file folders, and such, but it also supplies them with their coffee service and related paper products.

Janet Hall supervises an area responsible for the inventory of several of Smart Zone's office products. As such, she keeps track of the inventory needs of Smart Zone's retail stores and sources products from various vendors from all over the United States. She has developed strong relationships with store managers as well as many of Smart Zone's suppliers. Janet manages four men, all warehouse personnel who are responsible for stocking inventory and loading it on trucks for delivery to one of the many retail stores.

Under pressure from the CEO, Herb Crenshaw, to reduce costs, Janet had begun looking for alternative paper suppliers who could offer their products cheaper than Smart Zone's usual supplier. Janet had started buying from Peterson Paper because their bid was the lowest of four suppliers who were asked to submit a proposal for the business.

Herb was delighted with this supplier – the company delivers the product on time and it is of higher quality than Smart Zones' former supplier's product. In addition, Peterson will allow them to return any unsold paper at the end of the year.

Janet always signs off on the orders as they come in to make sure that the orders are correct and the payment terms accurate, and to ensure that the various office-supply items have not been damaged in any way. Lately, she has felt uncomfortable around Peterson's delivery person, Arthur Rolle. She discussed her concerns with a colleague and friend over coffee in the break room.

"I don't know this guy very well, but he makes me feel very uneasy. He stares at me, while he fondles himself," said Janet.

"He can't be shifting his underwear can he?" laughed Vanessa.

"It's not funny. He looks at me first and then starts playing with the front of his pants," said Janet.

"Well, what are you going to do? Herb seems to like this company and anyway, he probably thinks you can stand up to some pathetic character scratching himself. It's not like he is going to want to use another company after going through four proposals and interviewing other suppliers," Vanessa offered.

"Yeah, I know. He spent 10 minutes at the staff meeting telling everyone how pleased he was with the new arrangement we have. He isn't going to want to hear me complain about them," said Janet.

In the ensuing weeks, Arthur Rolle seemed to turn up at Janet's office for little, if any, reason. During these visits, he said he was stopping in to make a "customer service call" to ensure she was happy with the service and the product. Janet tried to be as dismissive as possible without offending him. The last time he arrived he suggested that Janet feel the muscles he was developing carrying boxes of paper to Smart Zone's warehouse and loading dock. Janet made light of his comment and said she was "too busy to engage in body building envy." During these visits, he continued to fondle himself in her presence.

Janet thought about trying to take this up with one of her male staff. After all, perhaps they could act as some sort of protection. After thinking about this for a time, she dismissed the idea. This wasn't the kind of thing she wanted her subordinates to know about – somehow she thought it might make her appear weak in their eyes. Anyway, bosses don't ask their employees for help. She tried to think of excuses for having them around, but this too was difficult.

"I can't just ask them to come and sit by me. Their job is out in the warehouse putting things away, stocking the shelves, and loading the trucks. What could I possible have them do in the office?" Janet confided in Vanessa.

"Well, I think you should just forget it. The guy is harmless. He isn't calling you at home or touching you or anything, is he?" Vanessa asked.

"Not yet, but I'm worried that that could come next. I find I am on edge around the noon hour when he typically shows up. He just scares me."

"Look, Janet. You could probably arm wrestle him to the ground. Maybe you should drop a heavy box on his toe. That might discourage him," Vanessa chuckled.

Janet felt angry with her friend. It was easy for her to make a joke of it when she was not face-to-face with him. Janet decided she had to take this up with Herb, but wondered what in the world she would say. Arthur Rolle's comments about his muscles could seem innocent enough, especially when taken in the context of his heavy-lifting activity. Janet wished that someone else had seen his behavior, but the two of them were always alone when he approached her. Nonetheless, she decided she would talk to Herb during their next regularly scheduled meeting.

### Discussion Questions

1.  Do you think an employer should be held responsible for the actions of his suppliers? Why, or why not?
2.  Assume that Herb finds this situation unacceptable, what should he do?

# LANDMARK CASES INVOLVING SEXUAL HARASSMENT

Two legal cases changed the way in which sexual-harassment law is interpreted, placing more liability on the employer. Prior to the 1990s, women who pressed charges for sexual harassment had the added burden of showing that they suffered adverse job consequences, such as loss of employment or demotion. In *Faragher* v. *Boca Raton* and in *Burlington Industries* v. *Ellerth*, the Supreme Court held that an employer is subject to liability to a victimized employee for an actionable hostile environment created by the employee's superior.

## Faragher v. Boca Raton

Faragher, a female lifeguard for the city of Boca Raton, Florida, filed suit against her employer, alleging that two of her immediate supervisors created a sexually hostile work environment by repeatedly subjecting her and other female lifeguards to uninvited and unwelcome touching, and to sexually suggestive and offensive remarks. The court ruled in Faragher's favor, even though she did not formally complain to higher management about her supervisors' conduct; she discussed the offensive conduct with another supervisor who failed to report it. The decision was overturned by the Eleventh Circuit Courts of Appeals. The court ruled that the two supervisors may have been harassing, but the City was not liable for their conduct. The Supreme Court reversed the case (seven-to-two), ruling that the City had not taken reasonable steps to prevent sexual harassment; it had a sexual-harassment policy, but never distributed it to the lifeguards.

"An employer can, in a general sense, reasonably anticipate the possibility of such conduct occurring in its workplace," wrote Justice David Souter, "and one might justify the assignment of the burden of the untoward behavior to the employer as one of the costs of doing business, to be charged to the enterprise rather than the victim."

Moreover, the court found that even though a supervisor may not explicitly threaten an employee, the threat is implicitly felt by the victim. Justice Souter wrote, "Supervisors do not make speeches threatening sanctions whenever they make requests in the legitimate exercise of managerial authority, and yet every subordinate employee knows the sanctions exist."

## Burlington Industries v. Ellerth

Ellerth, a former salesperson, alleged that she had been subjected to repeated harassment by one of her supervisors, Ted Slowik. Slowik was a middle manager who had authority to hire and promote employees with the approval of higher management. Ellerth told the court that Slowik constantly made offensive remarks and gestures and leered at her. She alleged that on three separate occasions he had made comments that could be construed as threats to deny her tangible job benefits.

The court ruled in Ellerth's favor, despite the fact that she suffered no retaliation for rejecting her supervisor's advances and was, in fact, promoted. In addition, Ellerth never informed anyone at a higher level even though she was aware that Burlington Industries had a policy against sexual harassment. Ellerth alleged that Burlington Industries employees engaged in sexual harassment and forced her eventual dismissal.

## Oncale v. Sundowner Offshore Services

Joseph Oncale worked for Sundowner Offshore Services with an eight-man crew on a Chevron oil platform in the gulf of Mexico. Oncale was forcibly subjected to sex-related, humiliating actions by three of his supervisors in the presence of the rest of the men. Oncale alleged that he had also been physically assaulted in a sexual manner and threatened with rape. He complained to his supervisors who did nothing to prevent the harassment and eventually he resigned from his job. He eventually took his case to court, claiming sexual harassment.

The case is important because the Supreme Court ruled that workplace harassment can violate Title VII, even when the harasser and harassed employee are of the same sex. In his opinion to the court, Justice Scalia wrote:

> If our precedents leave any doubt on the question, we hold today that nothing in Title VII necessarily bars a claim of discrimination "because of ... sex" merely because the plaintiff and the defendant (or the person charged with acting on behalf of the defendant) are of the same sex.

## Anita Hill v. Clarence Thomas

One of the most high-profile sexual-harassment allegations was against Clarence Thomas, a nominee for the US Supreme Court at the time of the allegations. Although the case was never tried, on October 11, 1991, Anita Hill, a law professor at the University of Oklahoma, was called to testify during the Senate confirmation hearings for Thomas. Hill's opening statement (below) at the hearings recounted Thomas' behavior towards her:

> I declined the invitation to go out socially with him and explained to him that I thought it would jeopardize what at the time I considered to be a very good working relationship. I had a normal social life with other men outside of the office. I believed then, as now, that having a social relationship with a person who was supervising my work would be ill-advised. I was very uncomfortable with the idea and told him so.
>
> I thought that by saying no and explaining my reasons my employer would abandon his social suggestions. However, to my regret, in the following few weeks, he continued to ask me out on several occasions. He pressed me to justify my reasons for saying no to him. These incidents took place in his office or mine. They were in the form of private conversations which would not have been overheard by anyone else.
>
> My working relationship became even more strained when Judge Thomas began to use work situations to discuss sex. On these occasions, he would call me into his office for reports on education issues and projects, or he might suggest that, because of the time pressures of his schedule, we go to lunch to a government cafeteria. After a brief discussion of work, he would turn the conversation to a discussion of sexual matters.
>
> His conversations were very vivid. He spoke about acts that he had seen in pornographic films involving such matters as women having sex with animals and films showing group sex or rape scenes. He talked about pornographic materials depicting individuals with large penises or large breasts involved in various sex acts. On several occasions, Thomas told me graphically of his own sexual prowess.

Because I was extremely uncomfortable talking about sex with him at all and particularly in such a graphic way, I told him that I did not want to talk about these subjects. I would also try to change the subject to education matters or to nonsexual personal matters such as his background or his beliefs. My efforts to change the subject were rarely successful.

Throughout the period of these conversations, he also from time to time asked me for social engagements. My reaction to these conversations was to avoid them by eliminating opportunities for us to engage in extended conversations. This was difficult because at the time I was his only assistant at the Office of Education – or Office for Civil Rights.

During the latter part of my time at the Department of Education, the social pressures and any conversation of his offensive behavior ended. I began both to believe and hope that our working relationship could be a proper, cordial, and professional one.

When Judge Thomas was made chair of the EEOC, I needed to face the question of whether to go with him. I was asked to do so, and I did. The work itself was interesting, and at that time it appeared that the sexual overtures which had so troubled me had ended. I also faced the realistic fact that I had no alternative job. While I might have gone back to private practice, perhaps in my old firm or at another, I was dedicated to civil rights work, and my first choice was to be in that field. Moreover, the Department of Education itself was a dubious venture. President Reagan was seeking to abolish the entire department.

For my first months at the EEOC, where I continued to be an assistant to Judge Thomas, there were no sexual conversations or overtures. However, during the fall and winter of 1982, these began again. The comments were random and ranged from pressing me about why I didn't go out with him to remarks about my personal appearance. I remember his saying that some day I would have to tell him the real reason that I wouldn't go out with him.

He began to show displeasure in his tone and voice and his demeanor and his continued pressure for an explanation. He commented on what I was wearing in terms of whether it made me more or less sexually attractive. The incidents occurred in his inner office at the EEOC.

One of the oddest episodes I remember was an occasion in which Thomas was drinking a Coke in his office. He got up from the table at which we were working, went over to his desk to get the Coke, looked at the can and asked, "Who has pubic hair on my Coke?" On other occasions, he referred to the size of his own penis as being larger than normal, and he also spoke on some occasions of the pleasures he had given to women with oral sex.

Angela Wright, another of Thomas' subordinates, claimed that she was also harassed by Thomas. Thomas fought back on all counts, claiming that the hearing was a "high tech lynching" and that all of the allegations were false, the product of a dissatisfied, bitter, and untalented civil servant. In the end, the Senate confirmed Clarence Thomas to the Supreme Court by a vote of 52–48. The hearing was interesting for a number of reasons. First, it profiled one of the most powerful individuals in the US judicial system and one who had formerly been head of the EEOC, the agency created to protect women and minorities from discrimination. Second, Anita Hill admitted that no one witnessed the egregious acts as they were alleged to have taken place privately in his office. The case highlights the difficulty of establishing proof when the alleged harassment happens in private. In the press, the case was characterized as "he said" versus "she said." And, third, many criticized Hill for waiting 10 years to report Thomas' conduct. The time lag brings into view the controversy over whether women should have to report incidents shortly after they happen. Proponents for sexual-harassment victims indicate that a woman may not report a case of sexual harassment for a variety of reasons: she may fear retaliation from her employer; she may worry about losing her job once she files a complaint; and even if she decides to complain and then quit her job, she may need a job reference from the individual who is harassing her. In her Senate testimony, Hill explains why she waited so long to report these incidents:

> I may have used poor judgment early on in my relationship with this issue. I was aware, however, that telling at any point in my career could adversely affect my future career, and I did not want, early on, to burn all the bridges to the E.E.O.C.

In 2007, Thomas wrote his memoirs and again recounted how Hill was a disgruntled employee, lacking competence and talent. Hill countered by asserting that she was telling the truth and by suggesting that Thomas was bent on denigrating her character.

## Cases Involving US Nationals Abroad

Four separate suits have been filed by women against Halliburton, an oil services company, and Kellogg, Brown and Root (KBR), the US's largest military contractor in Iraq, which was spun off from Halliburton in April 2007. The women worked for Halliburton and KBR in Baghdad. Two of these cases are described below.

### *Jaimie Jones* v. *Halliburton Co. et al.*

Jones alleges that Halliburton, KBR, and the US government are responsible for a hostile environment that led to her being sexually harassed and raped by several male employees. Jones alleges that she was forced to live on a co-ed floor in a male-dominated barracks where she was routinely subject to catcalls and partially dressed men. She says she complained to Halliburton and KBR managers several times about the living conditions and hostile atmosphere, and requested to be moved to another, safer location. Her request, according to her statement, went unanswered. In July 2006, Jones alleged that she was drugged and raped in her own room at the barracks by several Halliburton and KBR firefighters, as well as by her former boss. The suit alleges that Halliburton and KBR's conduct was unreasonable and negligent because they failed to enforce company policy on sexual misconduct, and because they failed to assist with the investigation of harassment. In addition, Halliburton and KBR apparently misrepresented the safety measures for women in Iraq because they knew that women had been subject to sexual harassment. Jones said that she would not have accepted the position in Iraq had she known about the hostile work conditions.

### *Tracy Barker* v. *Halliburton Co. et al.*

This case alleged quid pro quo harassment. Ms. Barker claims that her direct supervisor harassed her in exchange for favorable living and work conditions. She also alleged that a state department employee assaulted her and attempted to rape her.

## Class Action Suits

In recent years, class action suits have given more power to plaintiffs and put more pressure on defendants. Class action suits allow members of a protected class (women or racial minorities, for example) to file a lawsuit together. Companies pay much more attention to class action suits because they involve less financial risk for individual women who join them and large payouts for lawyers who prosecute. Lawyers take a percentage of the potential multi-million-dollar settlements that plaintiffs receive, so individual women do not need thousands of dollars to file a suit.

### Eveleth Taconite Company

In 1975, the Eveleth Taconite Company hired its first four women as the result of a consent decree: an out-of-court legal settlement whereby the accused party, in this case the Eveleth Taconite Company, agrees to modify or change its behavior rather than plead guilty or go through a hearing on charges brought before a court. In this particular case, the mining company agreed to hire women rather than admit to discrimination in its hiring procedures. Lois Jenson, the plaintiff in *Jenson* v. *Eveleth Taconite Company*, was one of these women. For 25 years she and other women were subjected to relentless sexual harassment in the form of sexual taunts, rude jokes, physical intimidation of all sorts, and adverse job assignments. For redress, Jenson approached the company, her union, and the State Department of Human Rights. In 1988, when the State Department of Human Rights told her they had done everything they could, she turned to Sprenger and Lang, a twin-cities law firm specializing in Title VII discrimination cases. Paul Sprenger urged Jenson to convince other women to join the suit, and in 1991 the case was given class action status. The case dragged on for several more years as the defense lawyers engaged in what has been referred to as a "nuts and sluts" defense, a strategy that portrayed the women as mentally unstable and of dubious character.

Finally, the Eighth Circuit Court reversed the trial court's award of nominal monetary awards to the women. The Eveleth Taconite Company was found to be liable and damages of $15 million were awarded to the women. In addition, boundaries for the conduct of the defense lawyers were set. In the case, defense lawyers had insisted on deposing a woman from her hospital bed as she was dying of cancer. Although Jenson was eventually vindicated, the stress of the lawsuit over so many years and the many interrogations to which she was subjected took a toll on her health; she became disabled and never worked again.

### Mitsubishi Motor Manufacturing Co.

In 1994, attorney Patricia Benassi filed a lawsuit on behalf of 30 women at the Mitsubishi Motor Manufacturing plant in Normal, Illinois. By the time the case was settled, there were 500 women plaintiffs and Mitsubishi would pay them $34 million, the largest settlement for damages of any sexual-harassment suit to date.

The women assembly line workers, secretaries, and clerical workers alleged that they had been subjected to a variety of actions contributing to a hostile work environment. One of the women, Sandra Rushing, described how men had put large wrenches and air guns between her legs to simulate penises. Others described how men had written sexual graffiti on the plant walls and on their cars, and how they had been physically intimidated at work. In the break room, men had placed photos on the coffee tables of prostitutes that had been hired for their sex parties. Many of the women claimed that they had been dismissed for complaining about the treatment or felt forced to resign.

As part of the settlement, in addition to the $34 million, the EEOC ordered that the company revise its sexual-harassment policy to include examples of sexually offensive behavior, a non-retaliation clause to protect the women, and disciplinary actions for offenders. The company was also instructed to institute sexual-harassment training.

### Caritas Christi Health Care System

In February 2006, several female employees came forward to complain about the advances of Dr. Robert Haddad, the President of Caritas Christi Health Care System. When the case became public, more women filed complaints about the President's leering gestures, unwelcome e-mails, and hugs and kisses at work. The President claimed that his Lebanese background accounted for his behavior and that these advances, including the hugs and kisses, were a matter of cultural difference – completely innocent and natural in Lebanese culture. After a careful investigation, Cardinal O'Malley, head of the Boston Catholic Diocese of which the healthcare system is a part, ultimately determined the hospital system's president had to be fired.

### Astra USA

Astra USA is the American subsidiary of the Swedish pharmaceutical company, Astra AB. This case is interesting because it demonstrates that harassment can go to the very top of an organization. The suit, brought by 79 women, accused the former president of Astra USA, Lars Bildman, and several other top executives of pressuring female employees for sex. In addition, the executives were accused of replacing older women with younger, more attractive ones.

EEOC lawyer James Lee remarked that there was an open season on sexual harassment fostered by the president of the company, managers, and even the company's customers and guests. A total of 79 female sales representatives and one man who spoke out against the harassment were awarded damages of approximately $10 million. The company fired Lars Bildman, took action against 30 employees and customers who participated in the behavior, and agreed to institute a sexual-harassment policy (*Business Week*, 1996; EEOC, 1998).

## The European Situation

The US Title VII law that made discrimination based on sex illegal acted as a catalyst to judicial decisions in the European Union. Therefore, the EU law parallels the US law. In spite of international attempts to eradicate sex discrimination, little international attention was paid to the 1979 United Nations Convention on all Forms of Discrimination Against Women (CAFDAW), primarily because some countries perceived the issue as a private internal matter that should not be intruded upon by international law. For some countries, national and cultural autonomy are privileged over a set of standard international laws (Earle & Madek, 1993).

Culture often determines whether or not an action or comment would be considered sexual harassment. Michael Rubenstein, co-editor of *Equal Opportunity Review* in London, said, "The French definition of sexual harassment is what we Americans would call assault and battery" (*Business Week*, 2004, p. 65). An unwelcome kiss or a sexist comment would not be considered harassment in France. In Germany, few cases have been filed as compared with the US or the UK, and 80% of cases that have been filed have been filed by men, rather than women. Men filed cases for backpay or reinstatement to their jobs because they were accused of sexual harassment and then punished by their employers.

In Britain, up until 1993 there was a cap on monetary awards for plaintiffs in sexual-harassment cases. This cap discouraged many women from litigating a sexual-harassment case. If a women had to choose between a long and often vicious battle with her employer with the possibility of a small payout, and a much larger settlement with her company for voluntarily resigning and not taking the company to court, her choice was obvious. In 2001, British law shifted the burden of proof in harassment cases to the employer. The removal of the cap on sexual-harassment claims and the shift in the burden of proof have brought significantly more cases to the fore. In July 2004, Merrill Lynch paid out $900,000 in an out-of-court settlement to Elizabeth Weston, an in-house lawyer for the company, who alleged another executive had made lewd comments about her breasts and sex life during a company Christmas party and, in 2003, a female trainee sales representative at a car dealership with only one weeks' service on the job was awarded £180,000 from an Industrial Tribunal, the UK employment court. The harassment, which consisted of groping and pinching of her buttocks, and lewd sexual comments by her line manager, was considered severe enough to leave her with post-traumatic stress disorder and make her likely to be unable to work in sales for several years. Still, the awards for sexual harassment in the UK can be very low for women who are near or at the bottom of the wage hierarchy because the awards are based on lost earnings during employment and on future financial loss of earnings. Loss of earnings are only relevant if the woman is not reemployed on terms equivalent to her former job. If she is not reemployed at the time of the judgment, the Industrial Tribunal makes an estimate of how long it will be before she is reemployed at an equivalent salary or wage, and makes an award based on this estimate of loss time in a job. The value of this estimate is influenced greatly by the persuasive ability of attorneys on either side of the case. In addition to the loss of earnings and future earnings, the court can award money for injury to feelings. This category generally pays out anywhere between £500 and £25,000 depending on the severity of the harassment.

Although the rest of Europe has been behind Britain in establishing laws to protect individuals against sexual harassment, a new European Union rule took effect in October 2005, and is expected to dramatically change the number of sexual-harassment cases that will be brought forward. The rule defines sexual harassment as a form of discrimination.

One gray area of the law concerns liability in the case of US citizens working for a US company abroad where the majority of employees are not US citizens. If sexual harassment is the norm in the host country, should it be ignored based on differences in cultural standards of conduct? Would a multinational company be liable for the actions of employees of another country where laws against harassment do not exist? To avoid possible lawsuits, multinational companies are defining uniform expectations of their workers world-wide as a response to more and more women taking overseas work assignments. In addition, they are training expatriates (individuals who work outside of their own country) in the culture and norms of the countries they will be placed in as a measure to avoid such situations. Recent cases have found US citizens working abroad for US companies to be protected under US law.

# Part III

# Gender Issues

Looking Ahead

# 9 Work–Life Balance

**Learning Objectives**

After completing this chapter, the reader will:

- understand the pressures confronting working adults (especially working women) that cause work–life imbalance.
- understand the different perspectives (models) of the work–non-work relationship.
- understand the effect of an "unbalanced" life on health.
- be familiar with cross-country comparisons of work–life balance.
- understand the benefits that accrue to organizations that provide work–life balance.

## The Importance of Work–Life Balance for Women

Many variations on the definition of work–life balance appear in the management and social-science literature. Some focus on the importance of equal time between family roles and work roles. Other definitions, rather than focusing on equal time commitment between these two roles, suggest that work–life balance depends on fulfillment, satisfaction, and energy available for the multiple roles that an individual fills (Kalliath & Brough, 2008). And still others suggest that balance in three areas is important: equality between work and family in terms of time, involvement, and satisfaction with the role (Greenhaus, Collins, & Shaw, 2002). Still other definitions have expanded the meaning beyond just balance between work and family, to the balance between work and non-work. This definition recognizes that single or married adults without children also need balance in their lives (Kalliath & Brough, 2008). Work–life balance can be viewed over a day, a week, or over a much longer period of time. At various stages in one's life, balance may be more important than at other times. For example, a woman may feel she needs more balance when she is trying to juggle the demands of early motherhood than when she is 50 and her children are grown up. She may need more time later in life when she is caring for an aging parent. No matter which definition of work–life balance is chosen, the element of time is involved in all of them. Lack of time for work or family will affect satisfaction, energy, and involvement in either role. Because of women's greater time commitment in family and domestic chores, they stand to be more affected than men by an imbalance between work and other pursuits.

More women are working today than ever before, yet women continue to shoulder most of the demands at home, whether they are taking care of children, cooking, cleaning, or running errands. Several demographic factors have contributed to the pressures on women and made these pressures greater for them than for men. First, women are more often single parents dealing with the financial strain and pressures of bringing up children on their own. In 2006, there were 12.9 million one-parent families in the US, of which 10.4 million were single-mother families (US Census Bureau, 2006b). Single mothers have a multitude of tasks to accomplish in any given day, without the support of a partner. Second, in 2005 the average age that women in the US had their first child was 25 (Center for Disease Control and Prevention, 2005). This coincides precisely with the time that women are trying to launch careers. Experts have recognized the importance of early childhood education on a child's cognitive and social development, and the importance of a mother bonding with her infant. Because of the importance of involvement with children at their most formative years, women will be more reluctant to leave a new-born or a young child for long periods of time. At the same time, they will feel the importance of proving themselves in their chosen career. Without the social support of a spouse, affordable childcare, extended family, and a workplace that supports parents, women will find it difficult to find a balance between work and family. A study of 623 men and women found that, for men, an increase in work-time investment reduced their time devoted to family, but an increase in a family-time investment did not affect time devoted to their work. For women, however, an increase of time in either role reduced the time devoted to the other role (Edwards & Rothbard, 2003). This study and others shared in this chapter will show that work–life balance is of particular concern to women.

Women experience different kinds of work–life pressures depending on their life circumstances. Women with young children need to find affordable childcare and make arrangements to drop off their children and pick them up according to the schedule of their daycare provider, while women with school-age children have to arrange to get them to after-school activities. Parents of teenagers may feel it important to have an adult presence at home during after-school hours. All parents have to make special arrangements when school hours are not synchronized with work hours; teacher workdays, breaks during the school year, and summer holidays make it difficult for working parents who may not be able to take time off from work to be with their children.

At the same time as women have increased their participation in the workforce, companies have asked employees to give more of their time. It is not uncommon in some industries and in some jobs for women to work 70–80-hour weeks. This increase in work commitment is particularly hard on women who are single mothers or who do not have partners who share equally in family responsibilities.

## Over-Employment: An Obstacle for Work–Life Balance

Before individuals on their own or with the help of organizations can act to provide a healthier balance between work and non-work, they will have to appreciate the root causes that disrupt the balance. As one of the main causes, some scholars have examined the concept of "over-employment," defined as a worker's inability to obtain reduced hours despite a willingness to proportionately sacrifice income (Golden, 2006). In the US, several large data sets have been used to estimate the percentage of employees willing to give up income in exchange for reduced hours. The General Social Survey and the Panel Study of Income Dynamics estimate that between 6% and 10% of employees are willing to reduce their hours for more free time (Kahn & Lang, 1995; Reynolds, 2003). Other estimates from different surveys are much higher; among workers on a fixed hourly schedule, over 50% were willing to sacrifice some income for reduced hours (Feather & Shaw, 2000). When asked whether they would prefer a raise or more time off, 37% responded "time off" (Schor, 1994). Friedman and Casner-Lotto (2003) found that 27% of unionized and 39% of non-unionized employees would exchange pay for more time off.

Several reasons have been postulated for over-employment in the United States. First, there is a growing use of compulsory overtime practices by employers (Golden & Wiens-Tuers, 2005). Second, since healthcare is a per-employee cost, the escalating cost of healthcare provides an incentive for employers to hire fewer workers and increase the number of hours each worker works. Because healthcare costs are rising faster than any employee-related cost, organizations have a financial incentive to try to reduce the number of employees and thereby reduce their overhead cost. Third, in today's global business environment, companies have an incentive to increase working hours for their employees, because extending production times reduces the average costs in manufacturing, and extending hours in the service sector is a way of responding to customer demands. Fourth, the reduced power of the labor unions makes it more difficult for employees to negotiate reduced hours, especially when the supply of workers exceeds demand. Employees feel the pressure to work longer hours as employers demand greater productivity owing to the global spread of technological capabilities. For example, workers in India can provide programming expertise to US companies, and call centers can operate from anywhere in the world, making it easy for employers to exercise the threat of shifting jobs overseas.

The growing trend in the United States supports what Jacobs and Gerson (2004) refer to as a "time divide." The "time divide" describes a situation in which workers either work full-time with little flexibility and with the rising demand of more hours or they work few hours and have more leisure time. The main way that employees approach their desired number of working hours per week is through a change in employer rather than by negotiating with their current employer (Altonji & Paxson, 1992; Drago, Black, & Wooden, 2004).

At the same time that companies are requiring more time from their employees, employees are asking companies to help them reconcile their work obligations with their personal lives. The increased labor market participation of women, dual-earner households, the growth of international competition, and information technologies such as e-mail, the Web, and telecommunications that blur the boundary between work and non-work time all contribute to an unhealthy imbalance between work and personal time. While extending hours can make companies more competitive, and therefore more profitable, extending the work day has a disparate impact on women. If women are already shouldering more of the home responsibilities, they will have an even harder time balancing work and family with an increase in their work day.

## Work–Life Balance at Both Ends of the Wage Hierarchy

Work–life balance is of concern to women at both ends of the wage hierarchy. On the one hand, women who work at the lower end of the employment hierarchy experience little control over their schedules, yet women at the higher end may feel compelled to work longer hours to stay on the management track.

At the low end, employees may have little choice over the hours they work, the number of weeks or months they work, or how much time they have between shifts. According to the US Bureau of Labor Standards, flexible schedules are most common among management, professional, and related occupations, but least common among construction and maintenance workers, production, transportation, and material-moving workers (2005).

Many employees at the lowest end of the payscale need to work the extra hours to make ends meet. Balance is sometimes a luxury that unskilled workers cannot afford, especially when their share of national income is falling. The wages and benefits as a percentage of gross domestic product (GDP) fell in many industrialized countries from 2000 to 2005. For example, in the United States the change in workers' wages and benefits from 2000 to 2005 was −2.5%. In Germany the change was −3.1% (Porter, 2006). The decline in wages makes it necessary for employees to take on extra hours. In the past, labor unions could bargain for flexible work hours and family–work balance. But, in the United States, labor unions have lost much of their bargaining power and more jobs are non-unionized, therefore decisions about workers' hours and pay are largely left up to the employer.

Some employers have flexible hours, but more for the convenience of the employer than the employee; workers may have to be available for various shifts and may be asked not to work if they are not needed. For example, consumer-oriented businesses such as retail and restaurants may ask employees to work extra hours when they are busy, and may reduce their hours when the customer demand is low. In the US, more than 75% of food-preparation workers, cashiers, orderlies and attendants, nursing aids, waitresses, and retail sales clerks work non-standard hours, defined as hours that deviate from a typical work day (i.e., from 8 a.m. to 5 p.m. with an hour for lunch) (Hamermesh, 1999). The majority of these workers attribute the reason for working non-standard hours to "the nature of the job" and "better arrangements for family or child care" (US Bureau of Labor Statistics, 2005, p. 3). In some cases, non-standard hours may be desirable if a couple has children. In these lower-level wage categories, if one parent works standard hours and the other non-standard hours, they can more easily and more cheaply manage childcare because one of the parents will be able to take care of the children while the other is working.

At the higher end of the wage hierarchy in the US, workers make more money, but have little say over their working hours. Women at this level often feel that using flexible hours, job-sharing arrangements, or taking a break from their careers will have an impact on their careers. For example, they may not be considered for promotion or for interesting assignments or training opportunities. Even when organizations agree to flexible hours and job-sharing situations, employees worry that management does so begrudgingly. For six years, Cynthia Cunningham and Shelley Murray, two executives, successfully shared the job of Vice President of Global Markets Foreign Exchange at Fleet Bank (now part of Bank of America), yet they felt little support for their job-sharing arrangement. They commented on their challenges:

> There was never a case where we couldn't get a project done because of the job share. Our clients [the retail division] were happy with our work, and we earned millions of dollars for the bank.... The real challenges came almost exclusively from a lack of management support and our immediate colleagues' suspicions about our arrangement.
>
> (Cunningham & Murray, 2005, p. 128)

In a study of office managers' attitudes toward employees wishing to organize alternative work arrangements, Powell and Mainiero (1999) noted that managers were more sympathetic to employees who desired special arrangements if their work was "non-critical" to the organization. Employees whose work was deemed as critical to the work unit, however, were less likely to be granted alternative work arrangements. Managers who expect their employees to work very long hours make it impossible for their employees to take advantage of company policies that offer flexibility. The emphasis with companies needs to change from hours worked to outcomes achieved.

In addition to experiencing lack of support for job-sharing arrangements and extended career breaks, most middle-management employees feel the need to stay connected to their organizations, even when they are on vacation. Management (SHRM, an association of members from over 140 countries, devoted to human resources development) polled human resource professionals to find out how their organizations handled vacation time (Victor, 2006). The HR professionals indicated that middle- and executive-level employees were expected to stay connected to the organization while on vacation via cell phones, pagers, laptops, and Blackberries more than non-management employees.

While the work culture encourages employees to work long hours, the lack of employment security in the US most likely dictates that workers cannot object too vehemently about extra hours or checking in with the office while on vacation. "Employment at will," a common-law rule in the US, holds that an employment contract of indefinite duration can be terminated by the employer or employee at any time for any reason (except for discrimination based on sex, race, or national origin). This employment status leaves very little employment security for the average worker in the United States, the only industrialized country that maintains "employment at will." Moreover, the categorization of employees into "exempt" (salaried workers) versus "non-exempt" (wage workers) provides little protection for exempt staff since they are exempt from (not covered by) the FLSA (Fair Labor Standards Act of 1938). The FLSA protects hourly workers to ensure minimum wage and overtime pay. Temporary workers, like exempt workers, are not covered by the FLSA, and do not benefit from many of the employment protections offered to full-time, permanent workers. Since the extent and influence of labor unions has waned from the early 1980s, workers cannot collectively resist having to work long hours should their employers wish it. The free-market perspective suggests that working hours should reach an equilibrium level resulting from bargaining between buyers and sellers; however, the sellers (individual workers) do not have as much market power as the buyers (large multinational companies) so that there is, in fact, no bargaining. The conditions are set by the employer.

It is true that some firms have instituted flexible work hours within the work day; these flex-time programs typically allow workers to modify their day slightly by starting an hour earlier and finishing an hour earlier, or by starting an hour later and finishing an hour later. Although firms make available these modified work schedules, many employees feel that they cannot take advantage of them. More than one in four workers are permitted to work a flexible schedule, yet only about one in ten is enrolled in a formal, employer-sponsored flex-time program (US Bureau of Labor Statistics, 2005). In the EU, two out of three European employees report that their work-time arrangements are set by their employers with no room for flexibility (European Foundation for the Improvement of Living and Working Conditions, 2008a).

## The Financial Penalty for Time off Work

Women in developed countries routinely take time off work to raise children. This time off, however, exacts financial and social penalties. Women in one study suggested that there was a stigma attached to people who use work–life balance benefits, as well as financial penalties to pay (Hewlett & Luce, 2005). Hewlett and Luce (2005) ran a multi-year taskforce called "The Hidden Brain Drain: Women and Minorities as Unrealized Assets." Their research included 2,443 women who were described as "highly qualified," with either graduate degrees or undergraduate degrees with honors. When women did decide to take advantage of leaving an organization to gain more flexibility in their lives, they intended to do so temporarily – in the business sector, on average women leave for only 1.2 years. Taking this time off, however, exacts a financial penalty; women in the business sector lose 28% of their earning power when they return to work. Across industry sectors, women lose an average of 37% of their earning power when they take three years or more off.

## Work Schedules in the US Versus Other Developed Countries

Some research shows that Americans are working longer hours than Europeans; as measured by total number of hours worked per capita, Americans work over 1,800 hours a year per capita compared with approximately 1,600 hours per capita in the UK and about 1,400 in Germany (OECD, 2004). These data also show that US workers are spending time at home to "finish or catch up" with work tasks; of 13.7 million wage and salary workers, about 10.2 million do job-related work at home on a regular basis without pay. Workers logged an average of seven unpaid hours at home (US Bureau of Labor, 2005, p. 1). A revision of the 1993 European Working Directive sets the maximum weekly working time for EU employees at 48 hours. However, an "opt-out" clause grants European Union employers an exemption from the weekly minimum if employees agree, either through collective bargaining or if it is written into the employment contract. It is possible for employees to work up to 65 hours per week. Currently, one in five employees in the United Kingdom works more than 48 hours (Boulin, Lallement, & Michon, 2006).

Governmental institutions and laws generally have effects on the degree to which people have control over their work. Most governments legislate maximum allowable work hours per week, rest breaks, and annual vacation leaves, but there are great differences among them. As Table 9.1 outlines, the United States has limited regulations in regard to working hours and annual leave as compared to the EU and Japan. The US Fair Labor Standards Act (FLSA) does not cover work breaks or meal breaks, nor does it cover salaried employees (executives, professionals, salespeople who are not on an hourly wage); about 27% of American workers are outside of the FLSA regulations, which means that they have very little power over their work schedules (Pedersini, 2008).

A cross-national comparison of European employment patterns conducted by Anxo, Boulin, and Fagan (2006) illustrates the positive effects that legislation can have over labor rates. Nordic countries have continuous labor market participation over the life course, especially at either ends of the age spectrum. Some 80% of women aged 25–54 are part of the workforce in Nordic countries. Women stay in the workforce over most of their lives in part because of strong social programs that help them with family commitments (parental leaves, childcare resources, income-compensated leaves, etc.). For example, Norway offers 42 weeks of paid leave at 100% of an individual's salary and 52 weeks at 80% of one's salary (Catalyst, 2007b). It is common for workers in Sweden to work some sort of flexible work arrangement. Additionally, Swedish workers are allowed a "flex bank," a system in which employees can bank hours that they work beyond the regular work day and use later. Sweden provides 96 weeks of maternity leave, 78 of which are paid at 80% of salary (European Foundation for the Improvement of Living and Working Conditions, 2008). France follows what

Table 9.1 Mandatory Rules on Some Basic Elements of Working Time

| | EU | Japan | US | Brazil | China |
|---|---|---|---|---|---|
| *Daily Working Time/ Overtime* | No specific industries, like road haulage, are subject to specific working time provisions. | Eight hours. | No specific industries, like trucking and aviation, are subject to maximum daily working time provisions for safety purposes. | Eight hours, no more than two hours of overtime. | Eight hours, no more than one hour of overtime (or three hours in special circumstances) a day and 36 hours a week. |
| *Weekly Working Time* | Maximum 48 hours on average each seven-day period including overtime. | 40 hours overtime premium must be paid (at least 25% of the hourly wage) and overtime cannot exceed 10 hours a week, 45 a month and 360 a year. | 40 hours, unless an overtime premium of at least 50% of the hourly wage is paid. | 44 hours. | 40 hours. |
| *Daily Rest* | 11 hours. | No. | No. | No. | No. |
| *Weekly Rest Period* | 24 uninterrupted hours and the daily 11 consecutive rest hours. | One day a week. | No. | One day a week, preferably on Sundays. | Saturdays and Sundays are the normal days off. |
| *Breaks* | If working day is longer than six hours. | If working time exceeds six hours (45-minute break) or eight hours (one-hour break). | No (some state legislation). | No. | No. |
| *Annual leave* | At least four weeks of paid annual leave, which may not be replaced by an allowance in lieu. | At least 10 days of paid leave, which can reach 20 based on a worker's seniority. | No. | 30 days. | Yes. |

Source: European Foundation for the Improvement of Living and Working Conditions. (2008). Wyattville Road, Loughlinstown, Dublin 18, Ireland.

Note
The information included in the table refers exclusively to EU level rules. National legislation may introduce further rules; for instance member states provide rules on daily working time and overtime.

the researchers call a "modified breadwinner model" where some women exit the labor force when they have young children, but the majority work full-time or adjust their hours for long part-time hours. In contrast to the Nordic countries, France has less social support and a higher unemployment rate, both of which limit women's full participation in the labor force. In Spain, even fewer women are in the labor force and those who are work full-time. The low provision of childcare, especially for young children, the low provision of guaranteed leave, and limited income replacement (paid leave is 16 weeks at 100% of salary) has an impact on female participation in the labor force. In the UK, a part-time model of work is common for mothers, even as their children grow older. In the UK, it is difficult to find full-time childcare – especially for the millions of commuters into London, who must start their day very early to arrive in the city by 8 a.m. or 9 a.m. In the UK, mothers are covered by a 39-week maternity leave – six weeks of which are paid at 90% of salary and the remaining weeks at a flat rate or 90% of salary, depending on which is lower. An additional 52 weeks is offered as unpaid leave. As in many countries since World War II, the UK government also provides a tax-free "child benefit," a monthly payment to parents to help raise their children.

In comparison with European countries, the United States makes even fewer accommodations for work–life balance. For example, the US did not pass legislation for maternity leave until 1993; by contrast, Sweden passed maternity leave legislation in 1891 and parental leave for fathers in 1974; Germany passed maternity legislation in 1883; and France in 1928 (Ruhm & Teague, 1995). The Swedish government expresses its commitment to reconciling work and family by affirming that women and men ought to be able to combine meaningful work with active parenting (Kimball, 1999). In contrast with European countries, the US follows a free-market model with little government support for childcare and paid leaves. The United States is one of the few industrialized countries that does not mandate a paid maternity leave for new mothers. (Although the US does not provide federal support, some states have provided paid leaves, notably California and Washington.)

Beyond the 12 weeks of unpaid leave provided by the US Family Medical Leave Act (FMLA), longer or paid leaves are up to the employer. Furthermore, companies with fewer than 50 employees are not covered by the FMLA. According to a survey by the Society for Human Resources, only 32% of US employers offered a paid family leave (Victor, 2006). To extend a maternity leave, many US employees use a combination of the Family Medical Leave provision, sick days, and their vacation allotment. The International Labour Organization has called for a *minimum* of 12 weeks' maternity leave and has recommended that employers offer 14 weeks, yet out of its 182 member states, 119 meet the minimum standard, only 62 countries provide 14 weeks or more, and 31 provide less than 12 weeks of leave.

Countries that do offer maternity benefits require various lengths of service with the same employer in order to qualify and notice periods. For example, in Switzerland an employee needs to work for the same employer for three months, while Zambia and Gambia require a two-year length-of-service. In Australia, a woman must give at least 10 weeks' notice before taking a maternity leave, while in Denmark, France, Greece, and Italy, no notice is required. These country comparisons clearly show the impact of institutional support from both governments and employers on labor-market participation and on work–life balance issues. Figures 9.1 and 9.2 provide a comparison of selected countries and their maternity and paternity leave benefits.

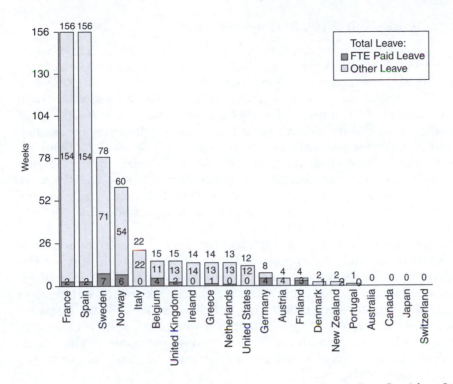

*Figure 9.1* Total and FTE Paid Leave for Fathers in Couples (source: Ray, Gornick, & Schmidt (2008)).

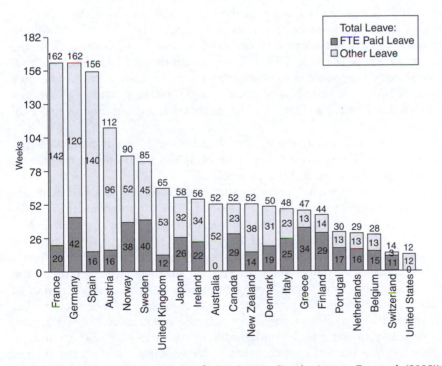

*Figure 9.2* Total and FTE Paid Leave for Mothers in Couples (source: Ray et al. (2008)).

## Theories of the Work–Non-Work Relationship

Whether we as a society value work–life balance depends on how we view the relationship between work and non-work time. Five models have been advanced that help describe the nature of the work and non-work realms and their interactions (Zedeck & Mosier, 1990). The segmentation model describes work and family as separate, with neither domain influencing the other. In the 1960s when women were about 32% of the US workforce, the two domains were treated as separate spheres largely because women took care of the household while men worked (Blood & Wolfe, 1960; Dublin, 1973). Many researchers have challenged the segmentation model, suggesting that work and non-work are two closely related activities that cannot be separated (Burke & Greenglass, 1987; Voydanoff, 1987). Still others argue that people separate the domains of work and non-work by actively suppressing thoughts about one domain while in the other (Lambert, 1990: Piotrkowski, 1979).

The spillover model acknowledges that work and non-work do indeed influence one another, and this influence can be either positive or negative. For example, if one is satisfied in one domain, one is apt to be satisfied in the other (Gutek, Repetti, & Silver, 1988); or if one is stressed or fatigued at home, it may be caused by stress or fatigue in the workplace (Eckenrode & Gore, 1990). Certain behaviors can spillover from one domain to the other – an employee may be irritable at work and he or she may bring that behavior home when dealing with children or a spouse, for example. Thus, spillover is often described in terms of mood, satisfaction with life, and behaviors that transfer from one domain to the other.

A third way of viewing the work and non-work relationship is through the compensation model, which suggests that what is lacking in one domain could be made up in the other. Two forms of compensation have been identified in the work–family literature (Edwards & Rothbard, 2000). First, a person may decrease involvement in the dissatisfying domain and increase participation in the potentially satisfying domain so as to spend more time in it or pay more attention to it (Lobel, 1991); and, second, an individual may respond to dissatisfaction in one domain by pursuing rewards in the other – financial or otherwise (Zedeck, 1992). To illustrate the first case, imagine that a woman has low status in the work environment and is dissatisfied at work. She may cut back on her work hours and spend more time at home. In the second case, suppose a woman is dissatisfied at home. She may work hard to pursue a promotion to make up for her unhappy home life.

The fourth model, the instrumental view, regards activities in one domain as facilitating success in the other. Thus, if one is happy and fulfilled when one isn't working, it will be easier to be successful and fulfilled at work.

The final model, the conflict model, proposes that high levels of stress and demands in both spheres produce conflict. Essentially, because of these high demands, the individual will find that meeting demands in one role means falling short in the other role (Burke & Greenglass, 1987). Greenhaus and Beutell (1985) identify three types of work–family conflict: time-based conflict, strain-based conflict, and behavior-based conflict. Time-based conflict occurs when an individual takes time to meet the demands of one role, which results in not having enough time to meet the demands of the other role. Strain-based conflict happens when stress or fatigue from one role makes it impossible to meet the demands of the other role. Behavior-based conflict occurs when behaviors necessary in one role are undesirable in the other role. For example, a young mother may feel that nurturing is necessary at home, while the same behavior is a detriment to her at work.

Various studies support the different views of how work and family interact. For example, most of the research supporting the conflict view is focused on women's inability to reconcile the two domains (Kalleberg, 2007). In our society, working women still bear the brunt of domestic house-cleaning and childcare (Andrews, 2004; Hochschild & Machung, 2003); women's earnings suffer more than men's earnings because of the time they spend on domestic obligations rather than work, and because they may exit the workforce entirely in order to take care of children (Shirley & Wallace, 2004). In their book *Work and Family – Allies or Enemies?*, Friedman and Greenhaus (2000) advance the instrumental, spillover, and conflict theories. On the one hand, work and family can be allies because resources derived from one role, such as money from one's job, can be applied fruitfully to benefit the family, and positive emotions from one part of life can spillover to the other domain. However, work and family can be enemies if one domain absorbs too much of an individual's attention and keeps him or her from fully participating in or concentrating on the other role. Exhaustion from working too many hours, for example, causes burn-out and can cause difficulty in a close personal relationship such as a marriage. A high psychological involvement in the family and putting family as the number one priority in one's life leads to a lower psychological involvement in work.

Friedman and Greenhaus view both domains of work and domestic life as mutually supportive; work provides psychological, economic, and behavioral support that has spillover effects to the domestic sphere. Money from work can be put towards children's education. In addition, psychological support at work makes one happier at home. Behavioral support from one's boss, for example, may mean he or she allows flexibility for employees to attend important events in their children's lives or take time out for family emergencies. In the other sphere, home life can provide support for work life. Behavioral support from a spouse who does his share of child-rearing frees a woman up to attend an important meeting, for example, and generally leaves a woman feeling less stress at work. Spouses or partners who are interested in their partner's work life and are proud of their accomplishments at work will have a positive effect on their partner's attitude toward work.

Several scholars have advanced the literature on how work and family interact. Some have suggested that how people manage the boundary between work and family should have a bearing on workplace policies (Rothbard, Phillips, & Duman, 2005). For example, those who clearly want the two domains segmented will be more satisfied with flex-time working arrangements and less satisfied with an on-site childcare provision. Those who like to integrate the two domains will find on-site childcare an attractive benefit because they are able to bring their children to work. Edwards and Rothbard (2000) agree with other scholars on the types of work and family interfaces, but they argue for a more comprehensive model of work and family relationships that, for example, can elaborate the strength of certain influences. For example, the spillover effect of mood may be more pronounced for negative rather than positive moods. In addition to more comprehensive models of the work–family interface, they suggest that more research needs to be done on the conditions under which different linkages occur.

## Work–Life Balance and the Impact of National and Regional Cultures

In addition to the five theories mentioned above, the culture of a nation or region has profound effects on what is considered the natural relationship between work and other activities. For example, countries may have a collectivist or an individualist tradition. The United States has an individualistic tradition in which individual achievement is prized and social safety nets are minimal compared to countries with a collectivist tradition. Countries with a collectivist mentality, such as China and Japan, believe in the cohesiveness and importance of the group over the individual. These views may lead employers to either leave individuals to fend more for themselves or to provide employees with more help and assistance. Cultures have unique ways of viewing the family unit; some perceive it as the husband, wife, and children, and other cultures, particularly those of Central and South America, think of the family as an extended and integral unit composed of grandparents, parents, aunts, and uncles. These difference in this definition of the family unit lead to differences in activities that are considered "family" time. The degree to which a culture segments work from personal affairs is another complicating factor. In many parts of Spain, for example, the work day is extended, but punctuated by long breaks during the day, where employees have time to go home for lunch. In China, work and pleasure are often combined, because business people frequently socialize with clients and colleagues. These cultural differences are bound to have an impact on company practices and policies (Powell & Francesco, 2009).

## Work–Life Balance over the Life Course

Work–life balance issues over lifetimes are very different from work–life balance issues over weeks and months. The availability of working hours for an individual will change depending on that person's life circumstances. A young mother may want to put in fewer hours than a woman in her mid-fifties, for example. As life spans increase in developed countries and people work for more years, the concept of work–life balance could more aptly be viewed over the whole course of a person's life. Traditionally, life is treated as having roughly three phases: initial education and early career, market work (which was usually seen as full-time in an eight-hour-day framework), and retirement (Anxo et al., 2006). Recently, this way of envisioning the sequence of work has been questioned. Now, many people take longer to finish school before entering the workforce (often choosing to attend graduate school), and remain longer in the workforce because they live longer, healthier lives. Some people choose to take career breaks to pursue more education and some choose never to retire, either because they want to remain in the workforce or because they need to stay in the workforce for economic reasons. Many employees have experienced discontinuity in their work lives because of company lay-offs or because of childcare responsibilities. Some choose to work part-time later in life either in a totally new career or in a career they have always had, but with reduced work hours. Clearly, to keep pace with individual circumstances over the life course, arrangements for work need to be more flexible and capable of departing from the traditional tripartite structure of initial education, uninterrupted career, and full retirement. The heterogeneity of the workforce, the fact that people have different preferences, and changes in the social structure necessitate more variety in work arrangements. Consider the increased number of divorces since the 1950s; women are often forced back into the workforce as a result of separation or divorce, and marriage occurs later as young people devote themselves to furthering their education and careers.

## Benefits of Work–Life Balance

Balancing work and other aspects of life is obviously good for individuals, but it is also of importance to organizations. Individuals will be more satisfied with their work lives if they feel they can strike a balance between work and their other interests, be they family obligations or leisure pursuits. Just as work–life balance benefits individuals, it makes organizations more productive, efficient, and safer. There are several examples of situations in which employees have been more productive when the two spheres of work and home are treated as interrelated. In a study of home-based versus office-based systems developers, the office-based employees who committed to a 9-to-5 schedule lost some of their most productive time. One-fourth of them reported that they were most productive outside the 9-to-5 timeframe. The home-based developers managed their time more productively in response to the needs of both their home and work (Bailyn, 1989). In another study, portfolio-analysis managers of a bank were allowed to work at home two days a week or have flexible hours. Although their supervisor was worried about the effect this would have on productivity, the portfolio-analysis managers reported that they could do their work at the times of the day or night that fit their most productive time and fulfill their other obligations. In addition, the employees became more willing to comply with their manager's request for documentation on financial reports (Rayman et al., 1999).

Workplace culture is key to business outcomes; managers who adequately staff their departments, offer flexible work schedules, and recognize the personal needs of their employees have more satisfied customers, lower absentee rates, fewer safety incidents, and improved corporate image (Yasbek, 2004). A study of 1,187 New Zealand employees indicated that employees' perceptions of employers that provided assistance with work–life balance issues contributed to job satisfaction, reduced work pressures, and a subsequent reduction in intentions to leave the organization (Forsyth & Polzer-Debruyne, 2007). In many cases, firms note that their corporate culture has an impact on company profits. The companies on *Fortune Magazine*'s list of 100 Best Companies To Work For in 2007 returned 18.1% for shareholders over the last three years, versus an average 10% return for the companies on the Standard & Poor's index. Some argue that work–life balance provides a positive attitude of exchange; if companies give their employees the "gift" of work–life balance, employees return the gift by providing discretionary effort when it is critical, thereby increasing productivity (Yasbek, 2004). A large-scale study of 732 medium-sized manufacturing firms in the US, France, Germany, and the UK reported that the US has the best management practices, but the worst work–life balance. According to this study, work–life balance is significantly associated with better management and higher productivity (Bloom & Van Reenen, 2006).

During economic recessions, the flexibility provided by work–life programs can be a cost-savings resource for companies. Providing employees with more time off through job-sharing, reduced hours, four-day work weeks, or working from home is one way of reducing costs and preventing lay-offs. Most employers do not want to lose valuable employees during tough economic times, and offering more flexibility may be one way to keep them (Frasch, 2009). Scan, a healthcare company, finds that offering employees the chance to work from home allows them to expand without incurring expensive fixed costs for real estate. Scan equips employees with office furniture, high-speed Internet, and Blackberries to keep in touch with the office. Besides saving companies money, employees find they can reduce their expenses and manage their time better when they work from home. Grace Renteria, an employee who works from home, says that she saves $15 a day that she used to spend on lunches, $70 that she spent weekly on gas, and $400 a year for wear and tear on her car (Conlin, 2009).

## The Business Risks Associated with Poor Work–Life Balance

Just as there are benefits for companies to encourage work–life balance, there are risks for not doing so. Consider the effect of a business organization working its employees too hard. Employees will likely make more mistakes, which will translate into poor quality of products and services. Employees are likely to feel disloyal and may search for other employers who will treat them better. In two separate studies, one with 545 fitness trainers and one with 603 managers, researchers found a significant relationship between the absence of work–life balance, job strain, and non-work-related reasons for quitting (Fisher-McAuley, Stanton, Jolson, & Gavin, 2003). Employee turnover is a significant cost to the employer in increased search costs for new employees, and in productivity – as newly initiated employees to a firm will not be as productive as experienced employees.

Moreover, in the age of the Internet, poor work–life balance policies cannot remain secret for long. It is easy for disgruntled employees to broadcast to their friends and to strangers that a particular company is not worth working for. Blogs, Web sites, and chat rooms communicate to potential employees both the virtues and ills of a company's practices. Websites such as "Companies that Suck" and "My3Cents" feature anecdotes by employees and customers of poor service, shoddy products, and unfair employment practices. The AFL-CIO has a website where users can enter a zip code or state to find employers who have violated labor laws. When potential employees are determining who they want to work for, they may put more stock in information from chat rooms and blogs than any company's marketing literature. Even Facebook groups have exposed companies to the wrath of employees who have felt mistreated, underpaid, overworked, or undervalued. The companies with poor reputations will suffer the consequences of bad press, while the companies with the best reputations will be poised to attract the most talented employees.

## The Toll of Work–Life Unbalance on Individuals

Occupational psychologist Peter Warr (1987) has identified several elements of work that produce satisfied and happy workers, as well as those elements that cause stress and dissatisfaction. Warr identified the lack of opportunity for control and autonomy as one of the causes of stress. When workers are expected to produce specific outcomes, but have little autonomy or control over the way that they do their work, including how much time they spend working, stress results. Other studies have established a direct relationship between the hours an individual works and stress. An Austrian work survey indicated that levels of stress rise proportionately with increases in working time (European Foundation, 2004). In an attempt to find out whether working hours affect health, a group of researchers undertook a meta-analysis – an aggregation of 21 independent studies. This statistical analysis found a positive correlation between total hours worked by employees and ill-health (Sparks, Cooper, Fried, & Shirom, 1997).

Surprisingly, some research suggests that when work–life flexibility is coupled with reduced or compressed working hours, the result may have a negative impact on workers' health. This is due to two trends: intensification of work and "densification" or the elimination of any unproductive time during the day (Anxo et al., 2006). The intensification of work in the US stems in part from the downsizing of the workforce in the 1990s. As employers cut workers, more demands were placed on individuals remaining in the workforce to produce the same number of goods with fewer resources; many worked longer hours to ensure that they would keep their jobs. Today, this intensification continues as the result of increased competition from both domestic and foreign companies.

The period between 1990 and 2000 in Europe offers an example of densification. As the collective working week was being reduced and part-time work was on the rise, working conditions became worse rather than better. Demands were placed on workers to finish all work in the shortened work period and to meet increased demands of customers.

## Specific Health Effects

Unrealistic demands on workers create stress. There are two kinds of stress: acute and chronic. Acute stress is the body's response to an event, such as an athletic contest, an important exam, or a public-speaking engagement. It is typically associated with the biological "fight or flight" response. Acute stress may actually help individuals perform better because all of their energy is focused on the task at hand. The body reacts quickly to prepare itself for either "fighting" or "fleeing"; it produces adrenaline and cortisol to help people react to the stressful event. Adrenaline, for example, increases the heart rate, elevates blood pressure, and boosts energy. After the threat is gone, these hormones return to their normal levels and heart rate and blood pressure return to normal as well.

Chronic stress is the body's response to continuous stress over a long period of time. It may be caused by long-term unemployment or untenable working conditions, for example. The demands placed on workers either because they are working more hours or because they are working compressed schedules are apt to produce chronic rather than acute stress.

The health effects of chronic stress are much more serious than those of acute stress. Highly stressed workers incur healthcare costs 46% higher than other employees (Goetzel et al., 1998). Chronic stress can contribute to heart disease, migraine head-aches, immunological problems, gastrointestinal problems, and many psychological disorders. Levels of cortisol, a steroid produced by the body, increase during stress, which can disrupt sleep patterns. Sleep deprivation leads to irritability and lack of con-centration. It is no surprise that when individuals are under stress for long periods of time, the quality of their work performance declines. Chronic stress can also cause or contribute to depression, chronic fatigue, and general unhappiness (Phelan et al., 1991; Roxburgh, 2004). It reduces levels of serotonin in the brain – the chemical associated with well-being – and it causes too much cortisol and adrenaline to be pumped into the system, creating a multitude of health problems, from allergic skin reactions, memory impairment, to weight gain or weight loss and high blood pressure (Mayo Clinic, 2009).

When people work too hard, they are prone to stress-related diseases such as arterio-sclerosis, colitis, auto-immune, and neurological problems (Sapolsky, 1998). A study of information-technology professionals found that when they spend most of their work week away from home at a client site, they are more prone to exhaustion and stress. When these so-called "road warriors" attempt to juggle family and job duties working at distant client sites, they are subject to unhealthy outcomes (Ahuja, Chudoba, Kaemar, McKnight, & George, 2007).

## Some Positive Company Examples

Many companies are realizing that providing work–life balance programs is good for the health of their employees and at the same time is good for their businesses as they help reduce absenteeism and promote morale. Some of the companies featured in this section have won awards for their work–life balance programs. SAS Institute, a soft-ware firm, has two on-site childcare centers, an elder care information and referral network, wellness programs, and a 58,000-square-foot fitness facility. Employees at SAS can work virtually, they can share jobs, and they can work flexible schedules. For nine years running, SAS Institute has been named as one of the "100 Best Companies to Work for in America" by *Fortune Magazine*. Jim Goodnight, SAS CEO, states that the company understands that it cannot separate its employees from their personal lives, and that the organization will reap the benefits of loyalty if it recognizes the *whole* person. For SAS Institute's efforts, it enjoys an employee turnover rate that is below the industry average. Because of its reputation as an employer that cares about work–life balance, SAS attracts the best employees and saves money by not having to recruit and train new employees.

Other companies that have been recognized on *Fortune Magazine*'s "100 Best Companies to Work For" include Google, REI, and Genentech. These companies have innovative work–life balance initiatives. Recognition by *Fortune* is particularly significant because its awards are based mainly on the opinions of employees gathered through employee surveys.

Google, for example, has a global education leave program that provides a full-time leave for up to five years with reimbursement of up to $150,000. Recognizing the time pressures of new parents, Google provides a take-out food benefit, which will reimburse up to $500 of take-out food for employees dealing with the first four weeks of their child's life. Several on-site facilities at Google help employees manage non-work activities better; Google has a laundry facility that employees can use and an on-site fitness center.

REI, an outdoor-equipment manufacturer and retailer, has instituted several work–life balance initiatives including a work–life employee assistance program that offers counseling and referral services and a sabbatical program. After 15 years of service, employees are rewarded with a month's paid leave. In addition, employees can request up to 12 weeks' unpaid leave a year. REI recognizes that parents who adopt children often need financial help as adoption costs are high. The company provides $3,000 in reimbursement for adoption costs.

Genentech, a leading biotechnology company, also has an adoption program, reimbursing employees $5,000 toward adoption costs and giving the primary caregiver six weeks' paid leave. Genentech has an on-site childcare center at its South San Francisco headquarters. The company's Lifeworks program offers counselors who provide resources and referral services for adoption, childcare, elder care, and help anticipating college expenses. Like the other companies mentioned above, Genentech has a sabbatical program giving full-time employees six weeks' paid leave after every six years of continual employment. In addition to all of these benefits, the company provides an on-site gym at its headquarters and provides employees at other locations free membership at a local fitness center.

NetApp, a company that provides data-storage and management solutions, has several work–life balance programs. Its adoption services program offers $10,000 a year for reimbursement of adoption costs and up to $20,000 over a lifetime. It also provides up to five days a year of paid time off for employees to engage in volunteer activities. Like many of the other firms, it offers recreational facilities; it has an on-site gym, a putting green, and an outdoor volleyball court.

Each of these companies has been on *Fortune Magazine*'s 100 list for several years running – NetApp for six consecutive years, Genentech for 11, REI for 12, Google for three years, and SAS for 11 consecutive years. Their CEOs and Board of Directors understand the importance of sticking with work–life balance initiatives, and have done their best to keep them operating even in tough economic times.

Many employers offer so called "comp" time to deal with any emergency, regardless of one's circumstances. Hewlett-Packard, for example, offers time off for all employees to deal with any issue. Eastman Kodak, American Express, and AT&T are just some examples of Fortune 500 companies that now offer domestic partner benefits to members of either sex (Human Rights Campaign Foundation, 2009). The most enlightened companies focus on output rather than actual time put in at the office, and they recognize that all employees have interests and obligations outside of work.

## Conclusion

While many of today's organizations have adopted "family-friendly" policies for the work environment, paradoxically many employees hesitate to use them. It's ironic that in an era of flexible work arrangements – gyms for people to use during their lunch break, opportunities for career breaks, job-sharing policies, and in many countries generous maternity and parental leaves – that relatively few employees use them. It is apparent that just having employee-friendly policies is half the equation. The other half must be a business culture that values work–life balance. Employees must feel that their managers support these policies or they won't take advantage of them. In the US, where "employment at will" holds, employees may risk their job security if they decide to work part-time or take career breaks. Employees who work part-time may be more vulnerable in environments where companies are downsizing because they may be viewed as less committed to their jobs.

There are several ways that companies signal to employees that they are not really committed to work–life balance. If the organizational culture encourages employees to arrive early, work through their lunch hour, and stay late, the chances are that few employees will feel comfortable using policies that allow them to balance their responsibilities. A culture of "face-time," a well-known phenomenon in which employees are judged on how much they are visibly present at work, is a powerful signal of a climate unfriendly to work–life balance. Such a culture tends to disadvantage women more than men; women with children have routine, on-going responsibilities that may make staying after business hours impossible. Women who cannot rely on caregivers, their own parents, or friends, may have to stay home to care for a sick child. If organizations have a culture that emphasizes outcomes rather than face-time, women will be more able to compete on a level playing field with men. Where employers provide senior-level employees job-sharing opportunities and allow or encourage both men and women at all levels of the organization to use flex-time arrangements to help them juggle their family responsibilities, all employees will feel it is more acceptable to utilize these policies. Individuals' needs vary during the course of their working lives; a young mother may need an extended maternity leave, while an older worker may need a break from work to take care of an aging parent or a troubled teenager (Anxo et al., 2006).

This life course approach is gaining traction in some organizations, especially in larger firms and in some countries. In Sweden among couples without children, women 60 years or older work just over 30 hours a week (Anxo et al., 2006). As many countries in the European Union are experiencing declining birth rates, it is important for older citizens to remain in the workforce. As employees age, they may not wish to work long hours and many may want to take longer leaves to learn a new skill.

Organizations embracing a life course approach to work–life balance need to understand the circumstances of all employees, not just women. If employers give flexible work arrangements to parents, but neglect the needs of single people, they risk alienating their workforce and causing resentment among employees. Single employees may begin to feel that they subsidize working parents and continually pick up the slack for them while they attend to family responsibilities during the work day.

The issue of work–life balance is important to everyone, but especially to women. American culture encourages individualism, hard work, and achievement without providing much social support for women in comparison to other industrialized nations. Many working women in the twenty-first century do not have the resources of an extended family network or a group of neighborhood women to help with childcare and other issues of importance to women. With divorce rates high, some women will be managing their work and family obligations without the support of partners. The mobile society of the US means that many women will not have family nearby to help with childcare. In their non-working hours, single mothers will undoubtedly feel the stress of providing for their children and helping them with their school work and other activities.

Ambitious women in particular may feel that they need to do it all: be the perfect mother, the perfect volunteer, the perfect wife, and the aspiring corporate worker. There is greater and greater emphasis, especially among affluent women, on providing everything for their kids, effortlessly. They may burn themselves out trying to ensure that their children have ever possible opportunity – being on an athletic team, private music lessons, tutoring to get into the best colleges.

The solution to providing more support for workers lies both with organizations and with government. More-generous leave times and greater flexibility can be mandated by governments to help all employees through different challenges during the life course, whether they be the illness of an elderly parent or the care of a young child. Corporations will find that allowing employees more flexibility pays off in terms of increased loyalty, decreased turn-over, and increased productivity.

## Further Reading

Anxo, D., Boulin, J.-Y., & Fagan, C. (2006). Decent working time in a life course perspective. In J.-Y. Boulin, M. Lallement, J. Messenger, & F. Michon (Eds.), *Decent working time – New trends, new issues*. New York, NY: Routledge.

Friedman, S.D. & Greenhaus, J.H. (2000). *Work and family – allies or enemies? What happens when business professionals confront life choices*. New York, NY: Oxford University Press.

Gambles, R., Lewis, S., & Rapoport, R. (2006). *The myth of work–life balance: The challenge of our time for men, women and societies*. London, UK: John Wiley & Sons.

Hochschild, A. & Machung, A. (2003). *The second shift*. New York, NY: Penguin.

# CASE STUDIES

## Case Study 1: A Tale of the Second Shift

Cynthia Barnes remembered the days when she woke at 6 a.m. to get her two young children, Jamie (age one) and Eileen (age three), ready for daycare. Those were tough times for her and her husband. Usually, her night's sleep was interrupted because Jamie was still waking up periodically. And then every morning just when Cynthia was enjoying deep REM sleep, her alarm would ring. She quickly showered, dressed herself, fed Eileen her favorite cereal and Jamie his mashed bananas, and got the children ready for their day at "Little Tikes," the daycare center located about 20 minutes from Cynthia's office. Cynthia's husband Greg was a graduate student at Georgetown University. Although he had a more flexible schedule than Cynthia, he was in the middle of trying to finish his dissertation in US history and was spending most of his waking hours at the national archives in downtown Washington, DC, or the university library. Understandably, Greg found it difficult to concentrate at home. He was willing to help get the children ready for daycare, but Cynthia enjoyed this time with them so she preferred to dress and feed them herself.

Cynthia had passed the CPA exams after college and now worked as an accountant in the budget office of Mercy Hospital. She liked her job and fully intended to work her way up the employment ladder to a senior accountant job. With the complexity of healthcare in the 2000s, there were budgets to keep up with, a multitude of billing forms to fill out, complex calculations to make, plenty of record-keeping, and always a different software package to learn. The hospital had a policy that allowed working parents to cut back on their hours or to work a more flexible schedule. After months of trying to work full-time, Cynthia decided she needed to take advantage of the hospital's policy. She was exhausted from managing two shifts – her work and her family responsibilities – and she was beginning to resent Greg. She and Greg had discussed the situation and they determined that the best course of action would be for Cynthia to cut back on her hours; she asked her supervisor if she could work out a schedule in which she had three mornings a week with her children.

Cynthia's supervisor was willing to accommodate Cynthia's request. The other accountants working with her had agreed that they would hire a temporary worker to fill in some of the work that Cynthia would not be able to do. Everyone seemed happy with the arrangement.

### Two Years Later

Cynthia's children were now in school: Jamie attended a pre-school and Eileen was in nursery school. During the last several years when Cynthia worked part-time, she had taken continuing education credits in accounting to keep abreast of new accounting procedures and the new software packages. She had also made sure that she attended all staff meetings. Now she was ready to go back to work full-time and to apply for a more senior-level job. She filled out the application for an Accountant Level III making sure to list all of her qualifications, training on software programs, and her continuing education credits.

In less than a week, her supervisor told her that she had not been chosen for the job. Vernon Ladner had been offered the job. Vernon had joined Mercy a year after Cynthia. He had worked full-time in the same position as Cynthia held during the time she took her partial leave.

Cynthia wondered if her part-time schedule had kept her from achieving the next step. She feared that the penalty she had paid to be with her children was management's impression of her as an uncommitted employee, or at least an employee who didn't have the ambition and drive to be promoted. Nothing could have been further from the truth. She knew other professional women at the hospital who had also chosen to work part-time while their children were young. They too seemed to be stagnating in their careers. Although the hospital had a part-time policy for all employees, she knew of no men in the professional ranks who had taken advantage of it.

### 15 Years Later

Cynthia was now 47-years-old and had gradually been promoted to higher-level positions in the accounting department. She was now an Accountant Level V and had substantial responsibility for the accounts dealing with all hospital suppliers. Instituting a new accounting protocol, she had saved the hospital thousands of dollars each year either by finding errors in what suppliers had charged the hospital or mistakes in what the hospital had paid suppliers. She planned on working until she was 65, and she had aspirations of becoming head of the department, a senior-level position, and a member of the hospital board of directors.

Cynthia's children had grown up. Jamie was now a gregarious 15-year-old, performing admirably in school and involved in after-school sports programs. Eileen had just finished her first year of college at the University of Washington in Seattle. Cynthia was very proud of her children; both were well-adjusted, independent, and happy. She and Greg had divorced three years ago, finding that their lives had moved in dramatically separate directions. Greg had long ago finished his doctorate and taken academic positions in the DC area. He liked spending his weekends either at academic conferences or playing tennis or golf. Cynthia, on the other hand, was interested in spending her free time with friends or in one of DC's many museums. In spite of the divorce, Cynthia and Greg got along, shared custody of the children and, fortunately, Jamie and Eileen were close to both of them.

Cynthia's newest challenge came in the form of a phone call from her only sibling, her younger brother Terry, who was an attorney living in New Jersey:

"I'm sorry to have to deliver bad news, Cindy. Mom went to the emergency room this morning. She's had another setback. She broke her hip as she got out of her car. I'm afraid the time has come for us to sell the house and find her an assisted living arrangement. With Dad gone, she can't really manage alone."

Cynthia paused for a moment in disbelief and then said, "Is she going to be OK? What do the doctors say?"

"She is going to be fine, but she will be in the hospital for at least four weeks. It was quite a break – they put pins and things in to hold the bone in place. Then they want to ensure that she has proper care at home. You know I would go there, but I am in the middle of a big court case and I just can't get away. There is no way I can get out of it," Terry replied.

"I'll be there as soon as I can and I'll call you when I get there. I'll have to make sure Greg can take Jamie, but I think it will work. Which hospital is she in?" Cynthia asked.

"St. Joseph's in downtown Boston."

"OK. I'll call when I get there. When will you be able to come?"

"This trial has been a bear. The judge takes no prisoners and I can't use any tactics to delay it. I really don't know when I can get away."

"What about one of your partners? Can't they take the case?"

"They're just as busy as I am and besides I just couldn't dump the case on them. There are too many files to read and reams of depositions. They'd never be able to get on top of it."

"Well, I'd like you to come."

"I'll try but I just can't leave in the middle of the case. If you need any money for anything just call me. Thanks for doing this, Cindy. I'll owe you one. We'll be in touch."

As she hung up the phone, she thought about all the things she had to arrange before leaving: flight arrangements, Jamie's care, and work. She would have to tell Mercy Hospital that she needed a leave of absence to deal with the emergency and that she would most probably have to be in Boston on and off for several months until her mother was healed and settled in an assisted living residence. She'd have to put the house on the market, look for a suitable place for her mother, and most important, convince her mother that this was the best option.

She knew that Mercy had a policy of giving employees support while they dealt with elderly parents, but she was unsure exactly how it worked. She was also worried that this new responsibility would again take her off the track for possible promotion to the head of her department, but she could see no other alternative. Mercy would just have to understand that her mother needed her help.

### Discussion Questions

1. How can working women avoid "the second shift?"
2. Does Cynthia have to take care of her mother? What other alternatives does she have? Are these alternatives acceptable in your view?
3. How does this case demonstrate that career paths and life choices for women are different from men's? Do they have to be?

## Case Study 2: A Manager's Dilemma and Time-Off

Orion Corporation manufactures various types of glass. Its largest market is for windshields of all kinds and tempered glass for residential construction. In recent years it has had a surge in business from an upbeat housing market, especially in the so-called sunshine retirement states such as Arizona, Florida, California, and parts of New Mexico like Santa Fe.

It has a workforce of 10,000, divided between its three regional manufacturing facilities and a large head office located in Miami, Florida.

One of the hallmarks of Orion Corporation and a major tool in recruiting talent to its headquarters has been its policies contributing to work and family balance and healthier lifestyles. Orion has a state-of-the-art fitness facility with the latest weight equipment and Nautilus machines, and a running track, an on-site daycare facility, and generous maternity and paternity leaves for new parents. Parents who are interested in adopting children are given a small stipend to help defray the cost of adoption. Managers at Orion are encouraged to use their own best judgment about giving employees freedom to handle family responsibilities such as looking after a sick child, attending an important school event, or taking time out to find appropriate medical care for an elderly parent. Flexible working hours allow employees to start work early and leave early or begin later and leave later than 5 p.m. Orion also has a job-sharing policy that allows employees to split a job between themselves and another individual. These policies are at the discretion of management; if an individual wants flexible work hours the arrangement must be cleared with his or her supervisor. Employees working in the regional manufacturing facilities also have an on-site fitness facility. All of the other benefits, with the exception of the daycare center, are available to plant employees. The company simply found it impractical and too expensive to set up daycare facilities for the regional plant employees.

Orion's CEO, Spencer Dax, believes wholeheartedly that employees should have balance in their lives. Dax is married and has three children: ages 10, 15, and 18. Although he values family time, he has made it very clear to managers that their units must produce. On more than one occasion he has said to managers, "Do what you think is right in terms of letting employees manage their work lives and their other responsibilities, but you better make sure that our profits stay high and your unit contributes." Some managers have remarked, "He gives us enough rope to hang ourselves. We're the ones who are held accountable if our teams don't reach our goals." Dax has given every employee a letter highlighting the various workplace policies and reiterating that specific work hours and time off are to be worked out with one's direct supervisor. The manufacturing facility employees have less flexibility because the plants operate on a three-shift system. Employees are scheduled far in advance for a particular shift and there is little flexibility in work hours unless there is an emergency. Most employees doing shift work are working the shift that they prefer. It is only when a co-worker becomes ill or has to go on leave for some reason that an individual may be asked to work a shift that he or she has not requested.

Marion Clark has worked for Orion for 10 years, gradually working her way into middle management as an information-technology manager. She started her career with Orion as a junior business analyst, but with advanced computer training made her way into better and better jobs. Marion has two children who are now in college. She remembers the days that she had to juggle daycare provision with an early morning meeting or a conversion of one informational technology system to another, requiring her to be in the office almost all night. Having raised two boys while working for Orion, Marion is sympathetic to the demands placed on parents and she tries to accommodate her staff.

Marion's staff includes Susan Lafferty, a senior system analyst; Joel Epstein, a systems analyst; Jeff Bigley, the helpline manager; Tom Wilkerson, network manager; Justin Finch, database coordinator; and Carla Wilkerson, administrative assistant.

Susan Lafferty is currently taking the first month of a six-month maternity leave. Susan began her leave on August 1, and plans to be back to work on February 3. The company provides for a three-month paid leave and allows employees to extend their leave, without pay, with permission of their supervisor. As a senior system analyst, Susan is a very valuable member of the team. She troubleshoots computer glitches and makes sure that the company's customer database operates flawlessly. Marion has covered Susan's job with two others from her staff, Jeff Bigley and Joel Epstein, who continue to perform their own jobs and fill in for Susan while she is on leave. Marion's department is constantly stretched; her five staff have to deal with all computer-related issues in the company. These issues range from providing computer training, manning a computer helpline, keeping up to date on viruses and building firewalls to prevent viruses from destroying computers, and recommending computer software programs and installing them.

Recently, Joel Epstein made an appointment to meet with Marion to discuss a pressing, personal issue.

### The September Meeting

Joel began, "Hello, Marion. Thanks for meeting with me. You know that I have been a sort of amateur science fiction writer for many years now. I love writing. It keeps me energized and it is really my main interest outside of work. Well … I just heard that I won a national science fiction writers' contest for a short story that I wrote. It's called "Wayward Galaxies" and …"

Marion interrupted, "Well, Joel, that is absolutely wonderful! I'm sure the competition was tough. Will it be published? I would be interested to read it."

"It's going to be published in an anthology of science fiction short stories. I'll give you an autographed copy when it comes out."

"That's great. I'm sure if it's autographed it will be valuable one day. After all, a first edition of Joel Epstein's 'Wayward Galaxies'!" Marion said encouragingly.

"Well, I wanted to talk to you about the prize I got. In addition to the honorarium of $5,000, I get to attend a month-long workshop with some really well-known science fiction writers. They will work with us on any of our drafts of stories. It's going to be held in Sedona, Arizona, in October and they pay for everything. It will be held at a nice type of retreat center. I'll need to take a leave from work to go."

"Wow … I'll need to think this over. October is a busy month for us. We'll be in the middle of a big conversion project. We have to convert data from our current billing system to a new customer program that integrates all customer transactions including all charges."

"Marion, I've been doing two jobs here. Mine and Susan's. I may be a single guy but I have important interests outside of work just like parents do. The writers workshop is a once in a lifetime opportunity. I can't ask them to hold it at another time. I don't see how you can give Susan six months off and not let me take a month off."

"It's just that I haven't got any bench left. Who could I get to fill in for you while you're gone? Our budgets are frozen and I can't even hire a temporary employee during our crunch times."

"I'm not asking for any pay while I am gone. I just want the time off."

"I appreciate that you would be willing to take the time off without pay. The company really doesn't have a provision to pay for things like this. But I still can't see how we will get the conversion done without you," Marion offered.

"Marion, you told us that you would try to work with us on balancing our lives with our careers. I've worked hard and have never taken any time off before, except, of course, my regular vacations. This is really important to me. It seems like this company gives all of the perks to parents. Well, just because I am not taking care of a kid, I have needs too."

"Let me think about this and get back to you in a couple of days. You have to understand that there are pressing business issues facing us and we are already stretched too thin. I really will try to come up with a solution and if you have one, please give me your ideas."

## Discussion Questions

1. Do you think Joel is justified in taking a leave off work? Why, or why not?
2. Should single employees have similar rights to employees who are parents?
3. What problems are associated with the company's policy about time off?
4. If you were going to try to accommodate Joel, what solutions could you propose?
5. Look at the information on the Family and Medical Leave Act of 1993 (Appendix 9.1). It does not cover the needs of same-sex couples or non-medical or non-caregiver situations. Discuss.

**Appendix 9.1: The US Family and Medical Leave Act of 1993**

Congress passed this act to provide eligible employees with up to a 12-week, unpaid, job-protected leave. Employers with 50 or more employees within a 75-mile area must follow the law. Smaller employers with fewer than 50 employees are exempt from it.

An employee is eligible if he or she has worked for the employer for at least one year or for 1,250 hours over the previous 12 months.

Under this legislation leave may be taken for the following reasons:

- to care for the employee's child (this includes the birth of a child, adoption, or foster care).
- to care for the employee's spouse, parent, son, or daughter in the event of a serious health condition.
- for the employee's own serious health condition, which makes the employee unable to perform his or her job.

Employees who take advantage of the Family Medical Leave Act are guaranteed to have their original job or an equivalent job back after their leave expires. Once they return to work, they cannot be denied the pay and employee benefits they had before their leave. Employees are entitled to continue their health benefits coverage while they are on leave.

Employees should give their employers 30 days' notice (or as soon as is practical) of their intention to take a medical or family leave.

---

**Case Study 3: Discrimination and Job-Sharing**

Job-sharing allows two people to share one position. In such an arrangement, the two individuals must coordinate their work, agree on work schedules, and communicate effectively with their manager about how tasks are being completed. Most job-sharers are highly motivated to ensure that the arrangement works well because they enjoy the freedom that working a part-time position affords. Some companies even extend employee benefits to both job holders, even though it will cost companies more money to do so.

At Pharmacare, a large pharmaceutical company located in Boston, Massachusetts, job-sharing is a policy that has been cautiously proposed by senior management. Pharmacare is a research-based company with approximately 80,000 employees world-wide – 25,000 are in sales and marketing, 20,000 concentrate on research and development, and the rest are in supportive positions such as information technology, human resources, manufacturing, finance, strategic planning, and other supporting staff positions. The company is currently working on drugs to prevent various cancers and auto-immune diseases. Its scientists have been involved in studying the role of various genes in the body in hopes of offering gene therapies that may cure auto-immune diseases such as leukemia and lupus. Pharmacare has 60 manufacturing sites in 30 different countries.

Pharmacare's policy about job-sharing reads as follows:

At the discretion of management, employees may share a job – each working half-time. Some jobs in the organization are more suited to this arrangement than others. Jobs in which responsibilities can be divided easily and positions that do not require a lot of client contact may be suitable. Individuals wishing to apply for a job-share should contact the human resources department for more information.

Janice Newman and Sandra Price are both research scientists at one of Pharmacare's labs, located at its headquarters. They have both appreciated their job-sharing arrangement in their current position since each has young children and wants to spend more time with them. Janice works on Monday through Friday from 8 a.m. until noon so that she is home with her two children after they come home from school. Sandra works Monday through Friday from 1 p.m. until 5 p.m. Sandra has a live-in nanny who takes care of her twin infants every afternoon until she arrives back home. Both Sandra and Janice have been willing to use their lunch hour to meet so as to ensure the smooth transition of work. Although Sandra's and Janice's manager, Mary Bynum, was at first leery about the arrangement, she soon discovered that it was working much better than she anticipated. The women worked hard, communicated well between each other, and kept her well-informed. The only additional burden for Mary has been in evaluating their performance separately and writing up two performance reviews each year.

"I have had to do the paperwork on two different employees for the same job which has added a little more work to my plate. But I honestly think I have gotten more out of two part-time employees than I would from either one of them alone. They seem to have energy and enthusiasm and great focus when they are here," Mary offered.

Since Janice and Sandra have operated in a job-sharing manner, their performance has been very good. Each has received "outstanding" or "very good" ratings since they've taken on the job-sharing arrangement.

Recently, Janice noticed a job posting in the employee cafeteria that caught her eye. She spoke to Sandra about it over one of their lunch meetings.

"This Lab Manager I position is perfect for us. We have both had lab supervision experience in previous jobs and at Orion we've both had excellent performance records. It's a major step up from what we are doing now. It would be an increase of about $16,000 a year – split in half it is a significant raise. I could use the money, couldn't you?"

Sandra responded, "Of course I could. Childcare is *so* expensive. I had no idea how much of my pay-check would be going toward that. How do you think Mary would feel about our applying?"

"She's always said that she'd support our careers. Now is the time to see if her words mean anything. I think she'll be receptive," Janice said.

"Who's managing the Lab Manager position?" Sandra asked.

"The posting says that Elliot Southern will be. I think he's OK. At least, I've never heard anything negative about him. He's worked in labs forever and really knows his stuff."

"OK, let's talk to Mary tomorrow and see what she thinks," Sandra offered.

### The Discussion with Mary

Janice opened the conversation, "Hi, Mary. Thanks for taking the time to meet with us. Sandra and I want to talk to you about a position that we would like to apply for. It really would be a great job for both of us and a promotion."

"We've talked it over and we think we would have no problem dealing with it. It fits both of our backgrounds very well," Sandra added.

"Do you mean another job-share?" asked Mary.

"Yes," they both said in unison.

"I'd be very sorry to have you go. Are you sure about this job? What is it?"

"It's the Lab Manager I job, reporting to Elliot Southern."

"Do you realize that you'd have to manage five lab scientists? That might be tough in a job-share situation," Mary said skeptically.

"We have both managed before and we have similar management styles and ways of working," Sandra said.

"Yes, but wouldn't it be hard for the lab scientists to adjust to that?"

"The company already has dual reporting relationships – they just aren't job-sharing ones. For example, there is a guy in information technology who reports to both the sales director and an IT senior manager."

"Hmm … that's true," Mary conceded. "It's just that I think you would have a hard time convincing Elliot Southern that it would be worth the trouble."

"Would you talk to him? You've got Tyrone who could move into our job. He has been eager to move up and he is very competent."

"I'm not really worried about finding a good replacement for the two of you, although I would be sorry to see you move on. I'll try to talk to Elliot, but to be honest with you, I don't think he will go for it."

### Mary's Discussion with Elliot Southern

"Elliot, How are you? I haven't seen you in ages. I guess we both have been buried in work. How's the enzyme research going?

"Sit down, Mary. Nice to see you. No breakthroughs yet on the enzyme work, but we are hopeful."

"Well, the reason I wanted to get together with you was to discuss Janice Newman and Sandra Price. They would like to apply for the Lab Manager I position that you have posted."

"Well, sure they can both apply. They just need to get the exact job description from human resources and send along a resumé."

"I mean they want to apply as one candidate. You know, a job-share. They do a job-share now and it's worked out really very well," Mary said.

"Well, maybe it works in a Lab Scientist role, but I'm not sure about a management job. I can't see how they would manage together. Staff need one person to call the shots. It gets really confusing if direction comes from more than one place. People get mixed messages. I really need someone who can keep close tabs on what's going on in the lab," Elliot countered.

"How much experience do the lab scientists have?"

"Well, let's see. About five or six years, I guess."

"Don't you think they are experienced enough to not require heavy supervision?"

"Well, there are other things the manager has to do besides manage staff. Set schedules, write up protocols, make sure that everything is running smoothly. It takes a detailed mind. I'd be worried that something would slip through the cracks."

"I understand how you feel. I was concerned about taking Janice and Sandra on in one job, but they have done such a terrific job. I think I've gotten more good work out of them than I would have had from one person doing the job alone."

"They have been so terrific that you are eager to get rid of them?" Elliot mused.

"Not at all. But I *do* think they have a right to move on if they see another opportunity."

"I just don't see how they would manage staff together. I am sure there are other opportunities for them in the company besides this one."

"Elliot, they really want this job. They have managed people before and they are extremely well-organized. I have not had to worry about supervising their work. In fact, they have given me extra time that I might have had to spend on someone less competent."

Mary could see that Elliot was beginning to straighten things up on his desk and he took a nuanced look at his watch. She took these as cues that he had other pressing things to do.

Mary stood up and said, "Think about it, Elliot. They really would be an asset."

### Mary's Follow-Up Meeting with Janice and Sandra

"Well, I met with Elliot and as I anticipated he was a little resistant to the idea. I think his big worry is not that you aren't competent, but that this would be a difficult position for the two of you to do together."

"Why?" Sandra asked.

"Because he is concerned about how the lab would be managed with two people trying to guide five lab scientists. He said that he worried about things slipping through the cracks."

"Has anything slipped through the cracks here?" Janice asked, slightly perturbed.

"No, you've both managed the arrangement very well."

"I don't see why we couldn't manage the Lab Manager role just as well. We keep each other well-informed about everything and we'd do the same thing with staff. We could even hold staff meetings together so everyone would be clear that we share the same expectations."

"That's a good idea. If you apply for the job, you are going to have to convince Elliot that you would have systems in place to make it work. To my knowledge, we don't have any managers in the company doing a job-share, so you would be breaking ground here," Mary said.

"Look the company says it wants to help employees deal with work and family balance. Managers should be able to take advantage of the same policies that non-managers get," Sandra said.

"Theoretically," Mary offered. "It's just that no one's done it before."

The three women continued discussing Mary's meeting with Elliot. Mary offered to write a letter of recommendation to Elliot highlighting the women's performance and job duties (see p. 220). Janice and Sandra decided they would formally apply for the job, knowing it would be an uphill battle.

### Elliot's Decision

Several weeks went by and Elliot announced that he had hired William Katz. In his announcement to the organization, he explained that Katz had many years of experience in laboratory work with not only Pharmacare, but other biotech companies. Privately, he told Mary that the job was too critical for him to consider a job-share situation.

*Appendix 9.2*

Mary Bynum

Pharmacare

270000 Industrial Park Drive

Miami, Florida

Elliot Southern

Director – Research and Development

Pharmacare

Dear Elliot,

I am writing to recommend Janice Newman and Sandra Price for the position of Lab Manager I. When I began to sit down to write this letter, I contemplated writing two separate recommendations – one for each of them, but I honestly see them as a unit. As you know, they have operated in a job-share situation in my department for the last two years.

As research scientists in my lab, they have carried out our efforts to discover drugs that prevent or mitigate the effects of auto-immune diseases. They have kept scrupulous lab notes and recorded all information; they both understand the latest technology; and they stay current with the latest scientific research. On occasion, they have come to me with recommendations for buying a piece of state-of-the-art equipment. Their recommendations have been solid and have improved lab operations. When I have had to be out of town for any reason, I have left them with the responsibility of managing the lab in my absence. They have never let me down.

Both Janice and Sandra are well-respected by their peers in part for their competence and in part for their common-sense approach. They have good instincts for managing people and they treat everyone with respect. They both have high standards not only for themselves but for others with whom they work.

I sincerely hope that you will consider them for this job opportunity. They are both exceptional employees.

Best regards,

Mary Bynum

Auto-immune Lab Manager

*Appendix 9.3: Internal Position Application – Pharmacare*

# Lab Manager I

This position is responsible for the supervision of lab technicians, approximately 10 full-time employees. The position requires supervision of staff who will be running lab experiments, planning laboratory work, and producing lab reports and documentation specifically for private and governmental grant work. The person selected will have managed employees in a scientific setting (preferably a lab environment) and will have knowledge of:

- quality-control procedures in a lab setting.
- testing procedures and reports analyzing results, progress, and recommendations.
- laboratory equipment.
- how to design work schedules for lab staff.

Further, the individual will:

- understand and implement safety standards and will maintain sufficient inventory of materials and supplies for performance of duties.
- utilize various software programs in reporting lab experiments.
- provide advanced problem-solving, troubleshooting, and interpretation of experiment results.
- stay abreast of latest technical procedures.
- communicate in a professional manner with doctors, patients, and other medical personnel with whom Pharmacare may be interacting.
- supervise a variety of personnel functions, including interviewing, hiring, performance appraisal, promotions, and vacation schedules.
- be able to confidently make decisions relevant to all laboratory procedures and keep his or her manager informed about all activities and major decision taken in the lab.

Minimum requirements: staff supervision in a lab setting, plus a relevant undergraduate degree in the biosciences or chemistry.

## Discussion Questions

1.  Do you think Pharmacare's policy should be more clear-cut or should managers be allowed to determine whether a job-share is appropriate?
2.  In your opinion, should the job of Lab Manager I be a job-share? Why, or why not?
3.  Could Janice and Sandra have handled their situation differently with Elliot Southern so as to convince him?
4.  In your view, is there any role that Human Resources might have played in this case?

## Other Activities

1.  In a group of four people, role play a job interview between the two women and Elliott. One individual should observe the role play and offer feedback.
2.  Read the article, "Two executives, one career," by Cunningham and Murray in *Harvard Business Review*, Feb. 2005. Discuss the challenges (both personal and professional) that the two women had in their job-sharing situation.
3.  Compare the labor laws in the European Union with those of the United States concerning part-time work. The following websites will be useful: www.eurofound.europa and the US Department of Labor's website: www.dol.gov.
4.  Interview your parents. Ask them how they balance (or balanced if they are no longer working) work with family demands. Find out if their employers provided flexible work arrangements, and if so, if they took advantage of them. If both parents work, ask them how they arrange to get non-work activities done.

## LEGAL CASES

Legal cases involving work–life balance center around job-sharing, part-time work, maternity leave, working from home, and work hours. In the US, employment law does not afford part-time workers all of the same protections as full-time workers. For example, they may or may not receive the same employment benefits that full-time workers enjoy. Moreover, employers are not obligated to consider requests to go from full-time to part-time employment. Part-time workers in the US are generally viewed as a flexible labor pool, hired when needed and let go when not required. The law surrounding part-time work in EU countries is stricter because of an EU Directive on Part-Time Work established in 1997. EU Directives require member states to comply, but give them a timetable for making changes to their laws and some flexibility in how they implement the law. In the UK the same hourly wage must be given to part-time and full-time workers who perform the same job, and accommodation of workers' requests for part-time versus full-time work must be given full consideration. In the US, the Pregnancy Discrimination Act (part of Title VII of the Civil Rights Act) guarantees a woman six weeks' unpaid maternity leave, while Canadian law allows at least 15 weeks of paid leave provided by the National Health Insurance system. The maternity leave benefits in EU countries vary, but they are generally longer than in the US and offer some pay. Here are a few representative examples of legal cases in some of these environments.

### *Nashville Gas Co.* v. *Satty*

Nashville Gas required Mrs. Satty, a customer clerk in the accounting department, to take a leave of absence for her pregnancy. After a seven-week absence from work, she sought re-employment with the company, but her former job had been eliminated due to cut-backs. Temporary employment was found for her at a lower salary than her former job. While in this temporary employment, she unsuccessfully applied for three permanent positions but each time was denied the job, which was given to another individual who had begun to work for Nashville Gas during her maternity leave. If she had been credited the seniority that she had accumulated before her leave, she would have been awarded the jobs for which she applied. While she was on leave, the company refused to pay her sick pay (as is paid for other medical disabilities) and she lost all of her accumulated job seniority. When she returned to work, her employer told her she would be employed in a permanent position only if no currently employed employee applied for the position. The District Court (and then the Supreme Court, on appeal) held that the policy of denying employees returning from pregnancy their accumulated seniority deprives them of employment opportunities and adversely affects their status as an employee because of their sex. There was no proof of any business necessity for the adoption of a seniority policy with respect to pregnancy leave. The policy of not awarding sick pay is not a violation of Title VII, per se, because as in a prior case, *General Electric* v. *Gilbert*, Supreme Court Justice Rehnquist argued:

> As there is no proof that the package [disability pay] is in fact worth more to men than to women, it is impossible to find any gender-based discriminatory effect in this scheme simply because women disabled as a result of pregnancy do not receive benefits; that is to say, gender-based discrimination does not result simply because an employer's disability-benefits plan is less than all-inclusive. For all that appears, pregnancy-related disabilities constitute an additional risk, unique to women, and

the failure to compensate them for this risk does not destroy the presumed parity of the benefits, accruing to men and women alike, [434 US 136, 142] which results from the facially evenhanded inclusion of risks.

(429 US, at 138–139; footnote omitted)

In the GE case, the cost of the disability program for men was no greater than for women and therefore was not considered to be discriminatory.

## BP Chemicals Ltd. v. Ms. Gillick and Roevin Management Services

In this UK case, Ms. Gillick had been supplied to BP from Roevin Management Services, an employment agency that had been contracted by BP to supply it with workers. Gillick received her pay from the employment agency, while BP paid a fee to the agency. Gillick had worked for BP for several years under this arrangement, until she left due to becoming pregnant. When BP refused to have her back in the same job after her absence, she filed a claim against them. An employment tribunal (ET) ruled that she could bring a discrimination complaint against BP and against Roevin. BP appealed that decision and lost. The Appeals Court said that the ET erred in deciding that Ms Gillick had a claim against BP as its employee. The ET had misconstrued the Sex Discrimination Act (SDA), which defines employment as "employment under a contract of service or of apprenticeship or a contract personally to execute any work or labour." For the Act to apply, however, a contract had to exist between the employer and the worker, and there was no contract between BP and Ms. Gillick.

The Appeals Court did decide that Ms. Gillick's claim could proceed under a different clause in the SDA, which makes it unlawful for an employer, who has a contract with another company to supply workers, to discriminate against those workers. This applied whether or not the individual was currently working. BP's appeal was therefore dismissed. The case is important because it settles the question about whether the UK's Sex Discrimination Act can be applied to agency workers and contractors, rather than employees of a company.

## Given v. Scottish Power Plc

Mrs. Given worked for Scottish Power from June 1979 until May 1994 as a clerical worker and then as an "Implementation Team Member," supervising 10–12 people. In March 1993, after discovering that she was pregnant, Given spoke to the Customer Service Manager about the possibility of a job-share because she knew that other team members had arranged them. The manager told her that this was impossible at her level. She asked her team leader if working from home, a career break, or part-time work were possible, but he also said no. After returning from her maternity leave, she raised the question of a job-share with the Personnel Officer, who told her she should consider downgrading herself to a team member, but even then he couldn't guarantee that she would get on. After trying again with the company's District General Manager, she was turned down. At that point, she resigned and took the issue of job-share to an industrial tribunal. The tribunal held that Mrs. Given was never told why the job was unsuitable for a job-share; her employers had not assessed the duties of her job or why they could not be fulfilled on a job-share basis. The tribunal was not satisfied that there were any meaningful "operational" difficulties with the proposed work arrangement and further said that the company's policy on job-share appeared to apply to the entire workforce. The tribunal found indirect sex and marriage discrimination and awarded Mrs. Given £35,000 on the basis that she had taken another job for lower pay. In determining the amount of the award, the tribunal considered her length of service with Scottish Power, the manner in which she was treated, injury to feelings, and career damage.

UK employers can refuse a request for flexible working conditions under the following conditions: it adds costs; it prevents meeting customer-service demands; the company cannot reorganize work among staff; there would be a detrimental effect on quality or performance; there would be insufficient work for the hours proposed by the employee; or there had been planned structural changes that interfere with the proposed work schedule.

# 10  Women Entrepreneurs
## Working *Their* Way

**Learning Objectives**

After completing this chapter, the reader will:

- understand the importance of women entrepreneurs in the US and other countries.
- understand the various motivations women have for starting a business.
- understand the research associated with women entrepreneurs.
- understand the obstacles that women entrepreneurs face.

Women entrepreneurs are a growing force in the US economy; in 1972, according to the US Census Bureau, only 4.6% of US businesses were owned by women. The number of women entrepreneurs has increased dramatically since the 1970s; in 1990, the number of female sole proprietorships (the simplest form of business ownership, one in which the owner does not share profits or losses with other employees) was 5.6 million, while in 1998 it had grown to 7.1 million. According to the United States Small Business Administration, in 1999, 9.1 million women owned businesses and employed 27.5 million people, adding $3.6 trillion to the economy. Most female-owned businesses are fairly small; 84% of women-owned businesses in 1997 were sole proprietors with average receipts of $31,000. The largest women-operated sole proprietorships had business receipts of over $200,000 – although this group constituted only 2.9% of female sole proprietors. Some women business owners operate small businesses alongside their salaried employment. These so-called "moonlighters" occupy 2.4% of the female labor force and are engaged in a variety of work (Lowrey, 2006). Women's businesses thrive in geographic areas that are densely populated; California, New York, and Texas are the three states with the highest proportion of women business owners. Cities such as Los Angeles, New York, San Diego, Dallas, and Houston can more readily support all businesses than smaller, rural areas (Lowrey, 2006).

In the UK, there has also been a rise in entrepreneurship among both men and women, although the pattern has been slightly different than that of the US. Data from the Labour Force Survey estimates that 1,013,000 women are self-employed, representing 7.6% of women in employment overall. While self-employment for men has grown over the last 20 years in the UK, the female share of self-employment over the same timeframe has remained stable. As in the US case, the employment pattern is stronger in some regions than others. The south-east part of England (which includes London) has the greatest share of entrepreneurs (Carter & Shaw, 2006).

There still appear to be sex-segregated professions, even when women choose to run their own businesses. In the US, the majority of women-owned small businesses are in direct sales, childcare, beauty shops, miscellaneous personal services, and real estate sales. The highest-income areas for women are in finance, insurance, and real estate. The US Office of Small Business Administration conducted a study of women-owned businesses, comparing data from 1997 and 2002. The largest share of women-owned business receipts from these two periods were in wholesale and retail trade and manufacturing. Although these business sectors had the largest receipts, the largest proportion of women had businesses in professional services, scientific and technical services, healthcare, and social assistance areas (Lowrey, 2006). Professional service is a large category, encompassing jobs that require substantial amounts of human capital. This category comprises occupations in community and social services, law, education, training, business and financial operations, computers, entertainment, healthcare support, etc. The pattern of women-owned businesses in European countries is similar to the pattern in the US; for example, in Germany, women business owners are primarily found in the trades and services areas, such as consumer-oriented-product companies and personal care services (Welter, 2006).

## Characteristics of Women Entrepreneurs

Who are these women entrepreneurs? Are female entrepreneurs different from male entrepreneurs? Social scientists have tried to answer these questions over the last 25 years. A 1984 study of 463 women uncovered that the average female entrepreneur was the first-born in her family, from the middle class, a college graduate in a liberal arts field, married with children, and had a supportive husband whose career was in a professional or technical field. These women chose retailing, hospitality, or the service industry as their business (Hisrich & Brush, 1984). In 1986, a follow-up study was conducted comparing female entrepreneurs with minority entrepreneurs. In this study, the women had middle-to-upper-class backgrounds, while minority entrepreneurs came from middle-to-lower-class families (Hisrich & Brush, 1986). Studies have examined the education level of women entrepreneurs. Sexton and Kent (1981) reported that women entrepreneurs had slightly lower education levels than female executives working for organizations. Other findings suggest that women entrepreneurs were less likely than male entrepreneurs to study engineering or computing, fields associated with high-growth business ventures (Menzies, Diochon, & Gasse, 2004). Women who choose non-traditional fields such as construction, technology, or manufacturing appear to have different characteristics from those who choose traditional female occupations; these women were older, had more education, and were more likely to have self-employed parents (Hisrich & O'Brien, 1982). Devine (1994) used the Current Population Survey Census Data to explore characteristics of females who are self-employed. According to this large data set, self-employed women are older, married, have the safety net of someone else's healthcare coverage, and have more than a high school education. A study collating data from US tax returns from 1985 to 2000 reported that 64.8% of women sole proprietors are married, 23.81% are single, and 10.87% are unmarried with dependents (Lowrey, 2005, p. 13). Because most women entrepreneurs are married, it is important for them to effectively structure their work and family life. Work and family-management strategies are a significant determinant of the ability of a woman to grow her business. Sharing roles with a partner can significantly help women reduce conflict between work and family (Shelton, 2006).

Several psychologists and sociologists have attempted to classify the types of individuals who are attracted to business ownership and are successful as business entrepreneurs. One such typology was proposed for female entrepreneurs by Langan-Fox and Roth (1995). Three types of female entrepreneurs were identified. The first, a managerial entrepreneur, has high ability to influence and exert power over others and resists being subordinated to someone else. She wants to control her own destiny. The second, a pragmatic entrepreneur, has the need to make money or to pass a business on to children. The third, a need achiever entrepreneur, has a high need for personal achievement and cares less about managing and controlling people. Geoffee and Scase (1985) identified four types of female entrepreneurs: conventional entrepreneurs attempt to combine their domestic and business responsibilities; innovative entrepreneurs are committed to entrepreneurship and do not subscribe to conventional gender roles; domestic types are committed to their conventional gender roles above entrepreneurship ideals; and radical types have low commitment to both entrepreneurship goals and typical gender roles. Senges (2007) analyzed 100 entrepreneurs involved in Internet start-ups in university settings. He reports four general characteristics that make up the entrepreneurial mindset: first, entrepreneurs believe in free will and have an internal locus of control. They subscribe to the idea that they control their actions and shape their environment. Second, entrepreneurs focus on their own values and are motivated by them. They are not influenced by the values of others. Third, they are pragmatic in nature and improve their ideas by trial and error. Fourth, they attempt to relate their idea and practice to the rest of the world. Senges refers to this characteristic as a concern for ethics and an interest in sustainability. Although Senges did not specifically analyze gender differences, his data are consistent with the characteristics of female entrepreneurs in other studies.

Whether or not women entrepreneurs are significantly different from male entrepreneurs is as debatable as whether men and women corporate managers are different. Some researchers have looked at the value systems of male versus female entrepreneurs, how men and women define success, and how they manage. The research on these questions appears to be divided, although some researchers find small differences. Women value equality more highly than males do, and men value family security more than women do (Fagenson, 1993). Self-fulfillment and goal achievement were important to female entrepreneurs (Buttner & Moore, 1997). Women defined success in three main ways: control over their destiny, fulfilling work, and fulfilling ongoing relationships with clients, while men mentioned achieving goals as most important (Reed, 2001). In terms of their business practices and management style, women emphasized quality rather than cost or customization of product (Chaganti & Parasuraman, 1996) and they used relational styles (Buttner, 2001). Women talked about mutual empowerment and teamwork in working with their employees. In several studies that compare the leadership styles of male and female managers, males seem to prefer a task focus with an emphasis on hierarchy rather than a relational, interactive style, which is more frequently observed in female managers (Alimo-Metcalfe, 1995; Burke & Collins, 2001; Lipman-Blumen, 1996). Female entrepreneurs seem to possess less ability than male entrepreneurs to generate innovative ideas – by pursuing new products or processes, or by going after niche markets (Bellu, 1993). Since male entrepreneurs are in manufacturing and high-technology fields in greater numbers than women, and women entrepreneurs are primarily focused in the service and retail industries, this finding seems expected – men have had more opportunity to apply innovative concepts (especially new product development) to their entrepreneurial activity.

In spite of the fact that the popular press and some institutions have focused on the differences between male and female entrepreneurs, there is much evidence that women and male entrepreneurs are more similar in personality and temperament than they are different. Masters and Meier (1988) found no significant difference between men and women entrepreneurs in their propensity for risk-taking. On dimensions of aggressiveness (Twenge, 2001) and attributes such as venture-innovation and risk-taking, Sonfield, Lussier, Corman, and McKinney (2001) found no significant differences between men and women. Several studies have found that where there are differences between male and female entrepreneurs, these differences have more to do with the social context and the industry than any gender traits. Anna, Chandler, Jansen, and Mero (2000) suggest that differences between entrepreneurs may be due more to the industry that they operate in; for example, in their study of women entrepreneurs, women in traditionally male industries such as construction, manufacturing, and high technology expected higher incomes and focused more on planning than women in more traditionally female industries such as retail or service. In the traditionally female industries, the entrepreneurs had a higher expectation for work–life balance.

## Motivations for Starting a Business

In addition to studying the nature of women's businesses, the characteristics of women business owners, and the size and type of their industries, social scientists have been interested in women's motivations for starting a business. Women decide to start their own businesses for a variety of reasons. Some say they had a desire to put an innovative idea into practice; others say they needed flexibility in their work lives; some say they wanted to work for themselves and be their own boss; and still others wanted to start their own business because they were frustrated with the lack of opportunity in the corporate setting. They felt they had gone as far as they could go because they had encountered a "glass ceiling." Several studies indicate that women desire independence, a sense that they control their own destiny, and a sense of self-achievement (Littunen, 2000; Orhan & Scott, 2001; Sarri & Trihopoulou, 2005). In one study of women and men with equivalent education (MBA entrepreneurs), the authors concluded that women were more motivated by family-related concerns and men were more motivated by wealth creation and career advancement. The study suggests that after they marry and have children, many women place greater value on flexibility (DeMartino & Barbato, 2003). Women entrepreneurs, more than male entrepreneurs, value the ability to pursue career goals in tandem with family responsibilities, and many recognize that running their own business offers them more say over how they will allocate their time between work and family interests (Gundry & Welsch, 2001; Stevenson, 1986; Orhan & Scott, 2001).

The wage gap between men and women may positively influence a woman's decision to leave paid employment for self-employment (Boden, 1996, 1999). A study of 31 female entrepreneurs detailed their reasons for starting their own businesses. However, in this study, social factors more than financial ones dominated: the women believed the limitations of their corporate roles were unfair, they resented having to go through an internal pecking order in order to get promoted, they felt their employers did not give them credit for their contributions – others took credit for their work – and the women lacked control over the rules and politics of the workplace (Reed, 2001). A Canadian study of 110 women small-business owners underplayed financial rewards and instead emphasized relationships, community building, and quality of life (Fenwick & Hutton, 2000). The study emphasized that women want to build mutually supportive relationships among their staff and networks of suppliers and competitors, make qualitative contributions to their communities, be known as reputable and reliable business persons, and sustain "quality of life" for themselves and their families.

Several economists have attempted to explain the reasons for women's interest in entrepreneurship. As we saw in Chapter 6, neoclassical economics suggests that networks that are thought to reduce transaction costs and increase efficiency do not serve women in the same way they serve men. Women are leaving the formal labor market to start their own businesses because in companies and other organizations they cannot penetrate male networks where information is shared, decisions are made, and careers are advanced (Weiler & Bernasek, 2001). From 2001 to 2003, there has been a decline in executive and managerial women on Wall Street. The percentage of women on Wall Street went from 41% to 37%, and the number of women in executive management positions fell to 17% from 21%. Part of this trend is certainly due to an economic downturn post-September 11, and certainly after the 2009 financial crisis the numbers of women have declined. However, women on Wall Street are also dropping out because firms are not providing the career paths they expected and because, even before they have families, women can see that balancing family responsibilities with work realities will be impossible (*Business Week*, 2004, p. 101). Similar to the situation in the US, the increase in women entrepreneurs in Germany over the last 10 years is due at least in part to economic conditions; many women found themselves unemployed and were pushed rather than pulled into entrepreneurial activity (Welter, 2006).

In one study, Scott (1986) found differences in motivations for men and women; women reported that they wanted a personal challenge and satisfaction from work, whereas men said they wanted to be their own boss. Kaplan (1988) found that women's motivations for self-employment had to do with their age. As women (and men) become older and more financially secure, they often want more than financial rewards for their work. They desire challenges, interesting work, and more freedom over how they do their work. The need for both personal achievement and autonomy are key motivators for women entrepreneurs (Langan-Fox, 2005).

## Women Entrepreneurs and Their Pay

"Business ownership has been one of the most effective means of improving women's economic well-being" (*Women in Business*, US Small Business Administration, October 2001, p. 1). In 1998, women-headed households with a business had an average income level 2.5 times higher than those without a business. Although this is an encouraging statistic for women who own businesses, there is still a significant pay gap between male and female entrepreneurs. Based on data from 1990 to 1998, women's average taxable receipts for head of household were $20,000; average returns for women filing jointly were $23,400; and for women filing singly, $23,600. Male entrepreneurs who are the head of household had receipts of $42,400; those who are married and file jointly had receipts of $69,900; and single male entrepreneurs had receipts of $45,200. These statistics do not tell us how hard the entrepreneurs worked, what type of business they have, or whether or not they worked full-time or part-time. The data is also taken over an eight-year period; women's earnings are steadily increasing every year. Figures gathered in 1999 by the US Small Business Administration indicated that the personal incomes of self-employed men and women are distinctly different: 83% of self-employed women earn less than $45,000 a year, while 59% of men earn less than $45,000 annually.

## Current Research on Women Entrepreneurs

Today, social scientists and behavioral economists are generally interested in four streams of research about women entrepreneurs: how they finance their businesses and their access to capital, their networks and degree of social capital, the growth perform-ance of their businesses, and opportunity structures for women entrepreneurs.

Financing and access to capital has changed dramatically since the 1970s. Histori-cally, women had been stereotyped as not being able to run a business as effectively as men and had been denied access to credit. Up until the Equal Credit Act was passed in 1975, women experienced overt credit discrimination. Banks and lending institutions perceived women business owners to be less successful than male business owners, yet these institutions perceived the women's business plans to be of the same quality as their male counterparts' plans (Buttner & Rosen, 1988).

More recent research has investigated the credit terms that are offered to men versus women (the interest rate charged and payment schedule), and the perceived attitudes of loan officers toward women entrepreneurs. Today, there is little if any evidence of systematic discrimination by banks (Coleman, 2000; Fabowale, Orser, & Riding, 1995; Fay & Williams, 1993). Some research suggests that women entrepreneurs will face higher interest rates than male entrepreneurs (Coleman, 2000) and higher require-ments for collateral for their loans (Coleman, 2000; Riding & Swift, 1990). Coleman argues, however, that bankers discriminate on the basis of the size of the business, rather than along gender lines. Women's businesses tend to be smaller than men's and bankers prefer to lend to larger, more established firms.

A recent study suggests that bank loan officers use a wide range of criteria to assess loan applications from entrepreneurs, and generally do not vary these criteria from one sex to another (Carter, Shaw, Lam, & Wilson, 2007). In this study, 35 male and female loan officers from one British bank were placed in focus groups and asked to respond to a variety of questions surrounding lending criteria and lending pro-cesses. While the results were generally encouraging for women entrepreneurs because little bias was revealed, there still were some gender differences among the respondents. Female loan applicants were more likely to be assessed on whether or not they had done sufficient research on their business idea, while male applicants were more likely to be assessed on whether or not they had supplied enough informa-tion about their business, their financial history, and their personal characteristics. Male bank officers were more likely to question the commitment of the loan appli-cant, especially if she was female. Female bank officers were more likely to emphasize the need to meet the applicant and to know the marital status of the applicant. Female bank officers use marital status as a signal of stability and responsibility, especially as a means of assessing men. The authors suggest that this difference may be due to gendered assumptions about women's comprehension of business activities and the potential integrity and capability of male entrepreneurs. The authors con-clude that banks see a lucrative market in women entrepreneurs and that the situ-ation for women is generally free of bias, although small differences between how women and men are assessed remain.

Although banks have an interest in lending money to any solid business venture, no matter the sex of the entrepreneur, some scholars maintain that gender socialization influences all parties involved in the credit decision. For example, researchers have found that mixed-sex entrepreneurial teams benefit women entrepreneurs in male-dominated cultures and industries (Godwin, Stevens, & Brenner, 2007). This is in part due to the stereotypes that people hold of women and the view that a mixed team of both men and women is more reliable than a women-only team, and in part due to the networks that men can bring to the newly formed enterprise. In 1994, 12.5% of women business owners reported believing that they had experienced gender discrimi-nation in their banking relationship (Read, 1994).

A second stream of research concerns itself with the availability of influential networks to women and their level of social capital.[1] Women may not start a business because they recognize that they do not have the influential contacts necessary to be successful or fear that, once they start their businesses, they will not be able to grow a business due to their lack of contacts. In short, they perceive that they are out of touch with key networks that could help them (Welter, 2006). Because women's participation in the venture capital industry has not kept pace with industry growth, and because women exit the industry faster than men, some scholars suggest that women are less likely to have social networks that overlap with venture capitalists. This will make it more difficult for them to receive financing from venture capital firms (Gatewood, Brush, Carter, Greene, & Hart, 2008).

In addition to studying the financing of businesses and social networks, researchers have been interested in the growth performance of women's businesses. In a qualitative study of 50 entrepreneurs, researchers separated the entrepreneurs by the level of revenue their firms produced. The high-growth entrepreneurs (mainly men) were those who had businesses that experienced growth of more than $1 million. They were motivated by the desire to be rich and the challenge of running a large business. These motivations were fueled by their strong identification with their business in terms of their self-concept and self-esteem. The modest-growth entrepreneurs (mainly women), by comparison, preferred to control the growth of their companies in line with their lifestyles and their family needs. They felt that adding employees or building their businesses would require too many personal sacrifices (Morris, Miyasaki, Watters, & Coombes, 2006). Both sexes must deal with the demands of family life on their business, but women may bear the brunt of these demands more heavily than men do. Some have argued that women may either deliberately or inadvertently limit the size of their ventures because of these demands (Aldrich & Cliff, 2003; Lowrey, 2005; Still & Timms, 2000; Stoner, Hartman, & Arora, 1990). In societies where a woman's role is linked to family and household responsibilities, entrepreneurship for women will be seen as less desirable (Baughn, Chua, & Newport, 2006). A study in Norway found that the lower funding levels of women's businesses are associated with the lower early growth of their businesses (Alsos, Isaken, & Ljunggren, 2006). The authors suggest that this lack of funding is due to the few women represented in venture capital firms that lend money. Similarly, in Canada, women entrepreneurs are less likely than their male counterparts to receive venture capital funding. This is most likely due to the smaller size of their businesses rather than any sort of gender discrimination (Jennings & Provorny Cash, 2006).

A final area of research has been concerned with the *perceived* opportunity structure by women who are interested in starting their own businesses. Researchers have been interested in finding out whether women perceive that there are obstacles or road blocks in their way. In a study of nascent women entrepreneurs from 17 countries in Europe, Africa, North America, and South America, women across all countries perceived themselves and the environment to be less favorable than the environment for male entrepreneurs (Longowitz & Minnite, 2007). Women had a greater perception of low opportunity, fear of failure, and the lack of networks than men did, and this negatively affected their propensity to envision themselves as entrepreneurs. One's level of confidence about skill-level and knowledge are positively correlated with starting a business. The fear of failure negatively influenced a women's propensity to start a business, while for men fear of failure was not an inhibiting factor.

Another study focused on the intentions of young business students in India, the US, and Turkey to pursue entrepreneurial activity (Gupta, Turban, Arzu Wasti, &

Sikdar, 2009). Both men and women perceived entrepreneurs to have characteristics similar to males, rather than to females. Only the women students perceived entrepreneurs as having "female" characteristics as well as "male" characteristics. This perception may in part explain the differences between male and female entrepreneurial activity, if women with more "feminine" characteristics assume that opportunities are closed to them or that they will have difficulty overcoming barriers. Some scholars have looked at how women and men identify opportunities and report that men and women use different processes for identifying them (DeTienne & Chandler, 2007). Although the processes were difficult, there were no differences in the innovativeness of their ideas.

Media portrayal of women entrepreneurs may contribute to the perception that there are more opportunities for men than women. Several studies focusing on such media portrayal of women entrepreneurs fail to portray them as a diverse group of individuals, and tend to focus on how women entrepreneurs are different from male entrepreneurs. Langowitz and Morgan (2003) examined the US business press for depictions of female entrepreneurs and compared these to surveys of women entrepreneurs. Their results show that the media portrays the female entrepreneurs as having common social characteristics, yet the survey data show a diverse group of individuals. A study of women in the German press found that women entrepreneurs are often portrayed in a sexual manner and are described as different from male entrepreneurs. The authors suggest that this depiction of women entrepreneurs pits them against their male counterparts and makes them more likely to be viewed as the exception, rather than the standard (Achtenhagen & Welter, 2003). Ahl (2004) also argues that showing women as different from men creates a picture of women entrepreneurs as outside the norm, and therefore inferior. Bird and Brush (2002) note that entrepreneurial activity has been described historically in male terms rather than female terms, or in terms that are gender-neutral. This framing of entrepreneurial activity as primarily a male domain could influence the perceptions of others toward would-be women entrepreneurs, as well as women's own perceptions of their abilities to succeed and to network with other business owners.

## Intrapreneurship – Women Entrepreneurs Within Organizations

Women who have entrepreneurial characteristics may find it possible to satisfy their need to invent and create within an organization, provided that organizations allows for creativity and innovation. Some organizations have encouraged this type of so-called "intrapreneurship" behavior in part to promote fresh ideas that may either save the organization money or increase its sales, and in part to keep good ideas within the corporation. A corporation risks losing talented, entrepreneurial employees who leave their organizations and create "spin-offs," small companies that may become competitors to the original firm.

Many companies have set up small groups of employees who are expected to come up with innovative ideas within the confines of the organizational structure. Lockheed Martin, for example, organized a small group of engineers responsible for delivering a new jet aircraft. The group came to be known as "Skunk Works" because it was allowed little interference from management, was encouraged to innovate, and had leeway to break some corporate rules. 3M corporation and Intel have also encouraged intrapreneurship. For example, 3M is known for giving its employees the freedom and time to create new ideas, independent of management oversight.

## Minority-Women Entrepreneurs in the US

Minority-women enterprises are on the rise; firms owned by women of color represent 20% of privately held firms, and they are growing at five times the rate of all US privately held firms (Center for Women's Business Research, 2007). The rate of women's business ownership is significantly higher among minorities than whites, as indicated by Figure 10.1. For example, white women owned 28% of women businesses compared to African American women, who owned 46%.

Many female minorities start their own businesses for the same reasons white women do. They want to exercise more control over their lives, use their education and experience, build their own wealth, and serve their own communities. Many say they are dissatisfied with the corporate experience; they encounter a "concrete ceiling" where both their gender and race are used to hold them back from achieving what they could achieve if the world were gender- and race-blind. Many minority entrepreneurs start a business catering to their own ethnic groups. These women say they started a business to exercise more control over their destiny. Unlike Latina, Asian, or American women business owners, African American women express commitment to being role models for others of their race and they want to make a difference in their community. African American women own 365,110 businesses in the United States and employ 200,000 people, contributing nearly $14 billion in sales revenue. African American women have an even more difficult time obtaining financing than white women do: 47% say they have trouble obtaining financing compared to 28% of white women. From 1997 to 2002, the number of African American firms owned by women increased by 17% (CELCEE Center for Entrepreneurial Leadership/Clearinghouse on Entrepreneurship Education, 04–04, March 2004, UCLA: Los Angeles).

Asian businesses, especially those run by Vietnamese people, have been influenced by two waves of immigration in the US – the first immediately following the Vietnam War in 1975, and the second from 1978 until the mid-1980s. These immigrants, the majority of whom settled in California and Texas, encountered a language barrier,

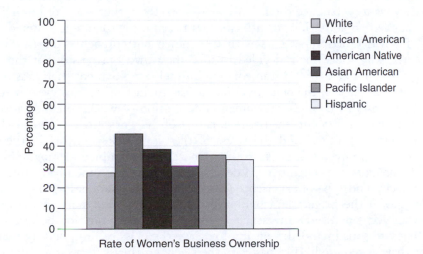

*Figure 10.1* Rate of Women Business Ownership by Race (2006) (source: Lowrey (2006). *Women in Business*, 2006. *A Demographic Review of Women's Business Ownership* (no. 280). Office of Advocacy, US Small Business Administration, p. 21).

cultural displacement, and they had few economic resources. Consequently, they started businesses serving their own communities – for example, opening small grocery stores or beauty shops. Most Vietnamese businesses are family funded and family run – with the majority of employees blood relatives. According to the National Women's Business Council, 32% of Vietnamese American small-business owners are women operating primarily in the personal service category – beauty and nail salons, for example. Many Vietnamese entrepreneurs are beginning to buy franchises or franchise their own businesses. This trend is happening especially in the fast-food restaurant sector.

As of 2004, Latinas represent 553,618 majority-owned, privately held firms in the US and employ about 320,000 people, generating $44.4 billion in sales revenue (National Women's Business Council, 2006). Latinas favor the service sector (about half of Latina firms are located here), the retail trade, transportation, communications, utilities, and construction industries. One difference between Latina women and other minorities is their decrease in entrepreneurship after the age of 34. This drop in activity is most likely due to different social expectations; many Latina women are expected to devote themselves to domestic responsibilities once they marry and have children. Another difference is in the number of employees Latinas typically hire – firms owned by Latina women are slightly less likely to employ people than other women-owned firms.

## Women's Entrepreneurship Around the World

Women-owned businesses around the world have grown dramatically since the early 1990s. According to the World Bank, one-quarter to one-third of all registered businesses in many countries are owned by women, and the start-up rates for women-owned businesses are overtaking those of men. Most of these businesses are small and in the informal sector of the economy, yet some are multi-million-dollar businesses employing thousands of people.

Women in other countries start their own businesses for many of the same reasons that women in the United States launch theirs. They want more independence in their working lives, they want to balance their family and work lives, they want to be their own boss, and they left to start their own businesses because they had encountered a "glass ceiling." From detailed interviews with 61 women entrepreneurs, a study in Canada investigated why the women decided to start their own businesses. For those women who lost their jobs and moved immediately into self-employment there was no hesitation in identifying lack of financial resources as the main reason. However, with more detailed questioning, many of the women cited erosion of working conditions, lack of a positive work environment, the political nature of the work environment, lack of autonomy in decision-making, and the stress of their job as key factors in their decision to leave an employer (Hughes, 2003). One study examined demographic characteristics of women entrepreneurs in 23 developed countries. Women had similar education levels, focus, and type of experience (Brush, 1992). In countries where there is an erosion of jobs in the private and public sectors, women often start their own businesses. In the UK, one study investigated women's motivations for becoming entrepreneurs. Their reasons included: wanting to escape the glass ceiling; finding that in organizations they lacked credibility based on their gender; they had been socialized to have high ambitions; and they wanted to balance work and family interests (Marlow, 1997). In Pakistan, women reported wanting personal freedom, economic security, and satisfaction (Shabbir & D'Gregorio, 1996).

In some countries, the political history and political climate have had a role to play in women's entry into entrepreneurship. In China, women have historically worked, and female professionals, because of the Communist Party's commitment to pay equity, were paid equally to male professionals. At present, approximately 17% of women-owned businesses in China hire more than 1,000 workers. In Poland, the transition from a centrally planned economy to a free-market system has provided the context for women entrepreneurs. Women entrepreneurs in Poland are more highly educated than their male counterparts (Zapalska, 1997a, b). In South Africa, women's entrepreneurial activity was seen as one way to repair an ailing economy and negate the effects of institutional segregation in a post-apartheid era, yet black South African women suffer from lack of business training and gender discrimination (Government of South Africa, 2005).

In some parts of the world, the obstacles for women entrepreneurs are far greater than for women in the United States. For example, in some countries, women lack training and experience in business, have difficulty securing financing, lack networks that could help them grow their enterprises, on occasion encounter hostility, and find it difficult to manage their personal and family responsibilities with business ones (Shragg, Yacuk, & Glass, 1992).

Some women are limited by discriminatory laws and cultural practices. For example, if land or inheritance is handed down to males, women have less capital than men; and if women are expected to remain in the home, they will not be accepted in the business community. Some governments make access to education and credit difficult for women. For example, in many African countries, custom law prevents women from rights to own property, and in some Middle Eastern countries, governments prevent women from owning their own businesses. In more traditional societies like Turkey, being a female entrepreneur helps one's economic status, but puts a strain on family and marital roles because women are not expected to hold a dominant role in the economy (Ozgen & Ufuk, 2001). In Ozgen and Ufuk's study of 220 married Turkish women entrepreneurs, the women defined risk as both economic and social and familial. About 45% of the sample stated that their entrepreneurial pursuits affected their roles in family life in a negative or very negative manner. The women entrepreneurs reported that there hadn't been any change in their domestic responsibilities, such as housework, since they started their businesses.

Female entrepreneurs in Kerala, India, are held back by their own avoidance of projects that might be considered "male." There is, as well, a cultural norm against extending credit to women, and women are often expected to discontinue their businesses after marriage (Krishnan Embram, 2003). Women are conditioned from childhood to defer to the most powerful male in her family, a father, brother, or uncle. Kerala men very often cannot tolerate a wife who earns a higher income. This gender socialization manifests itself in the type of products and the size of the business a woman owns; she is more likely to make garments or textiles or process food and her business will likely be small so as not to take away the social status of her husband. The government of India has recognized that it needs to provide female entrepreneurs with training on the nature of the product process and small-industry development to help them branch out into small-scale industries.

In the 1980s and 1990s, Japan suffered an economic downturn, but in the twenty-first century its economy has improved significantly. There are now many entrepreneurial opportunities in information-technology companies and Internet ventures. Because of the economic downturn, Japanese employers have changed their attitude toward the employment contract; they can no longer guarantee bright, young university graduates lifetime employment. This in turn has changed the attitude of employees. Young people in Japan no longer expect the stability and prestige that was once offered by large Japanese companies, and many have realized the freedom of owning their own businesses. For several reasons this entrepreneurial spirit has not engaged the female population as much as the male population. Traditional attitudes about female roles prevail. Japanese women are expected to take care of their own children, especially infants. Married women are not expected to strike out on their own.

Women in less-developed countries need access to capital and support from their immediate family with domestic work. The International Labor Office works to help women's businesses by providing training, working with governments to shape policy, and by working with other third-party organizations to help women start and maintain their businesses. Much of their work has been done in African countries – Tanzania, Zambia, and Ethiopia, for example. In these African countries there are several issues for women. First, women do not always have the education, marketing, management, and technical skills to launch a business, and they lack the sophistication to work with financial institutions to obtain financing. In Ethiopia, 85% of women starting businesses rely on their personal savings rather than credit. Second, many women prefer to have a limited commitment to their business because they are expected to be available to their husbands and families in the morning and in the evening to deal with domestic chores.

In addition to these personal factors, larger societal forces interfere. In most societies, women are traditionally not accepted as business owners and there is some resistance to dealing with women in this capacity. Even when women own their own property, they need permission from their husbands to use it as collateral for a loan. Corruption exists in many of these countries, and women are ill-prepared to deal with it; they aren't used to offering bribes primarily to male officials and they are not easily able to deal with bureaucratic rules, such as those governing licensure for their business. Finally, women are hampered by dealing only within their immediate, local market – only 5% deal outside of it. Trade liberalization and help from their governments in terms of obtaining contracts and training will help.

In Pakistan, women encounter some of the same barriers as in Zimbabwe, Swaziland, and Nigeria, for example. Nearly 70% do not use networks familiar to Western women such as women's support groups or chambers of commerce to help them in their businesses. A traditionally male-dominated culture makes breaking into business difficult, although this is changing. Many women complain of government red tape and the lack of support from their families who expect them to maintain strict gender roles. The ILO has interviewed a variety of women business owners including an exporter of precious stones, a woman who runs a medical clinic, a restaurateur, several clothing designers, and a woman who owns a transportation firm. All of them mentioned supportive family and friends who helped them to get started.

In spite of the challenges for women entrepreneurs in developing countries, their participation levels are increasing. In developing countries, cooperatives provide advantages for women entrepreneurs. (A cooperative is a legal entity of individuals who own and operate their own business together.) Cooperatives are formed along similar business objectives – for example, in Bangladesh there are dairy cooperatives and a wireless pay phone service called Village Phone, owned and operated by women. Members jointly set policies, share decision-making, and contribute capital. The advantages of cooperatives are several: first, they provide economies of scale because joint activities can be conducted at a lower cost; second, economies of scope afford joint production of goods and services which improve efficiency; third, owners in the cooperative have increased bargaining power with their suppliers; fourth, risk-taking is shared and the cooperative provides legal protection that limits individual liability; fifth, innovation is more likely when groups of people pool their talents and resources. Microfinancing and microcredit organizations such as BRAC, Opportunity International, the Grameen Bank, and others have provided loans to these cooperatives so that they can start and grow their businesses.

## Resources for Women Entrepreneurs

In recent years, help has been provided to women entrepreneurs by lending institutions, universities, the government, and non-profit organizations for funding, training, and advice. The Center for Women's Research has presented research to banks demonstrating the importance of women-owned businesses to the US economy, and banks have begun tailoring their products to the needs of women. Banks are beginning to recognize that women-owned businesses do well and represent a growing area of bank business. For example, Wells Fargo Bank began a Women's Business Services Program in 1995 to help women entrepreneurs understand their financing options and guide them through the application process. The bank reports that between 1995 and 2006, it has made loans worth $26 million to women small-business owners (Ossinger, 2006).

The Diana Project, named after the Greek goddess of the hunt, is a collaboration of scholars from 16 different countries whose objective is to provide education to both female entrepreneurs and to venture capitalists who invest in entrepreneurial activity. Based at Babson College in the US, the Diana Project provides information to investors about opportunities with women-owned businesses, and raises awareness for women seeking financing, especially in explaining how the funding process works and how to secure capital. In addition to its role in providing information to women entrepreneurs and potential funders, the Diana Project holds research symposia for scholars interested in entrepreneurship.

With the advent of Civil Rights legislation in 1964, the US government and state governments changed their policies to offer a greater number of women and minority businesses contracting opportunities with the government. However, because these contracts are often very large (multimillion dollar contracts), it is impractical for women business owners of smaller enterprises to bid on them. If this government work could be broken down into smaller contracts, women would have a better chance of winning contracts (Enchautegui, Fix, Loprest, von der Lippe, & Wissoker, 1997). The Small Business Administration (SBA), a government-backed agency, offers assistance specifically for women through its Office of Women's Business Ownership, designed to help start-up ventures. The SBA has about 90 centers in the US that offer loans, seminars, counseling, and programs for women wanting to start-up, maintain, or expand a business; a typical seminar would be one that explains how to read and understand financial statements (Ossinger, 2006). Other organizations have begun to sprout up to assist women business owners. A woman-based advocacy group called "Count Me In" partnered with American Express to launch "Make Mine a Million," an event where women presented their business plans to reach the $1 million mark in revenue. The winning plans received mentoring, marketing assistance, and a line of credit from American Express (Ossinger, 2006). "Angel investors," affluent individuals who provide venture capital for start-up companies, can also provide assistance to women. Golden Seed LLC is an angel investor group started by Stephanie Hanbury-Brown that lends money specifically to women. The group invests as much as $300,000 in a single company in exchange for an equity stake in the business, and they provide advice on how the company is run (www.goldenseeds.com).

Venture capital firms, firms that have private equity and invest it in non-public start-up companies, still seem to favor male-owned businesses; this could be because of women's lack of experience in presenting business plans, established networks of men who know venture capitalists and prefer to help each other, or women's lack of negotiation skills. Venture capital firms that do invest in women are uncommon, but are not non-existent. For example, Prolog Ventures has received "The Shattered Glass Award" from the Women's Technology Cluster in California for investing in companies led by female CEOs. Prolog Ventures invests in health sciences, environmental sciences, and consumer product firms. In addition to awards, other organizations such as Springboard enterprises, a non-profit, attempt to accelerate women's access to equity markets by educating women entrepreneurs and by giving them a platform to showcase their start-up ventures as they seek equity capital. Springboard gives women an audience with potential investors, provides coaching for potential business owners, and conducts local workshops and seminars for women entrepreneurs. The organization notes that as more women join venture capital firms, the chances of women garnering funding should increase. In addition to access to capital, access to major markets is important for women. Women sometimes find it hard to secure corporate clients because of lack of networks or outright bias. Although the government has begun to open up opportunities for women business owners, government contracts are still difficult for women to win. In 2008, women were awarded 3.4% of the total federal contracts (*Women in Business*, US Small Business Administration, 2008). Given their ready availability to earn contracts, women business owners earn only 29% of the expected dollars that they should earn from government contracts (Enchautegui et al., 1997). The importance of government contracts cannot be underestimated; corporate clients and the government are the two segments that produce the highest revenues and repeat business.

Some companies have recognized how difficult it is for women and minorities to garner business from large corporations. IBM has staffed a "global supplier diversity chief" whose job it is to find qualified minority suppliers in manufacturing and technology. The company has a supplier-diversity program that includes a mentor–protégé component, matching suppliers with IBM executives who may give guidance to minority entrepreneurs (Adu, 2005).

Science and technology are likely to be areas of entrepreneurship activity in the future. Universities are a fertile ground for male and female scientists who want to commercialize their discoveries. In a study of founders of university spin-out companies in the United States, women were under-represented compared to men. The reasons may be two-fold: women are under-represented in science departments at universities, and when they do engage in entrepreneurial activity they tend to be involved in teams with senior male colleagues (Rosa & Dawson, 2006). Universities across the United States provide laboratories for researching and designing potential business projects in fields such as computer science, biomedical engineering, and environmental science. These business incubators, as they are called, are often provided seed money from venture capitalists and from their universities to move their business from the idea stage to commercialization.

## Advice for Women Entrepreneurs

Several researchers have summarized what women entrepreneurs should do to ensure success. Of primary importance is the need to establish a track record as either a manager or technical employee. This track record is an important element that bankers use to determine credit risk. Women should compensate for their gaps in education by either obtaining more education, particularly in finance and marketing, or by hiring experts to fill the gap. Because women often bear the brunt of family responsibilities, they should assess the needs of their family before launching a business. Finally it is important to establish a strong support system of family, friends, and others in business, and to have the personal stamina and determination to succeed (Hisrich, 1989). Women in one study emphasized the importance of supportive husbands who believed in them and in their business and encouraged them (Reed, 2001). Solovic (2004) offers advice by cautioning women about the 10 mistakes people routinely make when starting a business.

1  They will be apt to misunderstand the commitment it takes to run a business.
2  They won't have strong support systems.
3  They won't have researched the market or the industry they intend to go into.
4  They will underestimate their costs.
5  They will over-project their sales.
6  They will fail to focus on the financials, especially cash flow and costs as they relate to revenues.
7  They will hire the wrong people, relying too much on referrals from family and friends.
8  They will seek confirmation for what they are doing, rather than the truth.
9  They will establish unnecessary business partners.
10  They will fail to have a solid business plan.

Springboard suggests that women pay attention to personal grooming and the pitch of their voice, as these suggest either self-confidence or the lack of it. In addition, they caution women to stay brief and get to the point quickly. Potential investors want to know what they will do, how they will do it, the experience of those who will run the company, and how they will make money (Greco, 2002).

Clearly individual women can benefit from advice from a variety of sources – organizations, family, friends, and other entrepreneurs. In addition to women playing a role, society needs to look to women for business ideas and innovations. In order to become or remain competitive, developed as well as developing countries are learning to harness the talents of individual women. Organizations in developing countries such as The Grameen Bank and the Bangladesh Rural Agriculture Cooperative (BRAC) are loaning money to women entrepreneurs through microfinancing programs because they recognize that small-business growth is and will continue to be a major part of countries' economies, and can make a difference in the lives of women and their families.

### Further Reading and Suggested Websites

Grameen Foundation website: www.grameenfoundation.org.

Gupta, V.K., Turban, D.B., Arzu Wasti, S., & Sikdar, A. (2009). The role of stereotypes in perceptions of entrepreneurs' intentions to become an entrepreneur. *Entrepreneurship: Theory and Practice, 33*(2), 397–417.

US Small Business Administration website: www.sba.gov.

## A CONVERSATION WITH FOUR ENTREPRENEURS

The following interview was conducted with four entrepreneurs. Mary works as an insurance agent representing a large insurance company, yet she is an independent contractor and owns her agency. Katherine is a certified financial planner and CPA who owns a fee-based financial advising business, and Laurie owns her own media company. Karen has owned two businesses – the first, an environmental biotech franchise, and the second a company that specializes in turning entrepreneurial engineering and medical ideas into viable products.

I: Tell me about why you decided to become an entrepreneur.

MARY: My parents had a great influence on me. They worked for themselves and I never saw them work a 9-to-5 day. My mom was a real estate agent and my father is a commercial developer. He buys properties and renovates them. All of my siblings also work for themselves. My older sister is an insurance agent, my brother is a builder and my other brother is in the mortgage brokerage business.

   I always wanted to rely on myself no matter what happened. Part of my motivation had to do with wanting a sense of financial security that I thought I could get from having my own business. No one could take it away from me as long as I did a good job. A family friend sort of recruited me to the insurance business. He said, "Teachers make the best agents because they can explain things to people in their terms."

KATHERINE: Before I became a financial advisor I was a social worker. I have always helped clients figure out how their finances impact their lives. I wanted to be on the creative end of something and I see helping people with their finances and having my own business fulfills that aim. I also wanted to cater to my own values, not someone else's. And finally, I started my business when I had a small child and I wanted a career where I could be flexible with my time.

LAURIE: I really had no control over becoming an entrepreneur. I was led into that direction from my former career as an attorney. I had been practicing in the entertainment and communication areas and after representing so many clients I became intrigued by the business side of it. I looked for an opportunity to put a toe in the water. I think entrepreneurs often don't have a choice. I really wanted to try my skills. I had a deep desire to forge my own territory – to build and create something.

KAREN: For me, it wasn't as if I had to get away from corporate America where I had worked before and had been successful, but I knew I wanted more than that environment could give me. It was a quality of life decision for several reasons. In my corporate career, there were too many layers of decisions and too many people to sign off on a decision before you could take action. I wanted more control over my time and more to show for my efforts than I get working for someone else. I also knew I wanted to enjoy life and I enjoy making things happen.

I: Did you have a work history before you became an entrepreneur?

MARY: Yes, I started out as a teacher after getting a degree in education. I taught high school for 4-and-a-half years, but thought I would never have financial security if I remained a teacher. Before becoming an entrepreneur, I had a few other jobs.... I worked for the Institute of Government and was a group secretary for several attorneys. I took the LSATS, but didn't really like law all that much. I think all of these experiences taught me something that helped me start my own business. I knew I was good at administration when I worked for the attorneys. They liked that I could multi-task and the fact that I took initiative.

KAREN: I started out working as a programmer for a large insurance company and worked my way up in the IT world. For the same company, I was a controller of a unit and then my last job before stepping out to run my own business was as the manager of a large service center for all of the insurance agents. I had 700 people in my area.

KATHERINE: From 1972–1985, I worked as a social worker in Washington, DC. I moved with my husband and decided to study for the CPA exam. I never intended to be an accountant but I thought the background would be useful. I passed it and then went on to take the CFP (Certified Financial Planner) designation. After I got that, I was an intern for a firm where I did tax advice and planning. When the firm was sold to a big-eight accounting firm, I couldn't see myself working there. I decided then to start my own business.

I: Did you have any reservations about owning your own business?

MARY: Well, not so much in my ability to make a success of it, but I did have reservations about the insurance industry. I had a poor impression of agents as sort of pushy, sleazy men. It is very true that the industry has been a good old boys' network. I helped a woman agent out and grew her business and I took several assessment tests – out of 52 candidates I did very well. I saw that I could be good at the business.

KATHERINE: I never had any doubts that the clients were there and that the business was there. I was lucky because I was able to have the back-up of a husband with a steady job and benefits. It's not so easy for entrepreneurs who don't have this. For example, 27% of self-employed people cannot afford medical insurance. If you are older it is even more difficult to afford it. I was able to finance my own business to start out and I worked from my home and didn't have a staff to begin with. I think people need to be aware of the vulnerabilities – they will need to be able to support themselves until they start making money.

LAURIE: I never had any reservations. I never wanted to go back. I loved the challenges.

KAREN: I really had no reservations, but I did spend a lot of money. I had to put all of my money into my first business and still wasn't ahead of the game. It came out alright because I sold the business after a few years. You just can't be afraid to fail. You have to persevere and have a high tolerance for risk.

I: What obstacles did you encounter along the way?

MARY: There were many. Perhaps the first had to do with my medical history. I had epilepsy as a kid, but had been cleared for it. The insurance company tried to block me from joining, because I had filled out an information form asking about my medical history. I put down that I had epilepsy as a kid. I had several doctors write letters telling the company that I was free of it and had been for many years. I just persisted so they dropped it.

KAREN: Financing is the biggest obstacle. Most businesses fail because they are under-capitalized. You project lower costs than you have and higher sales than you actually get. A second obstacle is understanding the market. With my first business, I should have actually gone out and asked restaurant owners if they would buy my environmentally friendly product. A third obstacle is really selecting the right business. Many people want to be an entrepreneur, but you really have to select something that you have a competency in and something that there is a strong market for.

KATHERINE: I really haven't found any obstacle.

I: Have you had any obstacles that have had to do with the fact that you are a woman?

MARY: Definitely. I was 25 at the time and naive about sexual politics at work. In 1994, after I had become an independent contractor, I went to a business-planning conference at Myrtle Beach, South Carolina. We were staying in two different condos. I was the only woman present. After the conference, I wanted to go out. None of the men wanted to go out, so I called an old buddy of mine – a guy that I had grown up with. I literally had known this guy since I was four years old! After a long evening, he was tired and so was I. He didn't want to drive all the way back to his house, some 25 miles away, so I told him he could sleep on the couch in my place. As it turned out, I gave him my bed and I took the couch. I never thought about how this might look. Well, the next day the rumors started to fly. Everyone was saying I had a man in my condo and had had sex with him. The next day, I was called to the Regional Office to talk to the Vice President. I asked for permission to tape record the interview, but he said "no." He didn't ask me for my version of the truth, he just told me that I had had a man in my room and had sex with him. He asked me to resign. I told him I wasn't quitting. He told me that I needed psychiatric help. He said the corporate world wasn't for me. That I was a square peg in a round hole. Well, as it turned out, I had a tape recorder in my pocket anyway, and I told him I had recorded the whole thing. He backed off, but told me he wanted me to apologize to every person who was at the conference and get their signature that I had done so. It made me so angry. I've seen men cheat on their wives, be drunk as coots, and I saw a male manager going at it with a female agent.

LAURIE: When I would go for financing at a bank, I encountered resistance to dealing with me one on one, as a female. I learned the trick of bringing along a male, even if he just sat there. I've never had a situation where I haven't been able to win someone over, though. People respect you if you are smart and you know your stuff. When I was an attorney, I think I was more conscious of people assuming things or trying to take advantage of me because I was a woman – I dressed conservatively, wore heavy, thick glasses, and pulled my hair back to make sure they took me seriously. I don't feel I have to do that now.

KAREN: Being an African American woman, I have sometimes felt that people, when they meet me for the first time, have perceptions about my race. I don't dwell on this but it is at the back of my mind sometimes, especially in certain parts of the country. Sometimes, I think I might do better talking to someone on the phone first. As a woman, I sometimes wonder if the financing issue might have been easier if I were a guy. But you can't dwell on these things.

KATHERINE: I guess I'm lucky. I haven't found any gender discrimination. Many financial planners are women and they do well.

I: What has been the hardest part about owning your own business?

MARY: For me, two things. Work–life balance. I hadn't taken a real vacation in 11 years. I was working 80 hours a week until recently when I got myself a "life coach." I had gained 30 pounds since my kids were born and work had taken over my life. She helped me work out a schedule where I got back to 35 hours a week, and I work out now for about a half an hour a day. My staff knows where I am all the time, but they fill in for me when I am not there. The second hardest part is managing employees. I was so nurturing it hurt me and my business. I think women have a natural desire to help people. I had to become tougher on employees. Before I tolerated it when people came in late or wanted to work their own hours. I still let people take off time to see their kid's play or something important, but I won't take poor attitudes or poor work performance any more. I've learned that two years with a good employee is better than 10 years with a bad one.

KATHERINE: Definitely managing the business. The talents for starting a business are different than the talents for maintaining and managing it. I'm not actually interested in growing my business. I want to be selective with my clients and if I grew it I would need a bigger infrastructure which would be even harder to manage.

LAURIE: For me, it's running the business. I love the building and dreaming part. The hardest part is managing it – hiring, doing the day-to-day follow-through. I think you have to believe in yourself and not get discouraged.

I: How has being a woman specifically helped you in this business?

MARY: I focus on women business owners for my business and when I do a good job for them they give me referrals. I have never had to advertise. I think the other aspect that I notice that distinguishes me and that is definitely a female thing is my ethics. I won't sell something to someone that they don't need no matter what the financial payoff might be for me. I still think of myself as an educator. I try to help people understand that they need to protect their income and always save a little. I helped a man from Honduras who speaks only Spanish get himself the right mortgage. It just made me feel good to help him.

KATHERINE: I am not sure if it is being a woman or my personality. I have an interest in family dynamics and maybe being a female is a bonus. Trust is very important to me and I think my clients trust me.

KAREN: For me, I am not sure it is being female or if it is simply the way I am. I read people well. I am personable and I make people feel comfortable. I make people feel good and I smile a lot. It helps me get my foot in the door.

LAURIE: Being a woman has absolutely helped me. When I am across the table from someone in a negotiation and I am perceived to be smart and know what I am talking about, it seems that people begin rallying around me. I don't think that happens to men as much. I think I stay away from aggressive tactics and I believe in the art of compromise. We don't live in a world of ultimatums and I can often work within a situation where I have to compromise and still get a lot of what I want. Women communicate well. I let people know what I am thinking and what my perspective is. That keeps the negotiation going rather than shutting it down. Women have so many assets – understanding, seeing other people's perspective, their nurturing side, patience.

I: What is the most important thing for people to know before trying to start a business?

KAREN: You have to know your own strengths and weaknesses. You have to be able to learn from your own mistakes. Most people don't succeed on the first go with a business. You have to hire good people and have others support you. I try to hire people who are smarter than I am. I want them to feel challenged at work. Life is short. Take advantage of every second and make sure that you are doing something you really like.

MARY: They need to be able to manage their own finances. It isn't good enough to have a business idea. I always tell people if they can't manage their own cash flow, they shouldn't go into business. They will just run it into the ground. If people do have an appreciation for money, but don't want to manage it day by day, they should get a good accountant who can do it for them.

KATHERINE: Be realistic and have a business plan. Figure out how you will support yourself when the times are lean. Manage your expenses so you don't get overstretched. Figure out where your business will come from.

LAURIE: You have to believe in yourself even when others may not believe in your idea. You have to keep going and not give up.

I:  Any final thoughts about entrepreneurship?

MARY:  You need high self-esteem to start a business. Many people don't have it when they are so young. You know the Japanese have a saying that you need three things in life: the sword, for a strong defense; the pearl, for economic security; and the most important thing – the mirror, self-knowledge. Because with self-knowledge, you can have the other two. That's a theory that I think is absolutely true.

KATHERINE:  Women in business can take advantage of many support groups who can give them advice and help them network. People in the same business don't have to be your competitors. We help each other with referrals and general knowledge. Not everyone is suited to be an entrepreneur. You have to be able to sustain yourself without a lot of stimulation from other people around you. You have to be disciplined with your time and you have to be able to promote yourself. Having good ideas is great, but you have to be willing to sell yourself.

KAREN:  I think you can't be afraid to try. If you fail, it isn't life or death. Life is about experiences. Just go on and do something else. Something you enjoy.

## Discussion Questions

1.  Compare the motivations of the four entrepreneurs.
2.  Do the women feel that being female has helped or hindered them?
3.  How did the women balance work and family (or other pursuits)?

# CASE STUDY

### Case Study 1: Two Entrepreneurial Titans – Mary Kay Ash and Anita Roddick

Arguably, no one embodies female entrepreneurship as fully as Mary Kay Ash, the founder of Mary Kay Cosmetics. The initial catalyst for starting Mary Kay Cosmetics was Ash's frustration with corporate life; when she was the National Director of Sales at World Gift Co., a direct sales company, she was passed over for promotion in favor of a male employee who she had trained. Dispirited, Ash quit World Gift and decided to take her personal savings of $5,000 to start Mary Kay Cosmetics. In 1963, she opened a storefront in Dallas, Texas, with her flagship product – a skin cream. (She had purchased the rights to it from the Heath family for $500.) Her motivation to become an entrepreneur was both personal and economic; she wanted to make money, be her own boss, not be limited by corporate politics, and create opportunities for other women. Within six to eight years, some women in the company earned over $100,000 per year. In 1964, the first annual Mary Kay convention was held in Dallas, where 200 women celebrated the company, its success, and their own. The company grew rapidly between 1974 and 1979; sales tripled and profits doubled.

Ash's business concept was to offer skincare products through a direct sales force of independent "beauty consultants." These sales consultants earned commissions from selling products. In 1981, direct selling was a $7.5 billion industry and was popular among women because they could work as much or as little as they wanted to. In the early days of the company, sales consultants sold the products through home beauty demonstrations. Today, in addition to product "parties" in the home, sales consultants sell through the Internet and in their workplaces, if they hold other jobs. The business model was very profitable because overhead cost were kept low (sales consultants worked from home and were not paid salaries). Mary Kay was known for her flamboyance and motivational strategies. Having spent 25 years in direct sales, she knew that recognition and rewards were important to salespeople. The annual Mary Kay conventions became legendary as a way to motivate and reward top saleswomen; pink Cadillacs, luxury vacations, and jewelry were awarded to top performers. In addition to motivating employees through these incentives, Ash provided career paths for women sales consultants. As women brought others into the company, they received higher commissions and could become eligible for higher-level jobs such as sales director, senior sales director, and national director.

Although Mary Kay Ash died in 2001, the company continues with her son at the helm. Today, it does business in 35 markets on five continents, and in 2008 had sales revenues of $2.6 billion. Much of its business is in emerging markets such as China (its second-largest market behind the US), Latin American countries, India, and Eastern Europe. Its product line has expanded greatly (make-up and toiletries have been added) and it now offers products for men such as face soap, shaving foam, and sunscreen. Manufacturing facilities are located in China and Dallas, and distribution centers are in many large cities in the US.

Like Mary Kay, Anita Roddick chose a product category she was familiar with – cosmetics and skincare. She founded The Body Shop, a company producing and retailing beauty products. The company was one of the first to focus on ethical sourcing of materials and fair trade with developing countries. It was also one of the first companies to prohibit animal testing of its products.

Roddick started a business with the aim of providing an income for herself and her two daughters. (Her husband, Gordon Roddick, was in South America for an extended period.) With inspiration from a small cosmetic store in San Francisco selling natural products, she decided to provide a limited number of quality skincare products in refillable containers and in small, sample sizes. After 15 different skin products were created in her garage, she opened her first shop in Brighton, England, in 1976 with a bank loan of £4,000. In the early days of her venture, her aim was to bring in £300 a week, just enough for her family to live on. With the success of the first store, a second store was opened six months later. Soon, every high street (shopping district) of every town in England had a Body Shop. The brand became widely recognized and synonymous with natural products.

Roddick was motivated by both financial security and political activism. She wanted to run an honorable business that did not establish hierarchies, but treated individuals equally. She was also interested in starting a business that furthered her activism. During her life, she had been involved in several causes including animal rights, environmentalism, anti-war protests, and defending human rights.

In the late 1990s and early 2000s, the company over-expanded, more competition entered the market – especially with availability of products online – and a recession hit in 2000. The Body Shop's profits declined dramatically and it was sold to L'Oreal in 2006, about a year after Anita Roddick died. Today the company sells make-up, skincare products, shampoos, bath products, and fragrances, and operates in over 2,300 stores in 61 countries across the world.

(Sources: Roddick, A. (1991). *Body and soul.* London: Ebury Press; www.thebodyshop. com; Kotter, J.P. & Stengrevics, J.M. (1981). *Mary Kay Cosmetics, Inc.* Harvard Business Online; Quelch, J.A. & Court, A.M. (1985). *Mary Kay Inc. Marketing Communications.* Harvard Business Online; www.MaryKay.com).

### Discussion Questions

1. Compare Ash's motivations to Roddick's.
2. These entrepreneurs chose different distribution methods (sales force versus retail shops) for the same product category. Discuss these methods and the pros and cons of each.
3. How did changes in the economy affect these businesses?

# 11  Policy and Organizational Practice

**Learning Objectives**

After completing this chapter, the reader will:

- understand the pros and cons of the various approaches that organizations have taken to equity and work–life balance.
- understand the role of governments, businesses, non-profits, and individuals in ensuring equity and work–life balance.

The previous chapters in this book identified many of the challenges women face in organizations. This chapter focuses on what companies, non-profit organizations, governments, and individuals can do to make the workplace more equitable.

Imagine that you are one of these three people:

- a woman who has worked her way through a corporation and risen to the ranks of senior management with all of its benefits and privileges.
- a man or woman in the organization with responsibility for encouraging more women and minority representation at senior levels.
- a newly minted college graduate looking for your first serious job.

If you are already at the top, you might be tempted to deny that obstacles still exist for women – you managed to reach the highest level, everyone else can too. This regrettable tendency fails to acknowledge what statistics tell us: there persists a dearth of women at senior levels. If you are at the top, you have a responsibility to influence the corporate environment, making sure that equitable practices are followed and everyone can achieve his or her potential. If, on the other hand, you are someone responsible for greater diversity in the workplace (perhaps someone in a human resources department or someone on a diversity taskforce), you are probably familiar with the statistics and eager to find out what programs or policies make for a better workplace. If you are the recent graduate and are job-hunting, you will want to understand the cultures of the organizations where you hope to work and how they treat their employees before agreeing to launch a career in any of them. If, as a recent graduate, you are a woman or a minority, this may be particularly important. You will want to be assured that you have the same opportunities as all other employees, be paid fairly, and be treated respectfully.

In all three of these scenarios, you would be wise to learn about the resources and interventions that help women and minorities achieve their potential. And it would be useful to know which efforts truly work and which do not produce lasting change.

## Interventions That Do Not Work in Isolation

Some organizational interventions are ineffective because they only *partially* address the issues of equity, representation of women and minorities in responsible positions, and work–life balance issues. Additional complementary efforts need to be taken with these interventions to make them effective. Communication with employees and managerial commitment, for example, improve the efficacy of these initiatives.

### Diversity Training

Business organizations have launched diversity programs to eliminate or minimize the "glass ceiling." Diversity programs often aim to bring minorities and women into influential positions in organizations. Many organizations take the view that diversity is good for business. They explain to their employees that their organization will be more successful if it mirrors the general demographics of their country, for example. A 2005 European Commission study reported that companies have the following business reasons for diversity:

- diversity provides a wider pool of high-quality candidates for jobs and helps in environments where there are labor shortages.
- it improves the corporate image.
- a more diverse workforce is more creative and innovative than a homogeneous one. With a diverse workforce that brings fresh ideas and new approaches, new products will more likely be developed.
- diversity opens up new markets. A diverse workforce is more likely to attract minority market segments – the gay and lesbian population or Hispanic population, for example.

Generally, four main approaches have been used to promote diversity: linking manager performance appraisals to diversity efforts, training employees on the benefits of diversity, establishing mentoring programs for women, and placing responsibility for diversity efforts with an individual or committee. A study in the US examined these efforts in 708 private-sector establishments (from 1971 to 2002) to find out which methods were most effective for removing barriers to women and minorities (Kalev, Kelly, & Dobbin, 2006). With data from the Equal Employment Opportunity Commission, the researchers tracked the change in managerial composition over the time period. Then they conducted interviews with human resource managers to determine the type of diversity efforts that were tried during the same period.

> The analysis reveals substantial variation in the effectiveness of diversity training. Some [training programs] increase managerial diversity across the board while others have meager effects, or positive effects for some groups and negative effects for others. The most effective practices are those that establish organizational responsibility: affirmative action plans, diversity staff, and diversity task forces.
>
> (Kalev et al., 2006, p. 27)

Diversity staff members are employees whose primary role is to ensure diversity in the organization and diversity taskforces are employees who take on the task of diversity management in addition to other organizational roles that they hold. Typically, diversity taskforces are comprised of employees from various parts of the organization who meet frequently to discuss diversity issues in the organization. Diversity employees and taskforces determine goals for the level of diversity they expect their organization to achieve.

Diversity training proved to be the least effective at increasing the proportion of women and minorities in management. Mentoring and networking, however, showed some modest effects to alleviate the glass ceiling for women and minorities. The most effective intervention by management was to appoint an individual as a diversity staffing professional, an advocacy committee with job responsibility for diversity, or to use affirmative action programs (Kalev et al., 2006). The authors note that where diversity initiatives are everyone's responsibility, but no one's primary responsibility, they fail because they can be easily ignored, as no one individual or committee has responsibility for implementing them. Importantly, the researchers also found that combining several methods can have a positive effect; having someone (or a group) responsible for diversity efforts in combination with education, training, mentoring, or networking, for example, can increase the effectiveness of diversity efforts.

Similar studies on the effectiveness of diversity programs have been conducted in the public sector. A large and multi-year study of diversity initiatives of US federal agencies analyzed promotion rates, voluntary turnover, and dismissals (as proxies for employment equality). The study found no evidence that diversity programs improved the environment for women or minorities (Naff & Kellough, 2003).

Ely and Meyerson (1999) found that organizations begin their diversity efforts with white, Western women, since they were the first to enter the managerial and professional ranks. To be truly successful, these organizations need to consider expanding their agenda to other identity groups such as African American women, Hispanic women, and gay and lesbian employees, since the experiences of these groups are likely to be different.

Some studies suggest that diversity training, rather than being simply ineffective, can be detrimental to minority advancement. One study tracked the effect of diversity training on the workforce composition of federal employees and found negative effects on the number of minority promotions (Krawiec, 2003). Other studies have produced similar results showing that diversity training programs actually activate bias (Kidder, Lankau, Chrobot-Mason, Mollica, & Friedman, 2004; Rynes & Rosen, 1995; Sidanius, Devereux, & Pratto, 2001). A study of 486 retail bank branches assessed whether employees' participation in diversity education influenced attitudes toward race, sex, age, and diversity in the length of tenure on the job. The results suggested a complex relationship among these factors; diversity education had a minimal impact on performance (Ely, 2004).

In conclusion, there are four main reasons why diversity programs often fail. First, they are not sustained efforts, but rather one or a few training sessions that employees are required to attend. It is unrealistic to think that diversity training sessions, frequently less than one day, will have much impact on the attitudes of employees. Some employees may even resent being forced to attend such training sessions. Second, diversity trainers may not be effective at changing people's attitudes that would, in turn, affect organizational change. Third, if they are not accompanied by goals for the number of minorities and women at various levels of the organizational, or followed by serious efforts to monitor organizational demographics, there will be little incentive to change. Fourth, diversity programs are often not comprehensive enough. Many diversity professionals emphasize that corporations need to think about diversity broadly. Firms need to welcome not only racial and gender diversity, but diversity of experiences, diversity in the age of its employees, and diverse ways of thinking. Moreover, without other interventions such as mentoring, taskforces, and serious efforts to recruit minorities and women into management positions, these programs will be less effective.

## Affirmative Action Programs

In addition to diversity programs, some organizations, especially in the US and Canada, have affirmative action programs that attempt to redress the imbalance of whites to non-whites in employment – particularly in the hiring process. The goal of affirmative action is to improve the number of women and minorities in job classes where they are underrepresented. These programs are sometimes resisted by non-minority employees, who see affirmative action candidates as somehow ill-equipped to handle the positions for which they have applied. For example, there is evidence that affirmative action programs are misunderstood by college students. In a study of 133 Canadian university students, 91% believed that employment equity produced reverse discrimination of white males (Leck, 2002). In the United States, a similar study showed that affirmative action was viewed negatively by university students (Kravitz & Platania, 1993). Although affirmative action programs are designed to provide opportunities for women and minorities, students in these studies equated them with quotas for minorities. Because of the potential negative attitudes of employees, it is important for senior business leaders to explain the benefits of diversity so as to prevent pitting white males against women and minorities. White males may perceive that these groups are given an unfair advantage. Bringing white men into the dialogue about why it is important to treat women and minorities fairly is an important part of both the affirmative action and diversity training approaches. Organizational leaders should stress that these programs are designed to attract high-quality candidates, not candidates who are unqualified for positions.

## General Skills Training for Advancement

In addition to considering the effect of diversity training and affirmative action on organizational demographics, we can consider whether training lower-level, low-paid workers results in their advancement. One study in the UK set about finding out the degree to which the government's emphasis on education and training might lift women out of low-paid work (Rainbird, 2007). Interviews with over 100 individuals from one local authority (local government) indicated that self-improvement through training underestimates the structural problems, such as lack of resources and entitlements to learning, facing low-paid workers. Even after lower-level employees are trained for more responsibility or higher-level jobs, there may be bias that prevents them from moving up or the lack of a clear career path for them to follow. Training by itself surely won't advance equality in organizations. Moreover, providing training for lower-level employees without a clear structure for fair advancement will only frustrate those who make the effort to better themselves. Instead of simply providing training, organizations need to combine training with fair, transparent systems of promotion and advancement. This will require work on changing organizational cultures to foster real equality of opportunity.

## Flexible Work Arrangements

Like diversity training and affirmative action programs, flexible work arrangements in and of themselves will not move the organization very far. Flexible work hours are laudable, but they cannot solve the problems of work–life balance for a number of reasons. First, work–life balance programs are often set up so that the manager approves the working schedule; if the manager does not want his or her employee to use flex-time, it is often impossible for the employee to do so. A manager may be reluctant to offer flexible work arrangements if all staff are needed to be present in meetings. Accommodating a part-time person or someone who works irregular hours may present a layer of complexity or complication that the manager does not want to take on. Most flex-time work arrangements are used by women who want to balance their childcare responsibilities with work. Men may find it difficult to convince their managers that flex-time is necessary to deal with a new-born or with a wife during a difficult pregnancy, and they may be stigmatized for using flex-time, when there is a perception that they do not need it. Until these arrangements are used by men as often as women, and in the same numbers, people in the organization will associate them with women and for women.

Second, flexible work arrangements are not as common with higher-level employees as with lower-level employees. How many senior-level managers work flexible hours as a matter of course?

Third, though offered by organizations, flexible work arrangements are not part of a routine, universal practice in the way that providing healthcare or retirement benefits to employees are. These arrangements are handled on a case-by-case basis and do not constitute an organizational practice or policy. Often there is nothing systematic in the way they are reinforced or implemented organization-wide, and as such they rarely have much impact on work–life balance across the organization.

Until both men and women begin to avail themselves of work–life balance programs in equal numbers, many believe that using them amounts to career suicide. As explained in Chapter 9, there are unspoken costs associated with work–life balance programs and a financial penalty for taking time off. Women who use work–life balance programs may suffer from the perception that they are not committed to their work. Typically women, rather than men, use company-sponsored childcare centers, which further stigmatizes them as being family-centered, rather than career-oriented (Connelly, Degraff, & Willis, 2002).

### Women-Only Leadership Courses

Many business organizations promote the advancement of women by establishing leadership training programs for women or by sending "high potential" women to leadership training programs geared exclusively to them and conducted by third-party providers. While admirable in theory, in practice these programs may not be very effective without a concerted effort to change the culture within the organization. What happens after the women return to their workplaces after a week away? Has anything changed? Will anyone follow up with them to find out how what they learned could be beneficial to their organizations? If mismanaged, these programs may even give the impression that women are deficient in their knowledge and skills compared to males, and therefore require a special program to correct their deficiencies. On the other hand, if these programs are well-managed and organizations communicate that they value the contributions of women and are investing in them, employees will be more apt to see the value of these programs. Most importantly, after these leadership courses women should have the opportunity to use the new skills they have learned.

In summary, many of the practices designed to improve the work lives of women and minorities do not succeed because they are half-heartedly embraced by the organization. In order for these practices to work, employees need to adopt a philosophy of fairness, and the most importantly senior managers in the organization have to want to change the existing order. Sustaining practices and programs that promote workplace equity often requires a change in the organizational culture and a change in employees' attitudes and behavior. At a minimum, organizations need to have clear, measurable goals for the programs they establish, communicate those goals to all employees, monitor progress toward them, and involve senior leaders in making employees accountable for achieving goals.

## Approaches That Do Work

### Changing the Culture

Organizational culture can be defined as shared symbols, meanings, practices, and the deeply embedded beliefs that guide behavior (Newman, 1995). Culture change does not happen overnight. It takes a concerted effort from senior leaders, human resource professionals, and managers to communicate with employees, to make their expectations clear, and to "walk the talk" by setting a good example of the behavior they desire in others. A starting point for organizational change is an honest appraisal of where an organization is in terms of its culture, followed by a dialogue about where it wants to go.

Terrance Larsen, CEO of CoreStates Financial Corporation, illustrates how important honest conversations are to bringing about a change in culture. As part of CoreStates' efforts to positively change the demographics of managers in the organization to include more women and minorities, he undertook a series of initiatives to open dialogue about the problem (Diversity Factor, 1998). First, he conducted a survey to help define the roadblocks for women and minorities. Then he shared the information from the survey with all of his employees, who then engaged in conversation about the data. Larsen credits his organization's work on diversity and values with the company's success in both improving the organization's finances and in retaining women at senior levels.

Meyerson and Martin (2001) caution against widespread cultural change programs that are focused on one set of values, however. They recognize three different types of culture change: the first is leader-led and shapes the culture according to the values of the leader. It is unambiguous – everyone knows what is expected. The second recognizes multiple sources of culture and is not leader-led. Rather, it is a combination of cultures, and is somewhat ambiguous and certainly not as clear-cut as the leader-led version. The values held by employees evolve more naturally. A third type is ambiguous, and disorganized – causing confusion among employees. A diverse workforce is apt to function best in the second version, where employees are allowed to express their own identities. Leader-led culture changes may alienate those who do not share the leaders' values and may produce calculated compliance, rather than a sincere following. The third version is simply too disorganized to be effective.

### Recognizing Different Approaches to Work

Managers should address gender and diversity in broad and all-encompassing terms by valuing all types of individuals, different approaches to work, and by encouraging constructive debate about workplace conflict. Different approaches to work will mean that managers allow greater diversity in *how* tasks are accomplished, and focus on outcomes. Organizations need to recognize that people of different backgrounds may have different thinking styles, different patterns of speech, and different value systems that affect how they approach work. Only through an open debate about issues will employees come to recognize the dynamics of power and privilege in organizations. Too often a politically correct atmosphere, in which companies focus on rules for dealing with people of different backgrounds, fails to change behavior. Instead, companies should focus on equipping employees with skills for building relationships and connecting with others (Ely, Meyerson, & Davidson, 2006). Organizations can provide opportunities for individuals of different backgrounds (gender, race, age, etc.) to work together on taskforces or committees. In this way, employees may begin to appreciate the different perspectives and skills that others bring to the table.

## Accountability of Senior Management

Appointing a specialist with accountability and authority to oversee the organization's diversity and work–life balance initiatives, and to monitor the organization's progress, is critical if such programs are to be successful. The individual or individuals with accountability must be senior enough to have influence in the organization; ideally, a senior-level manager reporting directly to the CEO would be chosen, or a senior committee with a reporting line to the CEO. Senior managers of an organization must have a sustained, coordinated commitment to diversity at the top of their organizations in order for women to succeed at those levels (Mattis, 2001). CEOs who are committed to diversity often articulate how diversity will help their companies succeed and will better reflect demographic changes in both the workplace and in their customer base (Giscombe & Matthis, 2002). One CEO even reflected upon how the diversity effort in his own organization opened his eyes to the invisible nature of white, male privilege:

> I didn't understand, when we started all of this [the diversity effort], that the rules around business are typically made by a bunch of guys who are kind of like me – and they fit guys like me. I don't think the rules were exactly created to fit us, but they do and they give us an advantage. I used to believe that all people had to do to succeed was to do what I did – conform to the rules. But over time I've been able to see how much easier it is for me to do that – and how the rules actually set up barriers to many other people.
>
> (Terrence Larsen, CEO of CoreStates Financial, as quoted in *Diversity Factor*, 1998, pp. 47–48)

As is illustrated in the above example, it is important for the dominant group to recognize that their own experience rising through the ranks of the organization may have been radically different from the experiences of other groups who have not been in positions of power and privilege.

Moreover, CEOs need to recognize that cohesive cultures do not necessarily mean homogeneous ways of working. People with different behavioral styles can be equally committed to the vision and purpose of the organization (Shelton, McKenna, & Darling, 2002). About three-quarters of companies studied by Giscombe and Mattis (2002) reported that they tie management bonuses and incentives, either formally or informally, to diversity efforts.

### Promoting Fairness in Interactions with Clients

Many professional service firms provide other businesses with expertise including consulting, investment banking, legal, and accounting services. In these firms and industries, women and men are sometimes excluded from assignments that should be gender-blind. For example, consider a managing partner in a law firm who goes along with a client's wish not to assign a woman or minority for the client's legal work. Or imagine the consulting firm that makes assumptions about the inappropriateness of a woman working on a client assignment in a male-dominated manufacturing company. Preventing women from taking client assignments based on their gender may severely affect their career progression. If women are pigeon-holed into certain assignments and not others, they will not develop the breadth of experience to be successful. To his credit, the former legal counsel of Oracle Software recognized this as a potential problem in his organization and established a policy for dealing with such discrimination. It is company policy for Oracle to clarify its stand on discrimination by the following statement, given to law firms that would supply attorneys to work for Oracle:

> We understand that your firm is and will continue to be an equal opportunity employer and that your firm will continue to actively recruit and promote women and minorities. We ask that the first person you consider for assignment to the case be a woman or a minority employee of your firm with appropriate experience. We also ask that you report to us annually the number and percentage of women and minority partners in the firm.
>
> (Ocampo, 1994)

### Successful Work–Life Balance Initiatives

Organizations need to understand the benefit of work–life balance, not only to individuals, but also to the bottom line. Employees who are able to better manage their domestic responsibilities will be more productive at work. A study by the London School of Economics found that the largest, most global, and best-managed companies offer their employees flexible hours, job-sharing, time banking, and working from home (Foroohar, 2006). British Telecom, a UK company, reports that 70,000 of its workers participating in flex-time are 25% more productive than its office workers. British Telecom's policy has saved the company £10 million in fuel costs and has been one of the driving reasons for new mothers to return to work (Foroohar, 2006). Allowing employees to work from home saves companies money that they would otherwise spend on office space, heat, and electricity. In order for these types of flexible policies to attract managers, workers at the highest levels have to use them. If the policies are perceived to be used by only lower-level employees, then middle- and upper-level managers will shun them. Importantly, it should be obvious to employees at all levels that these policies do not hinder career development. The company's newsletter or website can be a vehicle for highlighting employees who have successfully managed to work from home or successfully worked an atypical schedule. These examples will encourage others to follow suit, if they wish.

Redesigning jobs and work cultures is necessary to give women more equality. By taking into account individuals' personal lives when designing jobs, corporations are likely to improve worker productivity by making it easier for workers to focus on their work, while still meeting their obligations outside of work. Unfortunately family and personal needs are rarely addressed in job design – if treated at all, they are treated as an afterthought. It is necessary for corporations to rethink many of the policies and practices that they have taken-for-granted as immutable. What would happen if corporations focused equally on employee well-being and efficiency as Bailyn and Harrington (2004) suggest? Are corporations still concerned with "face time" – the time an individual is seen at the office – versus outcomes? Can employees do their jobs and also give back to the community? Is it acceptable to conduct volunteer activities during "work time?" Are flexible work hours perceived as deviations from the norm, and do they, therefore, demonstrate less commitment than full-time employment or employment during regular hours? These are questions that senior-level managers or human resource professionals need to ask.

Western culture (especially American culture) is preoccupied with the idea that the only productive time is structured work time in an office setting. Our assumptions about productivity are embedded in the notion of separate spheres of work and non-work time, neither of which is compatible with the other (Bailyn & Fletcher, 2003). Many organizations function according to old models of work in which the ideal employee is totally committed to work at all costs, and career development and reward systems are predicated on killer hours and unrealistic work schedules. This model increasingly does not serve men or women well. It can reduce efficiency, actual productive work time, and increase employee burn-out. As Bailyn explains, "Work designed around a less rigid, more encompassing sense of time follows a performance logic rather than one of control. Employees' lives are easier, and at the same time, work is more effective. Both time and energy expand" (2004, p. 1512).

Careers need to mesh better with individuals' personal lives, which may be very different during their early career years versus the years around their retirement (Moen, 2003). The life of a consultant can be grueling because, typically, the consultant must travel away from home Monday through Friday to be on the client site. Accenture Ltd has recognized that not all of its consultants want to be away from home and family on a constant basis. Under Accenture's flexible work arrangements, employees may work nine consecutive days on the client site followed by five days at home or work an eight-week period at the client site (with weekends off) followed by a full week at home (www.careers3.accenture.com).

Examples of successful programs and policies that organizations have implemented to promote cultural change, work–life balance, and equity for women and minorities are provided are in the following section.

## Successful Initiatives

### *Culture Change at Sandia National Laboratories*

Sandia, a multi-disciplinary engineering and science laboratory operated by Lockheed Martin Corporation for the US government, began a five-year cultural change program to address the perception of a hostile work environment toward women and minorities. In 1991, a US Department of Labor audit had revealed that more needed to be done at Sandia to address issues of diversity and inclusion, and the climate for women and minorities. In 1995, the exempt workforce (those in higher-level positions such as professional and managerial staff – salaried, not hourly employees) was composed almost entirely of men – 80% were men and 20% were women. Many of Sandia's organizational traits and its history worked against changing this gender imbalance. The organizational behavior was based on control, position power,[1] and the convergence of military, industrial, production-oriented, and research-based cultures that for years had been inhabited exclusively by men (Learson, 1998). Previous attempts to change this culture had centered on modest diversity training, while the new initiative would be a five-year plan aimed at "creating substantive and sustained change in the ways people interacted" (Learson, 1998, p. 34).

There were four phases to the new project: assessment, advocacy, planning, and implementation (which included both institutionalizing and operationalizing). The first step involved the Department of Labor audit and a consultant's assessment of organizational practices and the general climate. The second step, advocacy, involved identifying "diversity champions," people who would enthusiastically embrace diversity principles and actively influence others to do so. The top 100 executives at Sandia participated in a two-day conference about diversity. Before the conference, each executive was paired with a diversity champion, who discussed with the individual what diversity meant to them personally and what they might expect from the conference. The third step, planning, involved identifying diversity issues, especially barriers to success for women and minorities, in all of Sandia's divisions. Implementing, the last step, was intended to shift the ownership of diversity efforts away from the human resources department to individual managers. Vice Presidents reported out to their own work groups what they needed to change. Each Vice President wrote an action plan with the division's issues, plans, and commitments, with timelines for completion.

To ensure the diversity efforts had resources and enough power, the Vice Presidents each had an appointed diversity council with a budget. Each council made efforts to embed diversity into the ways the division operated, such as how it selected and promoted employees. In addition to the divisional diversity councils, a Corporate Diversity Team was given oversight for company-wide diversity efforts, such as establishing metrics to measure the organization's progress and planning educational programs across all of Sandia's divisions.

Sandia's efforts led to several improvements. Executives became more sensitive to including all employees in their communication and decision-making. For instance, at one point, Sandia needed to downsize its organization. The process, as reported by Learson (1998), was handled in a humane way, with sensitivity to people as one of its primary concerns. For the first time, Sandia included a "people objective" as one of its eight strategic objectives, which had implications for staffing, compensation, retention of staff, and promotion. Managing diversity became part of a manager's performance evaluation as a new management competency. Moreover, Sandia began implementing compressed work-week schedules, childcare referral services, elder-care programs, and networking groups for women, gays, lesbians, and bisexuals. Sandia now has two childcare centers for employees. In recognition of the importance of further education for career advancement, Sandia provides a tuition-reimbursement plan for advanced degrees for its employees. The lab credits the success of its diversity initiatives to strong support from both senior management and the diversity advocacy councils, management accountability, and its long-term, educational focus.

### Heller Ehrman – The Opt-In Project

Heller Ehrman, a New York law firm with multiple locations, had to address a problem similar to Deloitte's – that of women "opting out" of the workforce. In response to the exodus of women attorneys, Heller Ehrman formed an industry group to share best practices around ideas that will keep professional women in the workforce. The program, launched in 2006, is designed to bring industry leaders together to share concerns, discuss ideas, and find new solutions to keep women in professional service firms, financial service firms, and the high-tech industry in the workplace and in positions of leadership. Heller Erhman has recognized that workers are looking for career paths that can be tailored to their personal circumstances and companies are losing valuable talent by offering only one, straight-line career path for their employees. Areas that have been discussed include: keeping women engaged in their jobs if they choose to move "sideways" rather than up; and keeping employees connected to their firms if they choose to take a break from work.

## Award-Winning Examples

The National Association of Female Executives (NAFE) chooses the top 30 companies for women based on a range of characteristics. The 30 winners must have at least two women on their board of directors. They are also judged on the number of women in senior ranks compared to the number of men, and the programs and policies that support women. Catalyst also highlights leading companies in the area of diversity development in its Catalyst Award. The following organizations are examples of organizations from NAFE's top 30 companies and/or from the Catalyst award. These companies provide examples of the many programs, policies, and initiatives that have focused on promoting women and minorities in the workforce.

## Goldman Sachs

The Senior Women's Initiative at Goldman Sachs is designed to improve the process by which women are selected for senior-level jobs. Every four months, senior executives review the pool of talent for managing director positions. This frequent review of who is in the "pool" and the emphasis on improving the number of women selected for senior-level jobs has helped improve the ratio of women to men in the top jobs. The number of women managing directors and partners, the two highest job grades, doubled between 2001 and 2006. At the managing-director level, women went from 14% in 2001 to 17% in 2006. The number of partners increased during this timeframe from 7% to 14%. In 2006 and 2007, Goldman Sachs started a program called New Directions. It is designed to provide guidance and coaching for women who have left the workforce to help them make a successful transition back into the workforce. New Directions offers education about trends in the industry as well as an opportunity to network with employees who are currently in the workforce.

## PricewaterhouseCoopers

Like many consulting and accounting firms, PWC has few women at senior levels. The Unique People Experience (UPE) is intended to improve the representation of women at partner level. The first step in this initiative engaged PWCs leaders with staff to better understand the needs of individuals, and race and gender issues within the company. Senior leaders were encouraged to get to know individuals and their challenges both inside and outside of work. Results of surveys indicated that women and minorities wanted career flexibility with the ability to step on and off the fast track without penalty, the opportunity to network with a diverse set of individuals, and a dialogue about "bringing their whole selves to work" (Catalyst, 2007c). The second part of the initiative involved redesigning work to make teams of individuals responsible for clients, rather than individuals. These client portfolio teams, as they were called, resulted in a shift from a competitive environment to a cooperative one where teams divided the responsibilities equally and were rewarded as a unit. The formation of these client portfolio teams has been particularly good for women who may have worked excessively long hours. The teams meet monthly to monitor vacation time and personal time to ensure that people's lives are as balanced as they can be.

PWC has made other efforts to help employees balance their work and non-work lives. Like other corporations it offers alternatives to working a standard work schedule at the office by allowing job-sharing, flex-time, working from home or offsite, and a compressed work week. The firm shuts down completely between Christmas Eve and New Year's Day and managers are encouraged to have their employees use their vacation time. Vacation-time use is tracked so that managers whose employees do not use their vacation time will have to answer for this during their annual performance review. To cut down on the workaholic atmosphere at the company, the firm discourages sending e-mails over the weekend.

From 2001 to 2006, women's representation at partner level had increased from 12% to 16%, and turnover of women has decreased from 24% to 16%. Although this is certainly an improvement, the majority of partners and senior managers are still white males.

In a partnership with Duke Corporate Education, PWC instituted a program called Turning Point, the sequel to the Unique People Experience. Senior managers identified employees who were at risk of losing a healthy balance between work and the rest of their lives. Through facilitator-led small discussion groups, these employees began to identify their work–life challenges. "Instead of choosing one priority [work, family, community, etc.] over another, the program teaches the importance of making time for all of it, and provides tips on balancing responsibilities" (Weinstein, 2007, p. 1). In 2006, about 800 employees participated in the program. Along with the small group discussion sessions, larger groups (of about 100 employees) meet to watch skits featuring professional actors who highlight real work challenges. These skits provide a catalyst for discussion of real-life events. In one such skit, a young employee is depicted jet-setting across the globe on client assignments. When asked about relationships, he says he was very happy with his job, but hadn't time for relationships. The scene then moves forward to later in his career when he is satisfied with his career, but unhappy with his personal life (Weinstein, 2007). The combination of coaching in small groups with professional facilitators and the larger group sessions has stimulated dialogue and paid dividends to the firm; fewer employees leave the firm than before the program was instituted.

## Pepsi Co.

Pepsi Co. is not only known for promoting women to the highest levels of the organization, but it also has a reputation for promoting women and minority entrepreneurs. As the first woman CEO at Pepsi, Indra Nooyi assumed leadership in October 2006. Pepsi also has three women presidents running major business units. Several others developed valuable work experience at Pepsi that enabled them to compete for higher-level jobs. In 1982, Pepsi launched a purchasing program for minority and women business owners. The program actively pursues minority and women business owners as suppliers to Pepsi and asks its prime suppliers to provide information on how much they spend with minority and women business owners in their own enterprises. As an example of Pepsi's commitment to this end, Integrated Packing Corporation, a minority-owned firm, recently won a five-year, $75 million contract to supply Pepsi with corrugated boxes.

In addition to the program for minority and women business owners, Pepsi recognized the need to improve the environment for women of color in its own company through its Women of Color–Multinational Alliance. The program aims to create a culture of authenticity and honesty in all relationships and, specifically, further the dialogue about gender and race in the workplace. To generate commitment to the program, Pepsi makes bonuses available for senior managers who become active in the Alliance. Although the Alliance's efforts have been fairly modest to date, there has been some progress: from 2002 to 2006, the number of women of color in management has increased from 4% to 6.8%, and the turnover of women of color participating in the Alliance has been half of that for those not participating.

## Target

Target exceeds national and retail industry averages for employment of women and minorities in senior-level jobs. More than half of Target's attorneys are women.

One of the reasons for this success is its commitment from the top of the organization to employ women and minorities at the highest levels. Management is accountable to Target's board of directors for creating a diverse workforce. Organizations that position their incentives in such a way as to promote women and minorities will create more focus on the issue. Target has also created a pipeline to talented minorities for recruiting purposes, by forming alliances with specific organizations such as the National Black MBA Association, the National Association of Asian American Professionals, and the Hispanic Alliance for Career Development. Visibly supporting such organizations is a way for Target to signal to minorities that they are serious about recruiting them.

## Fannie Mae

Fannie Mae took a comprehensive approach to the promotion of women and minorities in their workplace. Several aspects of its approach are worth noting. First, it employed a Diversity Advisory Counsel to oversee the effort and to enable employees to directly address their concerns to this group. Second, it used a range of methods to educate and support its workforce, including formal and informal mentoring, career-development programs, and diversity training for both its employees and its customers, mortgage lenders. It also encouraged work–life balance by allowing employees 10 hours a month to volunteer to an organization of their choice (with pay), by providing a health-awareness program, and by recognizing the responsibilities that go with dependent care of children or older adults. Fannie Mae understands the importance of accountability and evaluation of these efforts. Monthly workforce profiles track the progress of minorities and women, and scorecards track retention and promotion. Managers are evaluated on their diversity efforts in their annual performance appraisal. Fannie Mae's efforts have worked; approximately 44% of managers and 40% at the officer level are women. Four of the 13 board members (about 32%) are women.

## Marriott Corporation

Marriott instituted its "Women and Minorities: Partners for the Future" program initially with a focus on promoting these groups to senior-level positions. Currently, the program is focused on all levels of management. Its three-pronged approach includes leadership training and opportunities for women, networking and mentoring activities, and an effort toward more flexible and alternative work arrangements with less emphasis on "face time." Biannually, the board of directors tracks the percentage of women executives. Additionally, managers are reviewed on their efforts toward diversity. Part of their annual bonus is dependent on their progress. Women are 35% of general managers of the company's North American Lodging Operations.

## *Bayer Corporation*

Bayer has made an effort to improve the proportion of women to senior-level positions and has promoted work–life balance programs. Recognizing that the path to top positions lies in science and technical training, and in international assignments, the company instituted the Delegate Career Development Program that guarantees women access to international assignments. Such assignments are crucial because they are seen to be essential experience for many top jobs. In addition, women are provided with opportunities for non-traditional assignments. An Alternate Career Path Program exists for women who may not be able to relocate. An Associate Development Program aims to increase the number of women and people of color in the "high potential" pool, who would be looked at for promotion. Bayer is also known for its programs to accommodate a better work–life balance. It has childcare on-site and extended leave for parents; the corporation will keep a job open for up to seven years after the birth of a child for a parent who wants to take an extended leave. Bayer also offers part-time, flex-time, job-sharing, tele-working, and sabbaticals for male and female employees.

## *ING Financial Services Corporation*

ING established a program entitled "Beyond Diversity: Building One ING Culture." Among the program's tenets is the importance of measuring the number of women in management and rewarding individuals' efforts to increase diversity. Metrics of the number of women in management are closely tracked at various levels in the organization so that the organization can clearly see where women are gaining influence and where they are not well-represented. Business units are rewarded for increasing the diversity of their employees: 10% of each business unit's bonus pool is linked to diversity measures. Because of the organization's focus on diversity, the number of women in senior management has increased from 25% to 50% and two executive women manage 80% of ING's US financial services businesses. Both of these individuals have profit and loss responsibility. This kind of experience is essential for moving to the highest level of the organization.

## What Do These Successful Efforts by Companies Have in Common?

In order to learn from these companies' experiences, it is important to identify what their programs and initiatives have in common. First, all of these companies took a hard look in the mirror in an attempt to identify the root causes of their problems. In each organization, there was an honest dialogue between employees and senior leaders. Second, the companies took a more comprehensive approach to a problem than is usually the case. For example, if the problem was retention of women, the organizations collected information on how many women were leaving, at which levels, and why, and then applied several methods to rectify the problem. Because the career trajectory for white women is often different than for women of color, the firms collected statistics on minority women.

Third, these companies' programs were sustained efforts lasting several years and are still in operation today. Fourth, these organizations recognized that advancement and retention of women was not due to women's lack of technical competence or their lack of preparedness for roles, but was more likely due to their desire for work–life balance and the opportunity structure of the organization. All of these companies took the position that the organization needed improving rather than the women.

## Other Organizations – Non-Profits, Research Organizations, and Think-Tanks

There are many organizations devoted to furthering the agenda of women and minorities in the workplace. Some are funded by corporation sponsorship, others are non-profits, and still others are governmental agencies; some provide advice, while others provide financial assistance or generate research and discussion on issues important to women.

### *The Center for Women's Business Research*

The mission of this organization is "to provide data-driven knowledge to advance the economic, social and political impact of women business owners and their enterprises worldwide." The organization attempts to set the national agenda to create insight on the status and achievements of women business owners. In addition, its purpose is to change the perception about the economic viability of women-owned businesses to raise awareness about their social and economic impact. Its research topics have included investigations of home-based businesses, motivations of women business owners, access to technology and capital, women as consumers, and minority women business owners (www.cfwbr.org).

### *Inforum*

Similar to the practices of the Center for Women's Business Research, Inforum collects data on women in the business arena, although it is focused at the state, rather than national, level. Inforum, a Michigan-based non-profit organization, highlights the progress of women in executive positions and on boards of Michigan's 100 largest public corporations. The organization publishes "Michigan's Leadership Index," a tool that compares Michigan companies and highlights those that are making the most progress in placing and retaining women at the highest levels. It also calculates salary levels of male versus female executives and tracks the progress of women of color. The index is published biannually, advertising the best and worst companies and industries for women, and creating a benchmark for companies in their executive-hiring practices. Although national data are useful, state-level data will raise the awareness of employers, potential women in the job market, and state governments about the practices of individual companies in their own backyard. Other states should follow Michigan's example.

### *The Hidden Brain Drain Task Force*

The Hidden Brain Drain Task Force has the mission is to create conditions that allow employers to retain and fully tap the productive energies of women and persons of color. Part of the Center for Work–Life Policy, the initiative was undertaken by leaders from both academe and the private sector. Of particular concern to this group is analyzing why women have not made more progress at the upper echelons of the labor market and to provide what they call "second-generation" solutions to the advancement of women and minorities. These second-generation solutions focus on educational opportunity, discrimination, and cronyism, and workplace policies that will help alleviate constraints that stem from family and community responsibilities. Among its activities, the Hidden Brain Drain Task Force has partnered with the *Harvard Business Review* to publish articles about issues related to women and minorities at work, such as re-employment in mid-life, talent development, and off-ramps and on-ramps (the phenomenon of women leaving and being able to re-enter the workforce in ways that don't disadvantage them). The general idea behind the articles is to garner widespread attention in both North America and Europe about these issues and to create a dialogue. In addition, US and European companies can benefit from learning about one another's policies; for example, family support policies tend to be stronger in Europe than the US, and EU governments are more heavily involved in providing incentives for work–life policies (Center for Work–Life Policy, 2006).

### The National Association of Women Business Owners (NAWBO)

This US organization fosters research and networking opportunities, and shapes economic and public policy to benefit women business owners. Both corporate and individual members may attend annual conferences and regional events to learn more about business issues of relevance to women. The Center for Business Research, the research arm of NAWBO, provides up-to-date data and research about women entrepreneurs.

### Catalyst

This organization offers advisory services for companies to create work cultures that attract and retain a diverse set of employees. Its annual Benchmarking Survey provides valuable data for member companies on the diversity profile of American executives and employees in the "executive pipeline." Catalyst Spectrum is a web-based service that equips companies with tools to implement effective diversity strategies. It gives members access to experts and to each other, offering practical examples. Catalyst Board Services offers services to senior women in organizations to prepare them as potential board members. Catalyst has published a wide range of research about women that is available to the general public via their website (www.catalyst.org).

### Wellesley Center for Women

The mission of this organization is to promote positive change for women and girls. It provides interdisciplinary research studies on gender equity, sexual harassment, childcare, adolescent development, and adult roles in both the home and at work. The organization has published some 50 research studies that provide information for the general public and for policy-makers. Information from this group can be accessed at their website (www.wcwonline.org).

### National Association of Female Executives (NAFE)

Owned by Working Mother Media, NAFE's stated mission is to empower women to achieve career success and financial security through education, networking, and public advocacy. NAFE offers workshops, brings in national speakers, and provides resources.

## International Efforts to Promote Equity at Work

It is important for students to understand how companies interact with non-profits and government. Because of globalization of production and labor, more and more governments and non-profit organizations (NGOs) are apt to seek universal standards of employment practices to ensure the health and well-being of their citizens. The best companies will support government and non-profit initiatives that seek fair employment standards. Support of these initiatives by corporations is not only morally responsible, but it also makes good business sense since this public support enhances the reputation of firms.

Most efforts by NGOs and governments are not legally binding, but rather are expressions of a commitment to improve the lives of women and minorities worldwide. For example, the Millennium Development Goals are statements by 189 UN nations to achieve broad equity goals by 2015. Two of these goals concern gender: the first is to promote gender equality and to empower women; and the second is to eliminate gender disparity in primary and secondary education by 2005 and at all levels of education by 2015. CEDAW (The Convention on the Elimination of all Forms of Discrimination Against Women) is part of the United Nations Human Rights Commission. Under CEDAW, 185 states have undertaken legal protections for women and established tribunals or courts. Although the United Nations has no formal authority over a nation's actions, the nations that have signed on to CEDAW submit reports every four years explaining the progress they have made toward goals.

The International Labor Organization (ILO), a UN agency, brings together employers, workers such as trade union representatives, and governments to agree on minimum standards of labor practices. Composed of 182 member states, worker representatives, and employers, the ILO promotes its Declaration of Fundamental Principles and Rights at Work, which include the following four tenets: the freedom for employees to engage in collective bargaining (joining a union), the elimination of forced or compulsory labor, the abolition of child labor, and the elimination of employment discrimination. Like many of the other international efforts, the ILO has no authority to punish or police its members, yet there are reporting mechanisms on the progress of countries and on abuses of the standards, the sharing of best practices, and peer pressure on member states, that encourage compliance with these minimum standards.

The United Nations Global Compact is an international framework for corporate social responsibility, based on internationally accepted principles. The Global Compact was born out of an address by Kofi Annan, the UN Secretary General, at the World Economic Forum where he challenged business leaders to join UN agencies and civil-society organizations (NGOs) to support a set of 10 universal principles – some of which apply to work and the employment relationship, and others that concern the environment. The Global Compact includes the four principles of the ILO and has added another work-related principle: to ensure that corporations are not *complicit* in human rights abuses. This principle is designed to highlight the importance of corporations managing their supply chains; for example, in cases where they do not own the factories where their products are made. Corporations willing to support the Global Compact are asked to write a letter to the UN Secretary General pledging their support and are requested to annually communicate their progress.

The Organization for Economic Co-Operation and Development (OECD) is an intergovernmental organization that fosters social and economic justice. Its 30 member countries are democracies and have market economies. The OECD countries make recommendations to businesses on a range of activities, some of which are related to fair work practices. For example, multinational companies are to provide notice to workers when any change might affect their livelihood. They are also to allow collect-ive bargaining, and companies that are doing business in foreign countries are expected to hire locals and provide training to employees to improve their skills. Although the OECD does not specifically address eradicating gender discrimination, its policies promote fair employment, particularly in situations where a developed country is con-ducting business in a developing country.

Although governmental organizations rarely have legal authority to punish non-compliance, they do serve a purpose in that they heighten awareness of the principles that businesses should follow and, in the court of public opinion, can make either a positive example out of an organization (or country) or a negative one. Consider the impact that the ILO had on Nike's sweatshop operations when they publicized the abuses in Nike's sub-contracted factories. Although Nike initially denied any respons-ibility for its sub-contracted facilities, the company was eventually forced to improve working conditions in these factories.

## Policy Issues – A Four-Pronged Approach

If equality between men and women is to be achieved in organizations, it must be pro-moted in the greater society. The most effective way of achieving equality between the genders is to engage four elements as part of a solution: the public sector (govern-ment), the private sector (corporations), the non-profit sector, and the individual citizen. In the United States, raising, educating, and caring for children is considered a private rather than public obligation for which parents bear the full responsibility. During the course of a person's early life, his or her parents pay for childcare, tutoring, books, counseling, extra-curricular activities, and college education. After children are nurtured, cared for, and educated, they emerge as responsible, adult citizens who con-tribute to the economy in several ways – as productive workers, as educators of the next generation, and as contributors to the economy as consumers and tax-payers. Although the state benefits in many ways, it places the burden of caring for children on the private sector and on parents. In many European countries, governments have instituted practices and policies that support parents as they raise their children. In the US, providing tax credits for childcare and providing more pre-school education in the public school system would help ease the burden on parents. Glass (2000) suggests that the legislative process require a family impact statement whereby state and federal legislation would spell out the consequences of proposed legislation on children and families. This notion is similar to procedures the EPA (Environmental Protection Agency) has put in place for issuing environmental impact statements and that federal agencies like the FDA (Food and Drug Administration) employ that protect consumers.

Corporations may resist more involvement in sharing the responsibilities of parent-hood. The most convincing argument for corporations to increase their involvement is that it will garner employee loyalty and higher productivity. Workers who can balance their work lives with their personal lives will not be distracted by domestic issues at work and will be happier, more engaged workers. Corporations that have begun to support their workers with more balanced hours, working from home, childcare centers, and the like must take an active role in educating other corporations that these practices are more than worth the money and effort. Conferences and websites, where corporations can share best practice, will help spread the word that initiatives to ease the burden on parents are, in the long run, cost-effective and not impossible to implement.

Corporations can also make sure that their culture is inviting to women and minorities. Having more women and minorities in influential positions sends a signal to other women and minorities that the organization takes their career development seriously. Managers should discuss their employees' personal goals as a regular part of the performance-appraisal discussion. The organization should recognize that different leadership styles are possible to reach a desired outcome; in this way, women should be able to achieve career success without mimicking a male leadership style. As different leadership styles emerge from both men and women, people in the organization will begin to understand that a variety of approaches and work styles can be effective.

Individuals are a third component of the solution. Women need to aggressively promote change and push to become influential members of senior management in organizations. Once there, they can influence decisions about job design, childcare, career breaks, selection and promotion of employees, and generally how businesses are run.

Non-profit groups are a fourth part of the solution. These groups can help educate corporations and citizens about the problems that working parents face and the potential solutions for providing more balance without compromising worker productivity. Like governments, they can put pressure on organizations to change their practices toward a more equitable workplace and toward more policies that offer workplace balance.

## Further Reading

Ely, R. & Meyerson, D. (1999). Moving from gender to diversity in organizational diagnosis and intervention. *Diversity Factor*, 7(3), 28–33.

Ely, R., Meyerson, D., & Davidson, M. (2006). Rethinking political correctness. *Harvard Business Review*, 84(8), 78–90.

Kalev, A., Kelly, E., & Dobbin, F. (2006). Best practices or best guesses? Assessing the efficacy of corporate affirmative action and diversity policies. *American Sociological Review*, 71, 589–617.

Meyerson, D. & Martin, J. (2001). Cultural change: An integration of three different views. *Journal of Management Studies*, 24(6), 623–647.

# CASE STUDIES

---

### Case Study 1: Promoting and Retaining Women at Deloitte Consulting

Deloitte, a large professional-services firm, is an organization known for its Initiative for the Retention and Advancement of Women (commonly known as the Women's Initiative, or WIN). Launched in 1993, since its inception WIN has been positioned as a business response to a business issue. Its mission is to "drive marketplace growth and create a culture where the best women choose to be." The issue, then, was that, while women were entering the firm at roughly the same rate as men, they were leaving the firm at much higher rates. The firm referred to this as "the gender gap in attrition." Moreover, Deloitte discovered women were not just leaving because of family obligations. In 1991, only four out of 50 candidates for partner were women in spite of the fact that half of its recruits were women (McCracken, 2000). The position of partner is the most prestigious in the organization and the most financially lucrative; partners are owners of the business and have an equity share in its profits. They are involved in all significant decisions that the firm might take.

The exit of female talent was affecting Deloitte's business in several ways: it was expensive (reducing the gender gap in turnover saved the firm $250 million over a five-year period); it was diluting the pool of partner candidates and therefore the quality of the partnership in the long run; and it was interfering with the firm's plans for growth. Since the inception of WIN, Deloitte has succeeded in not only eliminating the gender gap in attrition but also leveraging WIN as a platform for innovative talent strategies that benefit everyone.

Several elements distinguished Deloitte's initiatives. First, the very top of the organization championed the effort. The Women's Initiative was not driven only by the human resources department, but rather was seen as a company-wide initiative called for by the most senior people in the organization. This perception was important because employees could not easily ignore the initiative as something driven by one department interested in "people issues." Instead, it was viewed as a strategic imperative to address the lack of women in influential positions and the problem retaining women after they joined the organization. In 1992, the CEO, Mike Cook, had chaired a taskforce of both men and women to address the problem. The taskforce approached the issue very methodically by investigating it and gathering data to make a business case for change. To indicate his commitment to the Women's Initiative, Cook withdrew from the elite, men-only clubs of which he had been a long-standing member. "When Mike ended his long-standing memberships in these clubs, we knew he was serious," said Annette Tirabasso, a consulting partner. The current CEO, Barry Salzberg, is the WIN champion and attends all major WIN meetings.

Second, WIN is fact-based and continually does research, both internally and externally, to keep current on business trends and issues related to women. In 1992, the taskforce gathered data to understand the gender gap in attrition and learned that most women were not leaving to raise families, but rather to pursue other professional opportunities because they did not feel they could succeed in Deloitte's male-dominated culture. As a result, a series of two-day workshops, entitled "Men and Women as Colleagues," were held for all managers to help uncover gender-based assumptions that might have affected women. Tirabasso recalls some of the gender assumptions that were made during these workshops:

> Some of the men assumed that we [women] would be uncomfortable taking male clients to dinner or calling them for a working lunch or that we wouldn't want to travel if we were pregnant. Of course, we didn't have any problem calling up our clients and many of us didn't mind the travel. There were other assumptions about risk taking and

our potential. Men were assumed to have potential and women were assumed less able to take risks. The workshop helped to dispel a lot of myths.

(Interview, Annette Tirabasso)

Third, measuring the effects of the initiative and accountability were embedded in WIN from the beginning. Because Deloitte is a very data-driven firm, all of the firm's offices were instructed to monitor the progress of women in their offices. Local offices were asked to keep track of whether or not the top-rated women were receiving their proportionate share of the best assignments. Women tended to receive assignments without much global reach – projects in healthcare, non-profit management, and retail – while men received assignments in manufacturing, financial services, and mergers and acquisitions. Each Deloitte office was also required to complete an annual plan which would include its status in relation to a set of benchmarks such as the number of women, the gender gap, female promotions, female partner promotions, and flexible work arrangements. Each office was asked to describe the actions it planned to take to achieve its goals and these actions were made public for the rest of the organization to see (Rosener, 1999).

With office managers under the watchful eye of the CEO and the WIN taskforce, things began to change. Women started receiving more of the best client assignments and more informal mentoring took place.

The fourth element that has made Deloitte's effort unique and successful has been its transparency. From the beginning the company made public its findings. It held a press conference to launch the Women's Initiative and named an external advisory council to consult with WIN. Making its efforts public put the pressure on Deloitte to change, but also has given the firm tremendous visibility and eminence as a leader in women's retention and advancement in professional-services firms. Recognizing that technology is how people communicate, WIN launched a blog in 2005, which became available to anyone over the Internet and can be accessed through Deloitte's website.

Where is Deloitte's Women's Initiative Today? After over 17 years, Deloitte's initiatives for women are still in progress, but the firm has adapted as workplace issues for both men and women have changed. As discussions about work–life balance emerged, the senior managers at Deloitte recognized that many young men and women would sacrifice income for more flexibility and time to pursue non-work-related interests. By 1999, 800 people were on flexible schedules, and 30 people on flexible schedules had made partner.

The consulting life is difficult for anyone, and it is particularly tough on women with families since frequent travel is required. Often, consultants are away from their families for the entire week, arriving at home for the weekend and leaving again on Sunday evening. To address this suitcase lifestyle, Deloitte adopted a 3-4-5 schedule. Consultants working away from their home base would be away three nights a week, at the client site four days a week, and in their local office on Friday. Women with young children or women who are pregnant often request a local assignment for a period of time to avoid travel altogether.

Deloitte has regular programs for women in which speakers talk on a variety of topics. Recently, these programs have welcomed men as the topics are usually of interest to everyone. In 2005, 235 professional development events for women were held. And, in 2007, over 500 professional development and networking events were held, many of which were attended by men as well as women. Recognizing that technology is how people at work often communicate, Deloitte has launched the WIN online collaborative network, the purpose of which is for women to share best practices.

Deloitte's emphasis on the marketplace is also the result of the changing nature of the firm's clients, more and more of whom are women. Thus the composition of its management ranks has had to reflect these demographic changes. Facts supporting these demographic changes include the following: women influence 85% of automobile-buying decisions and purchase 65% of new cars (Wilbert, 2007). Women make 75% of all health-care decisions for themselves or their families, and women spend significantly more time online than men researching healthcare products such as pharmaceuticals, insurance plans, nutritional supplements, and vitamins (Fallows, 2005). Because WIN recognized the force of women in the economy, Deloitte sponsored a workshop called "Women as Buyers," designed primarily for male partners of the firm.

Perhaps the most innovative advancement in Deloitte's thinking about work–life balance is characterized by its Mass Customization Tool (MCC). Employees are encouraged to view their careers holistically by evaluating what they want over time in three major categories: their role, their desired location, and their preferred schedule and workload. One's role could vary from senior leader to individual contributor without management responsibilities; workload could be full or at some reduced level; location could be restricted to where one lives or completely unrestricted, meaning that a heavy travel schedule would be the norm. Restrictions to location could take the form of working remotely using technology or working a compressed work week. These dimensions of work life are intricately connected; for example, working three days a week would impact location and workload and the pace at which an individual could finish a project.

The organization realizes that at different times during their careers, employees will want to "dial down" (that is, reduce) or accelerate their work commitment. Individuals may wish to do so for a number of reasons – accelerating effort may be desirable when one has few other commitments and wants to concentrate on one's career to the exclusion of other pursuits. Dialing down may be useful if a family member becomes ill, if one wants to spend more time with children or a partner, if one wants to pursue a life dream (of competing in a triathlon, for instance), or if one simply needs a break from a more rigorous schedule. In an organization as large as Deloitte, it is not difficult to fill the holes that dialing down might create. If an individual chooses temporarily to work fewer hours or in a non-management role, it creates opportunities for all individuals who want to accelerate their commitment. The goal of MCC is to correlate an employee's talents, career aspirations, and evolving personal circumstances with the enterprise's shifting marketplace strategies and its resulting need for talent.

Deloitte's family-friendly policies appear to have had an impact; 77.5% of women return to work after a maternity leave. While an individual is on a parental leave, the firm tries to stay in touch by assigning a contact person to make sure that she or he is advised of work and social events. By 2007, in the US, women were securing 21% of partners, principals and directors at Deloitte. And the pipeline was robust: women were 38% of senior managers, 44% of managers, and 48% of senior consultants. In 2006, 134 women were selected as partners, principals and directors, a big improvement over the three women promoted in 1992. In 2009, Deloitte exceeded 1,000 women partners, principals, and directors in the US. Deloitte now has the highest percentage of female partners of the Big Four accounting/consulting firms.

### Discussion Questions

1. In your own experience, can you provide examples of when diversity improved the quality of thinking? The quality of a project?
2. Think about your future. How do you think you will approach work–life balance? Will you take time off work to care for children? How much time and energy will you invest in your career?
3. In your view, how should corporations deal with work–life balance issues? Consider the following: should men and women be treated the same? How should organizations balance the need for productivity with the needs of employees? What else do you feel is important for organizations to consider?

## Case Study 2: Best Buy's ROWE Program

Best Buy understands job and corporate culture redesign. It has initiated ROWE, Results Only Work Environment, that "seeks to demolish decades old business dogma that equates physical presence with productivity" (Conlin, 2006, p. 60). The goal of Best Buy is to rethink how employees are judged and to put the emphasis on outcomes rather than hours worked. At Best Buy headquarters in Minneapolis, there are no fixed schedules, no mandatory meetings, and people can fit in their work whenever and wherever it pleases them – as long as the job gets done. (The program is for exempt employees, rather than those on an hourly wage. Employees in the retail stores are not eligible for it.)

In practice, this means that many head office employees can come and go as they please; they will be assessed on their achievements, not how often, where, or when they work. For example, employees may start their work day from home and work into the wee hours of the morning should they choose to, or decide they prefer to work from a coffee shop rather than the office. If employees want to catch a movie during the day, go jogging, or go to the beach, they are free to do so – no one will monitor their activities. The "no meeting" rule means that employees are allowed to challenge whether or not a meeting is necessary to get the work done. Although critical meetings still take place, attendance is not required at unnecessary or unimportant meetings.

ROWE was the brainchild of two human resource employees at Best Buy, Jody Thompson and Cali Ressler. It started off as an experiment with flex-time, in which employees could pick one of four flex-time schedules without the approval of their manager. These two HR professionals kept track of employee productivity during the flex-time program. They found that the more control that they gave employees, the higher the productivity and the more likely employees were to stay with the organization. The ROWE program naturally grew out of this flex-time approach.

Even during the recent recession, Best Buy has made a commitment to keep ROWE going because it believes that a results-only culture is the best way to move forward.

Best Buy has had to ask for voluntary lay-offs, but it remains committed to ROWE because it knows that employees struggle during a recession and need to feel that they control aspects of their work lives.

### *Results of ROWE*

Two researchers at the University of Minnesota studied Best Buy's ROWE approach by analyzing the attitudes of teams at Best Buy who have adopted ROWE and those that have not (Moen & Kelly, 2007). A total of 658 employees responded to a survey asking questions about their work habits, productivity, and general health. The results of the study are striking. When compared with the non-ROWE employee groups, the ROWE employees report the following:

- greater control over when and where they do work.
- less work and family conflict.
- an increase in job security and lower expectations to leave the organization.
- lower likelihood of coming to work sick.
- more sleep than non-ROWE employees (more than seven hours a night) and more exercise.
- fewer ROWE employees do unnecessary work or low-value work.
- gain in energy for ROWE employees.
- fewer interruptions to their work for ROWE employees.

The report focuses on general health and satisfaction with work more than hard measures of productivity. However, one could assume that satisfied employees, who are in generally good health, are apt to be more productive at work. The approach seems to be working; average voluntary turnover has fallen and productivity is up 35% in some departments. For instance, a manager in the audit department stated that her group actually performed more audits than before ROWE was instituted, and her poorer performers were doing better. One interesting result of ROWE's program is the increase in involuntary turnover; Best Buy says this is because non-performers are weeded out of the organization. In addition, this style of working does not suit everyone (RenegadeHR, 2009).

### Discussion Questions

1. How does a company establish an organizational culture and sense of teamwork when its employees are coming and going? Do you see this as a problem? Why, or why not?
2. Does this approach fit well for all job functions? Why, or why not?
3. Given your personality, would you work well in this environment? Why, or why not?
4. For examples of how employees have used the ROWE program, watch the video available at http://renegadehr.net/best-buy-rowe.

# Notes

## 1 An Introduction to Women in the Workplace

1 The actual number of women in the labor force will be confirmed with the 2010 census.
2 The "glass ceiling" is a metaphor used to indicate an intangible, impenetrable barrier for women that prevents them from reaching the top of organizations.

## 4 Career Opportunities: Recruitment, Selection, and Promotion

1 "Opportunity structure" refers to the relationship of management positions in an institution which make occupants of one position natural candidates for promotion to another position.
2 By contrast with human capital, which is the result of investment in education and training, social capital is the result of investment in personal relationships that enhance one's opportunities.
3 "Reduction in force" is the term given for large-scale lay-offs of employees.
4 Companies use assessment centers to evaluate candidates for promotion. These centers can be staffed by employees of the company or by outside suppliers – for example, psychologists who offer their services to companies.

## 7 Gender and Communication

1 "Flaming" is slang for making personal insults or using obscene language in electronic communication.
2 A content analysis is a standard social-science practice in which the content of a communication message is studied (words, phrases, who speaks to whom, etc.).
3 Tag questions are declarative statements or imperative statements turned into a question by adding an interrogative: "I shouldn't do that, should I?"

## 8. Hostile Work Environments and Sexual Harassment

1 If an individual is working for a foreign employer outside the US, the rules of that nation apply. The issue here is the definition of control. Control is defined by whether the division operating outside the US is controlled by US management, whether the company uses centralized labor relations, and the degree to which operations are interrelated between the US-based operation and the foreign-based operation. When a company bases its human resources practices in a US division, rather than a foreign one, it has centralized labor relations.

## 10 Women Entrepreneurs: Working *Their* Way

1 "Social capital" (also discussed in Chapter 2) refers to the number and influence of social contacts that can help an individual receive benefits. In this case, help with a business start-up.

## 11 Policy and Organizational Practice

1 "Position power" is the power that one's position in an organizational hierarchy affords one, sometimes referred to as "power by title." For example, a supervisor has more position power because of his or her rank than a worker.

# Bibliography

Abbey, A. & Melby, C. (1986). The effects of nonverbal cues on gender differences in perceptions of sexual intent. *Sex Roles: A Journal of Research*, *15*, 283–298.

Achtenhagen, L. & Welter, F. (2003). Female entrepreneurship as reflected in German media in the years 1995–2001. In J. Butler (Ed.), *New perspectives on women entrepreneurs* (pp. 71–100). Charlotte, NC: Information Age.

Acker, J. (1990). Hierarchies, jobs, bodies: A theory of gendered organizations. *Gender and Society*, *4*, 139–158.

——. (1992). The future of women and work: Ending the twentieth century. *Sociological Perspectives*, *35*, 53–68.

Adams, M., Anderson, J., & Faroldi, J. (2004). *Louisiana employment law letter*. Retrieved October 4, 2006 from www.joneswalker.com/db30/cgi-bin/pubs/Vol.13No7.PDF.

Adler, N. (1994). Competitive frontiers: Women managing across borders. *Journal of Management Development*, *13*(2), 24–41.

Adu, K. (2005). Dedication to diversity: IBM's new global supplier diversity chief. *The Network Journal*, October. Retrieved October 26, 2009 from www.tnj.com/archives/2005.

AFSCME. (2007). *Unions increase women's economic security*. Retrieved October 1, 2007 from www.afscme.org/docs/wrfaq13.pdf.

Ahl, H. (2004). *The scientific reproduction of gender inequality: A discourse analysis of research texts on women's entrepreneurship*. Copenhagen: CBS Press.

Ahuja, M.K., Chudoba, K.M., Kaemar, C.J., McKnight, D.H., & George, J.F. (2007). ICT road warriors: Balancing work–family conflict, job autonomy, and work overload to mitigate turnover intentions. *MISQ Archivist*. Retrieved January 10, 2008 from www/misq.org/archivist/vol/no31/issue 1.

Aldrich, H. & Cliff, J. (2003). The pervasive effects of family on entrepreneurship: Towards a family embeddedness perspective. *Journal of Business Venturing*, *18*, 573–596.

Aldrich, H., Reese, P.R., & Dubini, P. (1989). Women on the verge of a breakthrough: Networking among entrepreneurs in the U.S. and Italy. *Entrepreneurship & Regional Development*, *1*(4), 339–356.

Alimo-Metcalfe, B. (1993). Women in management: Organizational socialization and assessment practices that prevent career advancement. *International Journal of Selection and Assessment*, *2*(3), 68–83.

——. (1994). Gender bias in the selection and assessment of women in management. In R. Burke & M. Davidson (Eds.), *Women in management: Current research issues* (pp. 93–109). London: Paul Chapman.

——. (1995). An investigation of female and male constructs of leadership and empowerment. *Women in Management Review*, *10*(2), 3–8.

Allen, T.D. & Eby, L.T. (2004). Factors related to mentor reports of mentoring functions providing gender and relational characteristics. *Sex Roles: A Journal of Research*, *50*(1–2), 29–139.

Allen, T.D., Day, R., & Lentz, E. (2005). The role of interpersonal comfort in mentoring relationships. *Journal of Career Development*, *31*(3), 115–169.

Alsos, G., Isaken, E., & Ljunggren, E. (2006). New venture financing and subsequent business growth in men and women-led business. *Entrepreneurship: Theory and Practice*, *30*(5), 667–686.

Altonji, J. & Paxson, C. (1992). Labor supply, hours constraints and job mobility. *Journal of Human Resources*, *27*, 256–278.

American Association of University Women. (2001). *Hostile hallways: Bullying, teasing, and sexual harassment*. Retrieved February 10, 2009 from www.aauw/org/research.

——. (2006). *Drawing the line: Sexual harassment on campus*. Retrieved February 2006 from www.aauw/org/research.

American College of Healthcare Executives. (2007). *A comparison of the career attainment of men and women healthcare executives*, December. Retrieved December 2, 2008 from www.ache.org/pubs/research/genderstudy.

*American Nurses' Association, et al., plaintiffs – appellants*, v. *State of Illinois, et al., defendants – appellees*, 85–1766 (United States Court of Appeals for the Seventh Circuit 1986).

Amott, T. & Matthaei, J. (1996). *Race, gender and work: A multi-cultural economic history of women in the United States*. Boston, MA: Southend Press.

Anastasopoulos, V. & Brown, D. (2002). *Women on boards: Not just the right thing ... but the "bright" things*. Ottawa: The Conference Board of Canada.

Andersen, K.J. & Leaper, C. (1998). Meta-analysis of gender effects on conversational interruption: Who, what, when, where, and how. *Sex Roles: A Journal of Research*, *39*(3–4), 225–252.

Anderson, J. (2006). Wall Street's women face a fork in the road. *New York Times*, August 6. Retrieved October 20, 2009 from www.nytimes.com.

Andersson, L.M. & Pearson, C.M. (1999). Tit for tat? The spiraling effect of incivility in the workplace. *The Academy of Management Review*, *24*(3), 452–471.

Andrews, E. (2004). Survey confirms it: Women outjuggle men. *New York Times*, September 15.

Anker, R. (1997). Theories of occupational segregation by sex: An overview. *International Labour Review*, *136*(3), 315–339.

Anker, R. & Melkas, H. (1997). Occupation segregation by sex in Nordic countries: An empirical investigation. *International Labour Review*, *136*(3), 341–363.

Anna, A.L., Chandler, G.N., Jansen, E., & Mero, N.P. (2000). Women business owners in traditional and non-traditional industries. *Journal of Business Venturing*, *15*(3), 279–303.

Anxo, D., Boulin, J.-Y., & Fagan, C. (2006). Decent working time in a life course perspective. In J.-Y. Boulin, M. Lallement, J. Messenger, & F. Michon (Eds.), *Decent working time – new trends, new issues* (pp. 93–122). New York, NY: Routledge.

Archer, D. (1999). Exploring "bullying" culture in the para-military. *International Journal of Man Power*, *20*(1–2), 94–105.

Arfken, D.E., Bellar, A.L., & Helms, M.M. (2004). The ultimate glass ceiling revisited: The presence of women on corporate boards. *Journal of Business Ethics*, *50*(2), 177–186.

Aries, E. (1977). Male–female interpersonal styles in all males, all females and mixed groups. In A. Sargent (Ed.), *Beyond sex roles*. New York, NY: West Publishing.

——. (1996). *Men and women in interaction: Reconsidering the difference*. New York, NY: Oxford University Press.

Aries, E.J., Gold, C., & Weigel, R.H. (1983). Dispositional and situational influences on dominance behavior in small groups. *Journal of Personality and Social Psychology*, *44*, 779–786.

Armstrong, M. & Baron, A. (1995). *The job evaluation handbook*. London: Institute of Personnel Management.

Asherman, I.G. & Asherman, S.V. (2001). *The negotiation sourcebook* (2nd ed.). Amherst, MA: HRD Press.

Atwater, D.M. & Jones, A. (2004). Preparing for a future labor shortage. *Graziedo Business Report*, 7(2). Retrieved May 11, 2009 from http://gbr.pepperdine.edu/042/laborshortage. html.

Awazu, Y. (2004). Informal network players, knowledge integration, and competitive advantage. *Journal of Knowledge Management*, 8(3), 62–70.

Axelrod, R. (1984). *The evolution of cooperation*. New York, NY: Basic Books.

Babcock, L. & Laschever, S. (2003). *Women don't ask: Negotiation and the gender divide*. Princeton, NJ: Princeton University Press.

Bahniuk, M. & Hill, S. (1998). Promoting career success through mentoring. *Review of Business*, 19(3), 4–7.

Bailyn, L. (1989). Toward the perfect workplace? *Communications of the ACM*, 32(4), 460–471.

——. (2004). Time in careers – careers in time. *Human Relations*, 57(12), 1507–1521.

Bailyn, L. & Fletcher, J.K. (2003). Work redesign: Theory, practice and possibility. *The Diversity Factor*, 11(1), 27–31.

Bailyn, L. & Harrington, M. (2004). Redesigning work for work–family integration. *Community, Work & Family*, 7(2), 197–208.

Baker, G., Gibbs, M., & Holmstrom, B. (1994). The internal economics of the firm: Evidence from personnel data. *The Quarterly Journal of Economics*, 109(4), 881–919.

Baker, J.G. (2003). Glass ceilings or sticky floors? A model of high-income law graduates. *Journal of Labor Research*, 24(4), 695–711.

Barnir, A. & Smith, K. (2002). Interfirm alliances in the small business: The role of social networks. *Journal of Small Business Development*, 40(3), 219–232.

Baron, J.N., Davis-Blake, A., & Bielby, W.T. (1986). The structure of opportunity: How promotion ladders vary within and among organizations. *Administrative Science Quarterly*, 31, 248–273.

Barrett, M. & Davidson, M. (2006). *Gender and communication at work*. Farnham: Ashgate.

Barron, L. (2003). Ask and you shall receive? Gender differences in negotiators' beliefs about requests for a higher salary. *Human Relations*, 56(6), 635–662.

Barron, R.D. & Norris, G.M. (1991). Sexual divisions and the dual labor market. In D. Leonard & S. Allen (Eds.), *Sexual divisions revisited* (pp. 153–177). London: Macmillan.

Bass, B.M. & Avolio, B.J. (1994). Shatter the glass ceiling: Women make better managers. *Human Resource Management*, 33, 549–560.

Bass, B.M. & Riggio, R.E. (2006). *Transformational leadership*. Mahwah, NJ: Lawrence Erlbaum.

Baugh, S.G. & Fagenson-Eland, E.A. (2005). Boundaryless mentoring: An exploratory study of the functions provided by internal versus external organizational mentors. *Journal of Applied Psychology*, 35(5), 939–955.

Baughn, D.D., Chua, B.L., & Newport, K.E. (2006). The normative context for women's participation in entrepreneurship, a multi-cultural study. *Entrepreneurship: Theory and Practice*, 30(5), 687–708.

Beck, D. & Davis, E. (2005). EEO in senior management: Women executives in Westpac. *Asia Pacific Journal of Human Resources*, 43(2), 273.

Becker, G. (1957). *The economics of discrimination*. Chicago, IL: University of Chicago Press.

——. (1964). *Human capital*. New York, NY: Columbia University Press.

——. (1971a). *The economics of gender* (2nd ed.). Chicago, IL: University of Chicago Press.

——. (1971b). *Human capital* (3rd ed.). Chicago, IL: University of Chicago Press.

——. (1985). Human capital, effort, and the sexual division of labor. *Journal of Labor Economics*, 3(1), 33–58.

Beckman, C.M. & Phillips, D.J. (2005). Interorganizational determinants of promotion: Client leadership and the attainment of women attorneys. *American Sociological Review*, 70(4), 678–701.

Belkin, L. (2003). The opt-out revolution. *New York Times Magazine*, 26, 42–47.

Bell, E. & Nkomo, S. (2001). *Our separate ways*. Boston, MA: Harvard Business School Press.

Bellu, R. (1993). Task role motivation and attributional styles as predictors of entrepreneurial performance: Female sample findings. *Entrepreneurship and Regional Development*, 1(4), 331–344.

Benko, C. & Weisberg, A. (2007). Implementing a corporate career lattice: The mass career customization model. *Strategy & Leadership*, 35(5), 29–36.

Bergman, M.E., Langhout, R.D., Palmieri, P.A., Cortina, L.M., & Fitzgerald, L.F. (2002). The (un)reasonableness of reporting: Antecedents and consequences of reporting sexual harassment. *Journal of Applied Psychology*, 87(2), 230–242.

Bernard, C. & Schlaffer, E. (1997). "The man in the street": Why he harasses. In L. Richardson, V. Taylor, & N. Whittier (Eds.), *Feminist frontiers IV* (pp. 395–398). New York, NY: McGraw-Hill.

Bernstein, A. (2005). Wal-Mart vs. class actions. *Business Week*, March 21, 73–74.

Bertrand, M. & Mullainathan, S. (2003). *Are Emily and Greg more employable than Lakisha and Jamal? A field experiment on labor market discrimination*. NBER Working Paper No. W9873, July. Retrieved February 25, 2010 from http://papers.ssrn.com.

Bielby, W.T. & Baron, J.N. (1986). Men and women at work: Sex segregation and statistical discrimination. *American Journal of Sociology*, 91, 759–799.

Bielby, W.T. & Bielby, D.D. (1988). She works for the money: Household responsibilities and the allocation of work effort. *American Journal of Sociology*, 93(5), 1031–1059.

Bilimoria, D. (2006). The relationship between women corporate directors and women corporate officers. *Journal of Managerial Issues*, 18, 27–61.

Bilimoria, D. & Huse, M. (1997). A qualitative comparison of the boardroom experience of U.S. and Norwegian women corporate directors. *International Review of Women and Leadership*, 3(2), 63–76.

Bilimoria, D. & Piderit, S.K. (1994). Board committee membership: Effects of sex-based bias. *The Academy of Management Journal*, 37(6), 1453–1477.

Bilimoria, D. & Wheeler, J. (2000). Women corporate directors: Current research and future directions. In M. Davidson & R. Burke (Eds.), *Women in management: Current research issues*, Vol. II (pp. 138–163). London: Sage.

Bingham, C. & Gansler, L.L. (2002). *Class action: The story of Lois Jensen and the landmark case that changed sexual harassment law*. New York, NY: Doubleday.

Bird, B. & Brush, C. (2002). A gendered perspective on organizational creation. *Entrepreneurship: Theory and Practice*, 26(3), 41–65.

Blair-Loy, M. (2006). *Competing devotions: Career and family among women executives*. London: Harvard University Press.

Blau, F.D. & Devaro, J. (2007). New evidence on gender differences in promotion rates: An empirical analysis of a sample of new hires. *Industrial Relations*, 46(3), 511–550.

Blau, F.D. & Kahn, L.M. (2000). Gender differences in pay. *The Journal of Economic Perspectives*, 14(4), 75–99.

———. (2007). Change in the labor supply of married women 1980–2000. *Journal of Labor Economics*, 25(3), 393–438.

Blau, F.D., Farber, M.A., & Winkler, A.E. (1998). *The economics of women, men, and work* (3rd ed.). New York, NY: Simon and Schuster.

Blood, R.O. & Wolfe, D.M. (1960). *Husbands and wives*. New York, NY: Macmillan.

Bloom, N. & Van Reenen, J. (2006). Management practices, work–life balance, and productivity: A review of some recent evidence. *Oxford Review of Economic Policy*, 22(4), 457–482.

Boden, R.J. (1996). Gender and self-employment selection: An empirical assessment. *Journal of Socio-Economics*, 25(6), 671–682.

———. (1999). Gender in equality and wage earnings and female self-employment selection. *Journal of Socio-Economics*, 28(3), 351–364.

Boisard, P., Cartron, D., Gollac, M., & Valeyre, A. (2003). *Time and work: Duration of work*. Dublin: European Foundation for the Improvement of Living and Working Conditions.

Booth, A.L., Francesconi, M., & Frank, J. (2001). A sticky floor model of promotion, pay, and gender. *European Economic Review*, 47(2), 295–322.

Borrego, A.M. (2001). Minnesota university settles sex-bias lawsuit. *The Chronicle of Higher Education*, January 5.

Boulin, J., Lallement, M., & Michon, F. (2006) Decent working time in industrialized countries: Issues, scopes and paradoxes. In J. Boulin, M. Lallement, J. Messenger, & F. Michon (Eds.), *Decent working time: New trends, new issues* (pp. 13–40). Geneva: The International Labour Organization.

Bowles, H.R., Babcock, L. & Lai, L. (2007). Social incentives for gender differences in the propensity to initiate negotiations: Sometimes it does hurt to ask. *Organizational Behaviour and Human Decision Processes*, 103(1), 84–103.

Bowles, H.R. & McGinn, K.L. (2005). Claiming authority: Negotiating challenges for women leaders. In D.M. Messick & R.M. Kramer (Eds.), *The psychology of leadership: New perspectives and research* (pp. 191–208). Mahwah, NJ: Lawrence Erlbaum.

Boyer, I. (1995). *The balance on trial: Women's careers in accountancy*. London: CIMA publishing.

Brady, D. (2003). Crashing GE's glass ceiling. *Business Week*, July 28, 76–77.

Brass, D.J. (1984). Being in the right place: A structural analysis of individual influence in an organization. *Administrative Science Quarterly*, 29(4), 518–539.

———. (1992). Power in organizations: A social network perspective. In G. Moore & J. Whitt (Eds.), *Research in politics & society* (pp. 295–323). Greenwich, CT: JAI Press.

Brass, D.J., Galaskiewicz, J., Greve, H.R., & Tsai, W. (2004). Taking stock of networks and organizations: A multilevel perspective. *Academy of Management Journal*, 47(6), 795–817.

Brescoll, V.L. & Uhlmann, E.L. (2008). Can an angry woman get ahead? Status conferral, gender, and expression of emotion in the workplace. *Psychological Science*, 19(3), 268–275.

Bridges, W.P. & Villemez, W.J. (1986). Informal hiring and income in the labor market. *American Sociological Review*, 51, 574–582.

Brister, K. (2002). Bell South faces bias suit. *The Atlanta Journal-Constitution*, May 3.

Brown, J. (1999). *Beauty and the geeks*. Retrieved February 4, 2009 from http://archive.salon.com/21st/feature/1999/03/cov.

Brush, C.G. (1992). Research on women business owners: Past trends, a new perspective and future directions. *Entrepreneurship Theory and Practice*, 16, 5–26.

Bryne, D. & Neuman, J.H. (1992). The implications of attraction research for organizational issues. In K. Kelley (Ed.), *Issues, theory, and research in industrial/organizational psychology* (pp. 29–58). Amsterdam: Elsevier Science.

Bu, N. & Roy, J.P. (2005). Career success networks in China: Sex differences in network composition and social exchange processes. *Asia Pacific Journal of Management*, 22(4), 381–403.

Burgess, D. & Borgida, E. (1997). Sexual harassment: An experimental test of sex-role spillover theory. *Personality and Social Psychology Bulletin*, 23(1), 63–75.

Burgoon, J.K. (1991). Relational message interpretations of touch, conversational distance, and posture. *Journal of Nonverbal Behavior*, 15(4), 233–259.

Burgoon, J.K., Buller, D.B., Hale, J.L., & DeTurck, M.A. (1984). Relational messages associated with nonverbal behaviors. *Human Communication Research*, 19, 351–378.

Burgoon, J.K., Buller, D.B., & Woodall, W.G. (1996). *Nonverbal communication: The unspoken dialogue*. New York, NY: McGraw-Hill.

Burke, R.J. (1984). Mentors in organizations. *Group & Organization Management*, 9(3), 353.

Burke, R.J. & Greenglass, E. (1987). Work and family. In C.L. Cooper & I.T. Robertson (Eds.), *International review of industrial and organizational psychology* (pp. 273–320). New York, NY: Wiley.

Burke, R. & Mattis, M. (2000). *Women on corporate boards of directors: International challenges and opportunities*. Dordrecht: Kluwer Academic Publishers.

Burke, R.J., McKeen, C.A., & McKenna, C. (1993). Correlates of mentoring in organizations: The mentor's perspective. *Psychological Reports*, 72(3), 883–896.

Burke, S. & Collins, K.M. (2001). Gender differences in leadership styles and management skills. *Women in Management Review*, 16(5), 244–257.

Burson-Marsteller. (1977). *Study of women directors*. New York, NY: Burson-Marsteller.

Burt, R.S. (1992). *Structural holes: The social structure of competition*. Cambridge, MA: Harvard University Press.

*Business Week*. (1996). Abuse of power – part 1: The astonishing tale of sexual harassment at Astra USA. Retrieved February 10, 2009 from www.businessweek.com/1996/20

——. (2004). Sex bias suit: The fight gets ugly. *Business Week*, September 6, 65.

——. (2005). Wal-Mart versus class action. *Business Week*, March 21. Retrieved from www.businessweek.com.

Buttner, E.H. (1993). Female entrepreneurs: How far have they come? *Business Horizons*, 36(2), 59–65.

——. (2001). Examining female entrepreneurs' management style: An application of a relational frame. *Journal of Business Ethics*, 29(3), 253–269.

Buttner, E.H. & Moore, D.P. (1997). Women's organizational exodus to entrepreneurship: Self-reported motivations and correlates with success. *Journal of Small Business Management*, 35(1), 34–46.

Buttner, E.H. & Rosen, B. (1988). Bank loan officers' perceptions of the characteristics of men, women and successful entrepreneurs. *Journal of Business Venturing*, 3, 249–258.

Cable, D. & Judge, T. (2004). The effect of physical height on workplace success and income: Preliminary test of a theoretical model. *Journal of Applied Psychology*, 89(3), 428–441.

Campbell, K.E. (1988). Gender differences in job related networks. *Work and Occupations*, 15(2), 179–200.

Campbell, K.E., Marsden, P.V., & Hurlbert, J.S. (1986). Social resources and socioeconomic status. *Social Networks*, 8, 97–117.

Capell, K. (2004). Sex-bias suits: The fight gets ugly. *Business Week*, September 6, 64–65.

Capelli, P. & Hamori, M. (2004). *The path to the top: Changes in the attributes of corporate executives 1980 to 2001*. Wharton Business School. Retrieved from www.Knowledge@Wharton.com.

Carli, L. (1989). Gender differences in interaction style and influence. *Journal of Personality and Social Psychology*, 56, 565–576.

——. (1990). Gender, language, and influence. *Journal of Personality and Social Psychology*, 59, 941–951.

Carlino, B. (1991). Marriott settles sex-bias lawsuit out of court. *Nation's Restaurant News*, January 7.

Carter, S. & Shaw, E. (2006). *Women's business ownership: Recent research and policy development. Report to the small business service*. Retrieved from www.berr.gov.uk/file38330.pdf.

Carter, S., Shaw, E., Lam, W., & Wilson, F. (2007). Gender, entrepreneurship, and bank lending: The criteria and processes used by bank loan officers in assessing applications. *Entrepreneurship: Theory and Practice*, 31(3), 427–444.

Cashdan, E. (1998). Smiles, speech, and body posture: How women and men display sociometric status and power. *Journal of Nonverbal Behavior*, 22(4), 209–228.

Casper, L.M. & Bianchi, S.M. (2002). *Trends in the American family*. Thousand Oaks, CA: Sage.

Cassirer, N. & Reskin, B. (2000). High hopes: Organizational positions, employment experiences, and women's and men's promotional aspirations. *Work and Occupations*, 27(4), 438–463.

Castilla, E.J. (2008). Gender, race, and meritocracy in organizational careers. *American Journal of Sociology*, 113(6), 1179–1526.

Catalyst. (2000). *Passport to opportunity: US women in global businesses.* New York, NY: Catalyst.

——. (2003). *Women on corporate boards: The challenge of change.* New York, NY: Catalyst.

——. (2005). *Women "take care," men "take charge": Stereotyping of U.S. business leaders exposed.* New York, NY: Catalyst.

——. (2006a). *Catalyst awards.* Retrieved December 20, 2006 from www.catalyst.org/awards.

——. (2006b). *Catalyst census of women corporate officers and top earners of the Fortune 500.* New York, NY: Catalyst.

——. (2006c). *Turnover and retention.* New York, NY: Catalyst.

——. (2006d). *Different cultures, similar perceptions: Stereotyping of Western European business leaders.* New York, NY: Catalyst.

——. (2007a). *The double-bind dilemma for women in leadership: Damned if you do, doomed if you don't.* New York, NY: Catalyst.

——. (2007b). *Quick takes: Maternity leave.* New York, NY: Catalyst.

——. (2007c). *PricewaterhouseCoopers LLP: Unique people experience.* New York, NY: Catalyst.

——. (2007d). *2007 census: Corporate officers and top earners.* New York, NY: Catalyst.

——. (2008). *Nissan Motor Co., Ltd.: Women in the driver's seat – gender diversity as a lever in Japan.* New York, NY: Catalyst.

Caven, V. (2006). Choice, diversity, and "false consciousness" in women's careers. *International Journal of Training and Development*, 10, 41–54.

Cawley, J. (2004). The impact of obesity on wages. *Journal of Human Resources*, 39(2), 451–474.

CELCEE Center for Entrepreneurial Leadership/Clearinghouse on Entrepreneurship Education, 04–04, March 2004, UCLA: Los Angeles.

Center for Disease Control and Prevention. (2005). *Women's health: Facts and statistics.* Retrieved February 25, 2009 from www.cdc.gov/women/mothers.

Center for Women's Business Research. (2007). *Minority numbers.* Center for Women's Business Research. Retrieved January 10, 2009 from www.womensbusinessresearch.org/content/index.php?pid=86.

Center for Work–Life Policy, The. (2006). *The hidden brain drain task force: Women and minorities as unrealized assets* [Electronic Version]. Retrieved December 21, 2006 from www.worklife-policy.org.

Chaganti, R. & Parasuraman, S. (1996). A study of the impacts of gender on business performance and management patterns of small business. *Entrepreneurship: Theory and Practice*, 21(2), 73–75.

Champion, D. (2001). Women and profits. *Harvard Business Review*, 79(10), 30.

Chao, G.T., Walz, P.M., & Gardner, P.D. (1992). Formal and informal mentorships: A comparison on mentoring functions and contrast with nonmentored counterparts. *Personnel Psychology*, 45(3), 619–636.

Charles, M. (1992). Accounting for cross-national variation in occupational sex segregation. *American Sociological Review*, 57, 483–502.

Charles, M. & Bradley, K. (2009). Indulging our gendered selves? Sex segregation by field of study in 44 countries. *American Journal of Sociology*, 14, 924–976.

Charles, M. & Grusky, D.B. (2004). *Occupational ghettos: The worldwide segregation of women and men.* Stanford, CA: Stanford University Press.

Charles, N. & James, E. (2005). He earns the bread and butter and I earn the cream: Job insecurity and the male breadwinner family in South Wales. *Work, Employment and Society*, 19(3), 481–502.

Chartered Management Institute. (2005). *Managers in the U.K., 2005*. Retrieved September 26, 2008 from www.managers.org.uk/content.

Chesterman, C. & Ross-Smith, A. (2006). Not tokens: Reaching a "critical mass" of senior women managers. *Employee Relations*, *28*(6), 540–552.

Chicha, M.-T. (2008). *Promoting equity: Gender neutral job evaluation for equal pay. A step by step guide*. Geneva: International Labour Organization.

*Christensen* v. *State of Iowa*. (1977). 563 F. 2d 353 at 355–56 8th Circuit.

Cialdini, R.B. & Trost, M.R. (1998). Social influence: Social norms, conformity, and compliance. In D.T. Gilbert, S.T. Fiske, & G. Lindzey (Eds.), *The handbook of social psychology* (4th ed., Vol. 2, pp. 151–192). Boston, MA: McGraw-Hill.

Clarke, L., Pedersen, E.F., Michielsens, E., & Susamn, B. (2005). The European construction social partners: Gender equality in theory and practice. *European Journal of Industrial Relations*, *11*, 151–177.

Class actions: What can you do to stem the tide? (2004). *Mississippi Law Letter*, pp. 1–3.

Cleveland, J.N. & Kerst, M.E. (1993). Sexual harassment and perceptions of power: An under articulated relationship. *Journal of Vocational Behavior*, *42*(49–67).

Cleveland, J.N., Stockdale, M.S., & Murphy, K.R. (2000). *Women and men in organizations: Sex and gender issues at work*. Mahwah, NJ: Lawrence Erlbaum Assoc. Inc.

Coats, E.J. & Feldman, R.S. (1996). Gender differences in nonverbal correlates of social status. *Personality and Social Psychology Bulletin*, *22*(10), 1014.

Coelho, A. (2006). Sexual harassment in the workplace: Definitions, cases, and policy. In A. Konrad (Ed.), *In cases in gender and diversity in organizations* (pp. 53–60). London: Ivey Publishers.

Cohen, L.E., Broshak, J.P., & Haveman, H.A. (1998). And then there were more? The effect of organizational sex composition on the hiring and promotion of managers. *American Sociological Review*, *63*(5), 711–727.

Cohn, S. (1996). Human capital theory. In P. Dubeck & K. Borman (Eds.), *Women and work: A reader* (pp. 107–110). New Brunswick, NJ: Rutgers University Press.

Coie, P. (2004). Remedial action after harassment allegations must be "prompt and effective." *Washington Employment Law Letter*, *11*(10), 1–3.

Coleman, S. (2000). Access to capital and terms of credit: A comparison of men and women-owned small business. *Journal of Small Business Management*, *38*(3), 523–542.

Colley, A. & Todd, Z. (2002). Gender-linked differences in the style and content of e-mails to friends. *Journal of Language and Social Psychology*, *21*(4), 380–392.

Collins, P.H. (1997). Comments on Hekman's "truth and method: Feminist standpoint theory revisited". Where's the power? *Signs*, *22*, 375–379.

Collinson, D. & Collinson, M. (1996). "It's only dick": The sexual harassment of women managers in insurance sales. *Work, Employment and Society*, *10*, 29–56.

Commission of the European Communities. (2006). *A roadmap for equality between women and men 2006–2010*. Commission of the European Communities, 1–22. Retrieved January 1, 2009 from www.ec.europa.eu/employment_social/news/2006.

Conlin, M. (2006). Smashing the clock. *Business Week*, December 11, 60–68.

———. (2009). Home offices: The new math. *Business Week*, March 9, 66–68.

Connelly, R., Degraff, D.S., & Willis, R. (2002). If you build it they will come: Parental use of on-site child care centers. *Population Research and Policy Review*, *21*, 241–273.

Cooper, E.A., Doverspike, D., Barrett, G.V., & Alexander, R.A. (1995). Sex bias in job evaluation: The effect of sex on judgments of factor and level weights. *Education and Psychological Measurement*, *47*(2), 369–375.

*Corning Glass Works* v. *Brennan* (1974). 417 U.S. 188.

Corporate Women Directors International Report. (2006). *CWDI report: Women board directors of the largest global and U.S. healthcare and pharmaceutical companies*. Corporate Women Directors International. Retrieved from www.globewomen.org/CWDI/order_form.htm.

Corsun, D.L. & Costen, W.M. (2001). Is the glass ceiling unbreakable? Habitus, fields, and the stalling of women and minorities in management. *Journal of Management Inquiry*, *10*(1), 10–25.

Cortina, L.M. (2008). Unseen injustice: Incivility as modern discrimination in organizations. *The Academy of Management Review*, *33*(1), 55–75.

Crawford, M. (1995). *Talking difference: On gender and language*. London: Sage Publications Inc.

Creighton, C. (1999). The rise and decline of the male breadwinner family in Britain. *Cambridge Journal of Economics*, *23*(5), 519–541.

Crompton, R. & Lyonette, C. (2006). Work–life balance in Europe. *Acta Sociological*, *49*(4), 379–393.

Cross, R. & Cummings, J.N. (2004). Tie and network correlates of individual performance in knowledge-intensive work. *Academy of Management Journal*, *47*(6), 928–937.

Crull, P. (1982). Stress effects of sexual harassment on the job: Implications for counseling. *American Journal of Orthopsychiatry*, *52*(3), 539–544.

Cunningham, C.R. & Murray, S.S. (2005). Two executives, one career. *Harvard Business Review*, February, 125–131.

Curhan, J.A., Neale, M.A., Ross, L., & Rosencranz-Englemann, J. (2008). Relational accommodation in negotiation: Effects of egalitarianism and gender on economic efficiency and relational capital. *Organization Behavior and Human Decision Processes*, *107*, 192–205.

Dahle, C. (2004). Choosing a mentor? Cast a wide net. *New York Times*, July, 259.

Dale, M. (2006). Workers triumph over Wal-Mart. *The News and Observer*, October 14.

Dalton, M., Ernst, C., Deal, J., & Leslie, J. (2002). *Success for the new global manager*. San Francisco, CA: Jossey-Bass.

Davidson, M.J. & Burke, R.J. (2004). Women in management worldwide: Facts, figures, and analysis – an overview. In M.J. Davidson & R.J. Burke (Eds.), *Women and men in management worldwide: Facts, figures, analysis* (pp. 1–18). Aldershot: Ashgate Publishing Ltd.

Davidson, P. (2006). Some particular themes: Nascent entrepreneurship, empirical studies and development. *Foundations and Trends in Entrepreneurship*, *2*(1), 32.

Davies-Metzly, S.A. (1998). Women above the glass ceiling: Perceptions on corporate mobility and strategies for success. *Gender and Society*, *12*(3), 339–355.

De Bruin, A., Brush, C.G., & Welter, F. (2007). Advancing a framework for coherent research on women's entrepreneurship. *Entrepreneurship: Theory and Practice*, *31*(3), 323–340.

de Janasz, S.C., Sullivan, S., & Whiting, V. (2003). Mentor networks and career success: Lessons for turbulent times. *Academy of Management Executives*, *17*(4), 78.

DeMartino, R. & Barbato, R.J. (2003). An analysis of the motivational factors of intending entrepreneurs. *Journal of Small Business Strategy*, *12*(2), 26–36.

DeMartino, R., Barbato, R., & Jacques, P.H. (2006). Exploring the career/achievement and personal life orientation differences between entrepreneurs and nonentrepreneurs: The impact of sex and dependents. *Journal of Small Business Management*, *44*(3), 350–368.

Dencker, J. (2008). Corporate restructuring and sex differences in managerial promotion. *American Sociological Review*, *73*, 455–476.

DeTienne, D.R. & Chandler, G.N. (2007). The role of gender in opportunity identification. *Entrepreneurship: Theory and Practice*, *31*(3), 365–386.

Devine, T. (1994). Characteristics of self-employed women in the United States. *Monthly Labor Review*, *117*. Retrieved October 22, 2009 from http://findarticles.com/p/articles/mi_m1153/is_n3_v117/ai_15161437.

Dey, J.G. & Hill, C. (2007). Behind the pay gap. *American Association of University Women Educational Foundation*, 64.

di Tomaso, N. (1989). Sexuality in the workplace: Discrimination and harassment. In J.R. Hearn, D.L. Sheppard, P. Tancred-Sheriff, & G. Burrell (Eds.), *The sexuality of organization* (pp. 71–90). London: Sage.

Dickens, L. (2006). Equality and work–life balance: What's happening at the workplace. *Industrial Law Journal*, 35(4), 445–449.

Dierks-Stewart, K. (1980). Sex differences in nonverbal behavior: An alternative perspective. In C. Berryman-Fink, C.L. Beryman, & V.A. Eman (Eds.), *Communication, language, and sex: Proceedings of the first conference*. Rowley, MA: Newbury.

Dingell, J.D. & Maloney, C.B. (2002). *A new look through the glass ceiling: Where are the women? The status of women in management in 10 selected industries*. Retrieved February 25, 2010 from http://search house.gov/htbin/search.

Diversity Factor. (1998). Moving on: A CEO's reflections. *Diversity Factor*, 6(4), 47.

Doeringer, P.B. & Piore, M.J. (1971). *Internal labor markets and manpower analysis*. Lexington, MA: D.C. Heath.

Doiron, D.J. & Riddell, W.C. (1994). The impact of unionization on male–female earnings differences in Canada. *The Journal of Human Resources*, 29(2), 504–534.

Donath, J. & Boyd, D. (2004). Public displays of connection. *BT Technology Journal*, 22(4), 71–82.

Dovidio, J.F. & Ellyson, S.L. (1985). Patterns of visual dominance behavior in humans. In J.F. Dovidio & A.L. Ellyson (Eds.), *Power, dominance and nonverbal behavior* (Vol. 22, pp. 105–124). New York, NY: Springer-Verlag.

Drago, R., Black, D., & Wooden, M. (2004). *Gender and work hours transitions in Australia: Drop ceilings and trap doors*. Melbourne Institute of Applied Economic and Social Research, Working Paper, No. 11, July 4.

Dreher, G.F. & Cox, T.H. (2000). Labor market mobility and cash compensation: The moderating effects of race and gender. *Academy of Management Journal*, 43(5), 890–900.

Dublin, R. (1973). Work and non-work: Institutional perspectives. In M.D. Dunnette (Ed.), *Work and non-work in the year 2001* (pp. 53–68). Monterey, CA: Brooks/Cole.

Duehr, E.E. & Bono, J.E. (2006). Men, women, and managers: Are stereotypes finally changing? *Personnel Psychology*, 59(4), 815–846.

Dunbar, D. (1990). Desperately seeking mentors. *Black Enterprise*, 20(8), 53.

Dunn, D. (1997a). Gender and earnings. In P. Dubeck & K. Borman (Eds.), *Women and work: A handbook* (pp. 61–64). New Brunswick, NJ: Rutgers.

——. (1997b). Gender-segregated occupations. In P. Dubeck & K. Borman (Eds.), *Women and work: A handbook* (pp. 91–93). New Brunswick, NJ: Rutgers.

Dziech, B.W. & Weiner, L. (1990). *The lecherous professor: Sexual harassment on campus* (2nd ed.). Boston, MA: Beacon Press.

Eagly, A.H. & Carli, L.L. (2007). *Through the labyrinth: The truth about how women become leaders*. Boston, MA: Harvard Business School Publishing.

Eagly, A.H. & Johnson, B.T. (1990). Gender and leadership style: A meta-analysis. *Psychological Bulletin*, 108, 233–256.

Eagly, A.H. & Steffen, V.J. (1986). Gender and aggressive behavior: A meta-analytic review of the social psychological literature. *Psychological Bulletin*, 100(3), 309–330.

Eagly, A.H., Johannesen-Schmidt, M.C., & van Engen, M.L. (2003). Transformational, transactional, and laissez-faire leadership styles: A meta-analysis comparing women and men. *Psychological Bulletin*, 129, 569–591.

Eagly, A.H., Makhijani, M.G., & Klonsky, B.G. (1992). Gender and the evaluation of leaders: A meta-analysis. *Psychological Bulletin*, 3(1), 3–22.

Eagly, A.H., Wood, W., & Diekman, A.B. (2000). Social role theory of sex differences and similarities: A current appraisal. In T. Eckes & H.M. Trautner (Eds.), *Development social psychology of gender* (pp. 123–174). Mahwah, NJ: Lawrence Erlbaum.

Earle, B.H. & Madek, G.A. (1993). An international perspective on sexual harassment law. *Law and Inequality*, *12*(1), 43–91.

Easton, A. (1994). Talk and laughter in New Zealand women's and men's speech. *Wellington Working Papers in Linguistics*, 6, 1–25.

Eckenrode, J. & Gore, S. (1990). Stress and coping at the boundary of work and family. In J. Eckenrode & S. Gore (Eds.), *Stress between work and family* (pp. 1–16). New York, NY: Plenum.

Edwards, J.R. & Rothbard, N. (2000). Mechanisms for linking work and family: Specifying the relationships between work and family constructs. *Academy of Management Review*, *25*(1), 178–199.

——. (2003). Investment in work and family roles: A test of identity and utilitarian motives. *Personnel Psychology*, *56*(3), 699–729.

EEOC. (1998). *Astra USA agrees to provide $10 million to victims of discrimination*. Retrieved February 11, 2009 from www.eeoc.gov/press/2-5-98.

——. (2000). *EEOC settles same-sex harassment suit for a half million dollars against major Colorado auto dealership*. Retrieved February 9, 2009 from www.eeoc.gov/press/8-4-00.html.

*EEOC* v. *Domino's Pizza, Inc.* (1995). Eleventh circuit, 909 F. Supp. 1529, 69, Cases 570, M.D. Fla.

Elliott, J.R. & Smith, R.A. (2004). Race, gender, and workplace power. *American Sociological Review*, *69*(3), 365–386.

Elsesser, K. & Peplau, L.A. (2006). Cross-sex – the glass partition: Obstacles to cross-sex friendships at work. *Human Relations*, *59*(8), 1077–1100.

Elvira, M.M. & Graham, M.E. (2002). Not just a formality: Pay system formalization and sex-related earnings effects. *Organization Science*, *13*(6), 601–617.

Ely, R. (2004). A field study of group diversity, participation in diversity education, and performance. *Journal of Organizational Behavior*, *25*(6), 755–781.

Ely, R. & Meyerson, D. (1999). Moving from gender to diversity in organizational diagnosis and intervention. *Diversity Factor*, *7*(3), 28–33.

Ely, R., Meyerson, D., & Davidson, M. (2006). Rethinking political correctness. *Harvard Business Review*, *84*(8), 78–90.

Enchautegui, M.E., Fix, M.E., Loprest, P.J., von der Lippe, S.C., & Wissoker, D.A. (1997). *Do minority-owned businesses get a fair share of government contracts?* Washington, DC: The Urban Institute.

European Commission. (2005). *The business case for diversity*. Retrieved April 10, 2009 from www.coference-board.org/worldwide/downloads/europeWorkplaceDiversity.pdf.

European Foundation for the Improvement of Living and Working Conditions. (2004). Long working hours in Austria. *News Updates*, December 1, Dublin.

——. (2008a). *Mind the gap: Women's and men's quality of work and employment*. Retrieved February 14, 2009 from www.eurofound.europa.eu/pubdocs/2008/39/en/1/ef0839en.pdf.

——. (2008b). *Revisions to the European working time directive: Recent research*. Retrieved January 20, 2009 from www/eurofound.europa.eu/publications.

European Professional Women's Network. (2009). *Third Bi-Annual European PWN Board Women Monitor 2008*. Retrieved August 25, 2009 from www.europeanpwn.net.

Eurostat. (2004). Women, science, and technology: Measuring recent progress toward gender equality. *Statistics in Focus*, Theme 9, Luxembourg, Eurostat.

——. (2009). Retrieved July 15, 2009 from http://epp.eurostat.eu/t.

Fabowale, L., Orser, B., & Riding, A. (1995). Gender, structural factors, and credit terms between Canadian small businesses and financial institutions. *Entrepreneurship: Theory and Practice*, *19*, 41–65.

Fagenson, E. (1993). Personal value systems of men and women entrepreneurs versus managers. *Journal of Business Venturing*, *8*(5), 409–430.

Fairlie, R. (2007). *Entrepreneurship in Silicon Valley during the boom and bust*. Santa Cruz, CA: Small Business Office of Advocacy.

Fallows, D. (2005). How women and men use the Internet. *Pew Internet & American Life Project*. Retrieved January 12, 2009 from www.pewinternet.org/ppf/r/171/report.

Fay, M. & Williams, L. (1993). Gender bias and the availability of business loans. *Journal of Business Venturing*, 8(4), 363–376.

Feather, P.M. & Shaw, W.D. (2000). The demand for leisure time in the presence of constrained work hours. *Economic Inquiry*, 38(4), 651–661.

Feldman-Schorrig, S.P. (1994). Special issues in sexual harassment cases. In J.J. McDonald & F.B. Kulick (Eds.), *Mental and emotional injuries in employment litigation*. Washington, DC: Washington Bureau of National Affairs.

Fenwick, T. & Hutton, S. (2000). *Women crafting new work: The learning of women entrepreneurs*. Proceedings of the Adult Education Research Conference (pp. 112–120). Vancouver: University of British Columbia.

Fernandez, C.D. (1995). Career comrades. *Hispanic*, 8(8), 46–47.

Fernandez, R.M. & Lourdes Sosa, M. (2005). Gendering the job: Networks and recruitment at a call center. *American Journal of Sociology*, 111(3), 859–904.

Ferris, G.R. & King, T.R. (1991). Politics in human resources decisions: A walk on the dark side. *Organizational Dynamics*, 20(2), 59–71.

Ferris, G.R., Buckley, M.R., & Allen, G.M. (1992). Promotion systems in organizations. *Human Resources Planning*, 15(3), 47–68.

Ferris, S.P. (1996). Women on-line: Cultural and relational aspects of women's communication in on-line discussion groups. *Interpersonal Computing and Technology*, 4(3–4), 29–40.

Fischer, E., Reuben, R.A., & Dyke, L.S. (1993). A theoretical overview and extension of research on sex, gender, and entrepreneurship. *Journal of Business Venturing*, 8(2), 151–168.

Fischlmayr, I.C. (2002). Female self-perception as a barrier to international careers? *International Journal of Human Resource Management*, 13(5), 773–783.

Fisher, R., Ury, B., & Patton, B. (1991). *Getting to yes: Negotiating without giving in*. New York, NY: Penguin.

Fisher-McAuley, G., Stanton, J.M., Jolson, J.A., & Gavin, J. (2003). *Modeling the relationship between work/life balance and organizational outcomes*. Conference paper presented at the Annual Conference of Society for Industrial–Organizational Psychology. Orlando, Florida, April 12, pp. 1–29.

Fishman, P.M. (1978). Interaction: The work women do. *Social Problems*, 25(4), 397–406.

Fisk, D. (2003). *American labor in the 20th century*. US Bureau of Labor Statistics, January 30. Retrieved September 2, 2009 from www.bls.gov/opub.

Fiske, S.T. (2002). What we know now about bias and intergroup conflict, the problem of the century. *Current Directions in Psychological Science*, 11(4), 123–128.

Fitzgerald, L.F., Swan, S., & Fischer, K. (1995). Why didn't she just report him? The psychological and legal implications of women's responses to sexual harassment. *Journal of Social Issues*, 51, 117–138.

Florea, N., Boyer, M., Brown, S., & Butler, M. (2003). Negotiating from Mars to Venus: Gender in simulated international negotiations. *Simulation and Gaming*, 34(2), 226–248.

Folbre, N. (1991). The unproductive housewife: Her evolution in nineteenth-century economic thought. *Signs*, 16, 463–484.

Fonda, S.J., Fultz, N.H., & Jenkins, K.R. (2004). Relationship of body mass and net worth for retirement-aged men and women. *Research on Aging*, 26(1), 156–176.

Foroohar, R. (2006). Myth and reality: Forget all the talk of equal opportunity. European women can have a job – but not a career. *Newsweek (International Edition)*, February 27.

Forret, M. & Dougherty, T. (2004). Network behaviors and career outcomes: Differences for men and women? *Journal of Organization Behavior*, 25(3), 419–437.

Forsyth, S. & Polzer-Debruyne, A. (2007). The organizational pay-offs for perceived work–life balance support. *Asia Pacific Journal of Human Resources*, 45(1), 113–123.

Fowler, J.L., Gudmundsson, A.J., & O'Gorman, J.G. (2007). The relationship between mentee–mentor gender combination and the provision of distinct mentoring functions. *Women in Management Review*, 22(8), 666–681.

Franco, V., Pirto, R., Hu, H.Y., Lewenstein, R., Underwood, R., & Vidal, N.K. (1995). Anatomy of a flame: Conflict and community building on the Internet. *Technology and Society Magazine*, 12–21.

Frank, T. (2008). *Talking Justice*. American Enterprise Institute, February 9, 2008. Retrieved April 29, 2008 from www.communities.justicetalking.org/blogs/day04/archive.

Frasch, K.B. (2009). Keeping work/life programs. *Human Resource Executive Online*. Retrieved February 28, 2009 from www.hreonline.com.

Friedman, S.D. & Greenhaus, J.H. (2000). *Work and family – Allies or enemies? What happens when business professionals confront life choices*. New York, NY: Oxford University Press.

Friedman, W. & Casner-Lotto, J. (2003). *Time is of the essence: New scheduling options for unionized employees*. Berkeley, CA: Work in America Institute, Labor Project for Working Families.

Fronczek, P. & Johnson, P. (2003). *Occupations: 2000*. Retrieved December 5, 2007 from www.census.gov/prod/2003.

Garfinkel, P. (2004). Putting a formal stamp on mentoring. *New York Times*, January 18, 3–10.

Gaskill, L.A.R. (1991). Same-sex and cross-sex mentoring of female protégés: A comparative analysis. *Career Development Quarterly*, 40(1), 48–63.

Gatewood, E.J., Brush, C.G., Carter, N.M., Greene, P.G., & Hart, M.M. (2008). Diana: A symbol of women's entrepreneurial hunt for knowledge, money and the rewards of entrepreneurship. *Small Business Economics*, 32(2), 129–144.

Geoffee, R. & Scase, R. (1985). Preliminary study of female proprietors. *The Sociological Review*, 31, 625–648.

Gender and Achievement Research Program. (2007). The Michigan Study of adolescent and adult life transitions. Retrieved October 10, 2009 from www/rcgd.isr.umich.edu/garp.

Gerhart, B. (1990). Gender differences in current and starting salaries: The role of performance, college major, and job title. *Industrial and Labor Relations Review*, 43(4), 418.

Gilbert, K. (2005). The role of job evaluation in determining equal value in tribunals – tool, weapon or cloaking device? *Employee Relations*, 27(1), 1–19.

Gilligan, C. (1982). *In a different voice: Psychological theory and women's development*. Cambridge, MA: Harvard University Press.

Ginsburg, R. (2007). *Ledbetter* v. *Goodyear Tire & Rubber Company*, Supreme Court (May 29, 2007, No. 05–1074). Retrieved January 13, 2009 from http:/supreme.justia.com.

Giscombe, K. & Mattis, M.C. (2002). Leveling the playing field for women of color in corporate management: Is the business case enough? *Journal of Business Ethics*, 37(1), 103–119.

Giuffre, R.A. & Williams, C.L. (1994). Boundary lines: Labeling sexual harassment in restaurants. *Gender and Society*, 8(3), 378–401.

Glass, J. (2000). Envisioning the integration of family and work: Toward a kinder, gentler workplace. *Contemporary Sociology*, 29(1), 129.

Gneezy, U., Nierderle, M., & Rustichini, A. (2003). Performance in competitive environments: Gender differences. *Quarterly Journal of Economics*, 118(3), 1049–1073.

Godwin, L.N., Stevens, C.E., & Brenner, N.L. (2007). Forced to play by the rules? Theorizing how mixed-sex founding teams benefit women entrepreneurs in male-dominated contexts. *Entrepreneurship: Theory and Practice*, 30(5), 623–642.

Goetzel, R.Z., Anderson, D.R., Whitmer, R.W., Ozminkowski, R.J., Dunn, R.L., & Wasserman, J. (1998). The relationship between modifiable health risks and health care expenditures: An analysis of the multi-employer HERO health risk and cost database. *Journal of Occupational & Environmental Medicine*, 40(10), 843–854.

Goldberg, C.B. (2007). The impact of training and conflict avoidance on responses to sexual harassment. *Psychology of Women Quarterly*, 31(1), 62–72.

Goldberg, J.A. (1990). Interrupting the discourse on interruptions. An analysis in terms of relationally neutral, power- and rapport-oriented acts. *Journal of Pragmatics*, 14(6), 883–903.

Goldberg, S. (1973). *The inevitability of patriarchy: Why the biological differences between men and women always produce male domination.* New York, NY: William Morrow.

———. (1993). *Why men rule: A theory of male dominance.* Peru, IL.: Open Court Publishers.

Golden, L. (2006). Overemployment in the United States: Which workers are willing to reduce their work-hours and income? In J.-Y. Boulin, M. Lallement, J. Messenger, & F. Michon (Eds.), *Decent working time: New trends, new issues* (pp. 209–234). Geneva: International Labour Organization.

Golden, L. & Wiens-Tuers, B. (2005). Mandatory overtime work: Who, what and where? *Labor Studies Journal*, 30(1), 1–23.

Goldin, C. (2006). The quiet revolution that transformed woman's employment, education, and the family. *The American Economic Review*, 96(2), 1–21.

Goldman, A. (2004). CostCo manager files sex-bias suit: The retailer is accused of denying women promotion to its top ranks. Class-action status is being sought. *Los Angeles Times*, August 18.

Gonas, L. & Karlsson, J.C. (2006). *Gender segregation: Division of work in post-industrial welfare states.* Aldershot: Ashgate Publishing.

Goodwin, D.K. (1995). *No ordinary time: Franklin and Eleanor Roosevelt. The home front in World War II.* New York, NY: Touchstone.

Gorman, E.H. (2005). Gender stereotypes, same-gender preferences, and organizational variation in the hiring of women: Evidence from law firms. *American Sociological Review*, 70(4), 702–728.

Gould, S. & Penley, L.E. (1984). Career strategies and salary progression: A study of their relationship in a municipal bureaucracy. *Organizational Behavior and Human Performance*, 34(2), 244–265.

Government of South Africa. (2005). *South African women entrepreneurs: A burgeoning force in our economy.* Department of Trade and Industry. Retrieved October 23, 2009 from www.thedti.gov.za/sawenreport2.pdf.

Granovetter, M.S. (1973). The strength of weak ties. *American Journal of Sociology*, 78, 1360–1380.

———. (1982). Who gets ahead? A review. *Theory & Society*, 11, 239–262.

Graves, L.M. & Powell, G.N. (1996). Sex similarity, quality of the employment interview and recruiters' evaluation of actual applicants. *Journal of Occupational and Organizational Psychology*, 69, 243–261.

Greco, S. (2002). Finding the perfect pitch. *Inc. Magazine*, June 1. Retrieved October 26, 2009 from www.inc.com.

Greenhaus, J.H. & Beutell, N.J. (1985). Sources of conflict between work and family roles. *Academy of Management Review*, 10, 76–88.

Greenhaus, J.H., Collins, L.M., & Shaw, J.D. (2002). The relation between work–family balance and quality of life. *Journal of Vocational Behavior*, 63(3), 510–531.

Greve, A. & Salaff, J. (2003). Social networks and entrepreneurship. *Entrepreneurship Theory and Practice*, 28(1), 1–22.

Gruber, A. (2004). Civil rights group decries shortfall in EEOC funding [Electronic Version].

*Government Executive*, October 6. Retrieved October 1, 2007 from www.govexec.com/dailyfed/1004/100604a1.htm.

Gruber, J.E. & Bjorn, L. (1986). Women's responses to sexual harassment: An analysis of socio-cultural, organizational, and personal resource models. *Social Science Quarterly*, 67(4), 814–826.

*Guardian*. (2008). You're fired!, *Guardian*, March 6. Retrieved from http://lifeandhealth.guardian.co.uk/women/story.

Guiller, J. & Durndell, A. (2007). Students' linguistic behavior in online discussion groups: Does gender matter? *Computers in Human Behavior*, 25(5), 2240–2255.

Gundry, L.K. & Welsch, H.P. (2001). The ambitious entrepreneur: High growth strategies of women-owned businesses. *Journal of Business Venturing*, 16, 67–86.

Gupta, V.K., Turban, D.B., Arzu Wasti, S., & Sikdar, A. (2009). The role of stereotypes in perceptions of entrepreneurs' intentions to become an entrepreneur. *Entrepreneurship: Theory and Practice*, 33(2), 397–417.

Gutek, B. & Morasch, B. (1982). Sex-ratios, sex-role spillover, and sexual harassment at work. *Journal of Social Issues*, 38(4), 55–74.

Gutek, B.A., Repetti, R., & Silver, S. (1988). Nonwork roles and stress at work. In C.L. Cooper & R. Payne (Eds.), *Causes, coping, and consequences of stress at work* (pp. 141–174). New York, NY: Wiley.

Gutnerhers, T. (2002). Progress? Not as much as you thought. *Business Week*, February 18, 108.

Hadjifotiou, N. (1983). *Women and harassment at work*. London: Pluto Press.

Hakim, C. (2002). Lifestyle preferences as determinants of women's differentiated labor market careers. *Work and Occupations*, 29(4), 428–459.

——. (2006). Women, career and work–life preferences. *British Journal of Guidance and Counseling*, 34(3), 279–294.

Hamermesh, D. (1999). The timing of work overtime. *The Economic Journal*, 109, 37–66.

Hannah, A. & Murachver, T. (1999). Gender and conversational style as predictors of conversational behavior. *Journal of Language and Social Psychology*, 18(2), 153–174.

Harcourt, W. (1999). *Women@internet: Creating new cultures in cyberspace*. London: Zed Books.

Hardman, W. & Heidelberg, J. (1996). When sexual harassment is a foreign affair. *Personnel Journal*, 75(4), 91–97.

Harriman, A. & Holm, C. (2007). *Equality at work: Tackling the challenges. International Labour Conference, 96th Session, Report I (B)*. Geneva: International Labour Organization.

Harrison, R.T. & Mason, C.M. (2007). Does gender matter? Women business angels and the supply of entrepreneurial finance. *Entrepreneurship: Theory and Practice*, 31(3), 445–472.

Haslett, B.J., Geis, F.L., & Carter, M.R. (1992). *The organization women: Power, and paradox*. Norwood, NJ: Ablex.

Haythornthwaite, C. (1996). Social network analysis: An approach and technique for the study of information exchange. *Library and Information Science Research*, 18, 323–342.

Headlam-Wells, J.E. (2004). Mentoring for aspiring women managers. *Women in Management Review*, 19(4), 212–218.

Hecht, M.A. & LaFrance, M. (1998). License or obligation to smile: The effect of power and sex on amount and type of smiling. *Personality and Social Psychology Bulletin*, 24(12), 1332.

Heilman, M.E. (1983). Sex bias in work settings: The lack of fit model. In B.M. Staw & L.L. Cummings (Eds.), *Research in organizational behavior* (Vol. 5, pp. 269–298). Oxford: Elsevier.

——. (1995). Sex stereotypes and their effects in the workplace: What we know and what we don't know. *Journal of Social Behavior and Personality*, 10(6), 3–26.

——. (2001). Description and prescription: How gender stereotypes prevent women's ascent up the organizational ladder. *Gender, Hierarchy, and Leadership*, 57(4), 657–674.

Heilman, M.E. & Parks-Stamm, E.J. (2007). Gender stereotypes in the workplace: Obstacles to women's career progress. In S.J. Correll (Ed.), *Social psychology of gender: Advances in group processes* (Vol. 24, pp. 47–78). Oxford: Elsevier Ltd.

Heilman, M.E., Wallen, A.S., Fuchs, D., & Tamkins, M. (2004). Penalties for success: Reactions to women who succeed at male gender-typed tasks. *Journal of Applied Psychology*, 89(3), 416–427.

Helweg-Larsen, M., Cunningham, S.J., Carrico, A., & Pergram, A.M. (2004). To nod or not to nod: An observational study of nonverbal communication and status in female and male college students. *Psychology of Women Quarterly*, 28(4), 358–361.

Henley, N.M. (1977). *Body politics: Power, sex and non-verbal communication*. Englewood Cliffs, NJ: Prentice Hall.

——. (1995). Body politics revisited: What do we know today? In P.J. Kalbfleisch & M.J. Cody (Eds.), *Gender, power, and communication in human relationships* (pp. 27–61). Hillsdale, NJ: Erlbaum.

Henningsen, D.D. (2004). Flirting with meaning: An examination of miscommunication in flirting interactions. *Sex Roles: A Journal of Research*, 50(7), 481–489.

Herring, S. (1993). Gender and democracy in computer-mediated communication. *Electronic Journal of Communication*, 3, 293.

——. (1994). *Gender differences in computer-mediated communication: Bringing familiar baggage to the new frontier*. Key note speech at Computer Professionals for Social Responsibility. Retrieved April 10, 2009 from http://cpsr.org/issues/womenintech/herring2.

——. (2005). Gender and power in on-line communication. In J. Homes & M. Meyerhoff (Eds.), *The handbook of language and gender* (pp. 202–228). Oxford: Blackwell Publishing.

Hewlett, S.A. (2002). *Creating a life*. New York, NY: Talk Miramax Books.

Hewlett, S. & Luce, C. (2005). Off-ramps and on ramps: Keeping talented women on the road to success. *Harvard Business Review*, 83(3), 42–52.

Hill, S. & Gant, G. (2000). Mentoring by minorities for minorities: The organizational communication support program. *Review of Business*, 21, 53–57.

Hisrich, R.D. (1989). Women entrepreneurs: Problems and prescriptions for success in the future. In O. Hagen, C. Richun, & D. Sexton (Eds.), *Women owned businesses* (pp. 3–33). NY: Praeger.

Hisrich, R.D. & Brush, C. (1984). The woman entrepreneur: Management skills and business problems. *Journal of Small Business Management*, 22(1), 30–37.

——. (1986). Characteristics of the minority entrepreneur. *Journal of Small Business Management*, 24(1), 1–8.

Hisrich, R.D. & O'Brien, M. (1982). The women entrepreneur as a reflection of the type of business. In K.H. Vesper (Ed.), *Frontiers of entrepreneurship research* (pp. 54–67). Wellesley, MA: Babson College Center for Extrepreneurship Studies.

Hochschild, A. & Machung, A. (2003). *The second shift*. New York, NY: Penguin.

Hodges, J. (2009). Presentation to Duke University Students, International Labour Organization, July 28, Geneva.

Hoff-Sommers, C. (2008). *The case against title-nining the sciences*. American Enterprise Institute for Public Policy. Retrieved May 11, 2009 from www.aei.org/publications/filter.all,pubID.28694.

Holmes, J. & Meyerhoff, M. (2003). *The handbook of language and gender*. Oxford: Blackwell.

Holmes, S. & France, M. (2004). Coverup at Boeing? *Business Week*, June 28, 84.

Holt, S. (2004). Company to pay settlement, change practices to end gender-bias case. *Seattle Times*, July 17.

Hornsby, J.S. & Karatko, D.K. (1990). Human resource management in small business: Critical issues for the 1990s. *Journal of Small Business Management*, 28(2), 9–18.

Hornsby, J.S., Benson, P.G., & Smith, B.N. (1987). An investigation of gender bias in the job evaluation process. *Journal of Business and Psychology*, 2(2), 150–159.

Horrell, S. & Humphries, J. (1997). The origins and expansion of the mail breadwinner family: The case of nineteenth-century Britain. *International Review of Social History*, 42(5), 24–64.

Hughes, K. (2003). Pushed or pulled? Women's entry into self-employment and small business ownership. *Gender, Work, and Organization*, 10(4), 433–454.

Human Rights Campaign Foundation. (2009). Domestic partner benefits: Prevalence among private employers. Retrieved January 16, 2010 from www.hrc.org/issues.

Hyde, J.S. (1986). Gender differences in aggression. In J.S. Hyde & M.C. Linn (Eds.), *The psychology of gender: Advances through meta-analysis* (pp. 51–66). Baltimore, MD: Johns Hopkins University Press.

Hymowitz, C. (2004). Corporate boards lack gender, racial equality [Electronic Version]. *The Wall Street Journal*. Retrieved December 1, 2004 from www.careerjournal.com.

Ibarra, H. (1993). Personal networks of women and minorities in management: A conceptual framework. *Academy of Management Review*, 18(1), 56–87.

Ibarra, H. & Andrews, S.B. (1993). Power, social influence, and sense making: Effects of network centrality and proximity on employee perceptions. *Administrative Science Quarterly*, 38, 277–303.

International Labour Organization. (2003a). *ILO yearbook of labour statistics* (62nd ed.). Geneva: International Labour Organization.

——. (2003b). *Time for equality at work*. Geneva: International Labour Organization.

——. (2004). *Breaking through the glass ceiling: Women in management*. Geneva: International Labour Organization.

——. (2008). *Global employment trends for women*, March. Geneva: International Labour Organization.

International Trade Union Confederation. (2008). *The global gender pay gap*. Brussels: Income Data Services. Retrieved July 29, 2009 from www.ituc-csi.org.

Jablin, F.M. & Krone, K.J. (1987). Organizational assimilation. In C. Berger & S.H. Chaffee (Eds.), *Handbook of communication science* (pp. 711–746). Newbury Park, CA: Sage Publishing.

Jackman, M.R. (1994). *The velvet glove: Paternalism and conflict in gender, class, and race relations*. Berkeley, CA: University of California Press.

Jacobs, J. (1993). Men in female-dominated fields: Trends and turnover. In C. Williams (Ed.), *Doing women's work: Men in non-traditional occupations* (pp. 49–63). Thousand Oaks, CA: Sage.

Jacobs, J.A. & Gerson, K. (2004). *The time divide: Work, family, and gender inequality*. Cambridge, MA: Harvard Business School Press.

Jacobsen, J. (1998). *The economics of gender* (2nd ed.). Malden, MA: Blackwell.

——. (2008). The human capital explanation for the gender gap in earnings. In K.S. Moe (Ed.), *Women, family, and work: Writings on the economics of gender* (pp. 161–176). Oxford: Blackwell Press.

James, D. & Drakich, J. (1993). Understanding gender differences in amount of talk: A critical review of research. In D. Tannen (Ed.), *Gender and conversational interaction* (pp. 281–312). Oxford: Oxford University Press.

James, E. & Wooten, L.P. (2006). Diversity crisis: How firms manage discrimination lawsuits. *Academy of Management Journal*, 49(6), 1103–1118.

Japanese Institute of Workers Evolution. (2007). Retrieved February 8, 2009 from www.jiwe.or.jp/english/evolusion/index.html.

Jennings, J.E. & Provorny Cash, M. (2006). Women entrepreneurs in Canada: Progress, puzzles, and priorities. In C.G. Brush, N.M. Carter, E.J. Gatewood, P.G. Greene, & M.M. Hart (Eds.), *Growth-oriented women entrepreneurs and their businesses: A global research perspective* (pp. 53–87). Cheltenham: Edward Elgar Publishing.

Johansson, C. (2003). Ohio-based Abercrombie & Fitch clothing chain accused of hiring discrimination. *Knight Ridder Tribune Business News*, June 18.

Johns, F., Schmader, T., & Martens, A. (2005). Knowing is half the battle: Teaching stereotype threat as a means of improving women's math performance. *Psychological Science*, *16*, 175–179.

Johnson, C. (1994). Gender, legitimate authority, and leader–subordinate conversations. *American Sociological Review*, *59*(1), 122–135.

Johnson, C.B., Stockdale, M.S., & Saal, F.E. (1991). Persistence of men's misconceptions of friendly cues across a variety of interpersonal encounters. *Psychology of Women Quarterly*, *15*, 463–475.

Jones, E.W. (1986). Black managers: The dream deferred. *Harvard Business Review*, *64*, 84–93.

Judge, T.A. & Ferris, G.R. (1992). The elusive criterion of fit in human resources staffing decisions. *Human Resource Planning*, *15*(4), 47–67.

Kahn, S. & Lang, K. (1995). The causes of hours constrains: Evidence from Canada. *Canadian Journal of Economics*, *28*, 914–928.

Kahneman, D. & Tversky, A. (1982). *Judgment under uncertainty: Heuristic and biases*. Cambridge: Cambridge University Press.

———. (2000). *Choices, values, and frames*. Cambridge: Cambridge University Press.

Kalev, A., Kelly, E., & Dobbin, F. (2006). Best practices or best guesses? Assessing the efficacy of corporate affirmative action and diversity policies. *American Sociological Review*, *71*, 589–617.

Kalleberg, A. (2007). *The mismatched worker*. New York, NY: W.W. Norton & Co.

Kalliath, T. & Brough, P. (2008). Achieving work–life balance: Current theoretical and practice issues. *Journal of Management and Organization*, *14*(3), 227–238.

Kanter, R.M. (1977). *Men and women of the corporation*. New York, NY: Basic Books.

Kaplan, E. (1988). Women entrepreneurs: Constructing a framework to examine venture success and business failures. In B.A. Kirchoff, W.A. Long, W. McMullan, K.H. Vesper, & W.E. Wetzel (Eds.), *Frontiers of entrepreneurship research* (pp. 625–637). Wesley, MS: Babson College.

———. (1994). Confronting the issue of race in developmental relationships: Does open discussion enhance or suppress the mentor–protégé bond? *Academy of Management Executive*, *8*(2), 79–80.

Kaufman, G. & Uhlenberg, P. (2000). The influence of parenthood on work effort of married men and women. *Social Forces*, *78*(3), 931–947.

Keashly, L. & Jagatic, K. (2003). By any other name: American perspectives on workplace bullying. In S. Einarsen, H. Hoel, D. Zapf, & C. Cooper (Eds.), *Bullying and emotional abuse in the workforce* (pp. 31–61). New York, NY: Taylor and Francis.

Keele, R.L., Buckner, K., & Bushnell, S.J. (1987). Formal networking programs are no panacea. *Management Review*, *76*(2), 67–69.

Kersten, D. (2003). Women need to learn the art of the deal: Pay gap linked to negotiation skills. *USA Today*, November 17, p. B07.

Kervin, J.B. & Reid, S. (2007). *Job gender and job devaluation in fifteen organizations*. Paper presented at the annual meeting of the American Sociological Association, New York, New York City Online. Retrieved from www.allacademic.com/meta/p184294_index.html.

Khurana, R. (2002). *Searching for a corporate savior*. Princeton, NJ: Princeton University Press.

Kidder, D.L., Lankau, M., Chrobot-Mason, D., Mollica, A., & Friedman, A. (2004). Backlash toward diversity initiatives: Examining the impact of diversity program justification, personal, and group outcomes. *International Journal of Conflict Management*, *15*(1), 77–104.

Kilbourne, B.S. & England, P. (1997). Occupational skill, gender and earnings. In P. Dubeck & K. Borman (Eds.), *Women and work: A handbook* (pp. 68–70). New York, NY: Garland.

Kilduff, M. & Krackhardt, D. (1994). Bringing the individual back in: A structural analysis of the internal market for reputation in organizations. *The Academy of Management Journal*, *37*(1), 87–108.

Kim, V. (2007). Four Sanofi staff bring sex bias suit. *Financial Times*, August 30. Retrieved January 30, 2009 from www.ft.com/cms/s/0/8657.

Kimball, G. (1999). *21st century families*. Chico, CA: Equality Press.

King, R., Winchester, J., & Sherwyn, D. (2006). You (don't) look marvelous: Considerations for employers regulating appearance. *Cornell Hotel & Restaurant Quarterly*, 47(4), 359–368.

Kinnick, K.N. & Parton, S.R. (2005). Workplace communication: What *The Apprentice* teaches about communication skills. *Business Communication Quarterly*, 68(4), 429–456.

Kleinke, C. & Taylor, C. (1991). Evaluation of opposite-sex person as a function of gazing, smiling and forward lean. *Journal of Social Psychology*, 131(3), 451–453.

Kluegel, J.R. (1978). The causes and cost of racial exclusion from job authority. *American Sociological Review, 43*(3), 285–301.

Klyver, K. & Terjesen, S. (2007). Entrepreneurial network composition: An analysis across venture development stage and gender. *Women in Management Review, 22*(8), 682–688.

Knapp, D.E., Faley, R.H., Ekeberg, S.E., & Dubois, C.L.Z. (1997). Determinants of target responses to sexual harassment: A conceptual framework. *The Academy of Management Review*, 22(3), 687–729.

Knapp, L.G., Kelly-Reid, J.E., & Ginder, S.A. (2008). *Postsecondary institutions in the United States: Fall 2007, degrees and other awards conferred: 2006–07, and 12-month enrollment: 2006–07. (NCES 2008–159)*. National Center for Education Statistics, Institute of Education Sciences, US Department of Education, Washington, DC.

Knoke, D. & Ishio, Y. (1998). The gender gap in company job training. *Work and Occupations*, 25(2), 141–167.

Koenig, B.L., Kirkpatrick, L., & Ketelaar, T. (2007). Misperception of sexual and romantic interests in opposite-sex friendships: Four hypotheses. *Personal Relationships*, 14(3), 411–429.

Kollock, P., Blumstein, P., & Schwartz, P. (1985). Sex and power in interaction: Conversational privileges and duties. *American Sociological Review*, 50(1), 34–46.

Konrad, A.M. (2006). *Cases in gender and diversity in organizations*. Thousand Oaks, CA: Sage.

Konrad, A. & Kramer, V. (2006). How many women do boards need? *Harvard Business Review*, 84, 22–24.

Konrad, A. & Pfeffer, J. (1990). Do you get what you deserve? Factors affecting the relationship between productivity and pay. *Administrative Quarterly*, 35(2), 258–285.

Kottis, A.P. & Neokosmidi, Z.V. (2004) Women in management in Greece. In M.J. Davidson & R.J. Burke (Eds.), *Women and men in management worldwide: Facts, figures, analysis* (pp. 19–31). Aldershot: Ashgate Publishing Ltd.

Kram, K. (1980). *Mentoring processes at work: Developmental relationships in managerial careers*. Dissertation Abstracts International, 41(5-B).

——. (1985). *Mentoring at work*. Glenville, IL: Scotts, Foresman & Co.

Kravitz, D.A. & Platania, J. (1993). Attitudes and beliefs about affirmative action: Effects of target and of respondent sex and ethnicity. *Journal of Applied Psychology*, 78(6), 928–938.

Krawiec, K.D. (2003). Cosmetic compliances and the failure of negotiated governance. *Washington University Law Quarterly*, 81, 487–544.

Krings, F. & Facchin, S. (2009). Organizational justice and men's likelihood to sexually harass: The moderating role of sexism and personality. *Journal of Applied Psychology*, 94(2), 501–510.

Krishnan Embram, M.K. (2003). *A study on women entrepreneurship in Kerala*. Doctoral Dissertation, Mahatma Gandhi University, Kottayam.

Kulik, C.T., Pepper, M.B., Roberson, L., & Parker, S.K. (2007). The rich get richer: Predicting participation in voluntary diversity training. *Journal of Organizational Behavior*, 28(6), 753–764.

LaFrance, M. & Henley, N.M. (1997). On oppressing hypotheses: Or, differences in nonverbal sensitivity revisited. In M.R. Walsh (Ed.), *Women, men, and gender: Ongoing debates* (pp. 104–119). New Haven, CT: Yale University Press.

Lakoff, R. (1975). *Language and woman's place*. New York, NY: Harper and Row.

——. (1990). *Talking power: The politics of language in our lives*. New York, NY: Basic Books.

Lambert, S.J. (1990). Processes linking work and family: A critical review and research agenda. *Human Relations*, *43*, 239–257.

Langan-Fox, J. (2005). Analyzing achievement, motivation, and leadership in women entrepreneurs. In S.L. Fielden & M.J. Davidson (Eds.), *International handbook of women and small business entrepreneurs* (pp. 32–41). Cheltenham: Edward Elgar Publishing.

Langan-Fox, J. & Roth, S. (1995). Achievement motivation and female entrepreneurs. *Journal of Occupational and Organizational Psychology*, *68*(3), 209–218.

Langowitz, N.S & Morgan, C. (2003). Breaking through the glass barrier. In J.E. Butler (Ed.), *New perspectives on women entrepreneurs* (pp. 101–120). Charlotte, NC: Information Age Publishing.

Latto, S. (2001). *University of Minnesota Duluth Newsletter*, March 20.

Lauzen, M.M., Dozier, D.M., & Horan, N. (2008). Constructing gender stereotypes through social roles in prime-time television. *Journal of Broadcasting & Electronic Media*, *52*, 200–214.

Lazarsfeld, P.F. & Merton, R.K. (1954). Friendship as a social process: A substantive and methodological analysis. In M. Berger (Ed.), *Freedom and control in modern society* (pp. 18–66). New York, NY: Van Nostrand.

Learson, B.E. (1998). Sandia National Laboratories influencing organizational culture change through line ownership of diversity. *Diversity Factor*, *6*(4), 33–39.

Leck, J. (2002). Making employment equity programs work for women. *Canadian Public Policy*, *28*, S85–S10.

*Legal News Watch*. (2004). Assistant manager files sex discrimination lawsuit against CostCo. *Legal News Watch*, August 18, 2004. Retrieved January 30, 2009 from www.legalnews-watch.com/416.

Leibowitz, A. & Klerman, J.A. (1995). Explaining changes in married mothers' employment over time. *Demography*, *32*(3), 365–378.

Leicht, K.T. & Marx, J. (1997). The consequences of informal job finding for men and women. *Academy of Management Journal*, *40*, 967–978.

Levesque, L.L., O'Neill, R.R., Nelson, T., & Duman, C. (2005). Sex differences in the perceived importance of mentoring functions. *Career Development International*, *10*, 429–443.

Levy, S. (2007). A missing online link. *Newsweek*, October 29.

Lin, N. (2001). *Social capital: A theory of social structure and action*. New York, NY: Cambridge University Press.

Lin, N., Vaughn, J.C., & Ensel, W.M. (1981). Social resources and occupational status attainment. *Social Forces*, *59*, 1163–1181.

Linehan, M. (2000). *Senior female leaders: Why so few?* Farnham: Ashgate Publishing.

Lipman-Blumen, J. (1996). *The connective edge*. San Francisco, CA: Jossey-Bass.

Littunen, H. (2000). Entrepreneurship and the characteristics of the entrepreneurial personality. *International Journal of Entrepreneurial Behavior and Research*, *6*(6), 295–310.

Lobel, S.A. (1991). Allocation of investment in work and family roles: Alternative theories and implications for research. *Academy of Management Review*, *16*, 507–521.

Longowitz, N. & Minnite, M. (2007). The entrepreneurship propensity of women. *Entrepreneurship: Theory and Practice*, *31*(3), 341–364.

Loprest, J.P., von der Lippe, S.C., & Wissoker, D.A. (1997). *Do minority-owned businesses get a fair share of government contracts?* Washington, D.C.: The Urban Institute.

Lorber, J. (2005). *Gender inequality: Feminist theories and politics* (3rd ed.). Los Angeles, CA: Roxbury.

Lowrey, Y. (2005). *US sole proprietorships: A gender comparison, 1985–2000*. Washington, DC: US Small Business Administration, Office of Advocacy.

——. (2006). *Women in business, 2006: A demographic review of women's business ownership*. Washington, DC: Small Business Administration, Office of Advocacy.

Lublin, J. (2004). Protégé finds mentor gave her a big boost, but shadow lingers. *Wall Street Journal*, September 7, p. B1.

Luchienbroers, J. (2002). Gendered features of Australian English discourse: Discourse strategies in negotiated talk. *Journal of English Linguistics*, 30(2), 200–216.

Luthans, F., Hodgetts, R.M., & Rosenkrantz, S.A. (1988). *Real managers*. Cambridge, MA: Ballinger.

Lyness, K.S. & Heilman, M.E. (2006). When fit is fundamental: Performance evaluations and promotions of upper-level female and male managers. *Journal of Applied Psychology*, 91(4), 777–785.

Lyons, B.D. & Oppler, E.S. (2004). The effects of structural attributes and demographic characteristics on protégé satisfaction in mentoring programs. *Journal of Career Development*, 30(3), 215–229.

Lyons, D. & McArthur, C. (2007). Gender's unspoken role in leadership evaluations. *Human Resource Planning*, 30(3), 24–32.

McCarthy, E. (2004). Women in management in Ireland. In M. Davidson & R.J. Burke (Eds.), *Women and management worldwide* (pp. 32–45). Aldershot: Ashgate Publishing.

McCracken, D.M. (2000). Winning the talent war for women: Sometimes it takes a revolution. *Harvard Business Review*, 78(6), 159–160, 162, 164–167.

McDonald, M. (2003). The mentor gap. *U.S. News and Business Report*, 135(15), 36–38.

McDonald, S. (2002). Hynix semiconductor settles Eugene, Ore., hiring dispute with recruiter. *Knight Ridder Tribune Business News*, July 26.

McDowell, J.M., Singell, L.D., & Ziliak, J.P. (2001). Gender and promotion in the economics profession. *Industrial and Labor Relations Review*, 54(2), 224–244.

McFarlin, D.B., Frone, M.R., Major, B., & Konar, E. (1989). Predicting career-entry pay expectations: The role of gender-based comparisons. *Journal of Business and Psychology*, 3, 331–340.

McGregor, J. (2006). Flexitime: Honing the balance. *Business Week*, December 11, 64–65.

McGuire, G. (2002). Gender, race and the shadow structure: A study of informal network and inequality in work organizations. *Gender and Society*, 16(3), 303–322.

McGuire, G. & Reskin, B. (1993). Authority hierarchies at work: The impacts of race and sex. *Gender and Society*, 7, 487–506.

MacKinnon, C. (1979). *Sexual harassment of working women*. New Haven, CT: Yale University Press.

McNabb, R. & Wass, V. (2006). Male and female earnings differences among lawyers in Britain: A legacy of the law or a current practice? *Labor Economics*, 13(2), 219–235.

McPherson, M., Smith-Lovin, L., & Cook, J. (2001). Birds of a feather: Homophily in social networks. *Annual Review of Sociology*, 27, 415–444.

Mahoney, R. (1996). *Kidding ourselves: Breadwinning, babies, and bargaining power*. New York, NY: Basic Books.

Mahoney, T., Rynes, S., & Rosen, B. (1984). Where do compensation specialists stand on comparable worth? *Compensation Review*, 16(4), 27–50.

Major, B. & Forcey, B. (1985). Social comparisons and pay evaluations: Preferences of same-sex and same-job wage comparisons. *Journal of Experimental Social Psychology*, 21, 393–405.

Major, B., McFarlin, D., & Gagnon, D. (1984). Overworked and underpaid: On the nature of gender differences in personal entitlement. *Journal of Personality and Social Psychology*, 47(6), 1399–1412.

Makri-Tsilipakou, M. (1994). Interruption revisited: Affiliative vs. disaffiliative intervention. *Journal of Pragmatics*, 21(4), 401–426.

Maltz, D.N. & Borker, R.A. (1982). A cultural approach to male–female miscommunication. In J.J. Gumperz (Ed.), *Language and social identity* (pp. 196–216). Cambridge: Cambridge University Press.

Marlow, S. (1997). Self-employed women – new opportunities, old challenges? *Entrepreneurship and Regional Development*, 9, 199–210.

Marsden, P.V. (1988). Homogeneity in confiding relations. *Social Networks*, 10(1), 57–76.

——. (1990). Network data and measurement. *Annual Review of Sociology*, 16, 435–463.

Marsden, P.V., Kalleberg, A.L., & Cook, C.R. (1993). Gender differences in organizational commitment. *Work and Occupations*, 20(3), 368–390.

Marshall, R. & Paulin, B. (1987). Employment and earning of women: Historical perspective. In K.S. Koziara, M.H. Moskow, & L.D. Tanner (Eds.), *Working women: Past, present, and future* (pp. 1–36). Washington, DC: Bureau of National Affairs, Industrial Relations Research Association.

Martin, B.A. (1989). Gender differences in salary expectations when current salary information is provided. *Psychology of Women Quarterly*, 13(1), 87–96.

Martin, L.M. & Wright, L.T. (2005). No gender in cyberspace? Empowering entrepreneurship and innovation in female-run ICT small firms. *International Journal of Entrepreneurial Behavior & Research*, 11, 162–178.

Massoni, K. (2004). Modeling work: Occupational messages. *Seventeen Magazine*, 18, 47–65.

Masters, R. & Meier, R. (1988). Sex differences and risk-taking propensity of entrepreneurs. *Journal of Small Business Management*, 26(1), 31–36.

Mattis, M.C. (1997). Women on corporate boards: Two decades of research. *International Review of Women and Leadership*, 3(2), 11–25.

——. (2001). Advancing women in business organizations: Key leadership roles and behaviors of senior leaders and middle managers. *Journal of Management Development*, 20(4), 371–388.

Maume, D. (2004). Wage discrimination over the life course: A comparison of explanations. *Social Problems*, 51(4), 505–527.

Maume, J. (1999). Glass ceiling and glass escalators. *Work and Occupations*, 26(4), 483–509.

Mayo Clinic. (2009). *Win control over the stress in your life.* Retrieved January 30, 2009 from www.mayoclinic,com/health/stress.

Meehan, Julie. Personal communication, May 10, 2007.

Mehra, A., Kilduff, M., & Brass, D.J. (2001). The social networks of high and low self-monitors: Implications for workplace performance. *Administrative Science Quarterly*, 46(1), 121–146.

Melkas, H. & Anker, R. (1997). Occupational segregation by sex in Nordic countries: An empirical investigation. *International Labour Review*, 136(3), 341–363.

Mencken, F.C. & Winfield, I. (2000). Job search and sex segregation: Does sex of social contact matter? *Sex Roles: A Journal of Research*, 42, 847–864.

Menzies, T., Diochon, M., & Gasse, Y. (2004). Examining venture-related myths concerning women entrepreneurs. *Journal of Developmental Entrepreneurship*, 9(2), 89–107.

Merton, R.K. (1957). *Social theory and social structure*. New York, NY: Simon & Schuster.

Metcalfe, B. (2006). Exploring cultural dimensions of gender and management in the Middle East. *Thunderbird International Business Review*, 48(1), 93–107.

Meyerson, D. & Ely, R. (2000). Advancing gender equity in organizations: The challenge and importance of maintaining a gender narrative. *Organization*, 7, 589–608.

Meyerson, D.E. & Kolb, D. (2000). Moving out of the armchair: Developing a framework to bridge the gap between feminist theory and practice. *Organization*, 7(4), 553–571.

Meyerson, D. & Martin, J. (2001). Cultural change: An integration of three different views. *Journal of Management Studies*, 24(6), 623–647.

Michael, J. & Yuki, G. (1993). Managerial level and subunit function as determinants of networking behavior in organizations. *Group and Organization Management*, 18, 328–351.

Mobley, G., Jaret, C., Marsh, K., & Lim, Y. (1994). Mentoring, job satisfaction, gender and the legal profession. *A Journal of Research*, 31(1–2), 79–98.

Moen, P. (2003). *It's about time: Couples and careers*. Ithaca, NY: Cornell University Press.

Moen, P. & Kelly, E. (2007). Flexible work and well-being study: Final report. Retrieved December 12, 2007 from www.flexiblework.umn.edu.

Money, J. (1955). Hermaphroditism, gender and precocity in hyperadrenocorticism: Psychologic findings. *Bulletin of The Johns Hopkins Hospital*, 96, 253–264.

Morahan-Martin, J. (1998). *Women and girls last: Females and the Internet*. IRISS International Conference, March. Institute for Learning and Research Technology, University of Bristol.

———. (2000). Women and the Internet: Promise and peril. *CyberPsychology & Behavior*, 3, 683–691.

Morris, M.H., Miyasaki, N.N., Watters, C.E., & Coombes, S.M. (2006). The dilemma of growth: Understanding venture size choices of women entrepreneurs. *Journal of Small Business Management*, 44(2), 221–244.

Morrison, A. & Von Glinow, M.A. (1990). Women and minorities in management. *American Psychologist*, 45, 200–208.

Morrison, T., Conaway, W., & Bordan, G. (1994). *Kiss, bow and shake hands*. Holbrook, MA: Adams Media Corporation.

Moules, J. (2004). Employers pay out £4.2m for bias claims. *Financial Times*, September 6, 4.

Muchinsky, P. (2004). When the psychometrics of test development meets organizational realities: A conceptual framework for organizational change, examples, and recommendation. *Personnel Psychology*, 57, 175–209.

Mulligan, T. (2001). EEOC sues brokerage in gender bias case. *Los Angeles Times*, September 11, C1.

Murdoch, M., Polusny, M.A., Hodges, J., & Cowper, D. (2006). The association between in-service sexual harassment and post-traumatic stress disorder among department of veterans affairs disability applicants. *Military Medicine*, 171(2), 166–173.

Murrell, A., Crosby, F., & Ely, R. (1999). *Mentoring dilemmas: Developmental relationships within multicultural organizations*. Mahwah, NJ: Lawrence Erlbaum Associates.

Naff, K.C. & Kellough, J.E. (2003). Ensuring employment equity: Are federal diversity programs making a difference? *International Journal of Public Administration*, 26 (12), 1307–1336.

Namie, G. (2007). *Workplace bullying survey*. Workplace Bullying Institute and Zogby International. Retrieved October 26, 2009 from www.workplacebullying.org/res/wbisurvey2007.

National Women's Business Council. (2006). *Fact sheet: Latinas and entrepreneurship*. Retrieved from www.nwbc.gov/ResearchRublications.

Nelson, R. & Bridges, W. (1999). *Legalizing gender inequality: Courts, markets, and unequal pay for women in America*. New York, NY: Cambridge University Press.

Nelson, T. & Levesque, L. (2007). The status of women in high-growth, high-potential firms. *Entrepreneurship Theory and Practice*, 31(2), 209–232.

Neumark, D., Bank, R.J., & Van Nort, K.D. (1996). Sex discrimination in restaurant hiring: An audit study. *Quarterly Journal of Economics*, 111, 915–942.

Newman, J. (1995). Gender and cultural change. In C. Itzin & J. Newman (Eds.), *Gender, culture, and organizational change* (pp. 10–29). New York, NY: Routledge.

Nkomo, S.M. & Cox, T. (1990). Factors affecting the upward mobility of black managers in private sector organizations. *The Review of Black Political Economy*, 18(3), 39–57.

Nussbaum, M. & Glover, J. (1995). Inequalities between the sexes. In M. Nussbaum & J. Glover (Eds.), *Women, culture and development*. Oxford: Oxford University Press.

Oakley, J.G. (2000). Gender-based barriers to senior management positions: Understanding the scarcity of female CEOs. *Journal of Business Ethics*, 27(4), 321–334.

O'Barr, W.M. & Atkins, K. (1980). "Women's language" or "powerless language"? In S. McConnell-Ginet, R. Borker, & N. Furman (Eds.), *Women and language in literature and society* (pp. 93–110). New York, NY: Praeger.

Ocampo, R.L. (1994). *On hiring women and minority attorneys: One general counsel's perspective.* Retrieved October 26, 2009 from http://carers.findlaw.com/diversity/articles/onhiring.html.

Office on the Economic Status of Women. (1982). *Legislative summaries, newsletter #60*, April. Retrieved February 5, 2009 from www.commission.leg.states.mn.us/ocsw/legsum.

Offstein, E.H., Morwick, J.M., & Shah, A. (2007). Mentoring programs and jobs: A contingency approach. *Review of Business*, 27(3), 32–37.

Ohlott, P.J., Ruderman, M.N., & McCauley, C.D. (1994). Gender differences in managers' developmental job experiences. *Academy of Management Journal*, 37(1), 46–67.

O'Murchu, I., Breslin, J.G., & Decker, S. (2004). Online social and business networking communities. *Proceedings of ECAI 2004 Workshop on Application of Semantic Web Technologies to Web Communities.*

Ones, D. & Anderson, N. (2002). Gender and ethnic group differences on personality scales in selection: Some British data. *Journal of Occupational Psychology*, 75(3), 255–277.

Organization for Economic Cooperation and Development (OECD). (2004). *OECD employment outlook 2004.*

Orhan, M. & Scott, D. (2001). Why women enter into entrepreneurship: An explanatory model. *Women in Management Review*, 16(5), 232–247.

O'Shea, T. & Lelond, J. (1998). *Sexual harassment: A practical guide to the law, your rights, and your options for taking action.* New York, NY: St. Martin Press.

Osman, S. (2004). Victim resistance: Theory and data on understanding perceptions of sexual harassment. *Sex Roles: A Journal of Research*, 50(3/4), 267–275.

Ossinger, J. (2006). The money game: Capital ideas, R11. *The Wall Street Journal*, September 25. Retrieved October 24, 2009 from www.wsj.com.

Ozgen, E. & Ufuk, H. (2001). Interaction between the business and family lives of women entrepreneurs in Turkey. *Journal of Business Ethics*, 31(2), 95–106.

Paoli, P. & Merllie, D. (2001). *Third European survey on working conditions 2000.* Luxembourg: Office for Official Publications of the European Community.

Parker, P. & Ogilvie, D.T. (1996). Gender, culture, and leadership: Toward a culturally distinct model of African-American women executives' leadership strategies. *Leadership Quarterly*, 7(2), 189–214.

Parks, M. (2006). *2006 workplace romance.* Society for Human Resource Development. Retrieved February 10, 2009 from http://moss07.shrm.org/publications/hrmagazine.

Parks-Yancy, R. (2006). The effects of social group membership and social capital resources on careers. *Journal of Black Studies*, 36(4), 515–545.

Paulson, M. (2006). Hospital crisis has some doubting O'Malley's leadership. *Boston Globe*, May 26.

Pedersini, R. (2008). *Working time in the EU and other global economies.* European Foundation for the Improvement of Living and Working Conditions. Retrieved January 20, 2009 from www.eurofound.europa.eu/publications.

Pekkarinen, T. & Vartiainen, J. (2004). *Gender differences in job assignment and promotion on a complexity ladder of jobs.* IZA Discussion Paper No. 1184, June. Retrieved from http://ssrn.com/abstract=562451.

Peplau, L.A. & Elsesser, K. (2006). The glass partition: Obstacles to cross-sex friendships at work. *Human Relations*, 59(8), 1077–1100.

Perry, D.G., Perry, L.C., & Weiss, R.J. (1989). Sex differences in the consequences that children anticipate for aggression. *Developmental Psychology*, 25(2), 312–319.

Perry, E.L., Davis-Blake, A., & Kulkit, C.T. (1994). Explaining gender-based selection decisions: A synthesis of contextual and cognitive approaches. *Academy of Management Review*, 19, 786–820.

Pfeffer, J., Davis-Blake, A., & Julius, D.J. (1995). AA officer salaries and managerial diversity: Efficiency wages or status? *Industrial Relations*, 34(1), 73–94.

Pfleeger, S.L. & Merz, N. (1995). Executive mentoring: What makes it work? *Communications of the ACM, 38*(1), 63–73.

Phelan, J., Schwartz, J.E., Bromet, E.J., Drew, M.A., Parkinson, D.K., Schulberg, H.C., et al. (1991). Work stress, family stress and depression in professional and managerial employees. *Psychological Medicine*, November 21 (4), pp. 999–1012.

Phillips, D.J. (2005). Genealogies and the persistence of gender inequality: The case of Silicon Valley law firms. *Administrative Science Quarterly, 50*, 440–472.

Piotrkowski, C.W. (1979) *Work and the family system.* New York, NY: Free Press.

Plant, A., Kling, K., & Smith, G. (2004). The influence of gender and social role on the interpretation of facial expressions. *Sex Roles: A Journal of Research, 51*(3–4), 187–196.

Podolny, J.M. & Baron, J.N. (1997). Relationships and resources: Social networks and mobility in the workplace. *American Sociological Review, 62*(5), 673–693.

Polacheck, S. (1981). Occupational self-selection: A human capital approach to sex differences in occupational structure. *Review of Economics and Statistics, 58*, 60–69.

Polacheck, S.W. & Xiang, J. (2006). *The gender pay gap: A cross-country analysis.* Retrieved July 28, 2009 from http://client.norc.org/jole/SOLEweb/Polachek.pdf.

Porter, E. (2006). After years of growth, what about workers' share? *New York Times*, October 15, p. BU3.

Posner, R. (1986). *American Nurses Association* v. *State of Illinois. US Court of Appeals for the Seventh Circuit*, #85–1766, January 24.

Powell, G.N. & Francesco, A.M. (2009). Toward culturally-sensitive theories of the work–family interface. *Journal of Organizational Behavior, 30*(5), 597–616.

Powell, G.N. & Graves, L.M. (2003). *Women and men in management* (3rd ed.). Thousand Oaks, CA: Sage.

Powell, G.N. & Mainiero, L.A. (1999). Managerial decision making regarding alternative work arrangements. *Journal of Occupational and Organizational Psychology, 72*, 41–56.

Powell, G.N., Butterfield, D.A., & Parent, J.D. (2002). Gender and managerial stereotypes: Have the times changed? *Journal of Management, 28*(2), 177–193.

PricewaterhouseCoopers. (2007). *Women step off the corporate ladder*, March 8. Retrieved December 5, 2008 from www.ukmediacentre.pwc.com/Content/Detail.

Prislin, R. & Wood, W. (2005). Social influence: The role of social consensus in attitudes and attitude change. In D. Albarracin, B.T. Johnson, & M.P. Zanna (Eds.), *Handbook of attitudes and attitude change* (pp. 671–706). New York, NY: Lawrence Erlbaum.

Puhl, R. & Brownell, K.D. (2003). Ways of coping with obesity stigma: Review and conceptual analysis. *Eating Behaviors, 4*, 53–78.

Pyle, J.L. (1999). Third World women and global restructuring. In J. Chafetz (Ed.), *Handbook of the sociology of gender* (pp. 81–104). New York, NY: Kluwer Academic.

———. (2001). Sex, maids, and export processing: Risks and reasons for gendered global production networks. *International Journal of Politics, Culture, and Society, 15*, 55–76.

Ragins, B.R. (1997). Diversified relationships in organizations: A power perspective. *The Academy of Management, 22*(2), 482–521.

Ragins, B.R. & Cotton, J.L. (1999). Mentor functions and outcomes: A comparison of men and women in formal and informal mentoring relationships. *Journal of Applied Psychology, 84*, 529–550.

Ragins, B.R., Townsend, B., & Mattis, M. (1998). Gender gap in the executive suite: CEOs and female executives report on breaking the glass ceiling. *Academy of Management Executive, 12*(1), 28–42.

Rainbird, H. (2007). Can training remove the glue from the "sticky floor" of low-paid work for women? *Equal Opportunities International, 26*(6), 555–572.

Rapleaf. (2008). *Rapleaf study reveals gender and age data of social network users*, July. Retrieved March 14, 2009 from http://business.rapleaf.com/company_press.

Ray, R., Gornick, J., & Schmit, J. (2008). *Parental leave policies in 21 countries: Assessing generosity and gender equality.* Washington, DC: Center for Economic and Policy Research, 1–23.

Rayman, P., Bailyn, L., Dickert, J., Carre, F., Harvey, M., Krim, R., et al. (1999). Designing organizational solutions to integrate work and life. *Women in Management Review*, *14*(5), 164–176.

Read, L. (1994). Raising finance from banks: A comparative study of the experiences of male and female business owners. *Frontiers of Entrepreneurship Research*, Babson College. Retrieved October 23, 2009 from www.babson.edu/entrep.

Reed, K.A. (2001). *Managing our margins: Women entrepreneurs in suburbia.* New York, NY: Routledge.

Rees, B. & Garnsey, E. (2003). Analysing competence: Gender and identity at work. *Gender, Work and Organization*, *10*(15), 551–578.

Reeves, M.E. (2000). *Suppressed, forced out and fired: How successful women lose their jobs.* Westport, CT: Quorom Books.

Reich, M.H. (1985). Executive views from both sides of mentoring. *Personnel*, *62*, 42–46.

——. (1986). The mentor connection. *Personnel*, *63*, 50–56.

Reid, L. (2002). Occupational segregation, human capital, and motherhood: Black women's higher exit rates from full-time employment. *Gender and Society*, *16*(5), 728–747.

Remick, H. (1979). Strategies for creating sound, bias free job evaluation plans. In *Job evaluation and EEO: The emerging issues* (pp. 85–112). New York, NY: Industrial Relations Counselors.

Renegade, H.R. (2009). *Smashing the clock: Best Buy's ROWE.* Retrieved October 16, 2009 from http://renegadehr.net/best-buy-rowe.

Reskin, B. (2000). The proximate causes of employment discrimination. *Contemporary Sociology*, *29*(2), 319–328.

Reskin, B. & Padavic, I. (1994). *Women and men at work.* London: Pine Forge Press.

Reskin, B. & Roos, P. (1990). *Job queues, gender queues: Explaining women's inroads into male occupations.* Philadelphia, PA: Temple University Press.

Reynolds, J. (2003). You can't always get the hours you want: Mismatches between actual and preferred work hours in the United States. *Social Forces*, *81*(4), 1171–1199.

Reynolds, J.R. (2002). Gender bias and feminist consciousness among judges and attorneys: A standpoint theory analysis. *Signs: Journal of Women in Culture and Society*, *27*(3), 665–704.

Riding, A.L. & Swift, C.S. (1990). Women business owners and terms of credit: Some empirical findings of the Canadian experience. *Journal of Business Venturing*, *5*, 327–340.

Robinson, W. & Paulson, M. (2006). Chief of Caritas forced out. *Boston Globe*, May 26.

Rogers, E.M. & Kincaid, D.L. (1981). *Communication networks.* New York, NY: Free Press.

Rosa, P. & Dawson, A. (2006). Gender and the commercialization of university science: Academic founders of spinout companies. *Entrepreneurship and Regional Development*, *18*(4), 341–366.

Rosener, J. (1999). Changing the workplace. *Harvard Business Review*, September 28, 4.

——. (2004). *Women on corporate boards makes sense* [Electronic Version]. Retrieved November 30, 2004 from www.womensmedia.com.

Rosenfeld, R.A. (1996). Women's work histories. *Population and Development Review*, *22*, 199–222.

Rosenthal, P. (1995). Gender differences in managers' attributions for successful work performance. *Women in Management Review*, *10*(6), 26–32.

Rosenthal, P., Guest, D., & Peccei, R. (1996). Gender differences in managers' causal explanations for their work performance: A study of two organizations. *Journal of Occupational and Organizational Psychology*, *69* (June), 145–152.

Roter, D.L., Hall, J.A., & Yutaka, A. (2002). Physician gender effects in medical communication. *Journal of American Medical Association*, *288*(6), 756–764.

Roth, L.M. (2009). Leveling the playing field: Negotiating opportunities and recognition in gendered jobs. *Negotiation and Conflict Management Research*, 2(1), 17–30.

Rothbard, N., Phillips, K.W., & Duman, T.L. (2005). Managing multiple roles: Work–family policies and individuals' desires for segmentation. *Organization Science*, 16(3), 243–258.

Roxburgh, S. (2004). There aren't enough hours in the day: The mental health consequences of time pressure. *Journal of Health and Social Behavior*, 45(2), 115–131.

Rubery, J. (1995). Performance-related pay and the prospect for gender pay equity. *Journal of Management Studies*, 32(5), 637–654.

Rubery, J. & Fagan, C. (1995). Gender segregation in a social context. *Work, Employment and Society*, 9(2), 213–240.

Ruble, D.N., Martin, C.L., & Berenbaum, S.A. (2006). Gender development. In N. Eisenberg, W. Damon, & R.M. Lerner (Eds.), *Handbook of child psychology: Vol. 3, Social, emotional, and personality development* (Vol. 3, 6th ed., pp. 858–932). Hoboken, NJ: John Wiley.

Ruderman, M. & Ohlott, P. (1994). *The realities of management promotion: An investigation of factors influencing the promotion of managers in three major companies*. Greensboro, NC: Center for Creative Leadership.

Rudman, L.A. & Glick, P. (2001). Prescriptive gender stereotypes and backlash toward agentic women. *Gender, Hierarchy, and Leadership*, 57(4), 743–762.

Ruhm, C.J. & Teague, J.L. (1995). *Parental leave policies in Europe and North America. NBER Working Papers 5065*, National Bureau of Economic Research, Inc. Retrieved January 19, 2009 from http://ideas.repec.org/p/nbr/nberwo/5065.html.

Rynes, S. & Rosen, B. (1995). A field survey of factors affecting adoption and perceived success of diversity training. *Personnel Psychology*, 48, 247–270.

Rynes, S., Rosen, B. & Mahoney, T.A. (1985). Evaluating comparable worth: Three perspectives. *Business Horizons*, 28(4), 82.

Sallop, L.J. & Kirby, S. (2007). The role of gender and work experience on career and work force diversity. *Journal of Behavioral and Applied Management*, 8(2), 122–140.

*San Francisco Chronicle*. (1998). $9.8 million sex harass payout: Drug firm had "Open season" on female employees. *San Francisco Chronicle*, February 6.

Sapolsky, R. (1998). *Why zebras don't get ulcers* (3rd ed.). New York, NY: Henry Holt and Co.

Sarri, K. & Trihopoulou, A. (2005). Female entrepreneurs' characteristics and motivation: A review of the Greek situation. *Women in Management Review*, 20(1), 24–36.

Savicki, V., Lingenfelter, D., & Kelley, M. (1996). Gender language style and group composition in Internet discussion groups. *Journal of Computer-Mediated Communication*, 2(3). Retrieved September 22, 2009 from http://jcmc.indiana,edu.

Schaef, A.W. (1985). *Women's reality: An emerging female system in the white male society*. Minneapolis, MN: Winston Press.

Schein, V. (2001). A global look at psychological barriers to women's progress in management. *The Journal of Social Issues*, 57(4), 675–688.

———. (2007). Women in management: Reflections and projections. *Women in Management Review*, 22(1), 6–18.

Schein, V.E. & Davidson, M.J. (1993). Think manager – think male. *Management Development Review*, 6(3), 24–29.

Schein, V.E., Mueller, R., Lituchy, T., & Liu, J. (1998). Think manager – think male: A global phenomenon? *Journal of Organizational Behavior*, 17(1), 33–41.

Schneider, K.T., Swan, S., & Fitzgerald, L.F. (1997). Job-related and psychological effects of sexual harassment in the workplace: Empirical evidence from two organizations. *Journal of Applied Psychology*, 82(3), 401–415.

Schor, J. (1994). Worktime in a contemporary context: Amending the FSLA. *Chicago-Kent Law*, 70(1), 157–72.

*Schultz* v. *Wheaton Glass Co.* (1970) 421 F.2d 259.

Schwartz, J. (2005). Always on the job, Employees pay with health. *New York Times*. Retrieved January 8, 2009 from www.nytimes.com/2004/09/05/health/05stress.

Scott, C.E. (1986). Why more women are becoming entrepreneurs. *Journal of Small Business Management*, 24, October, 37–44.

Sebenuis, J. (2001). Six habits of merely effective negotiators. *Harvard Business Review*, April, 87–97.

Seibert, S.E., Kraimer, M.L., & Liden, R.C. (2001). A social capital theory of career success. *The Academy of Management Journal*, 44(2), 219–237.

Seidel, M.D.L., Polzer, J.T., & Stewart, K.J. (2000). Friends in high places: The effects of social networks on discrimination in salary negotiations. *Administrative Science Quarterly*, 45(1), 1–24.

Senate committee considers equal pay legislation [Electronic Version]. *Women's Policy Inc.*, 11. Retrieved June 3, 2007 from www.womenspolicy.org/thesource/article.cfm?ArticleID=2308.

Senges, M. (2007). *Knowledge entrepreneurship in universities: Strategy and practice in the case of Internet based innovation appropriation*. Doctoral dissertation. Retrieved October 22, 2009 from www.maxsenges.com.

Sethi, S.P., Swanson, C.L., & Harrigan, K.R. (1981). *Women directors on corporate boards, working paper 81–101*. Center for Research in Business and Social Policy, University of Texas at Dallas.

Sexton, D.L. & Kent, C.A. (1981). Female executives and entrepreneurs: A preliminary comparison. In K.H. Vesper (Ed.), *Frontiers of entrepreneurship research* (pp. 40–46). Wellesley, MA: Babson College Center for Extrepreneurship Studies.

Shabbir, A. & D'Gregorio, S. (1996). An examination of the relationship between women's personal goals and structural factors influencing their decision to start a business: The case of Pakistan. *Journal of Business Venturing*, 11, 507–529.

Shaw, G.B. (1994). *Pygmalion*. New York, NY: Dover Editions.

Shelton, C.D., McKenna, M.K., & Darling, J.R. (2002). Leading in the age of paradox: Optimizing behavioral style, job fit and cultural cohesion. *Leadership and Organizational Development Journal*, 23(7), 372–379.

Shelton, L.M. (2006). Female entrepreneurs, work–family conflict, and venture performance: New insights into the work–family interface. *Journal of Small Business Management*, 44(2), 285–297.

Sherman, A. (1998). *Cybergirl: A woman's guide to the World Wide Web*. New York, NY: Ballantine Books.

Sherman, J.D., Smith, H.L., & Mansfield, E.R. (1986). The impact of emergent network structure on organizational socialization. *The Journal of Applied Behavioral Science*, 22(1), 53.

Shirley, C. & Wallace, M. (2004). Domestic work, family characteristics, and earnings: Reexamining gender and class differences. *The Sociological Quarterly*, 45, 663–690.

Shragg, P., Yacuk, L., & Glass, A. (1992). Study of barriers facing Albertan women in business. *Journal of Small Business and Entrepreneurship*, 9(4), 40–49.

Sidanius, J., Devereux, E., & Pratto, F. (2001). A comparison of symbolic racism theory and social dominance theory as explanations for racial policy attitudes. *Journal of Social Psychology*, 132, 377–395.

Simon, H.A. (1991). *Ellison* v. *Brady*: A "reasonable woman" standard for sexual harassment. *Employee Relations Law Journal*, 17(1), 71–80.

Singewald, D.R. (2007). EEOC guidance on workplace investigations. *New York Employment Law Letter*, 14(2), 1–3.

Single, P.B., Muller, C.B., Cunningham, R.M., & Carlsen, W.S. (2004). *A three year analysis of the benefits accrued by women engineering and science students who participated in a large scale e-mentoring program.* Paper presented at the ASEE Annual Conference and Exposition.

Skarlicki, D.P., Folger, R., & Tesluk, P. (1999). Personality as a moderator in the relationship between fairness and retaliation. *Academy of Management Journal*, *42*, 100–108.

Small, D.A., Gelfand, M., Babcock, L., & Gettman, H. (2007). Who goes to the bargaining table? The influence of gender and framing on the initiation of negotiation. *Journal of Personality and Social Psychology*, *93*(4), 600–613.

Smith, F.I., Tabak, F., Showail, S., McLean Parks, J., & Kleist, J.S. (2005). The name game: Employability evaluation of prototypical applicants with stereotypical feminine and masculine first names. *Sex Roles: A Journal of Research*, *52*(1–2), 63–82.

Smith, J.P. & Ward, M.P. (1985). Time series growth in the female labor force. *Journal of Labor Economics*, *3*(1), S59–S90.

Smith, R. (2005). Do the determinants of promotion differ for white men versus women and minorities? An exploration of intersectionalism through sponsored and contest mobility processes. *The American Behavioral Scientist*, *48*(9), 1157–1181.

Smith-Jentsch, K.A., Scielzo, S.A., & Weichert, M.A. (2007). An empirical test of gender-based differences in e-mentoring. In D.J. Svyantek & E. McChrystal (Eds.), *Refining familiar constructs: alternative views in OB, HR, and I/O* (pp. 27–43). Charlotte, NC: Information Age Publishing.

Smith-Lovin, L., McPherson, M., & Cook, J.M. (2001). Birds of a feather: homophily in social networks. *Annual Review of Sociology*, *27*, 415–444.

Solnick, S.J. (2001). Gender differences in the ultimatum game. *Economic Inquiry*, *39*(2), 189–200.

Solnick, S.J. & Schweitzer, M.E. (1999). The influence of physical attractiveness and gender on ultimatum game decisions. *Organizational Behavior and Human Decision Processes*, *79*(3), 199–215.

Solovic, S.W. (2004). Ten common mistakes start-up businesses make. *Women in Business*, May 1. Retrieved October 28, 2009 from www.allbusiness.com.

Sonfield, M.R., Lussier, R., Corman, J., & McKinney, M. (2001). Gender comparisons in strategic decision-making: An empirical analysis of the entrepreneurial strategy mix. *Journal of Small Business Management*, *39*(2), 165–173.

Sparks, K., Cooper, C., Fried, Y., & Shirom, A. (1997). The effects of hours of work on health: A meta-analytic review. *Journal of Occupational Health and Organizational Psychology*, *70*(4), 391–408.

Sparrowe, R.T., Liden, R.C., Wayne, S.J., & Kraimer, M.L. (2001). Social networks and the performance of individuals and groups. *The Academy of Management Journal*, *44*(2), 316–325.

Steele, C.M. & Aronson, J. (1995). Stereotype threat and the intellectual test performance of African Americans. *Journal of Personality and Social Psychology*, *69*, 797–811.

Steinberg, R. (1992). Gendered instructions: Cultural lag and gender bias in the Hay system of job evaluation. *Work and Occupations*, *19*(4), 387–423.

Stepson, L. (2000). *Equal remuneration for work of equal value: European perspectives.* Geneva: International Labour Organization.

Stevenson, L.A. (1986). Against all odds: The entrepreneurship of women. *Journal of Small Business Management*, *24*(4), 439–446.

Still, L.V. & Timms, W. (2000). Women's business: The flexible alternative work style for women. *Women in Management Review*, *15*(5), 272–282.

Stockdale, M.S. (1993). The role of sexual misperceptions of women's friendliness in an emerging theory of sexual harassment. *Journal of Vocational Behavior*, *42*, 84–101.

Stoltenberg, J. (2004). Toward gender justice. In P.F. Murphy (Ed.), *Feminism and masculinities* (pp. 41–49). Oxford: Oxford University Press.

Stone, P. (2007). *Opting out? Why women really quit careers and head home.* Los Angeles, CA: University of California Press.

Stoner, C.R., Hartmen, R.I., & Arora, R. (1990). Work/family conflict: A study of women in Management. *Journal of Applied Business Research,* 7(1), 67–74.

Stover, D.L. (1997). The stratification of women within organizations. In P. Dubeck & K. Borman (Eds.), *Women and work: A reader* (pp. 317–320). New Brunswick, NJ: Rutgers University Press.

Strangleman, T. (2005). Sociological futures and the sociology of work [Electronic Version]. *Sociological Research Online,* 10. Retrieved September 3, 2007 from www.socresonline.org. uk/10/4/strangleman.html.

Strout, E. (2003). Pay it forward. We explore a controversial question: Are female executives obligated to mentor younger women in sales? *Sales & Marketing Management,* 155(6), 44–47.

Stuhlmacher, A.F. & Walters, A.E. (1999). Gender differences in negotiation outcome: A meta-analysis. *Personnel Psychology,* 52, 653–677.

Tangri, S.S., Burt, M.R., & Johnson, L.B. (1982). Sexual harassment at work: Three explanatory models. *Journal of Social Issues,* 38, 33–54.

Tannen, D. (1990). *You just don't understand: Women and men in conversation.* New York, NY: William Morrow and Co.

——. (1993). *Framing in discourse.* New York, NY: Oxford University Press.

——. (1994). *Gender and discourse.* New York, NY: Oxford University Press.

——. (1995). The power of talk: Who gets heard and why. *Harvard Business Review,* September/October, 139–148.

Taylor, S.N. (2009). *It may not be what you think: Gender differences in predicting emotional and social competence.* Chicago, IL: National Academy of Management Conference.

Thomas, D. (2001). The truth about mentoring minorities: Race matters. *Harvard Business Review,* 79, November 1, 98–107.

Thomson, R. & Murachver, T. (2001). Where is the gender in gendered language? *Psychological Science,* 12, 171–175.

Thornton, E. (2005). Still marching to Purcell's drumbeat. *Business Week,* June 27, 38–39.

Tiedens, L.Z. (2001). The effect of anger on the hostile inferences of aggressive and nonaggressive people: Specific emotions, cognitive processing, and chronic accessibility. *Motivation and Emotion,* 25(3), 233–251.

Tiedens, L.Z., Ellsworth, P.C., & Mesquita, B. (2000). Sentimental stereotypes: Emotional expectations for high- and low-status group members. *Personality and Social Psychology Bulletin,* 26(5), 560.

Tiggerman, M. & Rothblum, E.D. (1997). Gender differences in internal beliefs about weight and negative attitudes towards self and others. *Psychology of Women Quarterly,* 21, 581–593.

Tijdens, K.G. (2004). Women in management in the Netherlands. In M.J. Davidson & R.J. Burke (Eds.), *Women and men in management worldwide: Facts, figures, analysis* (pp. 68–82). Aldershot: Ashgate Publishing Ltd.

Tirabasso, Annette. Personal communication, August 9, 2007.

Tischler, L. (2004). Where are the women? So what happened? *Fast Company,* 79, 52–60.

Torres, B. (2004). Fort Worth, Texas-based food, beer distributor settles hiring bias. *Knight Ridder Tribune Business News,* April 17.

Trinczek, R. (2008). *Working in Europe: Gender differences.* European Foundation for the Improvement of Living and Working Conditions, 1–14. Retrieved January 18, 2009 from www.fr.eurofound.eu.int/publications.

Tsui, A.S., Egan, T.D., & O'Reilly, C.A. (1992). Being different: Relational demography and organizational attachment. *Administrative Science Quarterly,* 37, 549–579.

Twenge, J.M. (2001). Changes in women's assertiveness in response to status and roles: A cross temporal meta-analysis, 1931–1993. *Journal of Personality and Social Psychology*, *81*, 133–145.

Uchitelle, L. & Kleinfield, N.R. (1996). On the battlefields of business, millions of casualties. *New York Times*, *3*, 14–16.

Unger, R.K. (1979). Toward a redefinition of sex and gender. *American Psychologist*, *34*(11), 1085–1094.

United States District Court for the Northern District of Alabama. Plaintiffs' Motion for Class Certification. Retrieved January 30, 2009 from www/cmht.com/pdfs/Bellsouthmotionfor-classcert.

University of Michigan Gender and Achievement Research Program. Retrieved September 22, 2007 from www.rcgd.isr.umich.edu/msalt.

US Bureau of Labor Statistics. (2000). February 14.

——. (2005a). *Work at home in 2004*, September 22, pp. 1–14. Retrieved January 7, 2007 from www.bls.gov/cps.

——. (2005b). *Workers on flexible and shift schedules in May 2004*, July 1, pp. 1–14. Retrieved January 7, 2007 from www.bls.gov/cps.

——. (2007). *Highlights of women's earnings in 2006*, September. Retrieved February 10, 2009 from www/bls.gov/cps/cpswom2006.pdf.

——. (2008). *Databook*. Retrieved February 13, 2009 from www.bls.gov/cps/wlf-databook-2008.pdf.

US Census Bureau. (2000). *Census 2000 briefs*. Retrieved February 12, 2009 from www.census.gov/population/www/cen2000/brief.

——. (2004). *Statistical abstract of the United States*. Washington, DC: Government Printing Office.

——. (2005). *Living arrangements of children: 2001*, July. Retrieved www.census.gov/population/socdemo/child/p70–104.pdf.

——. (2006a). *Current population reports: Median earnings of workers 15 years old and over by work experience and sex.* Retrieved February 2, 2009 from http://pubdb3.census.gov/macro/032006/perinc/new05_113htm.

——. (2006b). *Current population survey: 2006 annual social and economic supplement.* Retrieved February 25, 2009 from www.census.gov/apsd/techdoc/cps/cpsmar06pdf.

US Department of Education, National Center for Education Statistics. (2005). *Postsecondary institutions in the United States: Fall 2003 and degrees and other awards conferred: 2002–2003*, NCES 2005–154.

US Department of Labor Statistics. (2009). *Quick stats on women workers, 2008*. Retrieved September 1, 2009 from www.dol.gov/wb/stats.

US General Accounting Office. (2003). *Women's earnings: Work patterns partially explain difference between men's and women's earnings.* GAO-04–35, October.

US Small Business Administration. (2008). Retrieved October 24, 2009 from www.sba.gov.

Uzzi, B. & Dunlap, S. (2005). How to build your network. *Harvard Business Review*, *83*(12), 53.

Vallas, S.P., Finlay, W., & Wharton, A.S. (2009). *The sociology of work*. Oxford: Oxford University Press.

Van Haegendoren, M., Steegmans, N., & Valgaeren, E. (2001). *Mannen en vrouwen op de drempel van de 21 ste eeuw. Een gebruikershandboek genderstatistieken.* Brussels: Ministerie vror Tewerkstelling en Arbeid.

Victor, J. (2006). *Workplace vacation*. Society for Human Resources Management. Retrieved from www.shrm.org/hrresources/surveys_published/2006.

Vogel, D.L., Wester, S.R., Heesacker, M., & Madon, S. (2003). Confirming sex stereotypes: A social role perspective. *Sex Roles: A Journal of Research*, *48*, 519–528.

Voydanoff, P. (1987). *Work and family life*. Newbury Park, CA: Sage.

Wade, M.E. (2003). Women and salary negotiation: The cost of self advocacy. *Psychology of Women Quarterly*, *25*(1), 65–76.

Walby, S. (1988) *Gender segregation at work*. Minneapolis: University of Minnesota Press.

——. (1990). *Theorizing patriarchy*. London: Blackwell.

Walton, G.M. & Cohen, G.L. (2003). Stereotype lift. *Journal of Experimental Social Psychology*, *39*, 456–467.

Warr, P.B. (1987). *Work, unemployment, and mental health*. Oxford: Clarendon Press.

Warren, T. (2007). Conceptualizing breadwinning work. *Work, Employment and Society*, *21*(2), 317–336.

Washington University School of Medicine. (2004). *Women in health sciences – by the numbers: Healthcare managers and executives*. St. Louis, MO: Washington University School of Medicine. Bernard Becker Memorial Library Digital Collection.

Weichselbaumer, D. & Winter-Ebmer, R. (2002). *The effects of competition and equal treatment laws on the gender wage differential*. Working Paper No. 0307, Department of Economics, Johannes Kepler University, Linz.

Weiler, S. & Bernasek, A. (2001). Dodging the glass ceiling? Networks and the new wave of women entrepreneurs. *The Social Science Journal*, *38*, 16–19.

Weinstein, M. (2007). *PricewaterhouseCoopers: Balancing act (No. 2 in the training top 125)*, March 5. Retrieved February 11, 2009 from www.trainingmag.com/msg/content_display/publications.

Welter, F. (2006). Women's entrepreneurship in Germany: Progress in a still traditional environment. In C.G. Brush, N.M. Carter, E.J. Gatewood, P.G. Greene, & M.M. Hart (Eds.), *Growth-oriented women entrepreneurs and their businesses: A global research perspective* (pp. 128–153). Cheltenham: Edward Elgar Publishing.

Werwie, D. (1987). *Sex and pay in the federal government: Using job evaluation system to implement comparable worth*. New York, NY: Greenwood.

West, C. & Zimmerman, D.H. (1983). Small insults: A study of interruptions in cross-sex conversations between unacquainted persons. In B. Thorne, C. Kramarae, & N. Henley (Eds.), *Language, gender, and society* (pp. 102–117). Rowley, MA: Newbury House.

Westphal, J.D. & Stern, I. (2007). Flattery will get you everywhere (especially if you are a male Caucasian): How ingratiation, boardroom behavior, and demographic minority status affect additional board appointments at US companies. *The Academy of Management Journal*, *50*(2), 267–288.

Wilbert, C. (2007). Crazy for cars. *Pink Magazine*, February/March, 80–85.

Wilcox, M. & Rush, S. (2004). *The CCL guide to leadership in action*. San Francisco, CA: Jossey-Bass.

Williams, C. (1992). The glass escalator: Hidden advantages for men in the "female" professions. *Social Problems*, *39*(3), 253–267.

Williams, J. (2000). *Unbending gender: Why family and work conflict and what to do about it*. New York, NY: Oxford University Press.

Williams, S. (2004). Mentors help shatter glass ceiling in Columbus, Ohio. *Knight Ridder Tribune Business News*, September 4.

Willness, C.R., Steel, P., & Lee, K. (2007). A meta-analysis of the antecedents and consequences of workplace sexual harassment. *Personnel Psychology*, *60*(1), 127–162.

Wilson, F. & Thompson, P. (2001). Sexual harassment as an exercise of power. *Gender, Work and Organization*, *8*, 61–83.

Women's Policy Inc. (2007) *Senate committee considers equal pay legislation*, April 13.

Wood, J. (1994). Saying it makes it so: The discursive construction of sexual harassment. In S. Bingham (Ed.), *Conceptualizing sexual harassment as a discursive practice* (pp. 17–30). Westport, CT: Praeger.

Woodward, A.E. (2004). Women in management in Belgium. In M.J. Davidson & R.J. Burke

(Eds.), *Women and men in management worldwide: Facts, figures, analysis* (pp. 32–45). Aldershot: Ashgate Publishing Ltd.

Woolf, M. (2004). Women to be given advice on problems in workplace. *Independent*, June 7, 8.

Wren, B.M. (2006). Examining gender differences in performance evaluations, rewards, and punishments. *Journal of Management Research*, 6(3), 115–124.

Wright, E.O., Baxter, J., & Birkelund, G.E. (1995). The gender gap in workplace authority: A cross-national study. *American Sociological Review*, 60(3), 407–435.

Yancey-Martin, P. (2003). "Said and done" versus "saying and doing": Gender practices, practicing gender at work. *Gender and Society*, 17(3), 342–366.

Yancey-Martin, P., Reynolds, J.R., & Keith, S. (2002). Gender bias and feminist consciousness among judges and attorneys: A standpoint theory analysis. *Signs*, 27(3), 665–702.

Yasbek, P. (2004). *The business case for firm-lead work–life balance policies: A review of the literature.* Wellington: Labour Market Policy Group. Retrieved October 5, 2009 from www.dol.govt. nz.

Zapalska, A. (1997a). Profiles of Polish entrepreneurs. *Journal of Small Business Management*, 35. Retrieved October 29, 2009 from www.questia.com.

——. (1997b). Entrepreneurship and the development of small business in Poland. *Journal of Business and Behavioral Sciences*, 35(4), 76–82.

Zedeck, S. (1992). *Work, families and organizations.* San Francisco, CA: Jossey-Bass.

Zedeck, S. & Mosier, K.L. (1990). Work in the family and employing organization. *American Psychologist*, 45(2), 240–257.

Zelechowski, D. & Bilmoria, D. (2004). Characteristics of women and men corporate inside directors in the US. *Corporate Governance*, 12(3), 337–342.

Zetik, D.C. & Stuhlmacher, A.F. (2002). Goal setting and negotiation performance: A meta-analysis. *Group Processes and Intergroup Relations*, 5(1), 35–52.

Zimmerman, D.H. & West, C. (1975). Sex roles, interruptions, and silences in conversation. In B. Thorne & N. Henley (Eds.), *Language and sex: Difference and dominance* (pp. 105–129). Rowley, MA: Newbury House.

Zuber, A. (1999). EEOC suits put harassment on operators' front burner. *Nation's Restaurant News*, 33(5), February 1, 1–2.

# Index

*Italic* page numbers indicate tables not included in the text page range.
**Bold** page numbers indicate figures not included in the text page range.